Niger

the Bradt Travel Guide

Jolijn Geels

www.bradtguides.com

Bradt Travel Guides Ltd, UK
The Globe Pequot Press Inc, USA

21 JUN 06 : WATERSTONE'S – PF – £14.99

edition

I

Niger
Don't
miss...

Colourful architecture
Decorated house, Kandidja (JG)

Fascinating culture
Peul men performing at the
Geerewol Festival
(SR) page 28

Wetlands
Water lilies in October, near Kobadié
(JB) page 6

Striking landscapes
Camel train along the fringes of the Ténéré Desert and Aïr Mountains
(JG) page 190

Vibrant old towns
Hausa architecture in Birno, the old town of Zinder
(JG) page 213

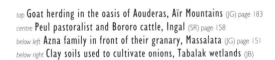

top Goat herding in the oasis of Aouderas, Aïr Mountains (JG) page 183
centre Peul pastoralist and Bororo cattle, Ingal (SR) page 158
below left Azna family in front of their granary, Massalata (JG) page 151
below right Clay soils used to cultivate onions, Tabalak wetlands (JB)

top **Along the River Niger, near Ayorou** (JG) page 118
above left **Fulani mother and child** (JB)
above right **Hausa man selling onions, Tahoua** (JG) page 155
below **Tuareg man pouring tea, Tchintoulous, Aïr Mountains** (JG) page 186

above left **Ancient mosque, Agadez** (JG) page 159
top right **Market scene, Maradi** (JG) page 209
above right **Baobab tree** *Adansonia digitata* (JB) page 6
below **Boudouma women creating a home, Doro** (JG) page 237

top left Member of a court of a traditional *chefferie*, Birni N'Konni (JG) page 149

top right Djerma woman carrying a *canarie* or water jar, Tillabéri (JG) page 115

centre Tuareg in traditional dress, Festival de l'Aïr, Iférouane (JG) page 187

right Truck prepares to leave for Bilma (SR) page 195

top **Cheetah** *Acinonyx jubatus* (MA) page 9
above left **Fennec fox** *Vulpes zerda* (MA) page 10
above right **Koutous Hills after rain** (GV) page 224
below **Dorcas gazelle** *Gazalla dorcus* (MA) page 9

Author/Contributor

When **Jolijn Geels** (known in Niger as Julie; e jolgeels@yahoo.com) from the Netherlands lived in Surinam as a young child, a travel bug must have bitten her, for she could never stay in one place for very long. After studying arts and culture, she lived in Spain and Scotland. A trip to Cameroon triggered her deep passion for Africa and she soon swapped her studio for hiking boots and a backpack. Since then she has travelled frequently to many corners of the continent, the Comoros Islands and Madagascar as both a backpacker and a tour leader. In addition to her work for Bradt Travel Guides, Jolijn is author of *Salut Vazaha!* – travel stories (in Dutch) about her journeys to remote areas in Madagascar – and contributor to various other publications. After the research for this guidebook, she has decided to work and live with the people of Niger.

CONTRIBUTOR

Joost Brouwer (e BrouwerEAC@wanadoo.nl) is a soil scientist and ecologist with more than 25 years' experience in agriculture, environment and social sustainable development. A native of the Netherlands, he has spent more than half of his professional life abroad, including a five-year stay as Principal Scientist at ICRISAT Sahelian Centre south of Niamey. He is author and co-author of more than 100 publications on various aspects of Niger, ranging from soils, millet and livestock, via vegetation ecology and Important Bird Areas, to wetlands, biodiversity and poverty alleviation. He also founded and maintains the Niger Bird Database, NiBDaB. At present he works as a consultant on tropical land use, biodiversity and their interaction.

PUBLISHER'S FOREWORD

Hilary Bradt

The first Bradt travel guide was written in 1974 by George and Hilary Bradt on a river barge floating down a tributary of the Amazon. In the 1980s and '90s the focus shifted away from hiking to broader-based guides covering new destinations – usually the first to be published about these places. In the 21st century Bradt continues to publish such ground-breaking guides, as well as others to established holiday destinations, incorporating in-depth information on culture and natural history with the nuts and bolts of where to stay and what to see.

Bradt authors support responsible travel, and provide advice not only on minimum impact but also on how to give something back through local charities. In this way a true synergy is achieved between the traveller and local communities.

I have known Jolijn for many years as an adventurous and thoughtful traveller in Madagascar. Her accounts showed an unusual sensitivity to the local culture so I used them as boxes scattered throughout my book. She went on to update our guide to Mali.

Jolijn was the perfect choice to write a book about a 'difficult' country such as Niger because she knows how to travel with an open mind and how to integrate properly with local people. We felt that Niger needed more than just a 'what to see and where to stay' approach. She has lived up to this promise superbly. Anyone reading her book will feel culturally enriched, even if they are not travelling to Niger.

First published May 2006

Bradt Travel Guides Ltd
23 High Street, Chalfont St Peter, Bucks SL9 9QE, England; www.bradtguides.com

Published in the USA by The Globe Pequot Press Inc, 246 Goose Lane,
PO Box 480, Guilford, Connecticut 06475-0480

Text copyright © 2006 Jolijn Geels
Maps copyright © 2006 Bradt Travel Guides Ltd
Illustrations copyright © 2006 Individual artists and photographers

British Library Cataloguing in Publication Data
A catalogue record for this book is available from the British Library
ISBN-10: 1 84162 152 8   ISBN-13: 978 184 162 152 4

Photographs *Text* Gamzaki Voyages (GV), Joost Brouwer (JB), Jolijn Geels (JG), Maurice Ascani/SOS Faune du Niger (MA), Sawadee-Reizen/Amsterdam (SR)
Cover Girl from Dogondoutchi (JG)
Back cover Tuareg man, Ténéré Desert (JG); Fennec fox, *Vulpes zerda* (MA)
Title page Sand dunes near Chiriet (JG); member of a court of a traditional *chefferie*, Birni N'Konni (JG); ancient mosque, Agadez (JG)

Illustrations Carole Vincer   **Maps** Alan Whitaker

Typeset from the author's disc by Wakewing
Printed and bound in Italy by Legoprint SpA

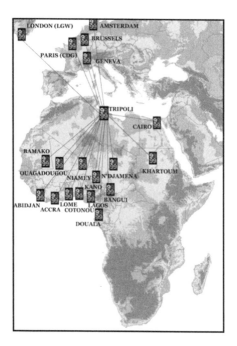

Contents

For key to map symbols, see page VII

Acknowledgements

During my research, I depended on many people who provided a wealth of information, transport, accommodation and practical assistance. Through their support, my ventures to many corners of the country produced the invaluable notes, documents and observations that made up the foundations of this guidebook. However, it is the long chain of highly valued and heart-warming encounters with so many Nigériens that made the journey an unforgettable one.

A great debt of gratitude is owed to Housseini Abdou-Saleye and Aha Issoufa, from whom I received a warm and unconditional welcome on more than one occasion.

Of all the people who shared their time and experience with me, I would like to especially thank: Amadou Nouhou, Ibrahim Boubacar, Mahaman Laminou, Hassimi Adamou, Moumouni Aoula, Boubé Gado, Abdulaye Maga and all the staff at the IRSH, Mahamadou Kelessi, Ibrahim 'Ahi' Almoustapha, Françoise and Nicholas Widmer, Moussa Kaka, Oumarou Keïta, Mamane Abou, Elh Idé Niandou, Ottavio Novelli, Maurice Ascani and Edith Maricaux in Niamey; Sarkin Arewa and Hamidou Salifou in Dogondoutchi; Abdouramane 'Soja' Kado, Abdou Nahantchi and Ben Halilo Mohamed in Birni N'Konni; Abdoulkarim Chaïbou in Dagarka; Moustapha Allasane and Abdul Raouf Sidi in Tahoua; Mr Moumouni, Elh. Kané, Barney Raymond, Doula Mokao, Ibrahim Manzo Diallo, Sidi Mohamed, Abdoussalam Mahadi, Mohamed Aghali Zodi, Hadizatou Baïlas and Mariama Alkabouss in Agadez; Birgi Raffini and Sidi Moumounia in Iférouane; Achmed Tcholli in Tchintoulous; Elh Habou Magagi, Sani Habou and Issoufou 'Ben' Bako in Maradi; Ibrahim Halidou, Abdullaye Bammo, Ibrahim Karamba, Abduramane 'Gabi' Gabidan, Sylvie Guellé and Marie in Zinder; Oumarou Yacouba and Laouali Salesou Dan Malam in Diffa; Modo Gaptia and Mohamed Barkaï in N'Guigmi. Apologies if I have left anyone out and apologies for omitting titles.

Also many thanks to all the local guides, fellow travellers and dear companions, of whom I would like to mention: all the staff of Taguelmoust Travels and Services in Niamey and Agadez; Elisabeth Knegtmans and Els Paardekooper; Karim 'Angaribou' Toudou; Rhissa Ilias; Michel Ligeour and Marion Mure, Martine Vermorel and Phillipe Dejucq; Richard Lees; Hassan, Florent and Apollinaire; Black and Sido; Bachir Mamane; Mamoutou A Guindo and Gilles Akakpo.

Thanks to those travellers who shared their stories: Thomas and Bethany Eberle; Yohan Quilgars, Belinda Aked and Wies Buysrogge.

I greatly appreciate the assistance received from the Nigérien consulate in The Hague (the Netherlands) and Afriqiyah Airways.

The team at Bradt Travel Guides should be acknowledged for commissioning this guidebook to Niger, and I am especially grateful to Tricia Hayne, Adrian Phillips, Anna Moores and Kate Lyons for their assistance and support throughout the process. Many thanks to Joost Brouwer for writing the excellent natural history section (in *Chapter 1*) and various other valuable contributions.

On my return to the Netherlands, I could not have finished writing this guidebook without the generosity and patience of Herman Snippe, who like no other has had to deal with the consequences of my passion for Africa.

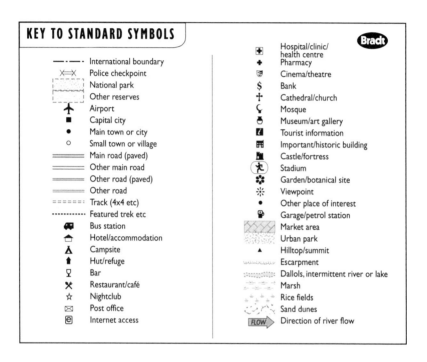

KEY TO STANDARD SYMBOLS

Bradt

—··—	International boundary
X—X	Police checkpoint
	National park
	Other reserves
✈	Airport
■	Capital city
•	Main town or city
○	Small town or village
═══	Main road (paved)
═══	Other main road
═══	Other road (paved)
═══	Other road
======	Track (4x4 etc)
··········	Featured trek etc
🚌	Bus station
⌂	Hotel/accommodation
▲	Campsite
♦	Hut/refuge
⛾	Bar
✕	Restaurant/café
☆	Nightclub
⊠	Post office
℮	Internet access

✚	Hospital/clinic/health centre
✚	Pharmacy
☺	Cinema/theatre
$	Bank
†	Cathedral/church
☾	Mosque
⚱	Museum/art gallery
ℹ	Tourist information
▦	Important/historic building
⛫	Castle/fortress
㊣	Stadium
✿	Garden/botanical site
☼	Viewpoint
•	Other place of interest
⛽	Garage/petrol station
▨	Market area
⋰	Urban park
▲	Hilltop/summit
	Escarpment
	Dallols, intermittent river or lake
	Marsh
	Rice fields
	Sand dunes
FLOW	Direction of river flow

FEEDBACK REQUEST

Only weeks after finishing the research, I hear of changed rates, new hotels being constructed and new travel agencies starting up business. How frustrating, the information is outdated even before it is written! But that just happens to be an unavoidable characteristic of a guidebook filled with data that is prone to change. It is something you as a traveller have to bear in mind at all times while using this guidebook, as prices might go up, bus schedules change and hotels shut down. To help us keep this guidebook as accurate as possible, do write to us with any additional information or changes that you feel should be included in the next edition.

Niger is an immense country where travelling can be very time consuming, especially when wandering off the tarred roads. Therefore, many places remained beyond the scope of this first edition. These may be destinations with very little in terms of tourist facilities, but all the more in terms of ethnic diversity and culture, nature and wildlife, archaeological and historical sites. While feedback on practical information is always useful, your personal story about any such place could be an enriching contribution for us as well as for future readers. Write to: 23 High St, Chalfont St Peter, Bucks SL9 9QE; ℮ info@bradtguides.com.

Introduction

A nasty bump in the road causes me to wake up suddenly. I have been dozing for a while, after a particularly bad stretch of road, on the long haul from Agadez to Zinder. It seems I am not the only one to wake up with a start. Other passengers also straighten their backs and resume conversations, without making much fuss about the bump that had jangled us all. I share a seat – that officially takes three – with Mariama and her three young daughters. It is not uncommon for two children to share one seat, but that is still one child too many, and the girls one by one take turns to stand in the aisle for a while, a discomfort they accept without the slightest complaint. As there is no alternative, I consent to being wedged in between Mariama and the window.

The view hasn't changed much. Maybe there are some more thorny bushes and acacias, but the arid and empty landscape still looks a hostile environment to me. The rains had seriously failed earlier in the year, and the signs of a forthcoming drought in this region are very noticeable already. Herds of cattle are headed to one of the few wells along the way, their lyre-shaped horns faintly silhouetted against a blanket of ochre dust, caused by so many hooves on dry soil. From the sleepy environment of the bus it looks picturesque, like a wide-screen film in slow motion and with no sound but the rumbling engine of the vehicle and the voices around me. I decide to leave it at that, and not even start to imagine the difficulties that might lie ahead for the herders and their livestock. Not now.

As the three girls change places again, my attention is drawn back to the inside of the bus. Communication with my four fellow passengers is limited. Mariama's French is hardly better than my clumsy attempts to speak some Hausa, but it sufficed for us to become friends for the duration of this journey. We share biscuits, groundnuts and smiles in our confined space. What a pity we can't really talk, though, as I like the casual conversations that sometimes unfold on long bus rides such as these: about the purpose of the trip, the final destination, are they going to see relatives or friends, where is home? And of what do they dream when they dream? On different occasions, when I asked Nigériens that same question, I was touched by the modesty of the most common answer: enough food for the family, fodder for the livestock, rain to feed the crops, and good health. The very basic necessities of life, for which many Nigériens have to struggle daily. Like the three children having to take turns in the aisle, they just accept this as a fact of life. Indeed, many Nigériens I had met along the way struck me with their adaptability and inventiveness, whilst keeping their lust for life and a good sense of humour. So while in many ways Niger seems a harsh country to be living in, it is truly wonderful to spend time with the hospitable Nigériens, whether they be Hausa, Peul, Djerma, Tuareg or Kanouri. Sharing a common language helps, of course, but its not a prerequisite to being comfortable among the people.

Again my attention is drawn back to reality as the bus pulls over and halts for one of the few stops between Agadez and Zinder. Time at last to stretch my legs.

Niger is not one of Africa's top ten travel destinations. In fact, until the 2005 coverage of the severe famine, many people hardly knew where to find Niger on the map, while others often confused Niger with its neighbour Nigeria. This book is solely about Niger: its history, society, nature and culture, and of course Niger as a travel destination. But how does 'spending a holiday in Niger' tally with all the negative reports about droughts, famine, insecurity and slavery? Can it be justified to travel in a poor country while there is so much suffering, and is it safe? Through this book I hope to put things in perspective, to shed some light on delicate issues, and to restore the balance as there is plenty of good news to be told about Niger, too. Despite all the difficulties, Niger is a wonderful country to be travelling in, and the Nigériens are among the most welcoming of peoples in Africa that I know.

When you are searching for information about Niger, you will notice that the emphasis lies on the northern region, from Agadez upwards to the Aïr Mountains and the Ténéré Desert. It is easy to see why, as this strikingly beautiful region has received more visitors over the years than anywhere else in Niger. The northern region has been highly developed for tourism, and therefore Agadez can be considered the tourist capital of the country. The real capital, Niamey, is hardly ever regarded as a tourist destination in its own right, but rather as a port of transit for those on the way to the north. In this guidebook, however, I have made an effort to balance the information about the different regions, as I feel that it should not be an automatic decision to head for the north; it all depends on what you are looking for, and Niger has a lot to offer.

THREE ZONES: SOUTHWEST – CENTRE AND NORTH – SOUTHEAST Parts Two, Three and Four of this guidebook each describe a zone that is made up of different regions (see map *Administrative regions*, page X). Chapters follow a geographical line-up, thereby occasionally cutting through district boundaries, but sticking to the roads and tracks in a (mostly) linear sequence. I have made an effort to include comprehensive practical information for those travellers who want to explore Niger independently, so precious time does not have to be spent trying to find out how Niger works. Some information will become outdated, but even then it should be useful as a guideline.

Part Two describes the southwesternmost zone and includes the capital Niamey, Tillabéri and Dosso. During the colonial era, this region was opened up for tourism, mainly to serve the French expatriates living in Niamey. Many of the facilities have degraded to a rather poor state over the last decades, while the region as a whole became little advertised. Once again, however, tourism in the southwest is developing, and with good reason. These regions are within easy reach from the capital, while this is also the zone that is dominated by the river Niger and its rich variety of wildlife. 'W' National Park is without doubt the best park in which to observe wildlife in the whole of west Africa, while the last viable herds of giraffe of west Africa have found a haven only 60km away from Niamey. Following the river Niger upstream not only provides almost guaranteed opportunities to watch hippos, but it is also a birdwatcher's paradise. To the south of the river Niger, little-known wetlands also prove surprisingly good birding areas. Add to this the picturesque villages and the magnificent and ever-changing riverine landscape, and you may wonder why so few people allow time for a visit.

Part Three describes the best-known zone, the immense region of Tahoua and Agadez, the Aïr Mountains and the Ténéré Desert. The south of this region, especially around Birni N'Konni, is a stronghold of indigenous beliefs where animist ceremonies still take place. Further north is the region where the Woodabe Peul and Tuareg dominate, where the Cure Salée and the Geerewol gatherings take

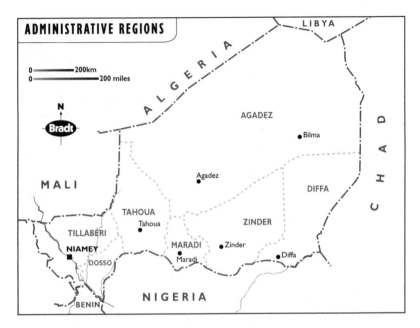

ADMINISTRATIVE REGIONS

0 ——— 200km
0 ——— 200 miles

N

Bradt

ALGERIA

LIBYA

MALI

AGADEZ

Bilma

Agadez

DIFFA

CHAD

TAHOUA

Tahoua

ZINDER

TILLABÉRI

NIAMEY

MARADI

Zinder

DOSSO

Maradi

Diffa

NIGERIA

BENIN

place, and where long caravans still leave for Bilma to buy salt and dates. The rocky massifs of the Aïr and the ochre and orange sand dunes along its fringes are striking to the eye, while the many archaeological remains and the dinosaur graveyards are mind-boggling sites. Tourism can be a package deal or a tailor-made journey, and either way it will be highly rewarding. And of course there's Agadez, historical city and seat of the Aïr sultanate, and a sprawling tourist centre too: Agadez has more travel agencies than the rest of Niger as a whole. Yet out in the desert expanses, tourists are accommodated with ease.

Part Four describes the zone stretching from Maradi to Lake Chad – regions that have seen few travellers thus far. Located near the Nigerian border, Maradi is a buzzing centre of trade. Further to the east, Zinder is first of all a historical town rich in Hausa culture and architecture, while it also harbours one of the two remaining sultanates in Niger. Yet more towards the east, the regions of Diffa and Lake Chad are home to the nomadic Peul and the little-known Toubou and Kanouri. Villages and hamlets are scattered throughout the region, but along the southern edge of the Sahara the landscape becomes arid and desolate. Here, the sparse population live in temporary settlements. At the end of the tar is N'Guigmi, with one of the biggest camel markets in the region. From there, the ancient riverbed of the Dilia Valley, leads to the beautiful but little-visited Termit Massif.

LANGUAGE AND SPELLING Is it Hawsa, Haoussa, Hausa or Haussa? Tamashek or Tamajeq? And what about Birnin Konni versus Birni N'Konni, or Miria versus Myrriah? There is no unequivocal answer: different documents and maps use different spellings. My approach in this guide has been to stick with those spellings that are most commonly used.

The national language of Niger is French, and only very little English is spoken. For vocabulary and phrases in French, Hausa, Djerma and Tamashek, see *Appendix 1*, page 239. I have sometimes included French words in the text, as they may be of practical use.

Part One

GENERAL INFORMATION

Location Niger is a landlocked country, bordering Algeria, Benin, Burkina Faso, Chad, Libya, Mali and Nigeria

Size 1,267,000km², which is larger than France, Spain and Portugal together, or four times as large as the UK and Ireland together

Capital Niamey

Administrative divisions Eight regions: Agadez, Diffa, Dosso, Maradi, Tahoua, Tillabéri, Zinder, and the urban region of Niamey

Flag Three equal horizontal bands of orange (top), white and green with a small orange disk (representing the sun) centered in the white band

Political system Multi-party republic, independent from France since 3 August 1960

Head of state President Mamadou Tandja (since 22 December 1999)

Prime minister Hama Amadou (since 31 December 1999)

Population 11,900,000 (2003)

Population under 18 years 6,700,000 (56%)

Fertility rate 8.0 (2003)

Annual number of births 662,000

Birth rate 53 births per 1,000 population

Death rate 19.5 deaths per 1,000 population

Life expectancy 46 years

Urban population 2,618,999 (22%)

Population per km² 9

Population growth rate 3.3% per annum

Population living below poverty line (less than US$1 per day) 7,616,000 (64%)

GDP US$2.8 billion (2003)

GDP per head US$200 (2003)

Main languages French (official language), Hausa, Djerma, Peul, Tamashek

Religions Islam (90%), Christianity and animism (10%)

Lowest point River Niger: 200m

Highest point Mont Bagzane: 2,022m

Time GMT+1

Electricity supply 220 volts

Money CFA franc = 100 centimes

Exchange rate £1 = CFA956, €1 = CFA656, US$1 = CFA518 (May 2006)

Measures Metric system

International telephone code 227 (no area code)

Internet code .ne

Emergency telephone numbers Police: 17; Fire brigade: 18

Background Information

GEOGRAPHY with Joost Brouwer

Niger is a relatively flat country, with most land lying between 200m and 500m above sea level. The geological formations immediately underlying the flatter areas are mostly sediments from the Tertiary period that lasted from 65 million to two million years ago. During that time relatively sandy sediments were deposited in two enormous basins covering most of the west and most of the east of the country. In many places the higher parts of the virtually horizontal sediments are capped by erosion-resistant laterite, or ironstone as it is also known. The resulting extensive, laterite-capped plateaux are separated from one another by wide and shallow valleys. Where the plateaux meet the valleys, isolated inselbergs or table mountains 10–50m high are often found.

Much older rocks come to the surface in the extreme southwest (west of the Niger River), down the middle of the country (from the Aïr and surroundings in the north to virtually the border with Nigeria), and in the northeast (Djado Plateau area and south to Bilma). The major mountain areas of Niger are associated with these older rocks: the extremely scenic Aïr Mountains go as high as 2,022m, the Djado Plateau lies at approximately 800–1,000m, and the highest point of the much smaller Termit Mountains or Massif in the central east is 710m above sea level.

Owing to their height the mountainous areas receive more rainfall than the surrounding plains, but their vegetation is still very much adapted to extended dry periods. In the geologically recent past, approximately 10,000 years ago and coinciding with the end of the last ice age at higher latitudes, all of Niger was much wetter than it is now. A legacy of that wetter period is the extensive network of now mostly dry valleys and drainage lines. These former drainage systems cover the entire country and run towards the Niger River in the southwest and towards Lake Chad in the southeast. Some of the more spectacular sections of these drainage systems are in the Dallol Bosso and Dallol Boboye near Baléyara, 100km east of Niamey, where there are sheer cliffs 70–80m high.

On top of all the rocks, but especially in the dry valleys in the Tertiary basins, recent, wind-blown coversands are often found, up to tens of metres deep. The pale yellow-to-orange colours of these sands, and the grey-green of the leaves of the more drought-tolerant bushes and trees, dominate the scenery in southern Niger for most of the year, except where there is permanent water. These subdued colours make the transformation into a riotously green landscape at the start of the rainy season all the more remarkable.

CLIMATE, VEGETATION AND LAND USE with Joost Brouwer

Geology and climate are the two main factors that determine what vegetation is found where, what animals are found where, and what human activities take place where. In very general terms the weather in Niger could be described as hot, dry and dusty. But that doesn't do justice to the differences between for instance the desert and the more vegetated south. In the desert the difference between day and night temperatures can be more than 30°C, reaching near freezing at night in January and February. In the vegetated south on the other hand, in the lead-up to the rainy season it sometimes remains more than 35°C even at night. Nor does 'hot , dry and dusty' do justice to the temperature differences between the seasons, which again are more extreme in the arid north than in the more vegetated south.

Weatherwise the year can be divided into three seasons. If we take the capital Niamey in the southwest as an example, the dry and cool season lasts from October through February. Night temperatures can drop below 20°C, which is considered quite chilly by local standards. During the day the temperature usually reaches between 30°C and 35°C, but it is a very dry heat and therefore to most people only uncomfortable during the middle of the day. As the cool season progresses, dust hazes, caused by *harmattan* winds, become more common. The dry and hot season, from March through May, is characterised by the dusty *harmattan* wind and steadily rising temperatures, which in Niamey may be around 45°C during the hottest days in April and May. During the peak of the hot season night temperatures stay above 30°C consistently, and humidity builds up as a prelude to the rains. These are the worst months of the year, quite taxing healthwise and very uncomfortable even for Nigériens. The dust storms that occur then, in the run-up to the rains, can be quite dense and of biblical proportions. Relief comes with the first showers of the rainy season that lasts from June through September. The temperature drops to just over 30°C during the day and about 25°C at night immediately following rainstorms, and the atmosphere is beautifully clear then. However, the rain falls in relatively few storms of often great intensity, reaching 50mm (2 inches) or more per hour: flood damage to bridges and road culverts is quite common, while off-road conditions can be difficult. Despite the discomforts, it is lovely to see everything so green during the rains.

Some 1,460 plant species have been recorded in Niger, of which four are considered endemic. Many more no doubt remain to be discovered. Many of these species do not have an English name, making it necessary to refer to them by their scientific name. Except in the mountain areas, rainfall and vegetation zones in Niger run more or less east–west (see map *Vegetation and rainfall*, opposite) From north to south, they can be described as follows.

DESERT ZONE In the north, where annual rainfall is less than 100mm and very erratic, there is the Sahara, with a desert climate. There are many rocky areas and gravelly plains, as well as huge sandy dune areas such as in the Ténéré. Vegetation is very localised and scarce, and mostly limited to annual grasses and herbs that germinate, flower, set seed and die off in only about a month following one of the rare rainfall events. Only along sand-filled dry riverbeds, where water is stored in the soil, strips of acacia trees may be found. The vegetation of the Aïr includes Mediterranean and Afromontane as well as Afrotropical species. Characteristic woody species are *Acacia*, *Rhus tripartita*, wild fig *Ficus salicifolia*, jujube *Ziziphus* and desert date *Balanites* species, and the saltbush *Salvadora persica*. The wild olive *Olea laperrinei* still occurs in the Aïr, too. Around oases there are also trees that live off the groundwater that comes to the surface from sometimes hundreds of metres down to form the oases. These include many date palms *Phoenix dactylifera*, for which oases are famous.

NORTHERN SAHELIAN ZONE To the south lie the Sahelian grasslands, which receive about 100–350mm of summer rainfall (June–August). The annual grasses are extensively grazed by livestock that come up from the south during the rains

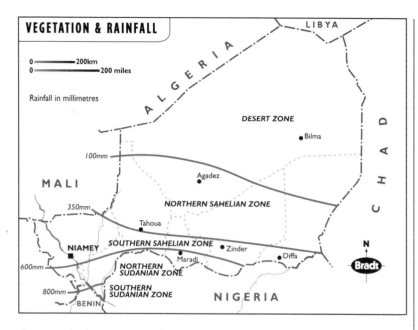

VEGETATION & RAINFALL

0 ▬▬▬▬ 200km
0 ▬▬▬▬ 200 miles

Rainfall in millimetres

LIBYA

ALGERIA

MALI

DESERT ZONE

• Bilma

100mm

• Agadez

350mm

NORTHERN SAHELIAN ZONE

Tahoua

SOUTHERN SAHELIAN ZONE • Zinder

NIAMEY ■

• Diffa

600mm

NORTHERN SUDANIAN ZONE

• Maradi

800mm

SOUTHERN SUDANIAN ZONE

BENIN

NIGERIA

CHAD

N

Bradt

for precisely that reason. Further south perennial grass and sedge species are also found. Trees and shrubs are rare in the northern part of this zone, but include acacia species, caper trees, maerua species, and desert date *Balanites aegyptiaca*. Further south the landscape is more wooded, but many of the trees and shrubs are still quite thorny to protect them against grazing, and they lose their leaves towards the end of the dry season. They include *Combretum*, *Boscia*, *Guiera*, *Sclerocarya* and *Commiphora* spp. Egyptian mimosa trees, *Acacia nilotica*, are often found along (usually dry) stream beds, where there is more water stored in the soil. Traditionally their pods and bark are used to tan hides. In drier localities gum arabic trees, *Acacia senegal*, are found, the major producers of gum arabic. Throughout the northern and southern Sahelian zones, and also in the Aïr, sodom apple, *Calotropis procera*, is found, an introduction-gone-wild from Asia. It is a very noticeable spindly tree or shrub with large grey-green leaves, all parts of which are used for various domestic, medicinal and construction purposes. It often occurs on disturbed or very degraded soils, including fallow fields.

The northern Sahelian zone is extremely marginal for millet cultivation, which is actually forbidden in the north. More and more desperate farmers are trying it anyway.

SOUTHERN SAHELIAN ZONE In the southern Sahelian zone (annual rainfall 350–600mm, June–September) millet fields often predominate, and in the higher rainfall areas, sorghum. Livestock also form an important part of the agricultural system, grazing on the crop stubbles and providing the farmers with manure. The original vegetation contains a variety of woody shrubs and trees of the tropical *Combretaceae* family, as well as other woody species, including doum or gingerbread palms, *Hyphaena thebaica*, in less dry positions. The leaves of doum palms are used for weaving mats, as can be seen near the Dallol Bosso along the Niamey–Dosso road. The herb layer is very varied and includes grasses, legumes and other species. In many farmers' fields gaos or apple ring trees, *Faidherbia* (or *Acacia*) *albida*, are found. Very unusually, most gaos lose their leaves at the beginning of the rainy

Joost Brouwer
The climax vegetation on the lateritic plateaux is the so-called 'tigerbush'. This vegetation type consists of bands of dense woody vegetation up to 6m high (mostly *Combretaceae* and *Acacia* species). The vegetation bands are separated from each other by strips of bare soil tens of metres wide. Because the bare soil is crusted, and rainstorms are very intense, rainfall hardly permeates the bare soil. Instead it runs off along the surface, down the negligible slope, to the bands of vegetation. Termites living under and around the vegetation keep the soil open there, allowing the run-off from the upslope to filter into the soil under the vegetation. From there the shrubs and trees can take the water up. This system allows the tigerbush vegetation to survive and stay green almost all year long in areas that are usually too dry for normal survival. In very low rainfall areas rainfall and run-off are of course less than in higher rainfall areas, but plant water use is about the same. To generate sufficient run-off for the trees and shrubs to survive, the bare strips of tigerbush in very low rainfall areas are therefore considerably wider than in higher rainfall areas.

season and regain them a couple of months later. They therefore don't compete for water with millet, and young millet plants are shaded from the harshest sunshine by the bare twigs of the gaos. Livestock rest under the gaos during the dry eason, and browse on leaves and pods, leaving behind their manure as fertiliser. The deep-rooted gaos also recycle nutrients that have leached to below the root zone of the millet plants. And many gaos are found on spots where soil fertility is relatively high due to previous activity of certain termite species. All this adds up to a tree that is much appreciated by farmers, and that has the most potential for agro-forestry of all the trees in the Sahel.

NORTHERN SUDANIAN ZONE The very south of Niger belongs to the northern Sudanian zone (annual rainfall 600–800mm, May–October) and is densely populated and cultivated (for sorghum mostly, but also for millet and cowpea). The original vegetation is a very varied woodland, which includes baobab, *Adansonia digitata*, red kapok or silk-cotton tree, *Bombax costata*, and various *Combretaceae*. The wood of *Proposopis africana* is much in demand because it is quite resistant to termite attacks. In farmers' fields in the very south karité or sheabutter trees, *Butyrospermum parkii*, are often left standing: from the fruit of this tree karité butter is made, which is used in foods and ice cream and also to make soap. Néré or African locust bean trees, *Parkia biglobosa*, are also found in millet and sorghum fields, as are tamarind trees, *Tamarindus indica*. The fruit of the latter is used to make very tasty soft drinks.

WETLANDS: VERY IMPORTANT RESOURCES ACROSS ALL DRY REGIONS Across all four rainfall and vegetation zones wetlands are found. Because water and nutrients are concentrated there, these wetlands are very productive and form extremely important resources for farmers, pastoralists, fishermen and collectors of natural products, as well as for wildlife.

The main wetland area in Niger is formed by the Niger River and its floodplains, which traverse the southwest of the country over a length of 550km. Fringing vegetation originally included dense stands of deleb palm trees, *Borassus aethiopum*, but almost all of these have been cut. The hydrology of the river itself has greatly changed over the past 40 years, because of the construction of dams for various purposes in upstream countries Mali and Guinea-Conakry. The fish catch has suffered accordingly. The Nigérien part of the other very large wetland, Lake

Chad in the southeast of the country, was dry for a number of years until 1998. The flow of the lake's main tributary in Niger, the Komadougou Yobé, has also greatly diminished. Again this is mostly because of the construction of dams in the upper reaches of the river, in this case in Nigeria. Along the major tributaries of the Niger River, between the river and Burkina Faso, gallery forests, containing among others, up to 35m-tall African mahogany trees, *Khaya senegalensis*, can be found.

In the inland parts of Niger there are more than 1,000 isolated wetlands of between 10ha and over 2,000ha in size. Most are run-off dependent. Some only contain water for a few months after the rainy season ends; others contain water all year round. Aquatic vegetation, where present, can vary from dense fringing stands of trees, via various herbaceous zones with grasses, sedges and wild rice, to dense patches of water lilies in the deepest parts. In more northern parts of the country wetlands include the usually dry riverbeds and oases mentioned above. Around the oases, in addition to palm trees, tamarisks can be found and sometimes rushes and reeds that emerge from the open water.

BIODIVERSITY AND PROTECTED AREAS with Joost Brouwer

BIOGEOGRAPHICAL REALMS Biogeographically most of Niger lies in the Afrotropical realm, one of the eight such realms that the world is divided into. What this means is that the plants, animals and ecology of the largest part of Niger are most similar to the plants etc of other African countries south of the Sahara. The Sahara itself is considered a part of the Palearctic realm, which covers north Africa, Europe, the Middle East and northern Asia. Migratory birds are of course not so concerned with human biogeographical classifications, and many species that breed in north Africa, Europe and western Asia spend the non-breeding season in Africa south of the Sahara, including Niger.

BIOGEOGRAPHICAL ZONES At a more detailed level, Niger is part of three biogeographical or ecological zones, to which the rainfall and vegetation zones mentioned in the *Climate, vegetation and land-use* section can be related: the very arid Sahara, the semi-arid western Sahel, and the sub-humid west African woodland/savanna. The World Wildlife Fund further subdivides the Sahara into lowland, mountain and Sahara-fringing zones. It also separates out the flooded savanna ecosystems surrounding Lake Chad. The Niger River and its floodplains in the southwest of Niger could be considered a separate ecological zone as well, as could the hundreds of isolated wetlands found throughout the lower third of the country. These isolated wetlands are situated mostly in the now usually dry valleys formed tens of thousands of years ago when the climate in Niger was much wetter. They include wetlands dependent on run-off or on groundwater, a limited number of artificial reservoirs, saline wetlands, and, in the north and east, oases. Some are permanent, others semi-permanent. The ones that only hold water for a few months each year are not even counted. Some isolated wetlands have no vegetation, some are surrounded by parallel zones of grasses, emergent water plants and water lilies, and others are covered by dense stands of acacia or are surrounded by palm trees. The variety of wetlands in Niger is quite astounding. Along the tributaries of the Niger River there are also some lovely sections of gallery forest, especially in 'W' National Park.

National nature reserves, IBAs (Important Bird Areas) and Ramsar sites in each biogeographical zone As all these ecological zones have their own characteristic plants and animals, it is important that all are included in the national nature reserve system.

The lowlands and the mountains of the Sahara are extremely well covered in the vast (77,360km²) National Nature Reserve of the Aïr and the Ténéré, which includes the Strict Reserve of the Addax Sanctuary.

The ecosystems of the fringes of the Sahara and the Sahel zones are even today hardly included in any protected areas. These zones contain only the Total Fauna Reserve of Gadabeji, 150km north of Maradi, but this is apparently badly degraded. The so-far-unprotected Termit Mountains 400km northeast of Zinder would be an excellent area to structure the conservation of desert-fringing and Sahelian ecosystems around. In these semi-arid zones two Important Bird Areas have been recognised by BirdLife International (see *Birds*, pages 10–12), but IBAs do not have any legal status as yet. The Dallol Bosso, a broad fossil valley bordered in some places by spectacular cliffs, traverses the desert fringe and Sahel zone from the border with Mali north of Filingué straight down to the Niger River at the border with Benin. Because of the presence of a number of small, groundwater-fed wetlands, the Dallol Bosso in its entirety (3,762km²) has been designated a Wetland of International Importance under the Ramsar Convention. Ramsar sites are wetlands that are considered to be of international importance because of their particular hydrology (how they receive their water), the presence of special ecosystems or of rare or endangered species, their importance for sedentary or migratory waterbirds, and/or their importance for sedentary or migratory fish. But in addition to wetlands the Dallol Bosso Ramsar site also includes large areas of adjoining semi-arid ecosystems.

The sub-humid woodland savanna in the very south of Niger is protected in the beautiful 'W' National Park (2,200km²), 150km south of Niamey on the borders with Benin and Burkina Faso, which is also a Ramsar wetland and an IBA. It borders the Tamou Total Faune Reserve and the Dosso Partial Reserve. There is also an IBA centred on Makalondi, 100km southwest of Niamey, which covers a combination of woodland savanna and small wetlands and ephemeral watercourses. The Ramsar site of the fossil valley of the Dallol Mawri (3,190km², designated in 2004), to the east and north of Gaya along the border with Nigeria, also contains an appreciable area of woodland savanna.

Of the wetland-related ecosystems, in addition to the three wetland sites just mentioned under the various biogeographical zones, the Niger part of Lake Chad (3,400km²) was designated a Wetland of International Importance under the Ramsar Convention in 2001. Similarly, two sections of the Niger River and associated floodplains along the border with Benin were designated Ramsar wetlands in 2001 (880km²) and 2004 (658km²) respectively. Three IBAs have also been recognised along the Niger River. A further eight IBAs are centred on isolated wetlands throughout the southern third of Niger (see *Birds*, page 10). Of these, Kokorou and Namga (668km²) were jointly designated Ramsar wetlands in 2001, making a total of seven Ramsar sites in Niger by 2005. Kokorou and Namga are also included in an African/Eurasian Waterbirds Flyway project, funded by the Global Environment Facility and due to start in 2006. A further five wetlands were in the process of being designated Ramsar sites early in 2006: the wetlands of Dam Doutchi, Lassour-Karandi, Tabalak, and the oases of Kawar and the Aïr.

FAUNA with Joost Brouwer

MAMMALS As in most countries, the number of mammals in Niger has greatly decreased. The difference is that in Niger this has happened mostly over the past 50 years rather than much longer ago, and that in Niger there are still some areas with very, very nice species. Their preservation is a matter of international importance.

About 130 species of mammals have been recorded in Niger. Unfortunately observations on the various species are not systematically collected, unless there is a project aimed at a particular species (see box *SOS Faune du Niger: Addax survey*, page 226). For many mammals it is therefore not clear what numbers still exist in Niger, if any. Statements below on the conservation status of individual species are based on the best available information, but do not go into the fine detail.

The mammals for which Niger is most famous, and for which it has the greatest conservation responsibility, are the species of the desert and desert fringes.

The last population of the scimitar-horned oryx, *Oryx damah*, until very recently lived in the grasslands on the edge of the Sahara in Niger and Chad, including the Ténéré Desert. It is now probably extinct in the wild.

The addax gazelle, *Addax nasomaculatus*, is a critically endangered species found in dunes and stony deserts. It is physiologically adapted to obtaining the water it needs from fodder. Formerly ranging from the Sudan to Morocco, populations probably still exist only in Mauritania, Mali and Niger (Termit area and/or Ténéré Desert). Like the Oryx it has suffered greatly from poaching, and probably from drought and competition with livestock.

The Barbary sheep (*mouflon* in French), *Ammotragus lervia*, is listed as vulnerable to extinction. Scattered populations still exist in mountainous areas and on plateaux throughout the Sahara, including in the Aïr and Termit mountains.

The Aïr region is known for holding small populations of cheetah, *Acinonyx jubatus*, and leopard, *Panthera pardus*. The only other areas in Niger where the two large cats might both still occur are 'W' National Park and the Termit Mountains. The cheetah may also still occur south of Bilma. Smaller cats that are more widespread include the caracal, *Caracal caracal*, sand cat, *Felis margarita*, African wild cat, *F. silvestris*, and serval, *Leptailurus serval*. In Niger, lions, *Panthera leo*, can only be found in 'W' National Park, although in the 1950s they were still common quite close to Niamey. Other larger carnivores in Niger include golden or common jackal, *Canis aureus* (throughout Niger), and side-striped jackal, *Canis adustus* (in the southwest). The spotted hyena, *Crocuta crocuta*, used to occur along the borders with Burkina Faso and Nigeria, and the striped hyena, *Hyaena hyaena*, throughout Niger. Unfortunately hyenas are often heavily persecuted, for example through poisoning, and they have disappeared from most of their former habitat in Niger. The spotted hyena still occurs in 'W' National Park. The most recent sightings of striped hyena are in the Termit Range and the Aïr. There are no recent observations of wild dogs, *Lycaon pictus*, in 'W' National Park, but according to the African Mammal Database (http://www.gisbau.uniroma1.it/amd.php) there are still some in the Djado Plateau area in the far northeast.

Similarly African elephants, *Loxodonta africana*, and African buffalo, *Syncerus caffer*, once roaming quite far north along the border with Burkina Faso and east along the border with Nigeria, are now restricted to 'W'. Among the buffalo there are quite a few red-coloured ones. Of the antelopes and gazelles only the red-fronted gazelle, *Gazella rufifrons*, is still relatively widespread in the southern half of Niger, but its range, too, is contracting. The Dorcas gazelle, *Gazella dorcas*, which is found as far south as the northern Sahel zone, is actually a species from north Africa and the Middle East. Most other species can now be found only in 'W' National Park, including the lovely striped-and-spotted bushbuck, *Tragelaphus scriptus*, two species of tiny duikers, the almost horse-sized roan antelope, *Hippotragus equinus*, with its large horns and stiff mane, two species of hartebeest with their strange elongated faces, oribi, *Ourebia ourebi*, Defassa waterbuck, *Kobus ellipsiprymnus*, and western Buffon's kob, *Kobus kob*.

Three species of monkey are also known from Niger: the olive baboon, *Papio hamadryas anubis*, and patas or red monkey, *Erythrocebus patas*, have a fairly wide, if patchy, distribution, including the Aïr Mountains. The vervet, green or tantalus monkey, *Cercopithecus aethiops*, is only found close to the border with Nigeria, including in 'W' National Park.

Other species worth mentioning that occur in Niger include the small rock hyrax, *Procavia capensis*, whose small hard droppings can be found at rocky outcrops throughout the savanna area and which are most closely related to elephants!; aardvark, *Orycteropus afer*, which used to occur throughout the grassland and savanna zone; warthog, *Phacochoerus africanus*, found only in the extreme southwest; honey badger, *Mellivora capensis*; African civet, *Viverra civetta*; Senegal bushbaby, *Galago senegalensis*; and north African crested porcupine, *Hystrix cristata*. In addition in various parts of Niger there are several species of foxes: pale or sand fox, *Vulpes pallida* (lower 60% of the country); Rüppell's sand fox, *V. rueppelli* (in the rest of the country, little overlap with the sand fox); and fennec fox, *V. zerda* (upper 60% of the country). Besides these, there are spotted-and-striped genet cats, hedgehogs, striped weasels, mongoose, squirrels and hares; almost all of these are nocturnal and most likely to be seen dead by the roadside. There are also numerous species of mice, rats and bats. Of the bats the most noticeable are the big fruitbats in Niamey that fly out over the Niger River at sundown.

In the Niger River there is a population of several hundred hippo, *Hippopotamus amfibius*, centred on the Ayorou area near the border with Mali. When the river is high following the wet season they disperse, coming down as far as Niamey and beyond and going back north again when the river level drops. If you are lucky you can see one from the Kennedy Bridge at the right time of year. Much harder to see are manatee, *Trichechus senegalensis*, which occur in the river from the border with Mali to the border with Nigeria. Spotted-neck otter, *Lutra maculicollis*, and Cape clawless otter, *Aonyx capensis*, are said to still occur in the Niger River as well, but they may also both be extinct in Niger. The isolated wetlands may be important drinking sites for certain larger mammals, but they have no particular species associated with them.

For giraffe you need to go to the giraffe project near Kouré, 60km from Niamey along the road to Dosso (see *Kouré and the Dallol Bosso Partial Reserve*, page 133). But if you really want to see a large selection of mammals in Niger, there is only one place to go: 'W' National Park (see page 122).

Details of mammal observations are always welcomed at the Niger Bird Database (see page 12).

BIRDS Bright green-and-yellow bee-eaters and sky-blue-and-orange rollers; huge-billed ground hornbills and tiny sunbirds; lone bustards at the edge of the desert, large flocks of storks and ducks from western Europe and Siberia: you can see them all in Niger. Not all at the same time, of course, because birdlife in Niger changes from place to place, and also from season to season. Habitats range from thick gallery forests along rivers in the south to bare rock and sand in the driest desert in the north. And each month certain bird species arrive in Niger, and others leave, as a part of their annual cycle.

Considering that Niger is landlocked and mostly quite arid, its avifauna is remarkably rich: approximately 530 species have been recorded to date, and new species are added each year. What is more, because there is little dense vegetation and it is easy to walk off the tracks, you can actually get to see many of those species relatively easily.

Resident bird species Because the Sahara and Sahel are so vast, and Niger is only a small part of these zones, Niger has no endemic bird species. As far as resident species are concerned, in and around the Aïr Mountains one can find ostrich and various large vulture species, Nubian bustard, cream-coloured courser, *Cursorius cursor*, desert eagle owl, *Bubo ascalaphus*, various species of sandgrouse, lark and wheatear, desert sparrow, *Passer simplex*, and trumpeter finch, *Bucanetes githagineus*. White-throated bee-eater, *Merops albicollis*, and yellow-breasted barbet, *Trachyphonus* *margaritatus*, are found throughout the drier parts of Niger, but the bee-eater only during the wet season. Arabian bustard, *Ardeotis arabs*, is also quite widespread, but much scarcer. The haunting, ventriloqual call of Saville's or red-crested bustard, *Eupodotis savillei*, can be heard throughout the southwest, especially during the rainy season. It can be quite some time before you actually see one, however.

Birds that you are likely to see in Niamey include Abdim stork, *Ciconia abdimi*, (nesting in many large trees during the rainy season), hooded vulture, *Necrosertes monachus*, black or yellow-billed kite, *Milvus migrans*, palm swift, *Cypsiurus parvus*, purple glossy starling, *Lamprotornis purpureus*, pied crow, *Corvus albus*, village weaver, *Ploceus cucullatus*, and Senegal firefinch, *Lagonosticta senegala*, and along the river the noisy spur-winged plover, *Vanellus spinosus*, and dirty-white cattle egret, *Bubulcus ibis*. Out in the country you are likely to see bright-blue and very long-tailed Abyssinian rollers, *Coracias abyssinica*, yellow, brown and green little bee-eaters, *Merops pusilla*, and possibly the red-with-a-green-head carmine bee-eaters, *Merops nubicus*. The huge nests found in trees in many villages are made by colonies of white-billed buffalo weavers, *Bubalornis albirostris*. For birds in the very south of the country, see 'W' *National Park* on page 122.

During the annual waterbird counts in January–February, more than 100 species of waterbird have been seen at Niger's wetlands. It is estimated that more than one million waterbirds are at those wetlands at that time of year. During the same counts more than 40 species of birds of prey have been seen. By and large the Afrotropical birds of prey move south for the dry season and make room for the European ones, but a few individuals often remain year round. How many Afrotropical waterbirds remain during the dry season depends on the rains during the preceding season, but there are always many thousands.

Migratory bird species Niger's richness in birds is due in no small part to the seasonal movements mentioned above. There are Afrotropical species that come north to spend the wet season in Niger, either to breed or following breeding further south. Other Afrotropical species breed near the edge of the Sahara and spend the dry season in the Sahelian or Sudanian zones. Many species from Europe and Asia come to spend the northern winter in all parts of Niger, others pass through once a year on a loop migration or twice a year on their way to and from wintering quarters further south. These species arrive in Niger along various routes. Some cross the Mediterranean Sea at Gibraltar and fly to Niger via Mauritania and Mali. Others cross the Mediterranean between Italy and Tunisia and cross the Sahara to 'make landfall' in the Aïr Mountains in the north of Niger. Others still fly via the Middle East down the Nile Valley and then west along the southern edge of the Sahara in Sudan and Chad until they reach Niger.

Bird ringing and satellite-tracking studies have linked Niger's birds to more than 40 other countries to date, with many more likely to follow. Those countries range from Mauritania to the Shetland Islands, across via Sweden and Finland to Russia east of the Ural Mountains, and on down to Tanzania, Zimbabwe and Congo-Brazzaville. Of the 530 species in Niger, 15% are thought to be at least partially Afrotropical migrants, and 32% are at least partially Palearctic migrants. A number of species have both resident and migratory populations.

Species that have been tracked by satellite to Niger include a short-toed eagle and two black storks from France, an osprey and a honey buzzard from Sweden, an osprey from Germany and a Montagu's harrier from the Netherlands. Abdim storks from Niger have been tracked as far away as Tanzania and Zimbabwe. Satellite transmitters are not small enough yet to track any of the thousands of ducks and waders that visit Niger from Europe and Siberia, never mind the countless small songbirds from the same general region.

Threatened bird species Only four globally threatened or near-threatened species occur in Niger. For the ferruginous duck, *Aythya nyroca*, Niger is probably not a very important country, but for pallid harrier, *Circus macrourus*, and lesser kestrel, *Falco naumanni*, Niger may be an important wintering area, and for Nubian bustard, *Neotis nuba*, an important area of residence. The enigmatic river prinia, *Prinia fluviatilis*, about which very little is known, has been reported from along the Niger River north of Tillabéri, and from near Diffa. It may also occur in 'W' National Park. The species that is closest to becoming extinct in Niger is the Sahelian subspecies of the ostrich, *Struthio camelus*, due to poaching and egg collecting: don't buy ostrich eggs, however beautiful they are! The large vulture species have also become much rarer in Niger, due to poisoning, and perhaps shooting or a reduction in carrion.

Important Bird Areas Important Bird Areas or IBAs are designated by BirdLife International, according to a number of criteria that include the presence of rare and endangered species; the presence of endemic (restricted range) species; the presence of groups of species typical for particular ecological zones; the presence of at least 1% of the population of a specific species that migrates along a particular route; and the presence of large congregations of colonially nesting birds, migratory birds or waterbirds.

In Niger 15 IBAs have been recognised. The species characteristic of the three ecological zones found in Niger are found mostly in only one or two of the present IBAs. This is an indication of how little is yet known ornithologically of the country. Of the 22 typical Saharan species that occur in north Africa, 14 are found in Niger, more precisely in the Aïr–Ténéré IBA. Some Saharan species are also found in the Dallol Boboye IBA 100km east of Niamey, and in the Dilia de Lagané IBA between Lake Chad and the Termit Mountains. All 16 typical Sahel species have been observed in Niger, mostly in Dallol Boboye and Dilia de Lagané IBAs. Some Sahel species are also found in the Aïr–Ténéré and in the 'W' National Park IBAs. Only a small part of Niger impinges on the northern edge of the Sudanian (savanna) zone. Of the 54 species deemed typical for this zone 26 have been reported from Niger, of which 21 are from 'W' National Park, and three additional ones from the Makalondi district (100km southwest of Niamey along the road to Ouagadougou), Dallol Boboye and Dilia de Lagané IBAs.

Eleven wetlands have been designated IBAs for being host to at least 20,000 waterbirds or to 1% of a flyway population. Of these three are river sites (including 'W' National Park), two are manmade reservoirs, and six are isolated wetlands. An additional eight wetlands (three river sites and five isolated wetlands) have met at least once the similar, but somewhat less demanding, criteria of the Ramsar Convention but have not yet been designated Ramsar sites. There is some overlap between wetland IBAs and Ramsar sites, but complete harmonisation is yet to take place. Almost all these important wetlands are in the 300–600mm annual rainfall zone.

Further reading All in all Niger is a fascinating country in which to watch birds, where much remains to be discovered by keen birdwatchers. This includes new species and new breeding records for the country, precise migration routes and wintering areas, and many details of the ecology of most species. For further information on the birds of Niger, see www.africanbirdclub.org (select Country Resources for Niger). Included are species lists for all 15 IBAs, as well as information on how to send details of all your own bird observations in Niger to the NiBDaB (Niger Bird Database). For other bird information see www.birdlife.org.uk and http://malimbus.free.fr/.

OTHER ANIMALS

Reptiles and amphibians On the island next to the Kennedy Bridge in Niamey crocodiles used to be worshipped. Crocodiles can no longer be found there, but there are still some in 'W' National Park, and also at isolated wetlands around Zinder. Similar isolated populations exist at inland wetlands in Mauritania and Burkina Faso.

Many species of lizard can still be found in Niamey. They include the medium-sized 'margouyas', found around many houses, the males of which have bright yellow-orange heads during the rainy season. There are also little striped ones with electric blue tails, and tiny geckos with big dark eyes and suction pads on their feet. Out in the countryside many other species await the patient observer.

There are all kinds of snakes, but most stay away from humans if they can. They include cobras and puff adders, as well as little vipers that hunt by ambushing, waiting for prey to pass by. At least 58 species of reptile are known from Niger. Because the atmosphere is so dry for a large part of the year, Niger is not a prime country for amphibians.

Fish There are a fair number of fish, mostly in the Niger River and its tributaries but also in wetlands that are isolated from other water bodies for most of the year. The most typical are perhaps the west African lungfish, *Protopterus annectens*, which are able to survive when their pools dry up by burrowing into the mud and sealing themselves within a mucus-lined burrow, and breathing air through their swim bladder instead of through their gills. Locally, during times of drought, they can be an important source of food. Commercially interesting species include north African catfish *poisson-chat* or *silure*, *Clarias gariepinus*, Nile tilapia, *Tilapia nilotica*, redbelly tilapia, *T. zilli*, and the very tasty Nile perch (*capitaine*), *Lates niloticus*, which can exceptionally reach 200kg. Also caught are bayad, *Bagrus bayad*, and *Auchenoglanis*, both catfish-like species. Some of the species mentioned have also been introduced into a number of isolated wetlands for fish production purposes.

For a list of 161 fish species that are found in Niger, see www.mongabay.com/fish/.

Invertebrates Much remains to be discovered about Niger's larger animals or vertebrates, but even less is known about its invertebrate butterflies, moths, dragonflies, spiders, scorpions, etc. If you have interesting observations and do not know what to do with them, just send them to the Niger Bird Database (see *Birds*, pages 10–12).

ENVIRONMENTAL CONCERNS with Joost Brouwer

THREATS Threats to Niger's ecosystems include degradation through prolonged droughts, unsustainable agricultural practices, clearing of new land for agriculture (often only marginally suitable), and overgrazing by livestock. Some of these problems are directly related to demographic developments: 3.3% annual growth in population means a doubling in just 20 years (see *Nigérien society*, page 31). Other problems are related to climatic changes: during the past 30 years annual rainfall everywhere in Niger has generally been roughly 100mm less than during the preceding 30 years. Illegal hunting and to some extent bush fires also have negative effects. Around urban centres the cutting of trees for firewood, charcoal or construction purposes is a major problem, as are lack of adequate facilities for the disposal of solid and liquid wastes. Plastic bags are everywhere around cities and villages, and garbage is sometimes used to fertilise fields without much sifting out of non-degradable items.

The floodplains of the Niger River are threatened by continued development for rice cultivation, as well as by the construction of further dams in Mali and Guinea-Conakry. There are also plans for the construction of dams in Niger itself. Virtually all wetlands in Niger are threatened by hydrological changes, erosion and/or sedimentation, and destruction of vegetation. This is caused by changing and inappropriate land use in their catchments, and by a lack of integrated local management that involves all stakeholders.

MANAGEMENT A number of ministries and departments are involved in natural resource management in Niger. However, means are very limited: only a very small number of people are responsible for guarding and managing wildlife throughout the country, including one national park and five reserves that cover 6.6% of the country or around 88,000km². Such numbers make active management, such as prevention of poaching and of illegal grazing, all but impossible, however willing the people involved.

Laws exist for the protection and use of water, soils, forests and trees on arable land, flora and fauna, but implementation and enforcement remain a problem. Wild natural resources are often not owned by anyone and, as wildlife is often not perceived to be useful, little reason is seen for saving wildlife or its habitat. Illegal hunting is also a big problem. On the other hand, older people have expressed an interest in conserving certain species of birds and mammals so that their descendants will be able to experience them, too. A few sacred forests still exist, mostly in the Gourmantché region in the very southwest of Niger, but fewer since the advance of Islam. In the Aïr Mountains, at Tchirzorene, a local marabout apparently successfully prohibits the exploitation of trees and animals. Plants and animals are also appreciated as sources of traditional medicine, and as environmental indicators. For instance, in large parts of Niger the arrival of Abdim storks, *Ciconia abdimii*, signals that the rains are about to arrive and that the fields should be prepared for the new cropping season.

Environmental legislation in Niger has been based primarily on French colonial laws, and in their absence on customary or Islamic law. Hunting was largely banned in 1974, but has been allowed again on a much wider scale since 1996. Conflicts between farmers and pastoralists over scarce resources such as grazing land and access to wetlands are ever more common. Traditional management structures are no longer adequate because of social, cultural, demographic and environmental changes. It is hoped that the proposed decentralisation of powers will give local people a bigger say, and a bigger interest, in the management of their resources.

THE FUTURE Ever since independence, Niger has demonstrated, through legislation and ratification of international conventions, its general wish to safeguard its natural heritage. Examples are on the increase of local stakeholders being involved more, and several NGOs (non-governmental organisations) concerned with the environment are establishing themselves. The general public, however, needs to be made more aware of the different aspects of natural resource conservation and their importance. The drive for self-sufficiency in food and in energy production often takes precedence over the wish to protect and restore the environment, even though all three are in the end inextricably linked and all three are mentioned in the 1984 Maradi Statement on Combating Desertification in Niger. In spite of a number of dedicated conservationists both within and outside the public service, because of a lack of funds and a lack of personnel, wildlife conservation in Niger continues to depend on international assistance, both governmental and non-governmental. Responsible eco-tourism can definitely play a role in nature conservation in Niger.

PREHISTORY

Palaeolithic Little is known about the Lower Palaeolithic period – from at least a million years ago until 90000BC – and no human remains have ever been found. Nevertheless, the discovery of an abundance of stone tools (usually quartz) leaves no doubt that different ancient civilisations were present in many corners of Niger this early in prehistory. The oldest traces, dating back to at least 300,000 years ago, have been found in the north of the Ténéré, in the region of Tafassesset, near the Algerian border, and in Tchigaï, near the border with Chad. Different acheulean layers (layers filled with small stone tools like points, leaf blades and scrapers) have been uncovered in the Adrar Bous (northeast of the Aïr Mountains), as well as in the regions of Bilma and the Djado. Most artefacts, especially in the northeast, have been traced back to the Mousterian and Aterian civilisation (90000–20000BC) in the Middle Palaeolithic period. Some relatively younger archaeological sites of this era (Upper Palaeolithic: from 10000BC) in the Mékrou Valley and the Adrar Bous area have produced very small microliths. Pottery was not yet known to these ancient civilisations, who lived as hunter-gatherers. The climate went through many changes, and varied from arid to humid in later periods.

Neolithic The climate became increasingly humid in the beginning of the Neolithic period (10000BC), and the levels of the Niger River and Lake Chad were at their highest ever. In the Aïr region, and later also in the Termit region, some significant techniques were introduced, such as making pottery, and the use of bows and arrows. By 7000BC, more arid times dawned and water levels gradually receded, while valleys in western Niger stood dry. Until 4000BC the northern Saharan regions were still fertile and wildlife was abundant. These regions were densely populated by people who lived as hunter-gatherers and fishermen. Lakes that have since dried up were numerous in this era. The practice of domesticated cattle-keeping spread from the Tassili region (Algeria) to the Aïr Mountains.

From 7000BC onwards, many civilisations had started burying their dead in different types of stone structures or *tumuli*. Some were no more than a pile of stones covering the body; others were more elaborate with different chambers and corridors. Artefacts like tools, decorative ornaments and pottery were sometimes buried with the dead.

The era from 4000BC to 2800BC was characterised by desertification of the central Sahara. The populations retreated to the south and the Aïr Mountains. Animal husbandry was now widespread, while agriculture was first introduced. Crops included millet and sorghum. The practice of hunting, fishing and food-gathering continued. Pottery was common, and techniques and decorations became more refined. The first copper and iron objects date back to this era and have been discovered in Azawagh (near Agadez) and Termit regions. Though techniques were still primitive, the metal objects soon replaced the use of most stone tools, but grinding stones and stone mortars (granite) remained in use. Bronze and brass alloys were manufactured in the later Neolithic. The whole Neolithic era has produced a rich heritage of rock engravings (see *Archaeological sites in the Aïr region*, page 180).

Post-Neolithic Following the Neolithic period, until the first centuries AD, climatic changes led to increasing aridness. The civilisations showed a tendency to diversify: animal husbandry became more common in the more arid regions, while agriculture was more intense in the southern plains, along the edges of Lake Chad and in river valleys, where permanent villages were created. Clearing of forest to develop more plots for agriculture intensified, and more crops – like vegetables, fruit and rice – were introduced. Metal-processing skills (copper, iron and bronze) developed over the centuries.

Many sites have been discovered in the Aïr region (Iwelen), Azawagh region, Termit and in the southwest of Niger, along the Niger Valley in particular. These sites reveal that funeral practices had changed, and some of the most remarkable archaeological finds include the burial ground near Bura (Téra region), where hundreds of ceramic and iron objects and ceramic statuettes – representing human figures – were unearthed.

The introduction of the Arab script in the 8th century coincided with the arrival of Islam. By then, several royal empires existed, but their early history remains veiled as no records exist. Since the Arabs had a tradition of recording history, more precise information is available from the 9th century onwards.

EARLY AND PRE-COLONIAL HISTORY The Songhay empire, with the town of Gao as capital, extended along the river Niger and into the Aïr Mountains in the north. The empire controlled the ancient trade caravan route from Mali in the west to the Aïr. The Kanem empire that existed around Lake Chad expanded over the eastern regions of Niger. In the 10th century, trade between the Arab civilisations along the Mediterranean coast, the Songhay empire, the Kanem empire and southerly states – along the Gulf of Guinea – developed, which in turn led to the rise of trade posts along the trans-Saharan trade routes. Through their regular contact with the Arabs, both the Kanem and Songhay empires converted to Islam.

In the rest of Niger, important developments took place in the 15th century. In the north, the Aïr sultanate was created. In the south, the seven Hausa city-states (see opposite) began to differentiate and they opened up more trade routes. In the east, the Bornou kingdom was founded by a king from the Seyfawa dynasty who had been expelled from the Kanem empire. More complex political structures developed. Islam gradually pushed its way south, though conversion often led to a syncretic mix of indigenous beliefs and Islam. Meanwhile, as the whole of Niger was wedged in between the Kanem and Songhay empires, for many centuries it was greatly influenced by these two polities.

The Songhay empire In the 14th century, the powerful Mali empire under Kankan Moussa had expanded its rule to the valley of the river Niger, engulfing the Songhay empire. It was under the first of two Songhay dynasties, the Sonni dynasty, that the Songhay empire became superior again. Sonni Ali Ber (1464–92) was a ruthless and great warrior, who pushed the boundaries of his empire from Timbuktu (Mali) well into the Niger Valley in the southwest of the country. Sonni Ali Ber was succeeded by his son in 1492, but was soon overthrown by one of his lieutenants, Mohamed Touré. He took the title of 'Askia' and founded the second Songhay dynasty: the Askia dynasty.

The Songhay empire reached its splendour under Askia Mohamed (1493–1528). He was a devoted Muslim and Islamic scholarship flourished under his rule. Askia Mohamed was a great warrior, but at the same time allowed smaller polities to continue to exist, as long as they were willing to pay tribute to him. After his pilgrimage to Mecca in 1496, Askia Mohamed conquered parts of Niger including Agadez and the Aïr. In return for taxes, he ensured the security of the region, which enabled trade in this zone to reach its maximum. He also managed to invade deep into Hausaland, where the city-states of Gobir, Katsina and Zaria succumbed to his power, while Kano had to pay tribute. In 1529, Askia Mohamed was overthrown by his own son, Askia Daouda (1529–83). The empire continued to prosper, until internal conflicts and threats from invading Moroccan troops caused the weakened empire to collapse after the Battle of Tonbidi (Mali) in 1591.

The Kanem and Bornou empires The Kanem empire reached the pinnacle of its glory in the 13th century, when Fezzan (Libya) was conquered. The empire now ruled over the whole north–south caravan route through eastern Niger, and created the important oases of the Kawar (Bilma) and the Djado. While the Kanem empire weakened as a result of recurring raids of nomadic groups, the Bornou empire took over the leading position under King Idris Alaoma (1571–1603). He conquered the whole region around Lake Chad, and the southern regions of Niger including the Damagaram. However, after Alaoma the Bornou empire rapidly declined. Though less influential than before, the Bornou empire withstood many attacks and raids, and continued to exist until 1893. It then collapsed under the onslaught of Captain Rabih Fadlallah, a native of Darfur in the Sudan who had set out to control trans-Saharan trade routes to the east of Lake Chad, but instead had moved on to conquer the Bornou empire.

The Hausa city-states The Hausa people are not so much one, but rather different ethnic groups unified through a common language. Differents waves of migrations from the Aïr and the Kanem and Bornou empires had brought these groups together in the northern regions of present-day Nigeria and the south of Niger in the 10th century, where the indigenous population soon assimilated with these new arrivals. Together, they founded the seven independent Hausa city-states of Daura, Kano, Katsina, Zaria, Rano, Biram and Gobir (see *Ethnic groups*, page 26), and each formed centres of trade and learning. Most Hausa embraced Islam in the 14th century, though many elements of the indigenous animist belief were incorporated in the new religion.

By the beginning of the 17th century, the Songhay empire no longer existed while the Bornou empire was weakened. This cleared the way for the Hausa city-states to expand their economic influence. They controlled an important section of the north–south trade route, which linked the Mediterranean to Nigeria and Ghana.

Under the rule of Bawa Jan Gorzo (1771–89), king of the Gobir city-state, times were difficult due to military invasions and attacks from the Tuareg, and instability reigned. At the same time, widespread criticism, even from within Hausa circles, targeted the dubious, syncretic Muslim practices of the Hausa and the exuberant lifestyle of their ruling class.

The Jihad of Ousman Dan Fodio The Peul Ousman Dan Fodio (1754–1817) was a brilliant Muslim scholar and one of many religious leaders who opposed the Hausa interpretation of Islam. In 1804, he launched a *jihad* or holy war on the Hausa states, to create the Peul empire of Sokoto, and most of the Hausa states succumbed to his violence. Meanwhile, a fairly young polity – the Damagaram, founded by groups of Kanouriphone from the east – stood up against Dan Fodio and managed to stay out of his reach. Many animist Hausa fled the region, while most city-states were usurped by the Sokoto empire. At its peak, this empire reached beyond the boundaries of the Hausa city-states, and the Islamic state of Sokoto stretched from Cameroon to Téra in the valley of the river Niger, where Dan Fodio's troops were halted by the Djerma leader Issa Korombé. Like the Damagaram, the Bornou empire managed to retain most of its territory. Towards the end of the 19th century, the power of the Sokoto empire decreased, allowing the Damagaram state – with Zinder as its capital – to emerge under Sultan Tanimoune (1851–85).

COLONIAL HISTORY
European explorers and expeditions While the Sokoto empire declined and the Damagaram state flourished, the first European explorers appeared on the scene in west Africa. The Briton Mungo Park travelled the river Niger in Mali in the early

years of the 19th century. Employed by the British government, the German Heinrich Barth set out on an extensive expedition between 1850–55. From Tripoli (Libya) he crossed the Sahara and the Aïr Mountains to Agadez, then continued south to Tessaoua, west to Say and all the way to Timbuktu (Mali), before returning east to Zinder, Lake Chad and the oases of the Kawar. The German explorer Nachtigal travelled from Libya through the Kawar to Lake Chad in 1870. Detailed reports of their ventures triggered an interest amongst European authorities in these regions. Besides economic considerations, central Sudan (the zone along the southern half of the Sahara) became important in creating a link between emerging eastern and western African colonial empires. The region around Lake Chad was considered crucial in this respect.

Unknown to the indigenous inhabitants, Great Britain and France had started to divide up African territory on paper. The line that was originally drawn to separate the French from the British intended range of influence was located north of the present-day frontier between Niger and Nigeria. The French then sent out Lieutenant Colonel Monteil in 1891–92 to determine the actual extent of British and French influence between the river Niger and Lake Chad. During this peaceful exploratory mission the first protectorate treaties were signed with the local authorities.

The conquest of Niger The scramble for central Sudan having been worked out on paper, the imperialist powers decided it was time to send in the army. In 1897, the Cazémajou mission was sent out to persuade the local authorities into signing treaties and forming alliances. Though it was a relatively calm expedition, it was stopped short by Sultan Amadou of Damagaram. He feared the position of the Damagaram would weaken if the French achieved an alliance with the forces of Rabih near Lake Chad, therefore he had Captain Cazémajou assassinated in May 1898.

The conquest took a different turn when the French sent out three military columns to converge on Lake Chad from the east (the Gentil mission coming from Congo), the west (the Voulet–Chanoine mission, coming from Timbuktu) and the north (the Foureau–Lamy mission who would meet the Voulet–Chanoine mission in Zinder). Their ultimate objective was to dispose of Rabih – who was still in control of the Lake Chad region – then push on eastward to establish a link to the Congo. The Voulet–Chanoine mission set out from the left bank of the river Niger in January 1899, leaving behind a trail of atrocities and destruction. The French government, who were informed about the excessive violations, sent out Lieutenant Colonel Klobb to take over command of the mission. Soon after he caught up with the column near Tessaoua, he was killed by Voulet and Chanoine's troops, who had been recruited on the way. These, in turn, revolted against the violent methods of their commanders and both Voulet and Chanoine were slain shortly afterwards.

The remaining French officers Joalland and Meynier took over command, and continued east where the Damagaram surrendered to the French after only a brief battle. In November 1899, they were joined by the exhausted and wrecked Foureau–Lamy mission, who had struggled their way through the Aïr to Zinder. The joint mission ventured to Lake Chad, where they met the Gentil mission. When the combined forces defeated Rabih in 1900, they had successfully established a link between the French African territories.

However, it did not mean that the French had gained full control over all the regions they had traversed. The Tuareg stood to lose their favourable position in trans-Saharan trade, even though the trade had already dwindled dramatically as a result of the violent battles during previous decades. The Kel Gress were among those who revolted against the French oppressors, and they found ready allies among other Tuareg groups of Damergou. In 1902, these rebel troops controlled the regions between the Aïr and the Damagaram, and they pushed further east, closing in on the French near Lake Chad. After a series of battles in which the French proved the more powerful, most Tuareg forces either fled to Nigeria or succumbed to the French, while a smaller group of Tuareg retreated northwards. Kaocen, an Izkazkazen Tuareg, was one of them, and he later was to play a significant part in a second Tuareg revolt in 1917 (see *The siege of the French garrison in Agadez*, page 161). By 1903, the French had strengthened their position in most of the military territory, and they established posts in Gouré, N'Guigmi (near Lake Chad) and Agadez.

In the Convention of 1904, the French and British agreed to delimit a new frontier between their respective territories (which was finally demarcated in an agreement in 1909), while the Military Territory of Niger was created by decree in December 1904. The territory stretched from Timbuktu to Lake Chad and included the left bank of the river Niger, and was governed from Niamey. In 1912, the 'new' Military Territory of Niger was created, and this territory now forms the current boundaries of Niger. The central administration was shifted to Zinder until 1922, when the Military Territory of Niger became a civilian-governed colony (the military remained in charge of the *cercle de Agadez* only). Niamey then became the capital of Niger, seat of the French governor (see *Niamey: history*, page 93).

The French colonial administration By 1908, the situation in most regions allowed the French to loosen their military strategy and start focusing on the establishment of a political administration. As the French lacked both the means and the manpower to establish 'direct rule' over the new territory, they sought to convert and incorporate the existing local authorities. This was a huge concession, since the traditional systems were feudal or aristocratic in character and not in compliance with the French administrative system.

Niger was divided into seven *cercles*, subdivided into *secteurs* (later *subdivisions*). The *cercles* and *secteurs* were all administered by French officers, later also French civilians. The *secteurs* comprised traditional political entities such as provinces and cantons (territorially defined entities), and tribes and *groupements* (ethnically defined entities, equivalent to nomadic and semi-nomadic groups). Traditional religious and political leaders were given the uniform title of *chef du canton* or *chef du groupement*, all with identical duties, obligations and prerogatives. They had to collect taxes and provide labour forces for public construction works. The indigenous population were called *sujets* or 'subjects' rather than civilians, and they did not enjoy any of the rights embodied in the Constitution.

In the administrative reorganisation process, the Djerma ethnie were given considerable preferential treatment. Though in the early days of the French conquest they had put up stiff resistance, the Djerma later showed the will to collaborate with the French more than any other ethnic group in Niger. As they were considered more malleable than others, the Djerma were allowed to form an elite, with many privileges like access to education and administrative posts. The Djerma have retained this favoured position ever since the early days of colonisation.

The era between 1922 and 1946 was the time of 'classic' colonial rule, with only moderate socio-structural changes and no clear administrative policy. The opinion of the colonised Nigérien population was sought but not acted upon, with the exception of some religious movements who created a temporary stir. Islam had become the favoured religion by the colonisers, as the Muslim organisation was more in concordance with French rule than indigenous animist structured entities.

Some extreme religious expressions, such as the animist Hauka movement and the Muslim Hammallist doctrine, that both seemed to undermine French authority, were suppressed by force.

Natural disaster struck in the form of a drought and locust invasion, leading to a serious famine in 1931. Tens of thousands of people died as a direct result, while many more fled the country to Nigeria. To absorb the effects of future droughts, the French introduced a system to bank local food supplies in millet granaries, while they also promoted different locust-resistant root crops, as well as cash crops to improve the national economy. Groundnut cultivation became one of the pillars of the Nigérien economy for a number of years. A short period of moderate prosperity was followed by another cycle of droughts between 1937 and 1940 and another economic crisis. During the years of World War II, Niger became a puppet in a theatre of opposing European forces on African soil, which resulted in an increased tension between Niger and its neighbouring countries. This effect was largely reversed after the war ended.

A significant shift in the principles of colonial policy followed the Brazzaville conference of 1944, when different European colonising nations stipulated their moral obligation towards the colonies. For the first time the voice of the Nigérien *sujets* was heard in the process that led to the Constitution of 1946, in which the French colonies were renamed Overseas Territories, unified under the French Union. The indigenous people – now 'citizens' – became involved in the shaping of their own future. The first Nigérien political parties, a local branch of the inter-African *Rassemblement Démocratique Africain* (RDA) and the *Parti Progressiste Nigérien* (PPN), were founded. In the years that followed, gradual reforms on an institutional level and the influence of other newly founded political parties paved the way for a new era of autonomy and finally independence.

INDEPENDENCE Niger achieved full independence on 3 August 1960. Hamani Diori, the leader of the PPN, became the first president of a repressive single-party civilian regime. Diori maintained close ties with France, and despite some unsuccessful coups, a weak economy and recurring ethnic conflicts, the political situation was generally stable for over a decade. Diori was re-elected in 1965 and 1970. The tide turned after a series of droughts between 1968 and 1974, when much of Niger's livestock perished and crop production plummeted. Diori was accused of corruption and lifting food aid supplies, and in April 1974 he was overthrown in a bloody military coup led by Lieutenant Colonel Seyni Kountché.

Kountché himself became the new president of a strict military regime, denouncing the previous civil constitution. The discovery of uranium in the northeast of Niger greatly helped to restore the economy after the severe droughts. However, as not all Nigériens benefited from the uranium boom, disparities in wealth only magnified, resulting in growing civil unrest. Having survived several coup attempts, Kountché died after a long illness in 1987.

His Chief of Staff, Ali Saibou, took over and embarked on a programme to dismantle the Supreme Military Council and articulate a new constitution. He created the *Mouvement National pour une Société de Développement* or National Movement of a Developing Society (MNSD) and held presidential elections in 1989, with himself as the only candidate. Consequently, Saibou was elected president. A new constitution – in which opposition parties were still banned – was adopted in 1990. The people of Niger were not satisfied with Saibou's shallow promises of a progressive approach that did not seem to materialise. In the north, a deep-rooted conflict between the Tuareg and the government had escalated in violence, marking the beginning of the Tuareg rebellion (see page 182). Meanwhile, students and union labourers participated in a wave of strikes and manifestations, calling for democratic reforms and the introduction of a multi-party system. After a national conference held in July 1991, Saibou's government was suspended and an interim government under Adamou Cheiffou was formed. Despite the deteriorating economy – largely a result of the steep decline in uranium prices – the transition government accomplished a few successes such as the adoption of key legislation (electoral codes and rural codes). Several independent newspapers appeared and were testimony to an increased freedom of the press.

The first free multi-party elections were held in 1993, and Mahamane Ousmane (MNSD) was elected president. The economy suffered even more after the devaluation of the CFA franc, and civil unrest prevailed in the following year. Meanwhile, rivalries within the multi-party coalition of nine political parties resulted in chaotic and inefficient government.

In January 1996, Colonel Ibrahim Baré Maïnassara used this governmental impasse to justify a military coup. He drafted a new constitution and promised elections for a new civil government, which were held in July 1996. Baré surfaced as president after highly fraudulent elections characterised by political manipulations and fiddling with ballot boxes. Baré was also accused of restricting the freedom of the press, violating human rights and nepotism. In response, international donors refused to restore multilateral and bilateral economic aid, while every aspect of the Nigérien economy was put under an IMF and World Bank direction that was more strict than ever. The situation went from bad to worse, as arrears in salary payments to civil servants and the military led to strikes, mutiny and general civil unrest. The fact that he succeeded in reaching a peace accord with the Tuareg in the northeast, ending a five-year rebellion, could not save Baré. In April 1999, a military coup was staged by the chief of his own presidential guard, Major Daouda Mallam Wanke. That Baré was assassinated in the process would later be described as 'an unfortunate accident' that served the general interest.

Wanke established a transitional National Reconciliation Council which had to prepare the way for a constitutional referendum, and legislative and presidential elections. The new constitution was approved in July 1999, and in October and November of that year, seven candidates stood in the election that was eventually won by Mamadou Tandja.

Mamadou Tandja The new president, a retired colonel and candidate for the MNSD, was by no means new on the political scene. After a military career he became Prefect of Maradi (1976–79), Minister of Interior Affairs under Kountché (1981–87), Prefect of Tahoua (1981–88), Ambassador in Nigeria (1988–90), Minister of Interior Affairs under Saibou (1990–91) and MNSD leader since 1991. He had run for president in 1993, but it was Ousmane who was elected on that occasion. At the age of 61, Tandja beat his opponents who included ex-president Ousmane and two former prime ministers. Tandja formed a coalition of the MNSD and the Democratic and Social Convention (CDS), while the legislature contained a total of five political parties. Hama Amadou (MNSD) was appointed Prime Minister, while Ousmane (now leader of the CDS) was elected Speaker of the National Assembly.

The new government was faced with no easy task, as the heritage of its predecessors included social and economic problems, arrears in wage payments in the public sector, general unrest especially among labourers and students, and extreme poverty. Despite economic restraint, salaries in the public sector were now paid more regularly, though the arrears were not yet fully compensated. In August 2002, a serious military uprising in Niamey, Diffa and N'Guigmi – motivated by poor pay and conditions – was brought under control within a matter of days.

In order to restore the pitiful economic balance, Tandja adopted plans for economic reforms mandated by the World Bank and the IMF, and in 2000 Niger qualified for the Heavily Indebted Poor Countries Initiative (HIPC). This allowed the development and implementation of an ambitious programme to improve the health and education sectors in rural areas: the *Programme Spécial*. Decentralisation was another important pillar of the government's central policy. The process of decentralisation had already been set in motion under Ousmane, and was a crucial part of the peace accords with the Tuareg. In July 2004, just before the end of Tandja's first term, successfully held municipal elections – the first of their kind in the history of Niger – marked an important phase in the process of decentralisation (see *Poverty reduction*, page 23 and *Aïr Mountains*, pages 182–3).

While Tandja's first term as president was no smooth run, it was marked by relative stability, unity within the coalition, and the will to move forward. Opposition voices criticised Tandja's poor use of financial and human resources – culminating in what was seen as an ineffective execution of the *Programme Spécial* – and he was also accused of being insensitive to public opinion.

Despite some heavy criticism, Tandja successfully ran for the presidency in 2004, and he was elected for another five-year term with 65.5% of the votes in elections that were considered generally free and fair. The legislature now contained seven political parties, and both Hama Amadou and Mahamane Ousmane were reinstated to their previous positions.

In March 2005, only months into his second term, Tandja shook the nation. As part of the IMF/World Bank mandatory economic reforms, Tandja was pressured into imposing a 19% VAT on basic food products such as millet, wheat flour, tea, sugar, rice and milk. The people of Niger felt betrayed by this measure that could not be rhymed with 'poverty reduction', one of the popular fundamentals of Tandja's electoral campaign. The timing was even more unfortunate against the backdrop of an imminent food crisis after drought and locust invasions had decimated livestock and the harvests of 2004. A series of mass demonstrations and general strikes, paralysing the nation for days, forced a partial climbdown.

Rather than allowing the independent media to act as an early warning system, Nigérien journalists who had covered the famine were arrested and silenced. By the same token, Tandja publicly denied that his people were starving. His comments on the famine were criticised both by the Nigérien people and the international community, but in rather opposite ways. Coverage of the famine showed a humanitarian disaster of immense proportions, and Tandja's denial of this shook the world. His own people had a different perspective: Tandja should have stressed that in fact famines are common in Niger, and every year many people die of starvation even when the international press is not around. The year 2005 was worse than previous years, but came neither as a surprise nor a shock to many Nigériens. They felt that Tandja should have pleaded for more structural and long-term food aid for this serious and recurring problem.

In September 2005, after a bountiful rainy season at last, Niger and the Nigérien government have started to recover from the crisis, and the political and social situation has calmed down once more during the months that followed.

ECONOMY

The economy is heavily based on the rural sector, which accounts for 42% of GDP, providing the livelihood of more than 85% of the population. Only a nominal part of Niger – mainly along the southern border with Nigeria – is arable, yet a surprisingly large proportion of the population is active in **agriculture**. Irrigation and soil improvement (manure and sometimes chemical fertilisers) are essential for the cultivation of the otherwise poor and dry soil. Principal food crops are millet, sorghum and rice. Requiring a lot of water, rice is produced in riverine areas. Millet and sorghum, on the other hand, can be cultivated in arid zones. In good years, agriculturalists can achieve self-sufficiency, but additional supplies often need to be imported. Most cash crops are produced in the southern regions (Dosso, Maradi, Zinder), and these include cowpeas, groundnuts and cotton. The region of Diffa produces red peppers. Owing to the favourable climatic conditions in parts of the Aïr Massif, some irrigated agriculture (onions, citrus fruits) is possible.

Animal husbandry is the second-largest activity of the country. Cattle exports are significant, though hard to quantify as official statistics lag behind the real numbers of animals that have crossed borders into Nigeria, Libya and other countries. Main livestock are cattle, goats, sheep, camels and some donkeys and horses. Goats and sheep represent the largest proportion of all livestock, while cattle and camels are highly valued as 'living capital' for the livestock trade. Some hides and skins are exported or locally traded for the manufacture of handicrafts.

Along the rivers in the southern regions and in places with permanent open water (Lake Chad and some other lakes), **fishing** takes place. Most of the fishing is done for local consumption, and to a lesser extent for export to neighbouring countries.

Hazardous climatic conditions make agriculture and animal husbandry the most vulnerable sectors of the Nigérien economy, with recurring extended droughts being the most debilitating factor. The drought of 2004 in combination with locust infestations caused the harvest to drop dramatically, while many cattle perished as a result of lack of grazing. This triggered a serious food crisis in 2005.

While the economy is heavily based on the rural sector, it is the mining sector that provides the greatest export revenue. Niger has some of the world's largest **uranium** deposits in Arlit, between Agadez and the Algerian border. When the uranium deposits were first being exploited in the 1970s, Niger's export earnings grew rapidly. In 1980 and 1981, the demand for uranium dropped dramatically, which resulted in a sharp decline in production. Despite this, the output is still 3,000 tonnes per year, representing 31% of national export revenue.

In recent years, some exploitable deposits of **gold** have been discovered. The first Nigérien gold mine – in the region of Tillabéri – became functional in October 2004. Other mineral resources include **phosphates**, **coal**, **iron**, **limestone** and **gypsum**. Niger has some **oil** potential, and in the region of Agadem – to the north of Lake Chad – some exploration is in progress.

Nearly half of the government's budget is derived from **foreign donor resources**. The most important donors are the World Bank, the IMF, France, the European Union, UN agencies, as well as a number of individual countries. Niger entered the IMF in 1963, and is represented in the IMF by the Ministry of Finances. In recent years, Niger has been granted partial debt relief by the IMF and the World Bank under the Heavily Indebted Poor Countries Initiative (HIPC). While this has provided more scope in the battle against poverty, it also means that the IMF and the World Bank have gained even more control over the economy and politics of Niger.

POVERTY REDUCTION

IMF AND POVERTY REDUCTION In 1996, the IMF and the World Bank created the Heavily Indebted Poor Countries Initiative (HIPC) to provide debt relief to the world's poorest and most heavily indebted countries. Not surprisingly, Niger was among the 27 countries elected for the initiative, but they would have to meet certain requirements first. In 2000, as Niger had shown three years of efforts to work towards a free-market economy, partial debt relief was granted. The World Bank, the IMF and members of the Paris Club reserved a total of US$1.2 billion in debt relief for Niger. The net present value (NPV) of this debt relief is equivalent to about half of Niger's total debt outstanding as of 2000. Niger developed a Poverty Reduction Strategy Paper (PRSP) which is based on four pillars:

- the creation of a macro-economic environment to promote economic growth
- the development of the production sector, especially in rural areas, to reduce vulnerability and increase income generation
- the improvement in access of the poor to quality social services
- the strengthening of human and institutional capacities, promotion of good governance, and decentralisation

In other words, partial debt relief significantly reduces Niger's annual debt service obligations, freeing funds for expenditure geared towards poverty reduction and reducing the constraints on economic growth. Niger has embarked on an ambitious programme that aims to diversify the economy; to privatise 12 state-owned companies, including water and telephone utilities; to improve the quality of and the accessibility to health services and education, especially in rural areas; to improve access to safe water and sanitation; to build capacities of the administration of civil society; to implement local development programmes, and so on.

SOME STATISTICS
- The UNDP Human Development Index ranked Niger 174th out of 175 countries in 2003.
- In 2003, the GDP per capita was estimated at US$200.
- Two-thirds of the population live below the poverty line, half of which can be considered extremely poor.
- Niger has a very narrow natural resource base: despite the decline of the demand for uranium, this sector still provides 31% of total export revenues
- Niger is highly vulnerable to external shocks such as droughts.
(Source: the World Bank Group and the World Nuclear Association)

DECENTRALISATION One of the key words in the whole HIPC process of poverty reduction is 'decentralisation'. At independence in 1960, Niger had been divided into 36 provinces (*préfectures*), headed by state-appointed governors (*préfets*). All major decisions had to be taken through the *préfecture* to a ministerial level, even when local issues were concerned. The urgency to strive for decentralisation already existed during the time of President Kountché (1974–87) and his political party, the MNSD. It was described as 'the development from the grassroots', where everything begins with the people rather than at the political top. The process of decentralisation was set in motion under President Ousmane (1993–96), though it turned out to be in very slow motion for many reasons. Bureaucracy, for one, but also the fear that the unity of the nation would be in jeopardy. And, last but not least, the lack of funds to get the process off the ground. Finally, after long years of refining the whole idea, the partial debt relief of the HIPC initiative pushed the doors to decentralisation wide open.

In June 2002, four new laws concerning decentralisation were passed. These laws determined to which degree the regions, departments and communities could – and should – eventually intervene and decide on local issues. The process of restructuring administrative and governance systems was sealed by the municipal elections held on 4 July 2004. Since the elections, Niger is divided into 265 much smaller districts (*communes*), each with its own democratically elected council and mayor (*maire*). Many of the national responsibilities were now transferred to district and community level, thus bringing the power closer to the people. It also means that local authorities now have to find their own ways to generate funds to contribute towards one of the main goals of decentralisation, that of poverty reduction.

HEALTH AND EDUCATION: *PROGRAMME SPECIAL*
Some more statistics
Health
- Infant-juvenile (<5 years) mortality per thousand live births (2001): 274
- Infant (<1 year) mortality per thousand live births (2004): 126
- Maternal mortality per 100,000 live births (2001): 700
- Vaccination ratio for different vaccines (2001): 30–50%
- Ratio of health officials to the population (2001):
  - doctors: 1 per 33,000
  - nurses: 1 per 9,000
  - midwives per woman of childbearing years: 1 per 6,650
  - pharmacists: 1 per 769,230
- HIV/AIDS seroprevalence (2002): 0.87% nationwide (50% among prostitutes)

Education
- Literacy rate among ages 15 and older (2002): 19.9%
- Access ratio in the first year of primary school (2002): 49.8%
- Ratio of age groups completing primary level education (2002): 25.6%
(Source: the Second Progress Report of the Poverty Reduction Strategy, June 2003–July 2004)

As part of the Poverty Reduction Strategy and in order to try to improve these sad figures, President Mamadou Tandja developed the *Programme Spécial*, in which he announced the construction of 1,000 classrooms, 1,000 health centres and 1,000 wells and boreholes. Since the beginning of the programme, which was initiated in 2003, these numbers have largely been achieved, and those who are familiar with the design of schools and health centres, will see the new buildings near rural towns and villages all over the country. Yet, it would be premature to call the programme an unqualified success.

Many of the health centres are no more than an empty shell, with no equipment and no medical staff, while new classrooms lack sufficiently trained teachers and school materials such as books. The programme did foresee the training of staff, but is lagging behind in this regard. Moreover, the training can hardly be called adequate, as a medical nurse – trained from scratch for this programme alone – receives no more than three months of education, while a teacher should master his teaching skills within nine months. After that, he or she is faced with large numbers of pupils, sometimes as many as 80 – of different ages and levels – in one class, and only a handful of books. The material for the health centres and schools is not included in the programme, and since decentralisation was effected in June 2004, local communities are expected to contribute towards the upkeep of stock and material. Thus far, while many communities have gained something from the *Programme Spécial*, they are now the ones struggling to make it actually work.

Nevertheless, despite criticism of the adequacy of the programme, new statistics (taken from the same source) do show some improvement in the overall situation. Some of the successes may indeed stem from the programme, but large-scale vaccination campaigns and campaigns to persuade the population to send their children to school have also had some effect. In 2004, the vaccination ratio for different vaccines had risen to 40–75%; infant-juvenile mortality had dropped to 252 per 1,000; the maternal mortality ratio had dropped from 700 to 500; the access ratio in the first year of primary school had risen to 55.2% (of which 40.3% are girls); while the ratio of age groups completing primary level education had risen to 32.2%. On the other hand, one doctor now has to serve 50,000 people, which is a significant increase. One can hardly say that these statistics are comforting, and clearly the battle is still on.

EVALUATION OF THE POVERTY REDUCTION STRATEGY In 2004, three years into the Poverty Reduction Strategy Programme, evaluation by the IMF and the World Bank concluded that the government had made serious efforts to improve living conditions, but that the results are insufficient. The diversification of the economy leaves much to be desired, although the macro-economic stability is considered encouraging. The process of decentralisation has significantly moved forward, but the formal transfer of authority to the local councils and mayors has fallen short of expectations. Moreover, the lack of funds for the 265 new districts means that for now there is little they can achieve.

Current indicators concerning health and education show that some progress has been made, but too little thus far. Many factors surface when it comes to explaining why progress is slowed down: time-consuming red tape procedures; lack of resources despite the partial debt relief; but also erratic rainfall patterns (note: only after the evaluation report had been published would the devastating effects of the drought and locust invasions of 2004 become clear). Another factor that gives cause for much concern is the high rate of demographic growth (3.3% per year). It means that even though there is some economic growth, it is unable to keep up with the population growth, and therefore does not have a noticeable effect on the per capita GDP. So while Niger is struggling to beat the statistics of poverty within the timeframe of the poverty reduction programme, demographic trends can be altered only in the long term. And that really casts a shadow over the future of Niger.

ETHNIC GROUPS

The Nigérien population consists of a colourful amalgam of ethnic groups. As a comment on this, a Nigérien stated: 'None of us can say that we originate from Niger. At some point in history we all crossed the invisible borders of what is Niger today. We can only say that some of us got here before the others did.'

HAUSA The majority of the sedentary peoples are Hausa (54%). Though they share the same language, customs, cultural habits, and social and political organisation, they are not one ethnic group, but rather various ethnic groups unified through a common language. There are various theories about the origins of the Hausa. One assumes that between the 10th and 15th centuries, different groups originating from central Sudan (as the Sahara region was then named) were ousted from the north by Berbers or Tuareg, or maybe they migrated, forced by droughts. They then somehow regrouped, founding the seven Hausa city-states of Daura, Kano, Katsina, Zaria, Rano, Biram and Gobir. These were located in what is now northern Nigeria, and the southern parts of Niger between Birni N'Konni and Zinder.

The Hausa developed solid socio-political structures, allowing them to make full use of the natural resources as well as their favourable position along trade routes. Religious life took a different turn when Islam was introduced in the 14th century. Though it did cause some duality, Islam did not fully replace the traditional animist belief and the two coexisted for centuries, merging into a syncretic religion. One significant sub-group of the Hausa is the Azna, or those Hausa that refused to convert to Islam in favour of their traditional beliefs. Within the groups of Azna that segregated from the city-states independently, one can distinguish between the Azna or Mawri people in the region of Dogondoutchi, and the Azna in the region of Birni N'Konni and Massalata (see the relevant chapters). These Azna still practise different animist rituals – based on spirit possession (the Bori cult) and fetishism – and show a deep respect for their spiritual leaders. Other (predominantly Muslim) Hausa sub-groups are the Adarwa, the Konnawa, the Gobirawa, the Katsinawa and the Damagarawa. These names refer to geographical locations where certain family lineages once firmly settled.

By the time the city-states eventually disintegrated or were usurped by other ruling entities, many Hausa had already dispersed. Today, Hausa still live in northern Nigeria, but also in parts of Ghana, Togo and of course Niger. The essence of their organisation had become so deeply intertwined with the essence of the Hausa identity as a whole, that many of the traditional elements of their hierarchic society survived the ravages of time, including the colonial penetration.

The Hausa can generally be characterised as hard workers with many skills. As they consider themselves 'owners of the soil', the Hausa cultivate the land, in farming communities with a strict organisation based on tradition. They also master many skills as craftsmen, whether it be with textiles, leather, metal or clay. But most of all, many Hausa excel as traders and merchants. Members of various Hausa lineages used to be easy to identify through facial markings or scarrings, which consist of sets of fine lines or geometrical patterns on the cheeks and temples. The use of these facial markings seems to be less common among the younger generations.

Not only is the Hausa language spoken by the largest ethnic group, but many others have adopted Hausa as their second language. Since many Hausa people are renowned merchants, theirs is the common language of a diverse group of traders. It is the dominant language by far from Zinder to Dogondoutchi; Hausa spreads across the Nigerian border and all the way north to Agadez.

DJERMA-SONGHAY Strictly speaking, the Djerma and the Songhay are two different ethnic groups, but their probable origins and their merging in the same western zone of Niger strongly link the two.

According to legend, the cradle of the Djerma had been the land of the Mandé (in what is now Mali). A fierce dispute with the ruling Peul forced the Djerma to flee. They scattered over eastern areas in Mali and into Niger, where some settled at the arid plateau of Zermaganda – north of the river Niger in the westernmost part of the country – in small autonomous kindred groups.

In the 15th century, the Songhay empire reached well beyond the boundaries of Mali. Some low-ranked groups of Songhay, the Sorko (fishermen or 'masters of the water') and the Gabiri (agriculturalists or 'masters of the soil') were already present in this western part of Niger. Then the Moroccan invasion of the Songhay empire pushed the Songhay aristocracy further east and into Niger, where they put up strong resistance against the invaders. However, in the 16th century the empire fell apart, demanding the social order be redefined and eventually leading to various migrations within the region. In the mean time, the Djerma also began to disperse towards the south. The gradual process of assimilation of various groups eventually led the Djerma to adopt the Songhay language.

Many sub-groups of the merged Djerma-Songhay prefer to describe themselves as Gabda, Kado, Tinga, Dendi, Sorko, etc. The history of some of these groups can be traced, as in the case of the Sorko. In other cases history becomes blurred, as it is not clear whether a group was indigenous to the region, whether it segregated from the Songhay or the Djerma at a later stage, or whether it somehow managed to preserve its original identity within one of the two ethnic groups.

The Djerma-Songhay now represent 21% of the Nigérien population, and most of them live in the region to the south of and along the river Niger, and in the southern parts of the Dallol Bosso and the Dallol Mawri. The majority are sedentary agriculturalists and fishermen.

Djerma or Zarma is the dominant language in this region, and is shared by different ethnic groups.

TUAREG They are often described as *Kel Tamashek* or 'the people who speak Tamashek', and Arabs use the name *moulathlamoun* or 'those who are veiled', but it is the term *Tuareg* that is commonly used for these people of the desert. The name refers to Targa, an important oasis in Fezzan (in what is now Libya) from where many Tuareg dispersed to different Saharan regions, not just to present-day Niger, but also to Algeria, Mali and Burkina Faso.

The society of the Tuareg is highly hierarchic in nature. Different families are united through a tribe or clan, and these in turn are regrouped in *groupements* or confederacies (eg: the Kel Gress, the Kel Owey, etc). Each confederacy has its own *chef*, who recognises the authority of the Sultan of Agadez, also known as the *Aménokal* (see also *The Aïr Mountains: history*, pages 179–80).

Apart from these divisions, the Tuareg traditionally recognise different social classes between clans or even between clan members. Through these classes, each family and each individual know their position within the community. However, the status or privileges that belong to each class are no longer generally acknowledged. The highest classes have sometimes been impoverished, while the class of the *captifs* has ceased to exist officially. The highest class is the *Imajeghen* or the nobles, and the *Imghad* are vassals. These classes were allowed to keep *Iklan*: *captifs* or slaves. These were the lowest class of forced labourers and herders. The *Ineslemen* represent the religious class, while the *Enaden* or blacksmiths form a special class of artisans who work with metal and wood. They are responsible for the manufacture of weaponry and utensils. The *Ighawelan* are freed captives or their descendants. Though key positions in the social hierarchy are reserved for men, some titles are passed on along matrilineal lines. Tuareg women are independent and are treated with deference.

By origin, Tuareg are nomadic traders and keepers of livestock (camels, goats and sheep), but a large proportion of the Tuareg are now semi-nomadic, while some families have become sedentary in places that allow irrigated agriculture. Some parts of the cooler Aïr Mountains with easy access to water have been transformed to highly productive green pockets. The Tuareg represent 10% of the Nigérien population.

PEUL There are numerous theories trying to pinpoint the origins of the Peul, and they couldn't be more diverse and are often incompatible. Basing their research on physical features, linguistic studies and historical accounts and legends, different scientists came to very diverse conclusions: the Peul could be descendants from Egyptian Jews who fled from their Roman persecutors; they would share linguistic rudiments with a nomadic people from Iran; the Peul could be of mixed blood and be partly Arab; or maybe there are links with Senegal, or even Asia. One theory, based on rock engravings found in the Tassili and Hoggar mountains in Algeria, relates how a people from Ethiopia migrated to the west thousands of years ago, when the Sahara was still a green and fertile zone with an abundance of wildlife. This people had cattle and may even have been the ones to introduce the Bororo breed, with lyre-shaped horns, to this zone. Owing to the changing climatic circumstances, they were gradually forced southwards, to the Sahelian zone and beyond. In the course of time, this people assimilated with other ethnies, diversifying into groups with varying features and skin colour, but with a similar cultural heritage and social structure. Names of different groups that pop up in this respect are the Fulani or Fulfulbe, the Toucouleur and the Peul.

In Niger, the Peul represent 9% of the total population, and they are spread out almost from east to west in the Sahelian zone, with some areas showing higher concentrations. Peul are passionate about their cattle. The herds are considered the family capital, not just for providing milk – an indispensable part of their diet – but also because cows can be sold for money to buy all the necessities of life (millet, sugar, tea, textiles, cooking pots, etc). All evolves around the well-being of their herds, forcing the Peul to cover huge distances to find suitable grazing. However, as a result of the increasing pressure on natural resources and the process of desertification, many pastoralists have become semi-nomadic with smaller herds per family, a tendency that is likely to continue. In some parts of the country, such as along the river Niger, separate groups of Peul have become sedentary agriculturalists. These Peul are well integrated into existing sedentary society, and while their original language is Peul, some have even adopted the Songhay language.

One particular group of Peul, the Peul Bororo or Woodabe, try very hard to hold on to their traditional way of living. They are concentrated in the region of Tahoua and the southern fringes of the region of Agadez. Every year, after the rains, the Woodabe gather for a special event, the Geerewol. This could be described as a celebration of male beauty, as young men try to look their absolute best as they line up to chant and dance.

KANOURI The term 'Kanouri' does not refer to a homogeneous group, but rather to a blending of ethnic groups. One of these was the Toubba, of Libyan or Egyptian origin. In the 9th and 10th centuries, they lived in the region of Kawar in the northeast of Niger, where they exploited the *salines* or salt pits. As they descended into the Kanem empire east of Lake Chad, they entered history as the Kanembou. During the era of the Bornou empire, the Kanembou spread all along the shores of the lake, where they mixed with the ethnic group the Sô. Their descendants are now known as Kanouri, while some kindred groups, like the Boudouma, Manga, Dagera and Mobeur, are also referred to as Kanouri. In the area around Lake Chad, the Kanouri grew to form the majority of the population. When the Bornou empire expanded towards the west, engulfing the Hausaphone Damagaram, the Hausa considered the Kanouri indigenous to the eastern regions. The Hausa named them the Béri-béri, a name widely used from Zinder to Lake Chad, which is still home to the Kanouri.

Though they are well represented in this region, the Kanouri make up less than 4% of the total population of Niger. Facial and body scarring is a less common practice in urban areas, but in traditional environments it still occurs. Typical is a series of fine lines on both sides of the face, and sometimes a vertical line from the forehead to the nose. Most Kanouri are sedentary agriculturalists or nomadic pastoralists, while a few – like the Boudouma – are fishermen.

TOUBOU The Toubou are the 'people of *Tou* or Tibesti' (in northern Chad), from where they migrated in waves to different regions of present-day Niger. Some Toubou settled in the region of Djado, the rocky plateau in the far northeast of Niger, while other groups found a new home in the Kawar, the region of Bilma. The Toubou lived side by side with the Kanouri – already present at the time – as separate groups. While the Kanouri traded salt, the Toubou owned the *palmeraies* or palm gardens for the cultivation of dates. During the era of the Kanem empire, some Toubou factions also travelled further south to Lake Chad and its environs, assimilating in the existing community of Kanembou and Sô, but only to a limited degree.

Their origins in Tibesti, as well as a rich cultural heritage – proudly defended by all – unify the Toubou as one ethnic group. However, as they were scattered over immense distances at different points in history, they have existed as many smaller factions and sub-groups. Various distinctions can be made, according to geography, lineage or livelihood to name a few. The Toubou themselves first of all distinguish between two linguistic groups: the Dazza (those living to the south of Ngourti) and the Tedda (north of N'Gourti; many of them live in Bilma). Besides this distinction, different classes or castes are recognised: the *amma megira* or nobles, and the inferior castes, the *azza* or artisans, and the *aggra* or (former) *captifs*. Even within the group of former *captifs*, several 'degrees' are recognised. These distinctions play an important role to this day, eg: a Dazza will never marry an *azza*. Conflicts within the Toubou population often stem from this hierarchic structure (see *N'Guigmi*, page 232).

The Toubou can be sedentary, semi-nomadic or nomadic, depending on the demands of their livelihood, which could be anything from farming and gardening (mostly date palms, but also millet and wheat), cattle keeping (goats, sheep and camels) and camel trading, or a combination of the three. They are a tough and fearless people, adapted to living in extremely harsh conditions. The Toubou live between Lake Chad, the Termit Massif, Kawar (Bilma) and at the Djado Plateau and represent less than 1% of the Nigérien population.

OTHER Other minority ethnic groups include Arabs (mainly from Libya), Gourmantché (who live in the region between the River Niger and Burkino Faso) and Europeans (mainly French). Together, they represent around 1% of the total population of Niger.

LANGUAGE

According to the 1999 constitution, **French** is the official language, but all other languages are respected and people are free to use the language of their choice. French was the latest of all the official languages to be introduced in Niger. It is spoken by around 20% of the population, a figure that is very much in accordance with the percentage of people who have had some form of education. All ethnic groups have their original language, while many variations and dialects exist within the different groups. The **Hausa** and **Djerma** languages have been adopted by many as the second common language in those regions where Hausa and Djerma ethnies are prevalent. **Tamashek** is the dominant language throughout the Aïr Massif.

As these are the four languages that are most widely spoken, lists of useful expressions and greetings in these languages are included in *Appendix 1*, page 239. English is rarely spoken in Niger. In the tourist industry, however, some people manage to speak English quite well. Do not count on it, though, and prepare yourself for a linguistic adventure. Some French expressions in the appendix assume a knowledge of the language, and are best described as typically 'African French', or 'Nigérien French' if you like. If you do not speak any French at all, it is best to bring a comprehensive phrasebook. Make an effort to learn at least the basic greetings, not just in French but rather in a local language, depending on your travel destination. This will be greatly appreciated and it breaks the ice, even if the rest of the 'conversation' is made up of gestures and grimaces.

TIFINAGH

Tifinagh (also spelt tchifinagh) is the alphabetic script the Tuareg use to write their language Tamashek. The discovery of older versions of this unique script unveils a long history.

Over 3,000 years ago, the first inhabitants of the Sahara, the ancestors of the Berber and Tuareg peoples, started engraving on rocks, depicting objects, utensils and the animals they knew. As time progressed, the images became less figurative and gradually evolved into geometric forms. These early signs, which have not yet been deciphered, are the origins of tifinagh. In Roman times, the speakers of Berber languages who lived all along the northern edge of Africa developed the Libye writing system after the first engraved characters found on rocks on various sites from Morocco to Tunisia. This primitive form of tifinagh is one of the oldest scripts in the world.

The key to deciphering the script came with the discovery of bi-lingual funerary steles, the most important one being the stele found in Dougga (Tunisia) in the mausoleum of the Berber king Massanissa, who reigned 2,200 years ago. This stele showed inscriptions in Libye and Punic, and dates back to 138BC. Numerous rock engravings of a more recent tifinagh script have now been identified in the Aïr Massif. While the Libye alphabet became redundant around 1,500 years ago (through the spread of Islam and the introduction of Arabic script), six signs have remained faithful to this ancestral script and are still used in tifinagh as it is known today.

Traditionally, tifinagh consists of 23 characters, only three of which are considered (semi) vowels. With so few vowels, one written word could have different meanings, depending on the pronunciation. To make it easier to read and pronounce the words, the *Association pour la Promotion des Tifinagh* (APT) defined an alphabet that includes five new vowels. The APT not only develops and studies the language, but also aims to preserve and stimulate the use of the script as part of the Tuareg heritage.

NIGERIEN SOCIETY

DEMOGRAPHY

The threat of population growth If a Nigérien woman lives to the end of her child-bearing years and bears children in accordance with age-specific fertility rates, she will give birth to eight children. High maternal mortality and an altogether low life expectancy mean that the real figure is lower. But of all live births, as many as 15% do not survive their first year, while 26% die before the age of five. It is one of the worst juvenile mortality figures in the world. Despite these sad statistics, the population growth is one of the highest in the world. Calculations show that if the population growth remains steady at 3.3% (some statistics show an even higher figure), Niger will have 22.5 million inhabitants by 2025, and a mind-boggling 45 million inhabitants by 2050. Already, the country's natural resources are insufficient to sustain the present population, and the pressure on them is increasing at an alarming rate. This demographic threat is often referred to as the 'silent crisis'.

Traditional *chefferies* under a new administration The history of Niger has been marked by many changes in ruling entities. The French were certainly not the first to restructure the authoritive powers in what is now Niger, but they somehow managed to impose a new administrative system on a melting pot of cultures, spread out over an immense territory. It was a long and by no means self-evident process, and the French could not afford to completely abolish the existing ruling class. Instead, traditional bodies of power were reshaped and renamed to incorporate them under the colonial administration (see *History*, page 17). To this day, different titles – together making up the body of traditional *chefferies* – are recognised by law, while their respective roles and benefits are also defined by law.

The *chefferies* – including the sultanates of Agadez and Zinder – are hierarchically ranked and all have their own, well-defined range of authority (over a town district, a village, a *groupement*, a district) which they are to use in relation to internal social matters: to protect individual and communal rights; to safeguard social cohesion; to see to it that administrative rules are respected; to defend religious tolerance and public order; and to defend the communal interest and the relationship with the central authorities. The traditional *chefferies* have close links with the people and their specific customs, and are generally well informed about the community they represent. As such, they cannot be ignored by the central administration, and *chefs* are often consulted by governmental bodies.

Slavery Slavery is deeply rooted in Niger's history, not just because Niger, like so many African countries, played a part in the slave trade, but even within society slavery has existed for centuries. Many ethnic groups are internally divided into different classes or castes, and more often than not these classes are hereditary. A son born in a lineage of blacksmiths or butchers will traditionally also become a blacksmith or butcher and even marry within his own class. Times are changing, however, and especially in urban areas the unwritten rules are applied less strictly, if at all. Nevertheless, remnants of the traditionally layered social system remain, and more so in rural areas. One such remnant is the existence of slavery. Slaves are at the bottom of the pecking order, with many obligations but only few, if any, priviliges. Those born into an established slave-class become the property of their masters, and are forced to work without pay, while they can be sold or passed on as a gift.

The slave trade was abolished at the beginning of the French occupation, and all forms of slavery were illegal according to French law. However, these laws did not yet apply to the indigenous population. Still, many slaves in Niger gained their freedom during the early years of the French occupation, while others simply fled from their masters and settled down in uncleared land. Nevertheless, the old aristocracy considered themselves owners of the land, thus reducing the runaway slaves to a rural, landless proletariat. Officially no longer slaves, they became a class of 'non-free' labourers, still very much at the mercy of the landlords. While the French were struggling to establish a colonial administration of Niger, it was best not to tamper too much with internal affairs, and the ongoing practices of slavery and the exploitation of the class of non-free labourers were issues that were left fairly undisturbed for a long period of time.

Even when slavery was prohibited under the 1999 constitution and the Penal Code, forms of slavery lingered on in some circles. The national human rights organisation Timidria ('solidarity' in Tamashek), founded in 1991, has been active to signal and expose the continued existence of – sometimes veiled – forms of forced labour and slavery. Growing awareness and international criticism led the Nigérien government to amend the Penal Code in May 2004, and those who are found guilty of slave possession and exploitation now face heavy penalties and up to 30 years' imprisonment. If that was a start, the next challenge remained: to effectively free the estimated 43,000 slaves and help them to rebuild their lives.

At first glance space does not seem to be a problem, with only nine people per km² of Nigérien land. However, given the climatic circumstances and the absence of vegetation and water in large parts of the country, Niger is largely uninhabitable, while another significant proportion of the land is unsuitable for either substantial agriculture or sedentary animal husbandry. It means that agriculture – mostly geared at self-sufficiency – is only possible in the southern zones, while pastoralists have to cover huge distances to find suitable grazing for their livestock. The transhumance of herds of cattle takes place along north–south axes, as the nomadic Peul and Tuareg move their livestock in search of good pastures. During and immediately after the rains, the northern zones provide enough food, while in the dry season pastoralists move south into the semi-arid regions.

The limits of the different agricultural and pastoral zones, as well as the overlapping agro-pastoral zone, are defined in the Rural Code: a comprehensive legislative package in which access rights to land and the use of natural resources are defined, while certain north–south bands of land have been designated as *couloirs de passage*, or transhumance corridors. These are meant to allow herds to pass into or through the agricultural zone without ravaging crops, at least in theory. Ideally, both groups know and respect this code: to avoid destruction of the crops by cattle, and to avoid agricultural use of land that was designated for pastoral use.

However, population growth, increasing desertification and soil degradation have forced both groups to expand the area where they make their living. Agriculturalists have had to claim more land – towards the north – to maintain sufficient harvests. The pastoralists, meanwhile, often need to move further south earlier in the dry season, especially when the rains have failed and the barren north then provides only little grazing for their cattle. Agriculturalists also do not always respect the boundaries of the transhumance corridors, and are tempted to cultivate the fertile corridors that are so rich in manure. The cattle, on the other hand, are tempted to trample the unfenced fields in search of better fodder.

Thus the overlapping zone, where the two groups compete for land and fodder, has become an expanding zone of conflicting interests and sometimes violent clashes. In years when the rains have failed, when both agriculturalists and pastoralists are struggling to save their means of existence, confrontations between groups can be so violent that they even result in the loss of life.

RELIGION

ISLAM Over 90% of the Nigérien population is Muslim. They believe that Mohammed was the last and the greatest of all the prophets. The *Qur'an* or Koran is the holy scripture of Islam, and it is composed of the revelations from Allah to the Prophet Mohammed. The Muslim faith is based on the five pillars of Islam:

- professing that there is no God but Allah
- praying five times daily, facing Mecca in the east
- giving alms to the poor
- daytime fasting during the holy month of Ramadan
- pilgrimage to Mecca

The times of prayer are announced from the mosque by the muezzin. While Muslims can pray in the mosque, at home, in the field or wherever they are, many believers go to the mosque for prayer and worship at least once a week, usually on Fridays at 13.00. Prayer is led by the imam, the religious leader. Children learn to memorise and recite the Koranic verses under supervision of a marabout in Koranic schools. The core of the Muslim community in Niger is in Hausaland, with the region from Maradi to Zinder being the most conservative. Nigérien Muslims are generally moderate in their views and tolerant towards other religions. Islam is often still embedded with elements of the indigenous animist beliefs, especially in traditional, rural areas.

ANIMISM Before Islam was introduced in what is now Niger, animist beliefs prevailed. Animists or *Azna* believe in the supernatural powers of *génies* or spirits. Only a very small percentage of the total population still practise animist rituals, while there is a growing tendency to convert to Islam. The stronghold of indigenous animist belief is in the region of Dogondoutchi and Birni N'Konni. For more detailed information on the traditional beliefs of the Azna, see *Dogondoutchi*, page 137, *Massalata*, page 151, and box *Arwa: ceremony of the Azna*, pages 150–1.

CHRISTIANITY Though many regional towns have a mission post and a church, only a very small proportion of the population is Christian. They are well integrated in society through their work in the health, education and development sectors, but remain a minority and conversion rates are low.

THE ARTS

MUSIC Outside Niger little is heard from Nigérien musicians, and yet the country hides many talents in many categories. In Niamey, young people with musical ambitions take courses at the **Centre de Formation et de Promotion Musicale 'El Hadj Taya'**, or TAYA for short. They can learn the basics, or proceed to more specialised classes for singers, dancers, solo instrumentalists or orchestras, while international professionals are occasionally invited to give workshops. TAYA has a documentation centre for traditional African music as well as a collection of traditional instruments from all corners of Niger. These are not just collectable items; they are used to promote and preserve traditional styles, and passing on the specific techniques to young musicians is one of the objectives of TAYA. Traditional music is often mixed with modern instruments (keyboards, saxophone, guitar, percussion) and styles, creating *musique tradi-moderne*, a new style that has become very popular. Rap music attracts many youngsters, and TAYA offers rap musicians opportunities to meet, share and develop new ideas. This initiative, called RAPZONE, holds informal sessions and concerts every Wednesday from 16.30, and it is also an occasion for visitors to enjoy the music and meet some of the young rappers. All hope to acquire some fame, and indeed TAYA has become the springboard for many musicians of all disciplines. TAYA is situated near the big mosque and the Centre Culturel Oumarou Ganda, and is open Monday–Friday, 07.30–12.30 and 15.30–18.30.

Traditional music Highly valued by the sedentary ethnies in Niger and other west African countries is the music of *griots* (female: *griottes*). They represent a special caste within their community and the profession of griot is hereditary and involves years of training. Griot music is a combination of melody and words, typically performed by one person who plays repetitive soft melody lines on a stringed instrument (often a one-stringed violin or the *molo*, a kind of lute), while he or she sings or recites the lyrics. Songs can be long historical epics and genealogies, poems of praise, or critical and provocative songs. While many lyrics are passed on from generation to generation, a talented *griot* will also improvise and add new songs to his repertoire. As *griots* are true verbal artists with historical knowledge and wisdom, they are both feared and respected. Their importance and power sometimes exceeds the limits of their community, as *griots* can reach a large audience on special occasions like important weddings and staged concerts.

Music plays an important part in **Tuareg** society and is used for all kinds of festivities and celebrations. Both Tuareg men and women play music, but traditionally there is a strict division between types of songs and dances played by either men or women, using different sets of instruments. The *tendé* ('mortar') is a drum, made from a wooden base or mortar with a stretched skin. This drum is fixed with rope between two wooden poles and held in place by rocks or boulders. It is often accompanied by hand-held drums and a deep-resonating drum made from a calabash, turned upside down in a bowl of water. One leading woman sings phrases to which the other women answer through rhythmic chanting, humming and clapping. While the *tendé* can also be played by men, the *imzad* is exclusively for women. The *imzad* is a one-stringed violin, and each instrument personally belongs to one woman, The *imzad* produces a delicate and emotionally moving sound.

The **Peul** know different songs and dances, all specific to different ceremonies and celebrations. The music of the Peul is vocal and rhythmic, and few instruments are used. One male leads the song, starting with a short phrase and melody, which in turn is repeated or answered by the other men. The singing is accompanied by clapping, clicking and hissing sounds, and stamping of the feet, while metal ornaments and tiny bells worn on the body jingle with each movement. As the men sway their bodies from one side to another, rhythms alternate and sometimes change into evocative syncopic patterns, creating a hypnotising effect.

Modern styles One style that is little commercialised is *tcherie-tcherie* (music 'that stirs jolly dust'). It is a happy and rhythmic kind of music played with modern instruments. It is more about entertainment than political engagement, and is popular at celebrations and marriages, as well as on informal stages and in the streets for festive occasions. Enthusiastic spectators stick banknotes onto the foreheads of the musicians to show their appreciation. There are no official concerts, but *tcherie-tcherie* is regularly played at weekends – mostly Sundays – in certain bars, like the Bar de l'Hotel de Ville (opposite the Centre Culturel Franco-Nigérien) and in several bars in the quarter around Hotel Terminus in Niamey.

There are various opportunities to enjoy the **musique tradi-moderne**, either in cultural centres, at concerts in bars or restaurants, or at one of the music festivals like the Prix Dan Gourmou (see *Public holidays and festivals*, page 74). Arguably the most famous among Nigérien bands is **Mamar Kassey**. The music is a swinging merge of styles based on the traditions of the Peul, Songhay, Djerma and Hausa. Since the mid-'90s, this band has performed in different countries in Africa, Europe and the USA. Mamar Kassey has released two albums: *Alatoumi* and *Denke-Denke*. The band **Etran Finawata** (meaning 'the stars of tradition') enjoys a growing international interest. Etran Finawata takes its inspiration from traditional Peul and Tuareg music, two very different musical sources. This creates a wonderful combination of polyphonic rhythmic chanting of the Peul Woodabe with Tuareg melody lines, accompanied by electric guitars and calabashes. Lyrics describe the nomadic life in the desert, but also cover themes like the changing identities of ethnic groups, prostitution, the threat of HIV/AIDS, peace and reconciliation. Etran Finawata is often invited to perform at the bigger music events and festivals, and in 2005 toured through several European countries. Other bands in this category include **Marhaba** (two albums: *Issa Bero* and *Bébé*), and the group **Dangana**, the winners of the 2004 Prix Dan Gourmou (one album: *Dangana*).

Most popular among the younger generation is Nigérien **rap** or **hip-hop**. This style mirrors international rap music, but with an African touch and rhythm. It all started in 1994, when some groups of students participated in school events, competing to be the best hip-hop dancers or the best rappers. Four groups emerged (Les Black DAPS, Wongari, Lakal Kaney and DLM), but none of these stayed together for more than a few years. In fact, this is a tendency among these young musicians, who are all looking for opportunities to perform, impatient to advance their careers whenever they get a chance. So it could well be that the groups that existed in 2005 will be history in 2006, but then the same rappers and their younger brothers will pop up in different guises. Some of the 2005 rap groups released albums, like **Wass-Wong** (*Anazoua*) and **Kamikaz** (two albums). Two other groups are **Diez D** and **Ras-Idris**.

More information For more information on Nigérien music, especially the modern styles, check the website of *Fofo* magazine (*www.fofo-mag.uni.cc; www.planeteafrique.com/fofomag*). This is the virtual counterpart of a printed magazine that was published through accessing foreign funds, but at the time of research it was unsure whether the paper version would continue to exist. The website gives in-depth information on bands of musicians and their schedules, and gives many links to other sites. For more information on the music of the Tuareg and the Peul, enquire at Restaurant Tamgak in Agadez. The owner is a music enthusiast who owns many albums and cassettes.

If you want to buy albums by Nigérien groups or recordings of traditional music, only a few titles are available from music stores in Western countries specialising in world music. In Niger, finding albums is again no easy matter. The shop Chants du Monde at the Maourey roundabout in Niamey has some albums and cassettes. Otherwise, ask for Masaki at Avenue Maurice Dellens, as copies are sometimes available from there. Albums and cassettes are occasionally sold at concerts. You can also enquire at the CCFN in Niamey or Zinder, as they often assist young musicians to record an album.

Some webstores offer albums of (traditional) Nigérien music. The Mediathèque is just one example, offering a selection of around 15 titles including traditional music from the Hausa, Djerma-Songhay, Peul and Tuareg ethnies. For more information, see www.lamediatheque.be/dec/pay/index.php?pays=niger.

CINEMA One could argue that the 'father of Nigérien cinema' was a Frenchman called **Jean Rouch** (1917–2004). He first went to Niger in 1941, where he was soon sidetracked from his work as a civil engineer by his fascination for traditional cultures and religions. Jean Rouch studied anthropology in Dakar (Senegal) and France, then returned to Niger in 1946. His footage of a hippo hunt on the river Niger (*Au pays des mages noirs*, 1946) marked the beginning of a long career as a film and documentary maker. The symbiosis of his field studies in west Africa and filming earned him fame in Europe, and his film *Les maîtres fous* (1955) was awarded the Grand Prix at the Venice Biennale. Jean Rouch described his later films as 'ethno-fiction', in which he increasingly added staged and improvised elements with the use of actors. *Moi, un noir* (1958) was particularly praised for its inventiveness. Some of his Nigérien friends and collaborators – like Oumarou Ganda and Moustapha Alassane (see opposite) – would continue to work closely with Jean Rouch, even when they had become respected filmmakers in their own right. Through his financial support, Jean Rouch helped to create the Institute for Research on Human Sciences (IRSH) in Niamey, and trained many young Africans cineastes in film technology. Even when he served as Director of the Cinématèque Française from 1986 to 1991, he continued to make films and documentaries in Niger and other west African countries, and his impressive oeuvre includes more than 150 titles. In 2004, Jean Rouch died in a tragic car accident in Niger, while he was on his way to a celebration of Nigérien cinema – the Festival International du Film d'Environnement (FIFEN) – where some of his films were going to be screened.

If Jean Rouch was the father of Nigérien cinema, **Oumarou Ganda** (1935–90) was the first Nigérien filmmaker. His career started in 1958, when he was assisting Jean Rouch. He first played a small part in one film, then the leading part in *Moi, un noir* by Jean Rouch. After having learnt the technical skills, he made his first film, *Cabascabo*, in 1968, an autobiographical account of the years he served in the French army in Indo-China. This anecdotic story of a displaced person, serving an alien cause in an alien country, received several awards at international film festivals. His second film, *Le Wazzou Polygame* (1970), a critical narrative of a polygamous marriage in Niger, received the Grand Prix du Fespaco in 1972. Other films like *Saïtane* (1972) and *L'exile* (1990) are also critical, yet loving portraits of Nigérien traditions and society. From his early days as a filmmaker, Oumarou Ganda managed to attract international attention and, as a pioneer in African filmmaking, he is now seen as the symbol of African cinema.

Another pioneer in Nigérien filmmaking is **Moustapha Alassane** (1942–) who was taught film technology by Jean Rouch at an early age. He then went to Canada, where he learnt all the tricks and dodges of animated cartoon making from Norman McLaren. His first film, *Aouré* (1962), an ethnographic document of a Djerma marriage, was soon followed by his first animated cartoon, *La mort du Gandji* (1963). Both films received multiple international awards. Of his extensive body of work, three more early films stand out: *Le retour d'un aventurier* (1965), a satire about Nigérien youths who mimic heroes from American western movies; *Bon voyage SIM* (1966), an animated caricature; and *FVVA Femme Voiture Villa Argent* (1969), a provocative portrait of a young man who will do anything to become a man of standing. While Moustapha Alassane dominated the Nigérien film scene in the 1960s, he has remained very productive and successful since then, and many of his films, documentaries and animated cartoons have received awards. For 15 years he served as director of the cinema section at the Institute for Research in Human Sciences (IRHS) in Niamey. Moustapha Alassane now lives and works in Tahoua.

LITERATURE Until the 1970s, Nigérien literature was dominated by **Boubou Hama** (1906–82), who wrote well over 50 titles in different genres and on different subjects such as history, geography, philosophy, fiction and drama. His body of work is all the more interesting as it reflects much of the colonial period and the early years of independence. Among the long list is a series of Nigérien tales and legends from different ethnic groups. Even for readers with a limited knowledge of the French language, these books are accessible and beautiful documents, generally available from bookshops in Niamey.

Numerous talented writers followed, and they produced a whole array of books covering many themes that are often very critical of traditional customs and sweeping social changes. Despite their dedication, Nigérien writers are faced with many obstacles when it comes to the publication and distribution of their work. Lack of funds is one recurring problem, and the low rate of literacy in Niger limits the number of potential readers. However, certain books are suitable to be used for theatre or cinema, while some writers deliberately focus on scriptwriting to create a 'happy marriage' between artistic expressions. Some examples are *Toula* by Boubou Hama, which was transformed to a film by Moustapha Allasane (see *Cinema* opposite); *Sarraounia*, the story of the sarauniya of Lougou (see box *Sarauniya,* page 140) by **Mamani Abdoulaye**, adapted for the screen by the cineaste Med Hondo; and *Talibo, un enfant du Quartier* by **Ide Mamadou** and filmed by cineaste and writer Ilbo Mahamane. *Talibo, un enfant du Quartier* pictures the story of a young Nigérien from a traditional family of marabouts, who is confronted with the destruction of his town district Gaweye, Niamey, in the early 1980s. This demolition was deemed necessary in order to modernise the capital through the construction of concrete 'monuments' like Hotel Gaweye and the Palais des Congrès, at the cost of all those people who lived in the old town district.

Hawad (1950–), a Tuareg poet and calligrapher from the Aïr region, deserves special mention. He writes in Tamashek, the language of the Tuareg, and in the traditional script, the tifinagh (see box *Tifinagh*, page 31), often accompanied by calligraphy. Many of his texts have been translated into French, and his publications are a combination of linguistic and visual art. In his *Testament nomade* (1987) he describes the anxiety of a nomadic people whose traditional lifestyle is changing under the pressure of external influences.

A selection of publications of Nigérien writers is included in *Appendix 2, Further Information*, on page 224.

THEATRE Niger has a rich history of theatre, partly because it has always been a very suitable way to reach people who are illiterate, or to entertain those who live well out of reach of cinemas. Theatre is also used as a medium to inform the population about issues like HIV/AIDS, national and regional politics, the importance of vaccinations and education, to name but a few examples. Furthermore, some forms of theatre can be seen as extentions of the tradition of storytelling. That tradition has lost ground but has not disappeared altogether, and can often rightfully be considered a form of art.

The capital and most regional towns have at least one stage for theatre, like the Maison des Jeunes et de la Culture (MJC), the Centre Culturel Franco-Nigérien (CCFN: in Niamey, Zinder and Agadez) and the Centre Culturel Oumarou Ganda (CCOG: Niamey). These cultural centres regularly stage plays and puppet shows. The best way to find out about their events programme is to enquire at the centres, but some major events will be announced through the media and posters.

One of the biggest events is the Pilotobé Festival, a touring caravan of actors and artists who perform in different towns. For more information, see *Public holidays and festivals*, page 74.

2

Practical Information

WHEN TO VISIT

When I ask Nigériens what season of the year they prefer, they usually fall silent at first. After some hesitation they name the months that they definitely do not prefer, as they are either too hot, too cold, too dusty or too windy. Eventually the answer invariably is: the rainy season. However, all admit that this is not because the violent winds and thunderstorms are something to look forward to, but the water is needed, the rain brings life, while temperatures drop to a pleasant level thereafter.

For visitors, the rainy season is probably the least practical season to explore the country, as off-road conditions can be extremely difficult, possibly turning journeys into hazardous expeditions. Even in those regions with very little rainfall, torrential rainstorms can cause sudden flooding, while the extreme winds and walls of dust that often precede such rains are highly destructive. So, if you think in terms of 'when to spend a holiday in Niger', the rainy season – from June through September – must be ignored. By the same token, the landscape and vegetation are refreshingly beautiful after the rains, when even the more arid zones are covered with a patchwork of green grasses and flowers.

In all other seasons it will invariably be dry and sunny, which should not automatically be taken as a guarantee of 'good weather', though. October and November are very warm, with temperatures rising to over 30°C during the mid-day hours, while the evenings are comfortable. In December, temperatures can drop quite suddenly, marking the beginning of the cooler months – from December through February. During the day, temperatures are generally pleasant, while occasional chilly winds can spoil that comfortable sensation. Winds sometimes carry dust, causing the atmosphere to turn rather hazy. Nights, on the other hand, can be very cold with temperatures dropping well below 10°C, especially in the desert regions. Undoubtedly, this has a considerable effect on any kind of camping expedition.

Usually during the course of February, temperatures start rising. Within weeks, warm clothes are discarded and memories of freezing nights soon fade during the hot daytime temperatures and warm nights. It is, however, only the beginning, as the hot season – from March through May – gets increasingly uncomfortable. Daytime temperatures often exceed 45°C in the shade, while nights offer little relief, becoming increasingly sticky as the rainy season approaches. These circumstances are physically very demanding and should not be underestimated. Bear in mind that Nigériens refer to these hot months as '*la saison morte*' – the dead season. People move only when they have to, while many stay immobile in a shady area until the evening brings some respite. Those who can afford it leave the air conditioning running around the clock.

To summarise, if you want to avoid the extreme heat and the rains, the best months to travel to Niger are from October to March. When your choice of timing depends mostly on temperatures, consider December, January and February, the cooler, sometimes even cold months. When dust is a serious problem, eg: because you are suffering from respiratory problems, October, November and December are the better months.

Obviously, you could also schedule your trip around special events like the *Cure Salée* or the *Festival de l'Aïr*. For more information and dates, see *Public holidays and festivals*, page 74.

TOURIST INFORMATION

Several governmental platforms are dealing with the development and promotion of tourism in Niger. Unfortunately, whatever the input of these platforms may be, they provide very little in terms of a public counter where independent travellers can get the information they need to plan their trip. The Tourist Board, with only one public office (Maison du Tourisme in Niamey), for instance, is no more than an empty shell. One reason to explain this void could be that there have been quite a few reorganisations in the hierarchical pyramid of tourism (eg: through the liquidation of the Office du Tourisme in 1998) as well as a temporary restructuring within the Ministry of Tourism in 2004. Nevertheless, there are a few places where independent travellers in search of information can present themselves.

The **Direction Régional du Tourisme** (DRT) is first of all the local governmental body that monitors private enterprises in the tourist industry. As a stronghold of knowledge in the field, their staff are usually willing to give independent advice on tourist destinations, tour operators, guides, hotels, etc. While they are not especially equipped to receive and inform travellers, I have found the direction and staff of the DRTs in Zinder, Maradi, Diffa and Agadez very knowledgeable and most helpful. The DRT can also be of assistance in case of serious problems, like the loss of a passport, and injury or illness.

Owing to its popularity as a tourist destination, it is perhaps not surprising that the only (private) platform intended to provide tourist information is to be found in Agadez. In 2001, a number of travel agencies joined forces in the **Syndicat du Tourisme du Niger**. Some of their objectives are to promote sustainable tourism and to improve the quality of all services provided in the tourist sector in the region, and this includes giving out information to tourists from the **Centre d'Information Touristique**. For more information, see *Agadez*, page 166.

If you are planning to book a trip through a **travel agency**, they could of course provide you with a whole array of information. In most **hotels** you should be able to get at least some idea about nearby travel destinations.

TOURIST TAX Tourist tax is payable for accommodation, and is CFA500 per person per night. Usually, this tax is already included in the rates for rooms.

As a result of the policy of decentralisation (see *Poverty reduction*, page 23), communities are now allowed to implement ways to generate income. In places where tourism already provides a good proportion of the economic resources in the private sector, the local authorities may decide to impose a tourist tax on all visitors. In 2005, when the idea of a community tourist tax was first launched, there did not seem to be any restrictions and therefore amounts may vary considerably.

TOUR OPERATORS

When your time is limited and you want to use that time in Niger efficiently, why not have a professional tour operator take care of all the logistics for you? Especially if you consider your French inadequate, or if you feel uncertain about travelling

Within Niger, tourist infrastructures are not evenly divided. The core of tourism lies in the north, where Agadez is the gateway to the desert. Tourism started to develop in this region from the 1970s onwards and played an increasing role in the local economy. During the Tuareg rebellion (see *The Aïr Mountains: the Tuareg rebellion* on page 182), tourist statistics dropped dramatically, but once the situation became calm again, business picked up where it had left off years earlier. One could argue that this happened solely because the northern region is the most beautiful part of the country, but that does not do justice to other regions with different, but no less beautiful landscapes and cultures.

These other regions, however, have not been made accessible to the same degree as Agadez and eventually it all becomes a vicious circle: poor accessibility means few tourists, means little income from tourism, means no money to improve facilities and develop a solid professional tourist infrastructure, means little reason to promote the region, means few tourists, etc. Many places are eagerly waiting to break free from this catch-22 situation, as people are desperate to improve their lives. Tourism is a beneficial sector, as it provides work for many, and moreover, it makes people feel proud about the culture and the country they represent.

The capital, the zone around the river Niger and some nature reserves (Kouré, 'W' National Park) escape from the stalemate to some degree. In the colonial years, expats living in Niamey needed their outings, and so some facilities popped up here and there. As a direct result the local people developed some idea of what tourism may enhance while making a little money in the process. It is not a thriving business, though, and many hotels and establishments have fallen into a rather derelict state. So while this particular region is easily accessible, it still doesn't work all that well. The majority of the tourists – whether they arrive through Niamey or not – still bypass the capital and environs, and head north as soon as possible in order not to 'waste' precious time.

The central and eastern zones are worst off. Regions like Maradi and Zinder and even Diffa and N'Guigmi have plenty to offer in terms of cultural heritage, historical sites and cultural and natural landscapes. For now, long listings of 'potential tourist sites that need to be developed' await patiently on desks, covered under a layer of dust until somebody finds the way and means to break the chain. Until that happens, tourism in these regions is a totally different experience altogether, but for those who do not mind the discomforts of travelling without all the amenities, for those who like to give new and relatively inexperienced travel agencies a chance to work, travelling to the far east of the country can be a very rewarding experience, too.

independently, this is definitely the more relaxing way to explore new horizons. Listed below are some European travel agencies and tour operators with experience in Niger. While some offer package tours in groups, others organise tailor-made tours. More often than not, these tour operators provide European tour guides as well.

UK and Ireland

Geographical Expeditions Ballycahill, Thurles, Tipperary, Ireland; ☏ +353 (0)504 54 252/+353 (0)87 81 62 947; e info@geographicalexpeditions.com; www.geographicalexpeditions.com

Tim Best Travel 68 Old Brompton Rd, London SW7 3LQ; ☏ 020 7591 0300; f 020 7591 0301; e info@timbesttravel.com; www.timbesttravel.com

France

Point Afrique Le Village, 07700 Bidon; ☏ +33 (0)4
75 97 20 40; f +33 (0)4 75 04 16 56; Paris
Branch: 26 Rue de la Grande Truanderie, 75001

Paris; f +33 (0)1 44 88 58 39; e
contact@point-afrique.com; www.point-afrique.com

Tour operators are concentrated in two cities: Niamey and Agadez. As Agadez has
been Niger's number-one tourist destination for decades now, the tourist industry
is well developed and developing still. You will have no problem finding a travel
agency with whom you can venture out into the desert. The problem will more
likely be to substantiate your choice, as all make wonderful promises and all travel
agencies work along more or less the same lines, albeit it for varying rates. On page
167 you will find a listing of tour operators working from Agadez. This list is
incomplete, but these names are a decent starting point from which to surf the web
and see what is on offer.

Travel agencies in Niamey are less numerous, and – contrary to their northern
counterparts – focus on different target groups. Some agencies mainly deal with air
ticketing, while some are primarily car rental agencies. Only a few act as tour
operators that provide full package deals, including transport, drivers and guides.
Some of these are listed in the *Niamey* chapter on page 105.

Following the Route Nationale 1 (RN1) towards the east, it becomes more
difficult to find local tour operators, and they have less experience in the field
simply because tourism isn't as developed as in other parts of the country. The few
agencies I managed to track down are mentioned in the relevant chapters.

If you see signposts for 'Hadj and Oumra' travel agencies, these focus solely on
organising pilgrimages to Mecca.

RED TAPE

VISAS AND TRAVEL DOCUMENTS Unless you are a citizen of a selection of north and
west African countries (members of the CEDEAO), you will need a visa to visit
Niger. When you meet the requirements, visas are issued without much ado. The
following documents are required to enter Niger:

- passport with at least six months' validity beyond the intended stay
- return or onward ticket, or a printed travel itinerary from your travel agent
- International Certificate of Vaccination against yellow fever

Applications for a visa can be submitted to the Nigérien **embassy** in your country.
If there is no Nigérien representation in your country, contact the nearest embassy.
You can send in the necessary documents by registered mail or by a courier service
such as DHL, or have it done through a visa service. Visa application forms can be
sent to you, but it is also possible to download the form from the internet. You will
need two, sometimes three copies with photographs attached, as well as a copy of
your return or onward ticket or travel document. The cost of a visa is around
US$35 or €30 (one month, single entry). This does not include return postage fees
or the – often substantial – handling fee charged by visa service agencies. It is
possible to apply for a long-stay or double-entry visa. Some embassies issue visas
for up to three months, but it is easy to have your visa extended in Niamey if you
can't get one directly from the embassy.

Alternatively, you can obtain a **visa on arrival** at Hamani Diori International
Airport in Niamey, or the international airport in Agadez. There is one catch,
though. Certain airline companies (eg: Air France) will not allow you on their
flights if you do not have a visa already. This regulation may actually change once
it becomes more widely known that visas are obtainable on arrival in Niger, but it

is advisable to check this well beforehand. Another complication when travelling directly to Agadez can be that the necessary documents sometimes run out, which causes delays. Therefore, if you are travelling with a local tour operator, check with them as they can prepare the visa application with the authorities on your behalf. If you are travelling independently, it is probably best to apply for a visa before starting out.

When you need to get your visa in Niamey, you have to fill out forms at the airport, and hand these in together with your passport, two photographs and CFA20,000 or €30 (one-month validity), or CFA50,000 or €75 (three-month validity). The following day, you can pick up your passport and visa at the **Direction de la Surveillance du Territoire**, next to the Telecentre du Passeport on Rue Heinrich Luebke. This is also the place to have your visa extended, when necessary. When you arrive in Agadez, the visa will be issued at the airport. Costs and requirements are the same.

In 1998, five countries – Benin, Burkina Faso, Ivory Coast, Niger and Togo – signed a convention for the implementation of a **visa d'entente**: a tourist visa valid for all five countries. A brilliant idea, but seven years down the road I still haven't heard from anyone who has actually managed to obtain a visa d'entente, so do not feel frustrated if you fail to get one. Belinda Aked from the UK gave it her best shot in August 2005:

> I tried various ways to obtain a visa d'entente. I first contacted the Benin consulate in London, who had heard of them; faxed the Nigérien embassy in Paris, who replied that they were not in circulation yet as they do not have the rubber stamps printed up and they couldn't give me any information as to when that was likely to happen. I decided to contact a visa agency in Paris, who said that they were unobtainable for the moment. So basically all the countries that are included, have obviously had a meeting at some point to agree the idea is good, sanctioned it, but have done nothing to put it into action as yet. I reached a dead end … I guess it just needs one to start the ball rolling!

✪ EMBASSIES AND CONSULATES ABROAD

Belgium 78 Av Franklin Roosevelt, 1050 Brussels; ☎ +32 02 648 59 60

Benin BP 352, Cotonou; ☎ +229 31 56 71; f +229 31 40 30

Canada 38 Blackburn Av, Ottawa, Ontario KIN 8A3; ☎ +1 613 232 4291; f +1 613 230 9808

France 154 Rue de Longchamp, 75116 Paris; ☎ +33 01 45 04 80 60; f +33 01 45 04 62 26

Germany Düürenstrasse 9, D-53173 Bonn; ☎ 0228 350 27 82/368 18 36; f 0228 350 27 68; e ambaniger@t-online.de

Italy Rome; ☎/f 090120145

Ivory Coast 01 BP 2743, Abidjan; ☎ +225 21 26 28 14; f +225 21 26 41 88

Netherlands (Consulate) Laan van Nieuw Oost Indië 14, 2593BT The Hague; ☎ +31 070 381 99 51; e info@falkenhage.nl; www.consulaatniger.nl

Nigeria 15 Adola Okeku St, Vivtoriat Island BMB 2736, Lagos; ☎ +269 61 23 00/61 23 30

Switzerland (Consulate) Rue Abraham Gevray 6, 1202 Geneva; ☎ +41 022 738 51 77; f +41 022 738 69 07

Togo (Consulate) Lomé; ☎ +228 221 63 73/221 63 13

United States 2204 R St, NW, Washington, DC 20008; ☎ +1 202 483 4224/7; f +1 202 483 3169; e ambassadeniger@hotmail.com; www.nigerembassyusa.org

GETTING THERE AND AWAY

✈ BY AIR
Arrivals in Niamey

The Hamani Diori International Airport (for *general information*, ☎ 73 28 81) sees around 22 international passenger arrivals and as many departures on a weekly basis.

Most incoming flights are by African airline companies, departing from their respective countries. The only exceptions are flights from Air France, Point Air and Go Voyages, arriving directly from Paris or Marseille. These flights represent the extremes of ticket prices, with Air France being the most expensive and Point Air offering some very cheap deals. By the same token, one can say that while Air France is reliable and scheduled flights will depart, Point Air sometimes cancels flights at short notice. However, it is worth checking out their special offers as well as new flight destinations, but remember to read the conditions before booking a ticket.

Flights by the African airline companies depart once or twice weekly to and from Niamey. Depending on where you are coming from (or going back to), choices to connect to one of these flights may soon peter out. Still, it is worth checking several options, as the fares might differ significantly. Consider booking through agencies such as Trailfinders (✆ 020 7938 3366), WEXAS (✆ 020 7581 8768), STA (✆ 020 7361 6262), or the Flight Centre (✆ 01892 530030) rather than phoning the airline directly.

Arrivals in Agadez In the tourist season, from October through February, Point Air and Go Voyages operate direct flights from Paris and Marseille to Agadez. These are all chartered flights, often scheduled in connection with package tours by the same companies. For more information on these companies, see *Chapter 7, Agadez*, page 162.

✈ Airline offices in Niamey

Afriqiyah Airways Sahel Airlines, BP 10154; ✆ 73 65 71/72; f 73 65 33; e sahelair@intnet.ne; www.afriqiyah.aero. Two weekly flights to Niamey from Tripoli (Tue, Sat).

Air Algerie Immeuble El Nasr; ✆ 73 38 98/32 14; www.airalgerie.dz. Weekly flights from Algiers (Mon).

Air Burkina ✆ 73 70 60/20 55; www.air-burkina.com. Two weekly flights from Ouagadougou (Mon, Sat).

Air France Immeuble Sonara; BP 10935; ✆ 73 31 21/73 31 22; f 73 29 15; e mail.cto.nim@airfrance.fr; www.airfrance.com/ne. Two weekly flights from Paris (Tue, Fri).

Air Ivoire Immeuble Sonara; ✆ 73 31 21/22; www.airivoire.com. Two weekly flights from Abidjan (Mon, Sat).

Air Senegal Immeuble El Nasr; ✆ 73 28 53/85; www.air-senegal-international.com. Two weekly flights from Dakar and Bamako (Mon, Fri).

Go Voyages Represented by Sahara Expeditions; ✆ 72 38 82/98 58 71; e sahara_expeditions2000@yahoo.fr; for reservations from France, ✆ +33 0 153 437 070; www.govoyages.com. Weekly flights from Paris on Sat from Oct–Mar.

Point Air Opposite Hotel Terminus; ✆ 73 40 26; f 73 68 93; e p-a@intnet.ne; for reservations from France, tel: +33 0 475 972 040; f +33 0 475 041 656; e contact@point-afrique.com; www.point-afrique.com. Several weekly flights from Paris and Marseille to Niamey and Agadez.

Royal Air Maroc Immeuble El Nasr; ✆ 73 28 53/85; www.royalairmaroc.com. Two weekly flights from Casablanca (Wed, Fri).

Sudan Airways ✆ 73 65 72; www.sudanair.com. One weekly flight from Khartoum (Wed).

Airline offices in Agadez

Go Voyages Represented by Dunes Voyages; ✆ 44 03 72/98 45 85; f 44 02 72; e dunes@dunes-voyages.com; www.govoyages.com. Weekly flights from Paris on Mon from Oct–Mar.

Point Air Represented by: Point Afrique; ✆ 73 40 26/28 99 89; f 73 68 93; e p-a@intnet.ne; www.point-afrique.com

Arriving at Hamani Diori International Airport When you have disembarked the aeroplane, walk to the terminal building, where you have to fill out an entry card and go through customs. If you do not yet have a visa, fill out some more forms and hand these in together with two photographs and 30 euro (see *Red tape*, page 42). Keep your Yellow Fever Certificate to hand, as health officials may ask to see it. Then proceed to the luggage belt and luggage check. Do not worry about changing euro to CFA francs, as the fixed exchange rate is common knowledge among everyone you will meet between the airport and your hotel, but make sure you carry some small notes and coins.

Once through the gate and in the arrivals hall, porters and taxi drivers swarm around the new arrivals, trying to find some heavy luggage to carry and passengers to take into town. Unsuspecting-looking tourists are popular, as they are often unaware of the value of the CFA franc. A porter should be more than happy with something like CFA300 (less than 50 eurocent) for carrying a suitcase or backpack to a taxi, but they have developed a habit of looking disappointed or even insulted in an attempt to get some more. As for the taxi: normally the rate per person for the distance from the airport into town should not exceed CFA600 (just under €1), which is *trois courses* or three times the typical fare. However, the taxi has been waiting for some time, it may be late at night and you have a lot of luggage – all sensible reasons for the fare to go up. Still, some taxi drivers boldly ask exaggerated prices. When you are lucky, the full fare for a taxi (taking up to four passengers) costs CFA5,000 (less than €8) and more would be a rip-off. Look for others to share a taxi with unless you do not mind paying that much, as there are no alternatives.

Departing from Hamani Diori International Airport When your plane leaves late at night or very early in the morning, do not forget to make prior arrangements with a taxi. Hotel staff will gladly be of help, and often they know a reliable taxi driver who is willing to work at inconvenient times. Expect to pay at least CFA2,500 for the ride, up to double that when you fill up the vehicle with people and luggage.

As Niamey usually sees only one departure at a certain time, procedures are pretty straightforward and feel almost informal. Access to the check-in hall is permitted only when groundstaff have taken their positions. Make sure your luggage is labelled through to your final destination. Fill out a departure card, then proceed to passport control, where you may have to wait for the officials to show up and wipe off the dust from their desks first. It's all very easy going. Some of the souvenir shops will open up for you to spend your last CFA francs or euro if you like, even for midnight departures. Then you may have to wait some more for the hand-luggage check. Remember to remove all sharp items from your hand luggage, as you will have to hand in anything from the pocket knife that has travelled with you for many years to nail scissors. Once through this last checkpoint, there is little else to do but wait for the boarding call.

BY RIVER Where the river Niger enters the country from the Malian border, the waterway is reasonably suitable for navigation. From October to January/February, water levels allow fairly big wooden vessels (*grandes pinasses* or *barques*) to shuttle between Ayorou and Ansongo, or even Gao in Mali. These are traditional, open boats, used to transporting merchandise as well as passengers. There is no fixed schedule for departures in either direction, but as long as the river does not become too shallow, there will be some sort of shipping traffic along this stretch. The journey between Gao and Ayorou takes several days, and should not be taken lightly: boats are typically jam-packed with merchandise and people, regular stops to load and offload have to be added to the travelling time, and overnight stops mean sleeping anywhere along the riverbank. It is an option, though. You would need to have your Niger (or Mali) visa already, as it is not definite that you will be able to get one at the border. If this sounds too adventurous for your taste, but you still like the idea of travelling by river, you can also hire a small, motorised pinasse to take you all the way in considerably less time. For more information, see *Tillabéri*, page 116; *Ayorou*, page 118 and box *River trips between Ayorou and Gaya*, page 118.

Approx 550km downstream, the river Niger exits the country not far from Gaya close to the Beninese border. The stretch of river between Niamey and the border is navigable from October through March. I would like to hear from travellers who have tried, and preferably managed, to travel this particular stretch of the river.

BY ROAD Niger is a landlocked country, bordered by Algeria, Libya, Chad, Nigeria, Benin, Burkina Faso and Mali. There are numerous border crossing options, but while some are easy and straightforward as it means just continuing driving on sealed main roads, other places are situated deep into the desert and very difficult to get to. In some cases security is a serious issue, and borders are sometimes closed for this reason.

Algeria Before the Tuareg rebellion and insecurity in Algeria virtually stopped all traffic between Niger and Algeria, the Sahara crossing from Tamarasset via I-n-Guezzâm to Agadez was a very popular one. Private expeditions and overland trucks were a common sight along this route and campsites at both ends thrived at that time. Then it suddenly stopped and for many years the border was closed. Nowadays, traffic between Niger and Algeria has resumed, although safety is still a concern. Before attempting to cross this part of the Sahara, enquire about the security at the embassy or consulate representing your country, or at the Algerian consulate in Agadez. When the circumstances allow overland travelling, remember that travelling in a convoy is always recommended, as a breakdown in the middle of nowhere can turn any desert expedition into a life-threatening situation.

Libya While crossing the Sahara between Algeria and Niger is an expedition, it is dwarfed by any journey between Niger and Libya. You would first have to get to, then through the Djado Plateau. Getting to the Djado region means days of driving through the *Grand Erg de Bilma*, which is equivalent to ploughing through thick sand. Awesome, and not to be taken lightly. The *piste* (for definition, see page 239) through the Djado Plateau is for the very experienced only, and even then it can only be attempted when the border is open. At the time of research, it wasn't, or at least that was the official statement. In reality trucks laden with goods and passengers do occasionally travel to Libya, but that is hardly an option. The reason why the border is officially closed is because the Djado Plateau has been the scene of banditry and smuggling more than once, and travelling through this region is highly discouraged by embassies. If crossing this border is one thing you had always wanted to do anyway, enquire at the Libyan consulate in Agadez or at the Libyan embassy in Niamey first. Also take travel advice from the embassy or consulate representing your country.

Chad For the same reasons, crossing into Chad just to the south of the Djado Plateau is no realistic option. The only feasible alternative is at the south end of the border between Niger and Chad, just north of Lake Chad. Again, this area is infamous for irregularities, but some battered vehicles attempt the journey from N'Guigmi via Mao to N'Djamena, a truly adventurous and physically demanding undertaking. For an account of this journey, see *N'Guigmi*, on page 235.

Nigeria By comparison with the above, crossing borders becomes a leisurely event along the south of the country. The main road from Diffa to Niamey, or the roads leading into Nigeria may not always be in a desirable state, but there is actually a road. The major border posts are between Zinder and Kano (via Magaria), between

Maradi and Kano (via Katsina), between Birni N'Konni and Sokoto, and between Dosso and Sabon Gari (via Gaya and Kamba). All of these are straightforward and public transport is frequent. See the various *Getting there and away* sections in the relevant chapters for information on public transport.

Benin Crossing into Benin from Dosso to Malanville via Gaya is very straightforward. The road is tarred and border formalities are not complicated as Nigériens frequently cross to Malanville to buy food supplies and goods at a lesser cost than in Niger. See the *Getting there and away* sections of Niamey and Dosso on pages 96 and 135 respectively for more information.

A new option will be to travel through the 'W' National Park into Benin. Joint efforts between the authorities and the Ecosystèmes Protégés en Afrique Sahélienne (ECOPAS) project should result in simple border formalities. Obviously, travellers need to meet all the necessary requirements like travel documents and visas as usual. It is the environment that makes this the most unusual border crossing. For more information, check with ECOPAS in Niamey (✆ 72 53 48, 59 34 03; e ecopas@intnet.ne).

Burkina Faso Travelling to Burkina Faso through the 'W' National Park is no different from the above, so check with ECOPAS in Niamey. Meanwhile, the most frequently used border post between Niger and Burkina Faso must be the one at Sambalgou, along the *Route Nationale* connecting Niamey to Ouagadougou. Traffic is frequent, and so is public transport. Comfortable coaches and buses shuttle between the two capitals daily. See *Niamey*, page 96, for more information.

Mali The only realistic option to travel overland from Niger to Mali is via Tillabéri and Ansongo. It is not a comfortable one, as the sealed road changes to a rough *piste* soon after leaving Ayorou. Sturdy trucks, converted into some kind of passenger vehicle, herald a tough journey that is nevertheless bearable, while all alternatives – like trucks crammed with merchandise, people and livestock – guarantee a true expedition your bones and muscles will not easily forget. For more information on travelling along this section, see the *Getting there and away* sections of Niamey and Ayorou on pages 96 and 118 respectively.

Further east the desert town of Andéramboukane is the only feasible destination before completing the full circle back to the Algerian border. Even this route is for the adventurous only. There is one reason to want to visit Andéramboukane: it is the location of a two-yearly festival, the *Tamadacht*, organised from Mali at the end of January. Otherwise, travelling this way is neither a shortcut nor a comfortable option to get to Mali. Moreover, the surrounding region is infamous for incidental robberies. Enquire about the security in the region before heading out there.

✚ HEALTH

With Dr Jane Wilson-Howarth and Dr Felicity Nicholson

TRAVEL INSURANCE Any money spent on travel insurance will hopefully be money wasted. Yet you should not even consider leaving home without at least some degree of health cover. It is essential that medical expenses as well as repatriation to your home country are included in the policy. Whether or not you insure your personal belongings is another issue. It is worth your while to shop around and compare premiums. Besides that, if you are a regular traveller, it may turn out to be good value to pay for a multi-trip or continuous policy. Check the small print as there may be restrictions, for example with regard to the duration of each separate trip.

IMMUNISATIONS AND MALARIA PREVENTION The only absolute requirement to enter Niger is an International Certificate proving that you have been vaccinated against **yellow fever**. This certificate is valid from only ten days after the vaccination has been administered, then it remains valid for ten years. If the vaccine is contraindicated for medical reasons then the doctor should provide you with an exemption certificate. Although this will not give you any protection against the disease it should allow you entry into the country. To be sure you would be advised to contact the embassy in the UK before you travel. All other vaccinations are optional, but it is highly recommended your immunisations for **diphtheria**, **tetanus** and **polio** (DTP) as well as **typhoid** and **hepatitis A** are up to date. The necessity to get immunised against other diseases, like **meningitis**, **hepatitis B**, **tuberculosis** or even **rabies**, very much depends on the nature of your trip. Seek advice about immunisations a couple of months before travel to schedule a vaccination programme if necessary. You can see your GP or visit a travel clinic, where updated information on the health situation and requirements of various countries is available.

There is no vaccine against **malaria**, but using prophylactic drugs and preventing mosquito bites (see page 55) will considerably reduce the risk of contracting it. Seek medical advice for the best anti-malarial drugs to take. Mefloquine (Lariam) is one of the most effective prophylactic agents, which is taken once weekly. This drug has gained a bad reputation (largely undeserved) as some people suffer unacceptable side effects, like depression or anxiety, severe headaches or changes in the heart rhythm. If you suffer from any of these then you should stop taking the medication at once, and seek medical advice. Minor problems such as dizziness and sleeping disturbances including nightmares are not considered a medical reason for stopping, but of course if they are unacceptable anyway then you would be advised to do so. If this drug is suggested then you should start at least three weeks before departure to check that it suits you. People who have had adverse reactions in the past, or who have a history of depression or anxiety, suffer from epilepsy or who have a family member with epilepsy, or have problems with heart rhythms should not be prescribed this drug in the first place. The chances are that you will not experience any side effects, in which case this could well be the best choice for you, despite all the negative reports. Another drug with less common and less severe side effects, is Malarone. It is rather expensive and so tends to be reserved for shorter trips. Malarone has to be taken only two days before starting a trip and for only one week afterwards. This drug is licensed in the UK for three months and is also available for children under 40kg in the paediatric form. It is prescribed on a weight basis, so it is helpful to know your child/children's weight/s in kilograms before you visit your doctor.

The antibiotic Doxycycline is an acceptable alternative anti-malaria agent. However, it cannot be used for those who are pregnant or breast feeding or for children under the age of 12. Also if you are on medication for epilepsy, Doxycycline may reduce the efficacy of this medication. The most common side effect, affecting around 1–3% of people, is sensitivity to sunlight sometimes resulting in allergic skin reactions. As staying out of the sun is hardly an option in Niger, this is something to bear in mind when deciding which drug to take. Your doctor or a travel clinic expert should be able to help you decide. Chloroquine and Nivaquine have been found to be less effective in recent years, and are used only when nothing else is suitable. Whatever choice you make, be sure to take the tablets meticulously and follow the directions for starting and stopping (unless there is a contraindication) to optimise protection. Do not take the drug on an empty stomach as this may cause nausea and heartburn. All malaria tablets are best taken with the evening meal and washed down with plenty of fluid.

TEETH Consider having your teeth checked before you leave. If you have lots of fillings, bring a dental emergency kit which is available from some pharmacies and dentists. Dental care is available in Niamey, see *Health*, page 107.

MEDICAL KIT In urban areas, travellers have access to medical advice and plenty of well-stocked pharmacies. When you venture out to remote areas, on the other hand, it is wise to take a medical kit. The following checklist is an example of what you may want to bring:

- plasters, dressings (Band-Aid) and sterile gauze
- a good drying antiseptic (iodine or potassium permanganate crystals, not antiseptic cream)
- aspirin and paracetamol
- antifungal cream
- a pair of fine pointed tweezers and nail scissors
- sunblock and lip balm
- eye drops
- insect repellent
- thermometer
- malaria tablets
- malaria treatment
- broad-spectrum antibiotics like amoxicillin (for chest, urine or skin infections)
- ciproflaxin antibiotic (for severe diarrhoea)
- condoms or femidoms

FURTHER READING Self-prescribing has its hazards so if you are going anywhere very remote consider taking a health book to help you. For adults there is *Bugs, Bites & Bowels, The Cadogan Guide to Healthy Travel* by Dr Jane Wilson-Howarth, and if travelling with children look at *Your Child Abroad: A Travel Health Guide* by Dr Jane Wilson-Howarth and Dr Matthew Ellis, published by Bradt Travel Guides.

TRAVEL CLINICS AND HEALTH INFORMATION A full list of current travel clinic websites worldwide is available from the International Society of Travel Medicine www.istm.org. For other journey preparation information, consult www.tripprep.com. Information about various medications may be found on www.emedicine.com.

Travel clinics

UK

Berkeley Travel Clinic 32 Berkeley St, London W1J 8EL (near Green Park tube station); ☎ 020 7629 6233

British Airways Travel Clinic and Immunisation Service 213 Piccadilly, London W1J 9HQ; ☎ 0845 600 2236; www.ba.com/travelclinics. The clinic offers a walk-in service (no appointment necessary): open Mon, Tue, Wed & Fri 08.45–18.15, Thu 08.45–20.00, Sat 09.30–17.00. Apart from providing inoculations and malaria prevention, they sell a variety of health-related goods.

Cambridge Travel Clinic 48a Mill Rd, Cambridge CB1 2AS; ☎ 01223 367362;
e enquiries@cambridgetravelclinic.co.uk; www.cambridgetravelclinic.co.uk. Open Tue–Fri 12.00–19.00, Sat 10.00–16.00.

Edinburgh Travel Clinic Regional Infectious Diseases Unit, Ward 41 OPD, Western General Hospital, Crewe Rd South, Edinburgh EH4 2UX; ☎ 0131 537 2822; www.link.med.ed.ac.uk/ridu. Travel helpline (0906 589 0380) open weekdays 09.00–12.00. Provides inoculations and anti-malarial prophylaxis and advises on travel-related health risks.

Fleet Street Travel Clinic 29 Fleet St, London EC4Y IAA; ℡ 020 7353 5678; www.fleetstreetclinic.com. Vaccinations, travel products and latest advice.

Hospital for Tropical Diseases Travel Clinic Mortimer Market Bldg, Capper St (off Tottenham Ct Rd), London WCIE 6AU; ℡ 020 7388 9600; www.thehtd.org. Offers consultations and advice, and is able to provide all necessary drugs and vaccines for travellers. Runs a healthline (0906 133 7733) for country-specific information and health hazards. Also stocks nets, water purification equipment and personal protection measures.

Interhealth Worldwide Partnership House, 157 Waterloo Rd, London SEI 8US; ℡ 020 7902 9000; www.interhealth.org.uk. Competitively priced, one-stop travel health service. All profits go to their affiliated company, InterHealth, which provides healthcare for overseas workers on Christian projects.

MASTA (Medical Advisory Service for Travellers Abroad) London School of Hygiene and Tropical Medicine, Keppel St, London WCI 7HT; ℡ 09065 501402; www.masta.org. Individually tailored health briefs available for a fee, with up-to-date information on how to stay healthy, inoculations and what to bring. There are currently 30 MASTA pre-travel clinics in Britain. Call 0870 241 6843 or check online for the nearest. Clinics also sell malaria prophylaxis memory cards, treatment kits, bednets, net treatment kits.

NHS travel website www.fitfortravel.scot.nhs.uk provides country-by-country advice on immunisation and malaria, plus details of recent developments, and a list of relevant health organisations.

Nomad Travel Store/Clinic 3–4 Wellington Ter, Turnpike La, London N8 0PX; ℡ 020 8889 7014; travel-health line (office hours only) 0906 863 3414; e sales@nomadtravel.co.uk; www.nomadtravel.co.uk. Also at 40 Bernard St, London WCIN ILJ; ℡ 020 7833 4114; 52 Grosvenor Gdns, London SWIW 0AG; ℡ 020 7823 5823; and 43 Queens Rd, Bristol BS8 1QH; ℡ 0117 922 6567. For health advice, equipment such as mosquito nets and other anti-bug devices, and an excellent range of adventure travel gear.

Trailfinders Travel Clinic 194 Kensington High St, London W8 7RG; ℡ 020 7938 3999; www.trailfinders.com/clinic.htm

Travelpharm The Travelpharm website offers www.travelpharm.com up-to-date guidance on travel-related health and has a range of medications available through their online mini-pharmacy.

Irish Republic

Tropical Medical Bureau Grafton St Medical Centre, Grafton Bldgs, 34 Grafton St, Dublin 2; ℡ 1 671 9200; www.tmb.ie. A useful website specific to tropical destinations. Also check website for other bureaux locations throughout Ireland.

USA

Centers for Disease Control 1600 Clifton Rd, Atlanta, GA 30333; ℡ 800 311 3435; travellers' health hotline 888 232 3299; www.cdc.gov/travel. The central source of travel information in the USA. The invaluable Health Information for International Travel, published annually, is available from the Division of Quarantine at this address.

Connaught Laboratories PO Box 187, Swiftwater, PA 18370; ℡ 800 822 2463. They will send a free list of specialist tropical-medicine physicians in your state.

IAMAT (International Association for Medical Assistance to Travelers) 1623 Military Rd, 279, Niagara Falls, NY14304-1745; ℡ 716 754 4883; e info@iamat.org; www.iamat.org. A non-profit organisation that provides lists of English-speaking doctors abroad.

International Medicine Center 920 Frostwood Dr, Suite 670, Houston, TX 77024; ℡ 713 550 2000; www.traveldoc.com

Canada

IAMAT Suite 1, 1287 St Clair Av W, Toronto, Ontario M6E 1B8; ℡ 416 652 0137; www.iamat.org

TMVC (Travel Doctors Group) Sulphur Springs Rd, Ancaster, Ontario; ℡ 905 648 1112; www.tmvc-group.com

Australia, New Zealand, Singapore

TMVC ℡ 1300 65 88 44; www.tmvc.com.au. 23 clinics in Australia, New Zealand and Singapore including:
Auckland Canterbury Arcade, 170 Queen St, Auckland; ℡ 9 373 3531
Brisbane 6th Floor, 247 Adelaide St, Brisbane, QLD 4000; ℡ 7 3221 9066
Melbourne 2nd floor, 393 Little Bourke St, Melbourne, VIC 3000; ℡ 3 9602 5788
Sydney Dymocks Building, 7th Floor, 428 George St, Sydney, NSW 2000; ℡ 2 9221 7133
IAMAT PO Box 5049, Christchurch 5, New Zealand; www.iamat.org

SAA-Netcare Travel Clinics Private Bag X34, Benmore 2010; www.travelclinic.co.za. Clinics throughout South Africa.
TMVC 113 DF Malan Dr, Roosevelt Pk, Johannesburg; ℡ 011 888 7488; www.tmvc.com.au.

Consult the website for details of 8 other clinics in South Africa.

IAMAT 57 Chemin des Voirets, 1212 Grand Lancy, Geneva; www.iamat.org

DRINKING WATER AND WATER PURIFICATION

The purest drinking water comes directly from closed wells, where the water is being pumped up to the surface. The source lies deeply embedded in the face of the earth, and could be either rainwater (filtered through layers of sand and soil) or fossil water. Bottled mineral water is taken from the same kind of source. It is expensive and not always available, though. Another downside of the use of mineral water is the fact that plastic bottles are used only once, then end up disfiguring nature or polluting the air when they are burnt.

Water towers (*chateaux d'eau*) have been installed in the bigger towns throughout Niger, and theoretically the water provided through these is treated, hence safe to drink. However, there are two reasons why you should be careful about this presumption. First of all, the water may contain fine dust particles. When the water is saturated with particles, the colour changes to a tell-tale shade of brown or orange, but most of the time a lower concentration remains invisible to the eye. Still, prolonged consumption of this water can cause damage to the intestines, and it is therefore recommended to filter tap water before consumption. The second potential risk of drinking tap water coming from water towers is that the system occasionally fails, allowing impurities to enter the water. Contamination of the drinking water doesn't happen very often, while the risk is higher when water levels run low.

In rural areas with no water towers, all water should be considered unsafe to drink without treatment. It could be contaminated with anything from faecal bacteria and microbes to worms and amoebic cysts.

The best method to sterilise impure water is by bringing it to the boil, as all microbes are killed this way. Any drink that has been boiled can be considered safe to drink, provided it is served hot or has been stored in a clean container. One easy way to boil your own supply of water is by using a miniature immersion heater. Obviously, this does not work when you venture out in the desert where sockets are hard to find. Chemical treatment does not render water safe to the same degree as by boiling, but it will deal with many bugs and is generally a good enough method. Types of chemical sterilising agents are iodine, silver and chlorine. Silver-based tablets have the advantage of being tasteless, while iodine is the most effective agent as it also kills amoebic cysts. Carefully stick to the prescribed dosage to avoid an unhealthy intake of iodine. To mask the foul taste of iodine or chlorine, add some lemon juice, vitamin tablets or powdered drink. Water filters are another alternative to purify water. There are different filter systems, and none of them comes cheap. The most reliable ones are a combination of a filter and a chemical, such as iodine. Ceramic filters are the most expensive, but also easy to clean and they leave no unpleasant taste. The minutest of bugs will still pass through the filter, though.

MEDICAL PROBLEMS AND DISEASES

It somehow seems unlikely that Niger will be the chosen destination for travellers who have never been to Africa (or other Third World countries) before. By the same token, travellers to Niger will probably at least have some basic knowledge of tropical diseases and annoyances. The list below is not complete but, extensive as it is, even to experienced travellers this may be a somewhat intimidating summary of nasty diseases. Keep things in perspective,

Dr Jane Wilson-Howarth

Long-haul air travel increases the risk of deep vein thrombosis (DVT). Although recent research has suggested that many of us develop clots when immobilised, most resolve without us ever having been aware of them. In certain susceptible individuals, though, large clots form and these can break away and lodge in the lungs. This is dangerous but happens in a tiny minority of passengers.

Studies have shown that flights of over five-and-a-half hours are significant, and that people who take lots of shorter flights over a short space of time form clots. People at highest risk are:

- those who have had a clot before – unless they are now taking warfarin
- people over 80 years of age
- anyone who has recently undergone a major operation or surgery for varicose veins
- someone who has had a hip or knee replacement in the last three months
- cancer sufferers
- those who have ever had a stroke
- people with heart disease
- those with a close blood relative who has had a clot

Those with a slightly increased risk:

- people over 40
- women who are pregnant or who have had a baby in the last couple of weeks
- people taking female hormones or other oestrogen therapy
- heavy smokers
- those who have very severe varicose veins

though. While most travellers encounter some minor upsets sooner or later, the chances of your catching a serious disease are slim, especially when you are aware of preventative measures or when you are able to recognise the early stages of a particular disease.

Diarrhoea Most experienced travellers will have some degree of experience with the phenomenon of **travellers' diarrhoea**, the relatively innocent type of diarrhoea caused by filth-to-mouth contact. The reason is not too difficult to understand: when your intestines are used to specific bacteria, they have learnt to build some kind of defence to thwart a bowel infection. However, when your digestive system is exposed to alien bacteria and microbes, the surprise attack can have debilitating effects for a few days. Even when you have taken all the usual precautions, you may have been exposed to noxious bugs through a handshake, a filthy doorknob or simply by handling money, followed by some kind of contact with your mouth. It is almost unavoidable, yet relatively harmless. As your body will look for ways to defend against the unknown enemy, a second assault will be less severe or may even go by unnoticed.

Though water can be the cause of this common problem, the main source is usually unhygienic food. To **prevent travellers' diarrhoea** or to limit its possible effects, you need to abide by a few rules concerning food:

- wash your hands regularly, especially after a trip to the toilet and before having a meal

- the very obese
- people who are very tall (over 6ft/1.8m) or short (under 5ft/1.5m)

A deep vein thrombosis (DVT) is a blood clot that forms in the deep leg veins. This is very different from irritating but harmless superficial phlebitis. DVT causes swelling and redness of one leg, usually with heat and pain in one calf and sometimes the thigh. A DVT is only dangerous if a clot breaks away and travels to the lungs (pulmonary embolus). Symptoms of a pulmonary embolus (PE) include chest pain that is worse on breathing in deeply, shortness of breath, and sometimes coughing up small amounts of blood. The symptoms commonly start three to ten days after a long flight. Anyone who thinks that they might have a DVT needs to see a doctor immediately who will arrange a scan. Warfarin tablets (to thin the blood) are then taken for at least six months.

Prevention of DVT Several conditions make the problem more likely. Immobility is the key, and factors like reduced oxygen in cabin air and dehydration may also contribute. To reduce the risk of thrombosis on a long journey:

- take a meal of oily fish in the 24 hours before departure
- exercise before and after the flight
- keep mobile before and during the flight; move around every couple of hours
- during the flight drink plenty of water or juices
- avoid taking sleeping pills and excessive tea, coffee and alcohol
- perform exercises that mimic walking and tense the calf muscles
- consider wearing flight socks or support stockings (see *www.legshealth.com*)
- the jury is still out on whether it is wise to take aspirin

If you think you are at increased risk of a clot, ask your doctor if it is safe to travel.

- avoid 'risky' food, like uncooked food or food that has been kept warm for some time, raw meat, ice cream, ice cubes, salads and peeled fruit
- street food that is prepared before your eyes and that is served sizzling hot is probably safer to eat than a luxury buffet that has been waiting for some time
- in short: peel it, boil it, cook it or forget it!

In the event your body has been invaded, **treating travellers' diarrhoea** is most of all a matter of common sense: relax, take all the rest you need, and be sensible about what you take in to get your bowels functioning properly again. Make sure you take plenty of clear fluids to prevent dehydration. Also avoid fizzy drinks or give them a good shake first. Sachets of oral rehydration salts give the perfect biochemical mix to replace all that is pouring out of you, as will any dilute mix of sugar and salt. Take any light drink you like, and add a four-finger scoop of sugar with a three-finger scoop of salt. A squeeze of lemon or orange improves the taste while it also adds a little potassium, which is lost during a bout of diarrhoea. Drink at least two glasses of liquid after every bowel action and plenty more if you are not eating. If you do feel like eating, stick to a bland, high carbohydrate diet and avoid greasy or spicy meals. When you need to travel and therefore need to reduce the number of times your body is flushing, consider taking Imodium (Loperamide). However, though this medicine is handed out as a matter of course to travellers, it can actually be harmful when you are suffering from more than a fairly innocent bug: if the diarrhoea persists, or if you are passing blood or slime, or if you develop a fever, these could be symptoms of a more serious problem like amoebic dysentery, giardiasis or cholera. In these cases, never take Imodium as it will be like a cork, fixing the source of the problem in your bowels for days and allowing the bug to reproduce. Once the cork leaves your body, the disease will hit hard again. If you show any of the above symptoms, make sure you take in plenty of fluids and seek medical advice as soon as possible as you will need some kind of treatment. Once the diagnosis has been made, most upheavals are easy to treat.

Cholera Outbreaks of cholera do occur, especially during the rainy season. Symptoms include extremely severe diarrhoea and sometimes vomiting, causing the patient to dehydrate rapidly. In acute cases the disease may be fatal within hours. Cholera usually affects the weak and those who live in poor hygienic circumstances. When you are generally healthy, you are unlikely to get the disease. To avoid infection, take the usual precautions that prevent any filth-to-mouth disease. Despite the odds against contracting cholera, if you suspect infection, start treating against dehydration and seek medical advice. For those who are working in very poor conditions and for those who have a pre-existing long-term medical condition (eg: diabetes, or a disease that affects the immune system) there is now an effective oral cholera vaccine (Dukoral). The course comprises two doses of vaccine given at least one but no more than six weeks apart. Ideally the second dose should be taken at least one week before entering Niger. This regime is suitable for those aged six years and over and is said to be at least 75% effective for two years. For those under six, a three-dose vaccine may be recommended. Seek medical advice at least eight weeks prior to departure.

Insect-borne diseases

Malaria Various types of malaria occur in Niger, the most common ones being *malaria vivax* and *malaria tertiaire*. The malaria mosquito thrives in the vicinity of open water, whether it be in towns or rural areas. In the north, malaria is less prevalent, the exception being Agadez where malaria is a serious health hazard. While malaria prophylaxis does provide a good degree of protection, there is still a slim chance of contracting the disease. However, the level of protecting agent circulating in your bloodstream will make the attack less severe.

Symptoms of malaria mimic those of bad flu and include fever, chills, joint pain, thumping headaches and sometimes vomiting and diarrhoea. Depending on the type of malaria, fevers may peak every three or four days, or stay fairly stable at over 38°C. If you show any of these symptoms, consult a doctor and have your blood tested. This is a standard procedure in most clinics and labs throughout the country, and it is the best way to either confirm or exclude malaria. Ideally, treating malaria should be left to a specialist. However, some travellers who venture well off the beaten track sometimes carry an emergency treatment. In Niger, Coartem is the drug that is generally used in such cases, and it is widely available without prescription at most pharmacies. Any decision to take this medication should not be taken lightly, but should be made only if medical assistance is out of reach and you cannot exclude the possibility of a malaria attack. Follow the instructions carefully and seek medical advice as soon as you are able. Beware of the danger of dehydration. If you know beforehand that you are going to be in a remote place, you should seek advice from a doctor or travel clinic expert about which standby treatment to take. The recommended regime is constantly changing, so it is best to take up-to-date advice prior to travel.

Symptoms of malaria may occur from as little as seven days after being infected, but remember that symptoms may still occur up to a year after infected mosquitoes got to you. So even when you are back home and while you are already planning your next trip, malaria could develop. Bear this in mind when you have flu-like symptoms and let your GP know you have travelled in a malarious country.

Dengue fever This disease is caused by a virus that is passed on by mosquitoes that bite during the daytime. Symptoms resemble those of malaria, and include strong headaches, rashes, excruciating joint and muscle pains, and fever. Treatment consists of complete rest, paracetamol and plenty of fluids to avoid dehydration. It occurs only very rarely in Niger, and is not considered a serious health hazard.

Avoiding insect bites The best way to prevent any insect-borne diseases and itchy lumps is simply to avoid being bitten. Malaria mosquitoes come out after sunset, and greedily attack any bare skin, preferably at ankle level. Limit the amount of exposed skin by wearing long trousers and sleeves, and apply insect repellent where necessary, even under your socks. The most effective repellents contain diethylmethyltoluamide or DEET in various concentrations (usually at least 50% for an adult). Though this is a most effective agent, some care should be taken as the chemical can damage the skin when it is used in combination with certain other skin products. As with all insect repellents, avoid contact with the eyes, mouth and food. If the fluid gets in your eyes, do not rub, and flush with plenty of water.

To keep away the mosquitoes while you sleep, the preferred method is by sleeping under a mosquito net, and better still when it is freshly impregnated with permethrin. Some hotels in Niger do provide nets, but do not count on it and many of the nets are damaged anyway. Close the holes using tape, or bring your own mosquito net. In most rooms you should be able to figure out a way to suspend it above your bed, sometimes with the use of rope, paperclips, screw hooks, clothes-pegs or iron wire. Be inventive!

There are some other, less effective ways to reduce mosquito attacks during the night. Switching on the air conditioning helps, while spraying the room or lighting a mosquito coil keeps them at bay for a short while.

Meningitis Meningitis is the inflammation of the cerebral and spinal membranes, and can be caused by viral or bacterial infection. The viral variety is less serious than the bacterial variety, which can be fatal within hours of the first symptoms appearing. Typical symptoms of bacterial meningitis include a throbbing headache, high fever, a stiff neck, sensitivity to light and sometimes a blotchy rash. If you show these symptoms, seek medical attention immediately. The disease is highly contagious, as it can easily spread through coughing, sneezing and kissing. Periodic epidemics of meningitis are more common in the windy, dusty season roughly from January through April. Symptoms of the viral variety include some or all of the following: headache, fever, photophobia, neck stiffness and general malaise. But those affected generally recover without treatment. Various forms occur in Niger, the most common being the bacterial types A and C. However, while Meningitis W used to be very rare, since 2000 there have been some sudden outbreaks in isolated pockets. Therefore the 'tetravalent' (A-C-W-Y) vaccination is now recommended for travellers.

Hepatitis A Hepatitis A is a contagious viral disease caused by faecal contamination of water, food or poor hygiene of the hands. Jaundice is a common symptom of this ailment of the liver, while the urine usually turns dark in colour. It takes weeks or sometimes months to fully recover from hepatitis A. The majority of travellers are advised to be immunised against the disease with hepatitis A vaccine such as Havrix Monodose or Avaxim. One dose of vaccine lasts for one year and can be boosted to give protection for up to 20 years.

Hepatitis B Hepatitis B is another viral disease that attacks the liver. Transmission is caused through direct contact with the blood or body fluids of an infected person, eg: by unprotected sex, dirty needles and contaminated blood or blood derivatives. The chances of contracting the disease are slim and depend on the nature of the trip as well as responsible sexual behaviour. Immunisation is recommended for longer trips (two months and over) and for those working in the medical field or with children. Ideally, three injections should be taken over a longer period to optimise the measure of protection. However, if time is short then there is a three-dose course of vaccine that can be given over 21 days (Engerix). This course will need to be boosted after a year to ensure that it remains effective.

Tuberculosis Various types of TB occur in Niger. Some caution is justifiable: statistics show that the number of TB cases in Africa is on the rise, while an increasing number of travellers throughout the world get infected, reintroducing the disease that seemed almost wiped out in developed countries. TB can be spread through oral and respiratory excretions (coughing, sneezing, kissing). In general, when you travel using private transport, you are less likely to be exposed to the bacteria than when you make use of public transport. Therefore independent travellers and those who intend to travel for extended periods of time may be advised to get the BCG vaccination. Seek medical advice at least eight weeks before travel if you have not had this vaccine. In the UK it is usually given between 11 and 14 years of age. In some countries, eg: the USA and Australia, the BCG is not given at all. They consider that TB is still treatable as long as it is detected. If you have a persistent cough (more than six weeks) and/or a fever (in particular night sweats) then go and see your doctor immediately.

Bilharzia or schistosomiasis This debilitating disease is caused by parasites found in infected fresh water. When the parasites penetrate the skin, this may lead to infection which can eventually cause irreversible damage to the intestines (*Schistosoma mansoni*) and the urinary system (*Schistosoma haematobium*). Therefore, though this disease is generally easy to treat, it is best avoided in the first place.

When someone with bilharzia excretes into fresh water, the eggs hatch and swim off to find a pond snail to infest. They develop inside the snail to emerge as torpedo-shaped *cercariae*, barely visible to the naked eye but able to digest their way through human or animal skin. This is the stage that attacks people as they wade, bathe or shower in infested water, such as stagnant pools or slow-moving water. The high-risk areas are reedy shores, especially near villages where infected people may defecate or urinate in or near open water. The river Niger is contaminated and so are most open waters, especially in the region of Tahoua. To be on the safe side, consider all rivers, stagnant pools or ponds as suspect. As it takes the tiny worm at least ten minutes to penetrate the human skin, you are not at risk when contact with water is brief, and followed by drying off thoroughly with a towel. Covering yourself with DEET insect repellent will protect you to a certain degree. Infection does not occur after drinking infested water, but the same water probably contains other unwanted bugs and should not be drunk in any event.

The only early symptom that may (or may not) occur after exposure to bilharzia parasites is a rash or itchy skin. Other symptoms that may be noticed two or more weeks after penetration include fever, a persistent, wheezy cough and sometimes blood in the urine. This last symptom may disappear after a while, while the infection lingers on. When you suspect you may have been exposed to the parasite, a simple blood test – done six weeks or more after exposure – will determine if infection took place. Treatment should then be straightforward, though a second treatment is sometimes necessary.

Animal bites

Rabies Contracting rabies should be avoided at all costs, as it is a particularly nasty disease with a 100% mortality rate. Therefore, stay clear of mammals, most of all yapping village dogs as dogs are common carriers. Moreover, dogs in Niger are hardly ever seen as pets and they are not used to being handled in a friendly way. Unless a dog is personally known to you, do not attempt to stroke or touch it. In the unlucky event you get bitten, scratched or even when licked over an open wound, always assume the animal is rabid and seek medical help as soon as possible. The incubation time can be very long, though the time is reduced when the bite or wound is nearer to the face. To reduce the risk of getting infected, scrub the wound with soap and pour on plenty of bottled or boiled water, then flood the bitten area with a strong iodine or alcohol solution. This also guards against wound infections including tetanus.

If you have not been immunised against rabies, you will need a full course of injections together with rabies immunoglobulin, an expensive and hard-to-come-by treatment. Therefore, if you are planning to travel to remote areas or if you expect to have contact with mammals, consider having the rabies pre-exposure vaccine. Ideally, three doses should be taken over at least 20 days Even when you have been immunised, you would still need at least two post-bite injections after a possible rabies exposure.

Snakes and scorpions Snakes may hide under rocks and in crevices, in holes and termite hills. They rarely attack unless provoked and bites in travellers are unusual. Snakes have no ears, so making a lot of noise to scare them off doesn't help, while stamping on the ground is an effective way to chase off most of them. The exceptions to this rule are puff adders and vipers, as they tend to lie still in ambush and even partly bury themselves in the sand when they feel threatened in any way. These species are highly venomous and bites are excruciatingly painful, sometimes even fatal. Most other snakes are relatively harmless and even venomous species will only dispense venom in about half of their bites.

Scorpions could also be described as 'shy' animals that will only attack human beings when they feel cornered. Often, they hide under rocks to avoid broad daylight, while they tend to be more active during the night and after rain. As scorpions do not like being exposed to direct sunlight, they will look for a place to hide towards sunrise. Bear this in mind when you camp out in the open: check your shoes for unwanted guests in the morning and watch out for scorpions that hide under your tent, ground sheet or luggage left outside. Like snakes, scorpions are almost inactive during the colder season, roughly from mid-December through February, especially when nights are cold. The chances of even seeing a snake or scorpion are very limited during this time of the year.

If you do get bitten by a snake or scorpion, try to stay calm as this helps to reduce the speed in which an eventual dose of venom spreads through the body. Remember that many snakes do not always dispense venom, and while scorpion bites can be very painful, they are rarely fatal. Many so-called first-aid techniques do more harm than good, as they involve cutting or sucking the wound. This invariably causes damage to the skin tissue surrounding the bite, allowing the venom to spread more easily; exactly what you intended to avoid. What you should do in the unlikely event of a bite, is the following:

- prevent movement of the bitten limb by applying a splint
- keep the bitten limb below heart height to slow the spread of any venom
- if you have a crêpe bandage, bind up as much of the bitten limb as you can, but release the bandage every half-hour to allow the blood to circulate for a few minutes through the affected limb

- do not use a tourniquet (as this cuts off the flow of blood completely), do not offer aspirin (as this dilutes the blood which in turn speeds up the spreading of the venom), do not apply ice packs or potassium permanganate. Administering paracetamol, however, is safe
- evacuate to a hospital which has antivenom, as this is the only effective treatment in the event of a snake bite
- ideally, capture the offending snake and show it to the doctor so he or she can be sure what antivenom to administer. However, the risk of another person getting bitten is real and beware: even a decapitated head is able to dispense venom in a reflex bite

Sexually transmitted diseases STDs and HIV infection occur in Niger, especially in urban areas (see *Health statistics*, page 25). Avoid infection by using a condom or femidom, preferably a well-tested brand bought before travel. Condoms are widely available in Niger and are advertised by stickers depicting a Peul hat and the brand name VISA.

Skin problems Symptoms of **fungal infections** include an itchy rash in the groin or flaking between the toes. As the climate is very dry for most of the year, this type of problem is not very common in Niger. However, if you are prone to fungal infections, bring an antifungal cream such as Canesten (Clotrimazole) and change socks and underwear frequently.

A fine pimply rash on the trunk is likely to be heat rash or **prickly heat**. Cool showers, dabbing (not rubbing) dry, and talc will help. If it's bad, you may need to check into an air-conditioned hotel room for a while. Slowing down to a relaxed schedule, wearing loose, baggy 100% cotton clothes and sleeping naked under a fan reduce the problem.

Respiratory problems Niger is a dry and dusty country for most of the year, with the amount of dust particles in the atmosphere occasionally building up to an unpleasant degree. This may induce irritation of the mucus membranes and lungs, and cause people to be more susceptible to colds or respiratory infections. The peak of respiratory complications seems to be from mid-December through January. Abandon all hope to inhale dust-free air when desert winds pick up and hazy skies turn the same colour as the soil. If you have respiratory problems, or if you want to avoid prolonged exposure to dust, cover your mouth using a turban, just like the local people will do.

HEAT AND SUN Whilst Niger 'enjoys' sunshine most of the year, it is not a country for sun worshippers in the Mediterranean sense of the word. The sun could well be a traveller's worst enemy when its damaging force is underestimated, and you wouldn't be the first one to suffer serious and sometimes long-lasting consequences after staying out in the sun just too long. Lips, ears and exposed skull are often the first victims of carelessness, resulting in sores and sunburn. Also, consider the risk of developing skin cancer due to excessive exposure to ultraviolet radiation. A hat and plenty of high-factor suncreams and lip balms provide some well-needed protection, but you should take protective action one step further: follow the example of the many Nigériens who routinely make an effort to avoid overexposure to direct sunlight. Long, loose garments covering most of the skin keep the ultraviolet radiation as well as the heat out. Try wrapping a long turban around your head as this is an excellent method of keeping your head relatively cool, illogical as this may seem at first.

Simultaneously, protective clothes keep dehydration levels down. As transpiration can swiftly evaporate into the dry air, you may not even be aware of the underestimated risk of dehydration. A signal of the first stage of dehydration is when you hardly pass urine or when your urine turns to a darker shade. The loss of salt and water can also cause headaches, nausea and muscle cramps, while the risk of developing bladder or kidney stones increases as a result of the higher than usual concentration of urine. Severe dizziness, sweating and fast, shallow breathing and a rapid, weak pulse signal a poor blood circulation caused by heat exhaustion. When these symptoms occur, do not take them lightly. Lie down, raise and support your legs to restore the blood flow to the brain. Water is your medicine; replenish fluids as much as you can, while some extra salt in the form of tablets or even table salt will help to restore the salt balance.

Prolonged exposure to the sun can cause heatstroke, which causes confusion, a strong pulse, slow, deep breathing and a high fever, eventually leading to a loss of consciousness and even death. Cooling down the casualty is crucial, so take the patient into the shade, remove excessive and tight clothes, apply wet sheets directly to the skin and fan to cause the evaporating moisture to cool the body as much as possible. Cool the head in the same way. Seek medical help as soon as you can.

SAFETY

When checking the governmental website for travel advice on Niger, you will find it littered with warnings about insecurity in various regions. This may put you off travelling in a country where apparently safety leaves much to be desired. Of course these warnings are there for a reason, but the background is rarely described. This section is about security, or, if you like, the insecurity in certain regions in Niger. While some of the topics discussed will sound intimidating, they are merely meant to put things in perspective, rather than to leave the false impression that Niger is a generally unsafe country in which to be travelling. On the contrary: insecurity isn't always what it seems, warnings do not apply to the country as a whole, and statistics aren't all that bad. To see why, it is necessary to make the distinction between the various types of crime and violence.

Petty theft occurs in all countries, pickpockets operate in many crowded areas, robberies can happen in a dark alley even in your home country. In this respect, serious warnings do apply to certain areas in Niamey especially after sunset (see box *Dangers and annoyances*, page 107), but most other towns throughout Niger can be considered surprisingly safe.

Gangs of criminals ('*coupeurs de route*') occasionally operate on certain stretches of (main) road, especially during the night. They put up an obstacle, obliging vehicles to stop, then seize valuables from their victims. For this reason, travelling at night is not recommended, while the more risky sections are sometimes closed for all traffic during the night. This type of villainy is targeting all types of vehicles and not simply those used by tourists and, again, is not unique to Niger: going on a holiday in Europe or the USA is no guarantee of avoiding similar situations.

Opportunistic robbers sometimes hold up tourist vehicles in remote regions. They are after money and other valuables, but no more than they can carry as they flee. Whilst these robbers usually carry arms to persuade their victims to part with their belongings, violence is uncommon. Many travel agencies in Agadez have had a vehicle in this situation at some point through the years, and, though it is a most unwanted situation to be in, it has never put them off continuing to work in the travel business.

More awkward are encounters with armed smugglers or bandits who want more than just a few loose items. Certain border regions especially are sensitive zones in this respect. While travel agents try to be aware of any signs of unrest and insecurity in the areas they intend to be passing through, every tourist season sees a few

During the era of the Tuareg rebellion, the whole of the Aïr Mountains region and parts of the Ténéré Desert were the scene of violence between the Tuareg and anyone representing 'the oppressive government' (*l'état oppressif*) (see *The Tuareg rebellion*, page 182). Peace was restored in 1995, when all rebelling parties were abolished and arms were handed in. Since then, there had been isolated pockets of violence, but on the whole the area had become calm enough to be opened up for tourism again.

One of the objectives of the Tuareg rebellion was to become more influential in national politics. A huge development, and one which should not be underestimated, after the signing of the peace accord, was that Rhissa ag Boula, a former leader of the Tuareg rebellion, was appointed Minister of Tourism in 1996. With several decades' experience in the field of tourism, he had very clear and catching ideas on how to boost the tourist industry in Niger. Highly respected by his kinsmen but considered a controversial person by others, Rhissa ag Boula managed to win the appreciation of many Nigériens during the years that followed. Perhaps more importantly, as a key figure in Tuareg circles, he played a crucial role in preserving security in the north of the country.

In January 2004, a politician, siding with the leading political party MNSD, was murdered. The assassins were arrested, but soon thereafter rumour spread that Rhissa ag Boula was linked to this liquidation. Though he claimed innocence, he stepped down from his post as Minister of Tourism. Days later he was incarcerated on suspicion of ordering the murder. However, though time went by he was not brought to justice.

During the months that followed, a series of brutal and violent attacks took place, the most violent being the indiscriminate shooting at a public bus; three civilians were killed, 11 were wounded and two police officers were taken hostage. The attacks were claimed by the FLAA (the former rebel party *Front de Libération de l'Aïr et de l'Azawagh*). Officially, the FLAA had ceased to exist on the day the Tuareg rebellion ended, but now the organisation seemed to have a new lease of life in order to free Rhissa ag Boula from imprisonment without trial. Matters got worse when the FLAA took four hostages (three police officers and a soldier) in the vast and inaccessible Tamgak Massif in the Aïr Mountains. For months the whole area was closed to tourists as the Nigérien army tried in vain to free the hostages.

It took months of intense negotiating to find a way out of this delicate situation. One major step was the eventual liberation of the four hostages. A remarkable second step can only be understood from within the Tuareg culture and jurisdiction: the family of the politician who was assassinated publicly pardoned Rhissa ag Boula, regardless of his involvement in the matter. From a traditional Tuareg point of view, this is a final and conclusive verdict, relieving the accused from further legal persecution. In fact, the mere question about 'guilty or not guilty' becomes irrelevant. According to the Nigérien penal code, a trial would still have to decide in the matter. However, in a country where traditional customs and constitutional law live side by side, the pardoning of Rhissa ag Boula by the victim's family was deemed sufficient to at least release him on probation.

On his return to Agadez, Rhissa ag Boula received an overwhelming and emotional welcome. To many of his own kind he was still the hero of the rebellion and a valuable former representative of the Tuareg in the government. Beyond any doubt, his release took the pressure off what was a delicate stalemate, and moreover, he could once again become a key figure in further discussions concerning the precarious events and other issues concerning the community of the Tuareg.

incidents where a 4x4 and many personal belongings are stolen. Travelling with a travel agency – or at least a local guide – in those areas that are considered risky, is highly recommended for various reasons: your local guide may pick up signals about (in)security while you are happily unaware, and should you find yourself in a precarious situation, your guide will be able to assess the situation better than you will. If there is anything positive to be said here, it must be that the chances of you featuring in Niger's crime statistics are very slim.

All of the above are acts of crime, with no political connotation. However, in 2004 up to the beginning of 2005 there were incidents – some of them very serious indeed – with a very different, political background. These incidents triggered fears that the security of the Aïr region was in jeopardy, with possible negative consequences for the tourist industry as an unwanted side effect. To understand where these incidents stem from and what the current implications for the security of the region are, see box *A Tuareg's pardon*, opposite. Bear in mind that the Aïr region measures 80,000km². While at some point a part of the mountain range was closed to travellers, elsewhere groups of tourists were happily travelling, oblivious of serious matters taking place hundreds of kilometres away. Maybe that is what sums up the essence of safety in Niger: it is a huge country where safety is certainly a matter to consider, but in the mean time thousands of tourists travel to Niger anyway to return home with happy memories only.

SAFETY FOR FEMALE TRAVELLERS Female travellers may feel more vulnerable to becoming the victims of petty crime, and before going to Niger for the first time I felt no different in that respect. However, after having travelled extensively in Niger, exploring many corners of the country on my own, I can honestly say that I felt generally safe, respected and even protected. Sometimes I took a few precautions – instigated by a combination of common sense and sometimes local advice – but these were the same or similar precautions I would take while travelling in a European country. On one occasion in Niamey, though, I knowingly ignored warnings, and this resulted in a nasty encounter in a dark street of notorious reputation. Through some much-needed assistance from bystanders, I managed to get away unharmed, but I should have known better!

As for unwanted attention from men, Niger must be one of the safest countries in Africa that I know. Especially in those areas that see few foreign visitors, the sight of a single female traveller rather causes people to raise their eyebrows and become overprotective, than to see this as an opportunity for harassment. Some urban areas felt different, but even then men who were looking for more than just having a Coke at my table could be easily discouraged without much ado. The most awkward experience that I had was in a rather tatty hotel with prostitutes and noisy, mostly drunk male guests. It probably wasn't the right place to begin with, but I just paid the nightguard some money and asked him not to stray too far from my door. I was disturbed by bed-bugs only.

In general, if you dress and behave respectably (see *Cultural sensitivity*, page 83), you will be met with respect. If a male is coming on too strong anyway, first of all try to discourage the unwanted company firmly but politely. When he persists, it may help to seek the attention of others.

WHAT TO TAKE

LUGGAGE As luggage will often be strapped on roofs of vehicles, a soft bag or pack is preferable to a hard suitcase. Take some precautions against dust, eg: use a light flightbag to wrap your bag or backpack and put a strap around it for easy handling. Bring a daypack to carry your hand luggage, and take all you need for the first few days on board with you, just in case your luggage is lost or delayed. Remember to put any medicines in your hand luggage, but do remove all sharp items before checking in for your flight.

CLOTHING To decide on your wardrobe, you need to have some idea of the temperatures you will face. Depending on your destination and the time of the year, temperatures can range from just above freezing point to 45°C. It is unlikely that you will have to cope with both ends of the scale, but it would be wrong to assume that Niger has a moderate climate.

In the coldest months, and most of all if you plan to go camping, do not underestimate the night temperatures, especially in the Aïr and desert regions. Cold winds may add to the discomfort, and the only sure protection from the cold is by dressing appropriately. A cardigan or jacket – or both – is a must. Fleece is a popular but synthetic material with a few downsides: a few sparks from an open fire are all that is needed to melt holes in the fleece, and in a dry climate, taking off your fleece can cause electrical sparks to lighten up the night! A woollen cardigan is a good – even better – alternative. Most woollen or fleece cardigans do not protect against strong winds, so bring a jacket for this purpose. Choose clothes that are suitable to use in layers, so you can add or remove a layer with ease. A locally bought turban protects against both the heat and the cold, but gloves are worth considering and are best brought from your home country. During the warm or hot months, loose-fitting clothes with long sleeves and long legs provide better protection against the heat than shorts and tiny shirts. Moreover, Niger is a Muslim country where it is not appreciated if you are underdressed (see *Cultural sensitivity*, page 83).

As for footwear, if you plan to go hiking, bring sturdy shoes with a good grip for slippery surfaces. Add some very light shoes or sandals to relieve your feet in the evenings.

CAMPING EQUIPMENT When you have booked a journey through a tour operator, they will most likely provide the essential camping gear, like cooking equipment, cutlery and crockery, and thin foam mattresses. If you are very attached to sleeping on a soft surface, the foam mattress in combination with a self-inflatable mattress makes a comfortable bed. Moreover, self-inflatable mattresses provide extra insulation. Bring your own sleeping bag, and check the possible night temperatures first. A three- or four-season sleeping bag is no luxury in the cold months, while a very thin sleeping bag will be enough in the hotter months.

Many travel agencies do not automatically provide tents, as you will sleep under the stars just like the local people during trips into the desert. There are, nevertheless, three reasons you may want to sleep in a tent: the cold, sandstorms, or snakes and scorpions. The last pose no threat in the cold months, as both snakes and scorpions are inactive at that time. An inner tent or a raised camping bed provide protection in those months and places when snakes and scorpions are active, and so would a mosquito net but it is not obvious how you could suspend it out in the open.

On longer journeys by 4x4 or with camels, water is carried in big jerrycans or traditional *guerbas* (a goatskin used as a water container), from which you refill your own water bottle. If you bring a metal one, it can double as a hot-water bottle to keep those feet warm during the coldest nights. Do not forget to bring a torch, and preferably enough new batteries to last your trip. Locally bought batteries can be very disappointing.

TOILETRIES In Niamey (and Agadez to a lesser extent) you can buy just about all you need. Lip balm is easy to get, but suncream or sunblock are difficult to find.

Tampax and tampons are available only in Niamey from the larger supermarkets and sometimes from drugstores, while condoms are cheap and widely available. Dental floss is a useful item, for flossing as well as for repairs. It is a strong material, and I once successfully used it to repair completely worn-out padding under a camel's saddle. Moist (toilet) tissues are ideal for freshening up during long-haul trips and after using the toilet. A special hand gel which cleans and disinfects will help to minimise the risk of bowel bugs. Insect repellents are available, but these do not contain DEET.

MISCELLANEOUS If you intend to stay in budget hotels, bring your own mosquito net as these are not always provided. Bring or buy a padlock and a couple of screw-eyes to secure your door when staying in accommodation of a debatable kind. A wedge to put under your door is another way to keep out unwanted guests while you are in. An inflatable pillow to provide neck support can come in handy if you want to sleep a little on long-haul journeys on tarred roads. Forget about taking a nap on all other roads.

PHOTOGRAPHIC EQUIPMENT Ordinary print film is available in Niamey and Agadez, while slide film is available only in Niamey (see *Shopping* and *Miscellaneous*, page 100). However, films may have been sitting in hot temperatures for a while, and this can badly affect the colours of your prints. It is best to bring a large supply; 100 or 200ASA films are best, while 400ASA is too sensitive for the sharp sunlight. A small (air)brush is essential to try to avoid the dust from damaging your film. Make sure to change a film in the best possible dust-free circumstances; still this is no guarantee that sand and dust will not find a way into your camera. Bring a dust-proof bag for particularly dusty days or sand storms, and consider a soft bag with good padding to protect your equipment on bumpy roads. See the *Photographic tips* box on pages 64–5 for more information.

MAPS The most widely available map is produced by the **Institut Géographique National (IGN)** in Niamey. At a scale of 1:2,000,000 it does not show a great deal of detail, but the overall view of the country is very clear; a rough classification of different zones of vegetation stand out at a glance, while the road system is depicted in a contrasting colour. The map was drawn in 1993, and although newer editions have been printed since, the only difference from the first edition is the front picture. Since 1993, the road system has been upgraded along a few stretches (eg: in the Tillabéri region) and is not fully up to date. However, for most travellers this will not have a big impact; it's still a useful map. In Niger, this map is available directly from the IGN, though stock often runs out. Otherwise you can try the better bookshops in Niamey, the small kiosk in Hotel Gaweye or the Syndicat du Tourisme in Agadez. Whether you buy the map in your home country or in Niger, the cost will be roughly the same (CFA15,000).

A new map, produced by **International Travel Maps (ITMB)** in Canada has the same scale but shows a very different picture. When I showed this map to the IGN board in Niamey, they exclaimed: 'What a wonderful map! The desert looks so green!' Of course the green is not about vegetation, but about elevation instead. Plenty of details like villages, wells, minor roads and tracks and community boundaries outshine the major road system – which is more up to date than on the IGN map – but the details can be very useful. You would be searching in vain for this map in Niamey, so order and buy it before travelling to Niger.

The IGN has a 1:50,000 map of the **Massif de l'Aïr**, depicting Agadez, Arlit and just about all of the Aïr Mountains. The road system is not always accurate, and it wouldn't be a detailed enough map to venture out on your own within the

2

Ariadne Van Zandbergen

EQUIPMENT Although with some thought and an eye for composition you can take reasonable photos with a 'point-and-shoot' camera, you need an SLR camera if you are at all serious about photography. Modern SLRs tend to be very clever, with automatic programmes for almost every possible situation, but remember that these programmes are limited in the sense that the camera cannot think, but only make calculations. Every starting amateur photographer should read a photographic manual for beginners and get to grips with such basics as the relationship between aperture and shutter speed.

Always buy the best lens you can afford. The lens determines the quality of your photo more than the camera body. Fixed fast lenses are ideal, but very costly. Zoom lenses are easier to change composition without changing lenses the whole time. If you carry only one lens, a 28–70mm (digital 17–55mm) or similar zoom should be ideal. For a second lens, a lightweight 80–200mm or 70–300mm (digital 55–200mm) or similar will be excellent for candid shots and varying your composition. Wildlife photography will be very frustrating if you don't have at least a 300mm lens. For a small loss of quality, tele-converters are a cheap and compact way to increase magnification: a 300 lens with a 1.4x converter becomes 420mm, and with a 2x it becomes 600mm. Note, however, that 1.4x and 2x tele-converters reduce the speed of your lens by 1.4 and 2 stops respectively.

For photography from a vehicle, a solid beanbag, which you can make yourself very cheaply, will be necessary to avoid blurred images, and is more useful than a tripod. A clamp with a tripod head screwed on to it can be attached to the vehicle as well. Modern dedicated flash units are easy to use; aside from the obvious need to flash when you photograph at night, you can improve a lot of photos in difficult 'high contrast' or very dull light with some fill-in flash. It pays to have a proper flash unit as opposed to a built-in camera flash.

DIGITAL/FILM Digital photography is now the preference of most amateur and professional photographers, with the resolution of digital cameras improving the whole time. For ordinary prints a 6 megapixel camera is fine. For better results and the possibility to enlarge images and for professional reproduction, higher resolution is available up to 16 megapixels.

Memory space is important. The number of pictures you can fit on a memory card depends on the quality you choose. Calculate in advance how many pictures you can fit on a card and either take enough cards to last for your trip, or take a storage drive on to which you can download the content. A laptop gives the advantage that you can see your pictures properly at the end of each day and edit and delete rejects, but a storage device is lighter and less bulky. These drives come in different capacities up to 80GB.

mountains. Yet, it is a very good map to give you some idea of where you are. Though you may be able to pick up a copy at the addresses mentioned above, this map is less widely distributed.

In theory, the IGN has a range of 1:200,000 maps, covering the whole country. In reality, only very few copies are available from the IGN in Niamey. It could even be that the last specimen is not for sale, as it is unclear when a new print run will be made available. When you are in desparate need of a detailed map, give it a go anyway. Sometimes staff are willing to photocopy a map in black and white on A3 sheets which you will then have to tape together. You would probably still pay the full cost of the map (between CFA5,000 and CFA10,000). Certain maps can be printed out in full colour. Make sure to agree on a price before you give the go-ahead.

Bear in mind that digital camera batteries, computers and other storage devices need charging, so make sure you have all the chargers, cables and converters with you. Most hotels have charging points, but do enquire about this in advance. When camping you might have to rely on charging from the car battery; a spare battery is invaluable.

If you are shooting film, 100 to 200 ISO print film and 50 to 100 ISO slide film are ideal. Low ISO film is slow but fine grained and gives the best colour saturation, but will need more light, so support in the form of a tripod or monopod is important. You can also bring a few 'fast' 400 ISO films for low-light situations where a tripod or flash is no option.

DUST AND HEAT Dust and heat are often a problem. Keep your equipment in a sealed bag, stow films in an airtight container (eg: a small cooler bag) and avoid exposing equipment and film to the sun. Digital cameras are prone to collecting dust particles on the sensor which results in spots on the image. The dirt mostly enters the camera when changing lenses, so be careful when doing this. To some extent photos can be 'cleaned' up afterwards in Photoshop, but this is time-consuming. You can have your camera sensor professionally cleaned, or you can do this yourself with special brushes and swabs made for the purpose, but note that touching the sensor might cause damage and should only be done with the greatest care.

LIGHT The most striking outdoor photographs are often taken during the hour or two of 'golden light' after dawn and before sunset. Shooting in low light may enforce the use of very low shutter speeds, in which case a tripod will be required to avoid camera shake.

With careful handling, side lighting and back lighting can produce stunning effects, especially in soft light and at sunrise or sunset. Generally, however, it is best to shoot with the sun behind you. When photographing animals or people in the harsh midday sun, images taken in light but even shade are likely to be more effective than those taken in direct sunlight or patchy shade, since the latter conditions create too much contrast.

PROTOCOL In some countries, it is unacceptable to photograph local people without permission, and many people will refuse to pose or will ask for a donation. In such circumstances, don't try to sneak photographs as you might get yourself into trouble. Even the most willing subject will often pose stiffly when a camera is pointed at them; relax them by making a joke, and take a few shots in quick succession to improve the odds of capturing a natural pose.

Ariadne Van Zandbergen is a professional travel and wildlife photographer specialising in Africa. She runs The Africa Image Library. For photo requests, visit www.africaimagelibrary.co.za or contact her on ariadne@hixnet.co.za.

$ MONEY

The Nigérien currency is the CFA franc, with CFA standing for *Franc de la Communauté Financièère d'Afrique* or Franc of the African Financial Community. It is a shared currency, in use since 1945 in the member countries of the *Union Economique et Monétaire d'Afrique de l'Oouest* (UEMAO) or West African Economic and Monetary Union (WAEMU). Apart from Niger, members are Benin, Burkina Faso, Guinea-Bissau, Ivory Coast, Mali, Senegal and Togo; all of them former French colonies. The coins and banknotes are issued by their common bank, the *Banque Centrale des Etats de l'Afrique de l'Ouest* (BCEAO) and can be used in any of these countries.

The value of the CFA franc has always been pegged to the former French franc, while nowadays it has a fixed rate with the euro: €1 = CFA655.957, usually rounded up to 656CFA. The exchange rate with other currencies fluctuates. In May 2006, the exchange rate to the US$ was: US$1 = CFA518. The CFA franc comes in notes of 10,000, 5,000, 2,000 and 1,000 and coins of 500, 200, 100, 50, 25, 10, 5 and even CFA1.

Since January 2005, old banknotes of a very different design have been withdrawn from circulation; consequently they are no longer valid. Though it is unlikely that old notes will still pop up, be aware that they are worthless so do not accept them as money. To have an idea of what these notes look like, many banks will still have the posters depicting the old notes, originally intended to inform people about their withdrawal.

EXCHANGING MONEY As the rate between the euro and the CFA franc is fixed, it is easy to see why the euro is the preferred hard currency in Niger. Changing euro to CFA francs is a straightforward matter, and most people working with foreigners in one way or another are well used to the fixed exchange rate. This means that in some of the places frequented by tourists – and usually when a bank is not too far off – the euro is readily accepted as a means of payment. Therefore, it is wise to bring some smaller notes in case you run short of CFA francs. While even coins are accepted by some (usually those who cannot afford to be fussy), use these sparingly, as they cannot be exchanged at banks. The only way for Nigériens to change euro coins to CFA francs is through a willing European traveller. Next in order of popularity is the US dollar, while some other hard currencies are taken by a few banks only. Therefore, if you travel with any other currency, plan carefully when and where to change enough money to CFA francs.

As the loss of travellers' cheques is covered by insurance, most travellers prefer to bring a mixture of cash and travellers' cheques. Even then, the preferred currency is the euro. Always retain the purchase receipt, as you may be asked to produce this at the bank. Credit cards are of little use in Niger. Some top-end hotels do accept payment by credit card, but outside Niamey there are only a few banks that give cash advances for Visa, MasterCard or the French Carte Bleue, the BIA bank in Agadez being one of them. A commission of CFA10,000 is charged for cash advances, regardless of the amount you require. Bear in mind that there is a limit to the amount that can be exchanged through travellers' cheques or cash advances given through credit cards. The maximum amount varies between banks, and your best chances for obtaining larger amounts are probably at the Ecobank in Niamey. Enquire also at their branches at the Hotel Ténéré and Hotel Gaweye, and expect to pay commission.

Changing money on the black market is a common practice in towns along the Nigerian border. The Nigerian currency, the naira, is preferred to the CFA franc. Most merchants deal in naira only, hence the presence of moneychangers at *taxi-brousse* stations and around markets. Even in some towns well away from any border there may be a thriving black market. On one occasion, a bank employee actually refused to change cash euro. Instead, she referred me to the black market, boldly saying that 'that is where we all go' to avoid paying commission to the bank. Hard currency other than the euro, and sometimes US dollars, is not accepted on the black market. Though officially it is illegal, changing money on the black market is generally tolerated and a fairly safe practise. No need to hide in a gloomy alley, the transaction is done openly at the table where the money-dealer has bricks of banknotes hidden, or simply laid out in front of him. Obviously, by-standers will be aware that you carry money with you, and some care should be taken not to fall into the hands of opportunists. For the euro, you will get the official rate or slightly less, but usually you'll get a better deal than at the bank if you take their commission into consideration. For the US dollar and the naira, make sure you check the current rate, but if you do not have that opportunity, trust that the majority of the moneychangers are reliable.

To check the latest official exchange rates, see www.oanda.com/convert/classic.

INTERNATIONAL MONEY TRANSFERS When all your cash and travellers' cheques have run out and when your credit card is damaged or lost, there is always the option to have money transferred to you from abroad. The most widely known agency for money transfers is Western Union. They are easily spotted through their signs in black and yellow. Many towns have at least one branch at the post office and one or more at various banks. When you are in need, you'll find one. Their services come at a price, though, and moreover, the commission is sometimes taken at both ends of the deal. Outside the UEMOA zone, the charges are more expensive still, eg: CFA37,000 to transfer any amount between CFA450,000 and CFA600,000. When you are in Niamey, it is worth checking out the commission charged by MoneyGram (↘ *73 92 30;* f *73 99 14*), who also arrange international money transfers. They are located next to Sahel Airlines in Rue Rivoli, not far from the *petit marché*.

BANKS IN NIGER Of the many banks in Niger, those listed below are the more useful ones when it comes to changing money. The telephone and fax numbers are taken from the main branch in Niamey. Services mentioned are generalised, so bear in mind that certain branches (especially those outside Niamey) have limited services. You should therefore always check the relevant chapter for more detailed information.

$ **BCEAO or Banque Centrale des Etats de l'Afrique de l'Ouest** ↘ 72 26 18. Travellers can only change cash euros here.
$ **BIA or Banque Internationale pour l'Afrique** ↘ 49 09 65; f 73 35 95. Cash (most currencies); travellers' cheques; credit card in some branches (Visa, MasterCard, Carte Bleue).
$ **Ecobank** ↘ 73 71 81; f 73 72 03. Cash (euro and US$); travellers' cheques; credit cards at some branches.
$ **Sonibank** ↘ 73 52 24; f 73 46 93. Cash (euro; US$ and other currencies in some branches only).
$ **BOA or Bank of Africa** ↘ 73 36 20; f 73 38 18. Cash (in Niamey only: most hard currencies).
$ **BINCI or Banque Islamique du Niger pour le Commerce et l'Investissement** ↘ 73 27 40; f 73 47 35. Cash (in Niamey only: euro and US$); travellers' cheques (in Niamey only: euro and US$).

GETTING AROUND

BY AIR Consider the immense size of Niger and the remoteness of certain cities and desert towns in combination with the extreme roughness of certain pistes, and you may agree that covering some distances by air to save time and energy would make sense. Travel agents and those Nigériens who could afford the expenses, for instance, would certainly make use of air shuttles between Niamey and Agadez, even Niamey and Zinder or Diffa. In reality, however, there are no scheduled domestic flights. In fact, Niger's airstrips are currently in such a state of deterioration that large aircraft would not be able to land safely anywhere other than Niamey and Agadez. Only small planes occasionally venture out to the remote areas, but you would have to know the right people in the limited aviation circles to be able to make use of any such flights.

Nigeravia is the only company which offers commercial flights to destinations within Niger, but the catch is that you'd have to charter a whole aircraft. Obviously, this is an extremely expensive way of getting around. For information, see *Niamey*, page 95.

BY RIVER Even the formidable river Niger – flowing 550km through Nigérien territories from Ayorou to Gaya – does provide a few options for a different means of travelling. Certain stretches are littered with tiny islands and rocky ilôts, while the water level may drop to such a degree that navigation becomes impossible. Traffic is therefore limited to pirogues (wooden dugout canoes or larger-size narrowboats made from bent planks) and pinasses (traditionally built wooden barges used for merchandise and passenger transport), which are hardly ever a more efficient means of transport than either a car or bush taxi. However, they do provide wonderful opportunities to see the riverine landscape and its wildlife from a different perspective.

Public transport by river is available, though there are no official harbours or ports that may serve as a departure point or a place to get information. As a general rule, you may assume that pirogues and pinasses will leave fully laden to meet local markets. Hence finding such a pinasse is a matter of asking around about markets and the options available at landing points. Rates are fixed to a certain degree, but being white and a tourist may push the fare up quite a bit. Always bargain and try to find out what others pay to travel a particular stretch of river. Travelling by public pinasse will guarantee a high degree of *couleur locale*.

In some places along the river, local guides may offer to take you out for a day trip to get the feel of the river or to try and find hippo. Expect to pay anything between CFA5,000 for an hour, up to CFA25,000 for a day trip. Obviously, the bigger the pinasse or the number of your party, the higher the rate. Booking a river trip through a travel agency is the more leisurely option and, again depending on the number of passengers, need not be very expensive. Only a few travel agencies in Niamey offer organised trips, but it is worth asking around since there is a growing interest in excursions of this kind. For more information, see the relevant sections in the *Tillabéri* and *Dosso* chapters.

BY ROAD As there is no railway in Niger, as domestic flights are virtually non-existent and as options to navigate the river Niger are limited, just about all travelling within the country has to be done by road. Given this inevitability, there is good news and bad news. The good news is that along the – mostly tarred – main axes, public transport is regular, affordable and comfortable. The bad news is that anywhere else, public transport is erratic and often physically demanding, while the only alternative is a costly one: to rent a 4x4 vehicle. Rates for a 4x4 vary and start at CFA60,000 per day, fuel not included. When lower rates are offered, there will probably be a catch, like bad maintenance, no insurance, no back-up in case the car breaks down completely. For more information on hiring a vehicle, see page 70.

On some main roads a toll is payable. This will go unnoticed when you are travelling on public transport, but not in private vehicles. The amount depends on the distance and the type of vehicle, for instance a minibus going from Niamey to Ayorou (225km) costs CFA500.

Buses Aïr Transport, Rimbo Transport des Voyageurs (RTV), Maissagé (or EHGM) and the Société Nigérienne de Transport des Voyageurs (SNTV) all provide similar services along most tarred roads at more or less the same rates. The quality of the buses or coaches may vary, but in general they are quite comfortable. Typically, there are three and two high-backed seats to the left and right of the aisle respectively. As these seats are usually covered with synthetic material that does not absorb any perspiration, many passengers bring a towel or blanket to sit on, which is marginally more comfortable. The windows are usually lined with curtains to keep the blinding and scorching sunlight at bay. SNTV seems to be the only company thus far with some air-conditioned coaches shuttling between Niamey and Arlit.

Though you may be tempted to pay a little more for the added luxury, you could be in for a serious disappointment: these coaches have no windows that can open, so if the air conditioning does not work (which is not exceptional), the vehicle quickly turns into an oven while you are the bun that is gradually being cooked.

The buses leave their departure point sometimes very early in the morning. Therefore it is advisable to reserve a seat, and preferably pay and collect your ticket the day before you intend to travel. If you do not mind the discomfort, you are allowed to sleep at the bus station rather than get up very early and hope to find a taxi. You should report at the bus station half an hour prior to departure (reporting time or *rendez-vous*, ie: the time mentioned in the various sections with bus schedules). Most companies will then call the passengers in order of booking: those who obtained their ticket early get the first choice of seats. The only places where long legs can comfortably stretch out are just behind the driver's seat, otherwise passengers will have to put up with a lack of legroom. The two seats at the opposite side of the aisle are reserved for the second driver and other staff. As the two drivers take turns at the wheel, they drive almost non-stop, with short stops in the bigger towns only. Water (in polythene bags) is sometimes available on board, but do not count on it and bear in mind that the water is not purified.

If you need to find a seat on a bus from a point between main stopping places, check for availability and book well beforehand. Yet, overbookings do occur. When it's your unlucky day, you may find that coaches from other bus companies have already passed, in which case you are stuck for the day unless you are willing to squeeze into a *bâchée* or bush taxi (see below). Another reason to book well in advance is when you are planning to travel just before or after public or Muslim holidays, like Tabaski and Id al Fitr. Buses tend to fill up quickly around such occasions.

Bâchées, bush taxis and trucks For destinations in between the bigger towns and for destinations off the main roads, there is a hotchpotch of vehicles to choose from. The most common ones are *bâchées* (usually a Peugeot 504 with nine passenger seats) and *taxi-brousses* (bush taxi: minibuses with 19 passenger seats). If the lack of legroom in the big buses worries you, travelling by *bâchée* or *taxi-brousse* is a challenge. Moreover, these vehicles are invariably worn down to a certain degree, and breakdowns are commonplace.

You will find this kind of transport along the main roads in smaller villages or at the *autogares* in bigger towns. Look for the ticket office somewhere under a ramshackle hangar or shelter. Before paying for your ticket, enquire how many passengers have booked for the same vehicle, as *bâchées* and *taxi-brousses* will leave only when full. Depending on the day and the destination, this may take up to several hours. The places in the front are usually slightly more expensive as they are considered the more comfortable seats. Whether or not this is really the case is questionable, as the front seat will take two passengers. Women are sometimes expected to travel in the back in any case as a compulsory protective gesture: statistics show that in case of an accident the front seat is not the best choice after all.

It is generally safe to leave your big bag or backpack somewhere near or in the ticket office while you wander around until all the seats have been sold, but take some precautions to make your bag look inconspicuous and inaccessible. A pair of trainers or sandals tied to your bag, for instance, could just be too much of a temptation. All luggage (together with a sizeable selection of furniture, bicycles, jerrycans filled with fuel, sheep and what not) will be tied on top of the roof, often almost doubling the height of the vehicle.

Some roads and *pistes* require a more sturdy kind of vehicle, like **Land-Rover**

pick-ups and **trucks**. ('*Piste*' is a French word that is generally used to describe a rough or sandy track in arid or desert regions. Such a track might be well defined and marked or just be a series of parallel tracks in the open desert.) While some of these are meant for passenger transport only, others are primarily meant for the transportation of merchandise. In the latter case, as many people as can possibly fit climb on top of the already heavily laden vehicle, where they will have to hang on to anything or anybody for the duration of the journey. This must be without any doubt the most exhausting way to travel and should never be underestimated. Where long distances are involved, the journey may include an overnight stop. Usually, this means sleeping in a very basic hotel or anywhere by the side of the road. Remember that you will be exposed to the scorching sun throughout the daytime, so come prepared and be self-sufficient, especially in water. Dehydration and heatstroke are serious threats and not uncommon on long hauls (see *Heat and sun*, page 58). Moreover, in case of a breakdown in a barren area, water (and shade) may not be available. Wearing a *taguelmoust* or turban is highly recommended.

Slightly less uncomfortable are the passenger trucks or pick-ups, where countless people typically have to stand in the back, again out in the burning sun for the duration of the trip. The same warnings and precautions as above apply here as well. To get some idea, see the travellers' account of a journey from N'Guigmi to Chad on page 235.

Hitchhiking Though hitchhiking is allowed in Niger, it is not a common or efficient way of travelling. Big buses will definitely not stop, while *bâchées* and *taxi-brousses* will stop only when they have any seats available. Obviously, the ride will then cost the usual fare. Private vehicles will generally ignore hitchhikers, unless you get a chance to talk the driver into taking you on board. Therefore, the best way to hitch a ride is to approach drivers at either a petrol station or a police checkpoint or barrier. Your best chances are with NGO vehicles, and these are clearly recognisable through logos. Always offer to pay for the ride.

Around town In the bigger towns, **shared taxis** provide the most regular, sometimes only means of public transport. Since there are very few places where taxis line up, it is a matter of waiting for one to pass by on a thoroughfare. All taxis are white and numbered, hence easy to spot. Shared taxis take up to four adults and as many children as can be squeezed in. A ride typically costs CFA200 per person for an average distance, and if the driver expects you to pay more, he should discuss so beforehand and not on arrival at your destination.

If you do not fancy a possible delay as other passengers are being picked up and dropped off, you should specify that you want a *location*. In that case, the taxi will take you straight from A to B, but you will have to negotiate the fare beforehand. For shorter distances, CFA1,000 should be enough. Taxi drivers patiently waiting outside the bigger hotels, however, will charge more than that. See also *Niamey: getting around*, page 97.

When taxis are rare or totally absent, it is likely that *kabou-kabous* or 'taxi-motos' are the only alternative. The motorbikes may be anything from brand new and sturdy to ramshackle and *fatigué* (tired), while the drivers are almost without exception young and very cool. With a casual '*On y va?*' they will let you know they are ready to go. While it is a fine way to travel around town, do check the state of the motorbike and bear in mind that young, inexperienced and often unlicensed drivers and worn-out motorbikes can be a risky combination in Nigérien traffic. Be fussy, as accidents do happen.

Hiring a vehicle While travelling by public transport between the bigger towns is still relatively comfortable, all that changes quickly as soon as you leave the tarred roads. Unless you have a tight budget, plenty of time and stamina, you will most likely end up hiring a vehicle, or more specifically a 4x4 (unless you mean to be driving around Niamey only). You will have to cough up a small fortune, but in return you get the luxury of your own vehicle, usually with driver. Expect to pay no less than CFA60,000 to CFA80,000 for a day, and this usually does not yet include the fuel. Though it is a lot of money indeed, it is also a reasonable rate, if only considering the high expenses of maintenance due to the rough road conditions. Therefore, be wary if you are being offered a 4x4 for less than the above since there is usually a catch.

In Niamey, there are a few car rental agencies who rent out vehicles with or without drivers (see *Niamey*, page 97). Outside the capital, options are limited to travel agents, who will prefer to sell you a whole package, including a guide, a cook, camping material, food, etc. Depending on where you want to go, this may be well worth considering.

ACCOMMODATION

In 2005, as Niger was preparing itself for the 5th Jeux de la Francophonie (the Francophone equivalent of the Commonwealth Games), a newspaper printed an inventory of all the officially registered and licensed **hotels** all over the country. The total showed an astonishingly low figure of 57, 13 of which are in the capital with another 13 in the best structured tourist destination, Agadez. Officially, this leaves only 31 hotels for the rest of Niger (some of which are in a poor state, while others are actually brothels), a tell-tale figure from a country where tourism is not evenly developed over the regions.

Especially in Niamey and Agadez, there is a whole range of hotels – from basic to very luxurious – to choose from. Prices vary from CFA5,000 to CFA80,000 or more, with most of the accommodation on offer being in the CFA15,000–25,000 range. This means that budget accommodation is very rare, while the rooms starting at CFA15,000 sometimes have very little appeal whatsoever. In fact, many hotels that once must have been real beauties are now in a desperate state of decay. Meanwhile, rates may have been fixed or even gone up, sometimes leaving a huge gap between what you might expect and what is really there. One reason must be the fact that the Tuareg rebellion caused a dramatic decline in the numbers of tourists visiting Niger, leaving rooms vacant, the cash till empty and the morale to keep up standards low. In a number of cases, a change of management in this less favourable era has been an extra catalyst in the downward spiral.

On the whole, while it is certainly possible to find comfortable and even excellent hotel rooms, accommodation in Niger may cost a small fortune and this is something you should be well aware of when budgeting your trip. A tourist tax of CFA500 is payable per person per night, and this is usually, but not always included in the price. While just about all hotels and lodges do serve breakfast, this is hardly ever included in the price for the room. The price and quality match the standard of the accommodation, and hovers between CFA500 for some bread, jam and Nescafé, and up to CFA3,000 for a breakfast buffet that will please gourmands.

Besides the official listing of hotels and the occasional unlicensed hotel, some Catholic and Evangelic missions and NGOs have *chambres de passage* or guest rooms. While these rooms are usually inexpensive and clean, more often than not they are clearly not on offer for tourists. Instead, they are primarily intended for religious people attending conferences etc and for NGO employees and guests. Even if tourists are allowed to stay, priority is always given to those visitors the rooms were originally built for. Other than in towns or villages where there is no

2

alternative, I would therefore generally discourage even considering making use of these rooms. Of course there are always exceptions to the rule, and some of these are mentioned in the text.

In rural areas, but also in some towns, you may find a **campement**. As the word suggests, it is most likely a place where camping is allowed at a nominal and often negotiable fee. However, *campement* first of all refers to an enclosed area with some kind of accommodation, like basic rondavels, comfortable bungalows, canvas tents or traditional huts. Facilities like a restaurant or bar may be limited or missing altogether. The setting as a whole could be anything from 'basic but charming' to 'luxurious and expensive' and the rates will reflect this.

In places where there is no accommodation whatsoever, local villagers or NGO employees may put you up for the night. Whether you are given a *chambre de passage*, a place to pitch your tent, the use of an empty classroom or a woven mat in a simple homestead, in rural areas where visitors are a rare commodity, you are likely to meet both curiosity and warm hospitality. Always offer to pay.

Note: in accommodation listings in the following chapters, the abbreviations 's/c' and 'AC' are used, denoting rooms which are self-contained and/or air conditioned.

✖ FOOD AND DRINK

Whether or not your journey in Niger will be a refined culinary experience depends on a few factors, like your destination (urban or rural?) and your budget. And your personal taste for food, of course. In those towns that are developed for tourism, you are likely (very likely) to find certain familiar types of food prepared in a familiar way, like French fries, pepper steak or grilled chicken, green peas or beans in a gentle tomato sauce. French bread will be available in many places, just like *La vache qui rit*, the processed cheese that seems to follow travellers all over francophone Africa. It is a reminder that Niger once was a French colony, and the former colonisers did a thorough job in leaving behind a culinary heritage. In Niamey and a few top-end restaurants elsewhere, you could have anything from liver pâté, frogs' legs, seafood and lamb *à la provençale*, accompanied by fine wines. The capital has plenty more international options (Chinese, Lebanese, Italian etc) to choose from. However, you probably didn't travel all the way to Niger for spring rolls or *osso bucco*.

Different ethnic groups live on specific diets, depending on their preferences (eg: pastoralists prefer meat and milk, but not fish) and depending on what is available. For most Nigériens, the staple food is millet (or some other kind of cereal) which has been pounded in a mortar, then boiled with water to make solid porridge. To add flavour and nutrients, the porridge is accompanied by a sauce and sometimes meat or fish. There are plenty of ways to spice up a sauce, and though it may be an acquired taste, the combination of *pâte de mille* or porridge and sauce can be very tasty. Boiled rice, couscous, noodles or bread can replace the porridge, and as long as the meal is filling, it's a good meal by Nigérien standards.

The southern regions of Niger, as well as the cooler Aïr Mountains, are more suitable for agriculture, so fresh fruits and vegetables are part of the daily diet of those living in these areas. In the riverine zones, meals will often consist of fish-and-something. The fish can be smoked, cooked in sauce or grilled, complete with head and fins. More refined or extravagant meals are often reserved for special occasions, such as marriages or certain Muslim holidays. Then the meal is composed around meat – sheep in all likelihood as it is the meat preferred by many. So if you are looking for a meal that does not have any of the expensive ingredients imported from France, there is still an ample choice. It all depends on the occasion and your location.

Below is a small selection of local specialities and some drinks that you may come across, whether it be in a restaurant, in a foodstall near the bus station, or somewhere in the desert.

Koulikouli or **Tourteaux** Groundnuts are pounded to a greasy paste, pretty much like peanut butter. The paste is then squeezed dry by hand, an elaborate process to separate the oil from the solid matter. The dry paste is rolled to form balls the size of a golfball. These are dried, then roasted or fried. In dry conditions, these balls can be preserved for months. Some nibble on the koulikouli as they come (give it a try, they are rock solid!), but they are more generally ground again, then used as a condiment for meat or cooked meals. Koulikouli are widely available in the region of Maradi, though as they preserve well, they are sold in other places too. See also box: *Maradi, the groundnut capital*, page 206.

Kilichi Very thin slices of beef are first laid to dry in the sun, then they are grilled. This is an efficient way to preserve meat in a dry climate. Kilichi comes in different varieties: salted only (dark in colour); salted and spiced (the red variety); or generously rubbed with ground koulikouli and chilli powder (the thickest and chewiest of the three). This is a speciality of Maradi and Tessaoua, where vendors-on-bikes will carry stacks of the wafer-thin and crispy slices of meat. Delicious! In Niamey, look for kilichi in the vicinity of cinema Sonni Ali Ber.

Sugared groundnuts Yet another Maradi special is caramelised groundnuts. They are sold in used bottles, often with the Johnnie Walker label still on them. In Maradi one bottle costs a mere CFA500, while the price increases or even doubles the further away you are from Maradi.

Halawa A chunky kind of fudge, made from cane sugar and lemon juice. The fudge is cut into strips, bars or cubes, then sold by street vendors. I found halawa in different towns, usually on a tray on the head of a vendor.

Bourabousko au Karassou A couscous variation made from millet with garden sorrel and butter. A curious combination that can be found in the region of Diffa.

Tchoukou or **takomért** The Hausa call it *tchoukou*, the Tuareg say *takomért*, and both are varieties of cheese, made by the Peul and Tuareg. The final flavour depends on the milk that is used – cow, goat, sheep or camel – and the amount of salt that is added. It is rich in flavour and full of character, and comes in local varieties. Pieces of cheese can be thin, rather sweet and a bit crispy, while others are over 1cm thick, moist and salty. I found the former near Tahoua and Abalak, while the latter seems more typical of the Aïr region.

La boule or **foura** A typical Tuareg brew or porridge, made from pounded, cooked millet. The millet is mixed with salt and spices, ground dates or ground *takomért*, or a mixture of the above, then diluted with water or milk. As *la boule* or 'the ball' keeps very well in a dry climate, the mixture is often prepared, rolled into balls and then left to dry for later use. The balls have to be ground again before adding the water or milk. Depending on the ingredients, the flavour varies from rather nondescript to a sweet-and-salt mixture. A very nourishing porridge, but also an acquired taste.

Toguella The best bread of the desert, made of wheat flour and water. It is cooked directly in 'pre-heated' sand, so the whole process starts by making a good fire. The dough is shaped until it looks like a thick pizza base, and is put directly on hot sand (after the embers have been removed). It is then covered with hot embers and sand, and left to cook for a while. When it is ready, the bread is removed and thoroughly dusted off. Most likely, the bread will then be torn to bits, and soaked in a sauce before serving.

Mechoui An entire sheep, filled with couscous or rice, then cooked in a traditional clay oven until the meat is moist and tender. It takes a long time to prepare but the result is a delicious meal to feast on with a group of people. Not from any region specifically.

Bissap, jinjimbre and **jus de tamarin** Three natural juices, made from hibiscus flowers, ginger and tamarind. As the juice is boiled first, then left to cool down, it is safe to drink. The juice is sold in small polythene bags at bus stations or sometimes in bars or street stalls. Some supermarkets (like Haddad and Score in Niamey) sell the natural but undiluted version by the bottle. It is inexpensive and a good thirst quencher, as you can dilute to taste and mix with other drinks.

Solani or **Kossam** Small bags filled with curdled milk or drinking yoghurt. It comes in different flavours, is inexpensive (CFA100–125), widely available and usually comes chilled. Street vendors will chant 'Solani solani!' as they scavenge for more customers. As it is a popular drink, the chances of buying one that is past its 'best before date' are slim.

Tea Sooner or later you will get to taste the tiny glasses of bitter-sweet tea. Vendors at bus stations sell tea by the glass, but the real experience is a more elaborate ceremony that involves three rounds of tea, made from the same leaves and handfuls of sugar in a tiny enamel teapot. The first serving is 'bitter as death', the second is 'mild as life', and the third one is 'sweet as love'.

PUBLIC HOLIDAYS AND FESTIVALS

PUBLIC HOLIDAYS

Most Christian holidays (Easter being the exception) and national holidays have fixed dates:

1 January	New Year's Day
March-April	Easter Monday
24 April	Concord Day
1 May	Labour Day
3 August	Independence Day
18 December	Republic Day
25 December	Christmas Day
31 December	New Year's Eve

Concord Day On this date an agreement between Tuareg and the government was signed in Ouagadougou, thus ending the Tuareg rebellion.

Labour Day Celebrations take place in Niamey and the larger towns.

Christmas Day and **New Year's Eve** May well pass by unnoticed for those who are travelling in rural areas. On the other hand, in cities like Niamey and Agadez, celebrations and festivities take place.

Muslim holidays are based on the lunar calendar – a lunar month counts as either 29 or 30 days – and therefore the dates vary from year to year.

Leilat al Kadr	Celebration of the 27th day of Ramadan
Id al Fitr	End of Ramadan
Tabaski	Feast of Sacrifice
Mouloud	Celebration of the Prophet's birthday

As the start of each lunar month is determined according to visual sighting of the new moon, dates vary locally. Therefore, the dates below can be one day off the actual dates.

	2006	2007	2008	2009	2010	2011
New Year	31 Jan	20 Jan	10 Jan; 29 Dec	18 Dec	8 Dec	27 Nov
Mouloud	11 Apr	31 Mar	20 Mar	9 Mar	26 Feb	15 Feb
Start of Ramadan	24 Sep	13 Sep	1 Sep	22 Aug	11 Aug	1 Aug
Id al Fitr	24 Oct	13 Oct	2 Oct	21 Sep	10 Sep	31 Aug
Tabaski	10 Jan; 31 Dec	20 Dec	9 Dec	28 Nov	17 Nov	7 Nov

Ramadan During this lunar month Muslims fast during the day. Many restaurants are closed during the day, but life resumes in the evenings.

Id al Fitr Marks the end of Ramadan.

Tabaski Commemorates the father of all believers, Abraham. According to the Koran, the faithful Abraham was willing to do as Allah had commanded: to immolate his only son, Isaac. As Abraham was about to make the sacrifice, Isaac was replaced by a ram. Tabaski is the feast of sacrifice, and all who can afford it will sacrifice a sheep as a token of their belief. After the morning prayers at the mosque, the Imam sacrifices the first sheep. The streets go quiet as families get together for the ritual sacrifice of a preferably white and male sheep. The rest of the day is spent preparing the meat and feasting on it. The day after Tabaski is the day when the rest of the meat is shared with the poor, when people venture out on the streets and visit family and friends. Unless you are invited to celebrate Tabaski within family circles, the first day will feel like a solemn and quiet day. It is usually on the second day that some festivities take place.

Mouloud The celebration of the Prophet's birthday is marked by praying, reciting Koran texts and sometimes singing. In certain locations, the following day (or days) is the scene of festivities, like in Timia, an oasis in the Aïr Mountains (see *Timia*, page 186).

Muslim New Year Not an official holiday, but sometimes reason for some celebration anyway. The end of the Bianou festival in Agadez is ten days after this day (see box *Bianou*, page 174).

FESTIVALS AND SPECIAL EVENTS Niger boasts a long list of festivals and special events, some of which go back a long way. Certain traditional gatherings, like the Cure Salée and Geerewol, were firstly special occasions for one or more ethnic groups but have been reshaped to a certain extent for the benefit of visitors. Meanwhile, particular rituals or celebrations are meant for a select group, and you will only be able to witness these on special invitation. Sometimes grafted on ancient traditions, other festivals are novelties that have been especially designed to promote various cultural manifestations and to attract a wider public from both Niger and abroad. A third category of special events are the sometimes exuberant Muslim celebrations. These religious events have no fixed dates, as the dates are determined according to the lunar calendar in which a 'month' counts as either 29 or 30 days.

Practical Information PUBLIC HOLIDAYS AND FESTIVALS 2

The list below is by no means complete, but includes a variety of festivals from all of the above categories. If I have missed an important event or if you want to share your experience of a visit to one of the festivals, please send us your story.

Festival de l'Aïr The first Festival de l'Aïr was held in 2001, and one of the reasons to organise this event was to provide opportunities for Tuareg leaders and confederacies to have meetings and discussions about issues concerning the Tuareg community. Another good reason, of course, was to promote the region for tourism. If you happen to be travelling in this region towards the end of December, the Festival de l'Aïr is an event you should not miss. The date is fixed at 27–29 December, and though there have been discussions about switching the location between different communities in the Aïr Mountains, it now seems that the festival will continue to be held in Iférouane. For transport to Iférouane, see *Agadez*, page 166. For more information on the programme, contact the organisation in Agadez (✆ *98 62 20*) or Niamey (✆ *98 58 71;* ✆/f *72 38 82*). See also box *Festival de l'Aïr*, page 188.

Bianou One week after Tabaski is the start of the Bianou festival, unique to the town of Agadez. For more information, see box *Bianou*, page 174.

Hawan Kafou or corrida At the end of Ramadan, Zinder stages a special event that is not held elsewhere in Niger. It is a kind of bullfight, and takes places at the sultanate. For more information, see *Zinder*, page 222.

Cure Salée Once a year, towards the end of the rainy season, thousands of the nomadic Tuareg and Peul Bororo and their cattle regroup in the region of Ingal and Teguidda N'Tessoumt. As this region is rich in salts and minerals, the nomads bring their cattle for the Cure Salée, which literally means 'salt cure'. As the animals consume the salty grasses and water, they replenish vital minerals, while the purgative action cleanses their bowels of parasites. The large-scale gathering is primarily about this salt cure, but it serves many more purposes as it is one of the few occasions where so many nomads are reunited in one place. The many factions take the opportunity to have meetings to discuss political and social issues according to their tradition, but also with representatives from the central government. Meanwhile, medical services are present for vaccination campaigns, consultations and counselling. The Cure Salée is also an occasion for different festivities, such as camel races, music and dance, while all the nomads are dressed up in their best costumes. It is the ensemble of these traditional festivities that attracts large numbers of visitors. As the Nigérien government is becoming more and more involved in the event, the date that marks the beginning of the Cure Salée is now determined by officials in Niamey. However, the exact date is sometimes not revealed until shortly before the event, and it can even be postponed at the last minute. Expect the Cure Salée to take place in the second half of September. Local tour operators should be able to inform you, and to provide the means to get to the location.

Geerewol Every year after the rains, thousands of the nomadic Peul Bororo gather for a Geerewol (also spelt Guerewol or Guérouel). This one-week celebration reunites two unrelated lineages and involves different exuberant dances and ceremonies. The most striking dances are a manifest of male beauty, which is largely determined by facial features such as big, bright eyes, white teeth, and a long, narrow nose. To emphasise these features, the men lighten the skin of their face with ochre, yellow and white, they blacken their lips to stress the whiteness of their teeth, while a black line around the eyes accentuates the white of their eyes. In addition to that, they adorn their faces with a series of red and white dots and lines. These preparations take hours, after which the unmarried men of one lineage line up for a slow dance with rhythmic chanting, clicking, hissing and stamping. Rolling their eyes and exposing their white teeth, they try to win the approval of young women of the other lineage, who then point out the most handsome and well-dressed men. The courtship may result in sexual relationships for the duration of a night or the whole festival, but this does not have to lead to marriages.

Different Geerewols are planned during or just after the Cure Salée, which also takes place at the end of the rainy season, usually in the second half of September. The gatherings are mostly concentrated in the triangle between Ingal, Agadez and Teguidda N'Tessoumt. The Bororo welcome visitors to their festivities, but as there are no fixed dates and no fixed locations, you will have to trace them first. Most local tour operators will be able to inform you, and they can also provide vehicles to take you to the site of a Geerewol.

Animist gathering in Massalata This is a very serious event for the Azna or animist community. Once a year, thousands of animists gather to perform a long ceremony in which they consult the *génies* about the coming year. This ceremony follows a strict protocol, so if you consider attending, you must be willing to adapt and blend in. For more detailed information, see box *Arwa: a ceremony of the Azna*, pages 150–1.

Traditional wrestling *La lutte traditionelle* or traditional wrestling is probably the most popular sport in Niger. Most towns have a special arena – used exclusively for this sport – in which two men try to knock each other over, cheered on by enthusiastic crowds. The actual wrestling can be over within minutes, but the mental battle that precedes that short time is just as important and thrilling to watch. The opponents are dressed in a traditional outfit, little more than a kind of skirt or loin cloth with long tassels and decorations. On their naked upper bodies, the men wear bundles of *gris-gris* or charms, meant to protect the individual from weakness, or rather to invoke weakness in the opponent. Before the physical fight begins, it is the mental game of intimidation that is worth seeing, as the two men circle around one another like predators, touching the ground with a flat hand to seek the support of *génies*.

At some point in January or February, a national wrestling competition takes place, every year in a different town. This tournament is the best occasion to enjoy both the competitors and the crowds, but preceding the national event are the locally held qualifying rounds. There is only one way to find out about dates: just ask around in any of the towns with an arena.

Pilotobe Once a year, a long caravan of international actors, storytellers and other artists travels around Niger to perform at various locations: in cultural centres, in schools, on market squares and street corners. A huge undertaking, leading to spectacular and surprising shows. The caravan halts for four or five days in Zinder, Agadez and Niamey, but some of the theatre companies will also make stops in other towns (Maradi, Diffa, Tahoua, Dosso and Tillabéri). The preforming artists are from Niger, neighbouring countries, Belgium and France. It does not matter if you do not understand all that is spoken, as many shows are visually attractive. In 2005, Pilotobe took place over two weeks in March, but enquire at cultural centres to find out about future programming.

2

Le Prix Dan Gourmou The late Dan Gourmou was a composer and musician from Tahoua who introduced novelties in Nigérien traditional music and encouraged others to follow in his steps. In 1987, when he was still alive, the Ministry of Culture organised a musical contest and named it after him. Since then, the Prix Dan Gourmou has become one of the major music festivals in Niger, held every two years in Tahoua, Dan Gourmou's place of birth. It features both traditional musicians and young musicians that represent a new style, the *musique tradimoderne*. This is modern music based on the traditional, and combines modern instruments with the *doumdoum* and the *molo* (see *The arts*, page 34). In 2003, the festival was won by Dangana, a group of youngsters from Zinder who since then have done very well both in Niger and in France.

The festival lasts several days and takes place very two years in September–October. For more details, enquire at the Centre Culturel Franco-Nigérien in Niamey or Zinder (and in Agadez once the new CCFN has opened its doors).

Festival de l'Eau This 'Water Festival' is an international sporting and cultural encounter in Tillabéri, and a bit of a novelty: the festival has been held twice, most recently in March 2005. For more information, contact the organisation in Niamey at the Palais des Sports (*the NGO Taghlamt;* ✆ *72 55 57/29 13 27*) or in Tillabéri (✆ *71 14 73;* e *organisation.taghlamt@caramail.com*), or enquire at the Centre Culturel Franco-Nigérien in Niamey.

Festival International de la Mode Africaine (FIMA) The founder of this international fashion festival, the famous African designer Alphadi, called the initiative 'positive madness'. In 1999, the extravaganza took place near the Falaise de Tiguidit, an awesome location in the middle of nowhere, 60km to the south of Agadez. The three-day festival was attended by an invited 1,500 guests – some of whom were top international fashion designers, like Yves Saint-Laurent and Jean-Paul Gaultier of France – and was an event full of controversial paradoxes. The fashion show itself was highly praised, but could it be justified that a country as poor as Niger spent huge sums of money on a festival that was targeting an elite and not the people of Niger? At the same time, Islamic associations heavily criticised the event as a 'ceremony of perversion' with half-naked models parading on the catwalk. Nevertheless, the FIMA has been staged four times since, the latest having been held in Niamey in December 2005. To find out about future events, enquire at the Centre Culturel Franco-Nigérien in Niamey or go to www.fima2005.net.

Salon international de l'Artisanat pour la Femme SAFEM SAFEM is both a commercial and a cultural celebration that aims to promote the work of female artisans. Every event focuses on a different region of Niger, but all the regions are represented by many craftswomen and men. The international event is organised and sponsored by DANI, a programme that has proven very successful in the promotion of arts and crafts in Niger (see *Handicrafts and what to buy*, page 80). Apart from the presentation of the various products, SAFEM invites many musicians, dancers and actors for animated performances. The two-yearly celebration is held in November–December at the Village Artisanal de Wadata in Niamey. For more information, contact the organisation at safem@intnet.ne, or go to www.niger-eu/safem2005.

FIFEN The first Festival International du Film d'Environnement de Niamey took place in September 2004. For more information, enquire at the Centre Culturel Franco-Nigérien in Niamey.

RTT Concert Radio Télévision Ténéré or RTT, a local broadcast station based in Niamey, is very popular amongst music-loving youngsters, as much of their output covers Nigérien rap and other modern music. Every year towards the end of January, a national concert celebrates yet another year of the promotion of these musical expressions through RTT. The spectacle lasts throughout the night, featuring the best Nigérien musicians and bands who are cheered on by an audience of thousands of enthusiasts. As the concert switches between towns, enquire at RTT in Niamey for future locations. RTT is located at Rond Point Maourey in Niamey. Alternatively, enquire at the Centre Culturel Franco-Nigérien in Niamey.

HANDICRAFTS AND WHAT TO BUY

HANDICRAFT PRODUCTS Niger is very rich in arts and crafts. All ethnic groups have their specific objects related to their culture, and most products that are offered to visitors are either traditional utensils or decorative objects and jewellery, or items that are derived from these. Some artisans are truly skilful and their work is highly valued.

Silverwork or **jewellery** is the work of Tuareg men. The artisans' or *bijoutiers'* preferred material is pure silver, sometimes in combination with (imported) semi-precious stones, like agathe. Modern materials include nickel and gold, synthetic beads (replacing wooden beads) and coloured glass. There are numerous items, shapes and styles to choose from. Striking are the 21 Tuareg crosses, each of them emblems of a community or region, and worn as necklaces or earrings. Well-known examples are the *croix d'Agadez* and the *croix d'Ingal*. Very eye-catching are the necklaces with agathe, typically worn by women. If you are interested in jewellery, note that there is a big difference in the prices for silver or nickel items. Silver is heavier than nickel, it has a somewhat whiter colour and is less shiny than nickel. The advantage of nickel is that it does not require polishing, but some people are allergic to the metal. Some ready-made 'silver' objects are in fact made of an alloy (forget about hallmarks to verify the quality of the material) and will etch and turn black easily. Most jewellers are fair and will tell you what quality they are selling.

All over Niger you will find high-quality **leatherwork**. The Tuareg use leather for bags, wallets, cushions, small pouches, sandals, sheaths for daggers and swords, but also to adorn and personalise camel saddles. Elaborate decorations are done by women, in a distinct and refined style. All these items are still very much in use. In some shops you may find used objects that are full of character. The Tuareg find it somewhat hilarious that tourists sometimes prefer used and worn items, but they will happily sell it anyway. In the regions of Maradi and Zinder, many tanneries provide plenty of raw material for the production of *maroquinerie* or leatherwork of a different style. Numerous Hausa artisans patiently cut up dyed hides, then glue and sew them together again to make colourful patchworks and patterns. Objects include shoes and sandals, all types of handbags, duffle bags, wallets, hassocks and cushions. Some of the leather is of very good quality; strong and supple, yet inexpensive. The best quality hides are from a goat breed called *le rouge de Maradi* or 'the red Maradi goat'. If you get the opportunity to visit a tannery, you will appreciate the whole process from wet skin to finished product even more.

Basketwork and **woven mats** are produced by women throughout Niger. Mats are used to sit or sleep on, but nomads often use mats to build (and rebuild) their huts. The material that is often used are the leaves of the Doum palm tree. Very decorative mats are made from narrow, dyed strips. These are

2

woven into 15–20cm-wide lengths, then sewn together. Baskets are sometimes manufactured in combination with leather, and various types are used for storage of dry foods.

Earthenware fragments found in remote desert areas are silent witnesses to the fact that **pottery** has been practised for thousands of years. In different regions pottery is still being produced – mostly by women – as long as the raw material is present. Along the river Niger, pottery is concentrated around Boubon, where Djerma and Bouzou women produce huge *canaris* or water jars and other items (see *Boubon*, page 115), while another pottery centre is in Miria, just east of Zinder (see *Miria*, page 223). In the Aïr Massif, pottery is less common than it used to be. Many potters have now adapted to the needs of tourists, and some now produce decorated dishes, teapots and cups and other European-style objects.

Different types of **beads** are used for necklaces. Some tiny beads are made of argile, while chunky and colourful beads can be from natural stones or coloured glass in various shapes and shades. Not all beads are produced locally. While in some places ready-made necklaces are for sale, you could also look out for market stalls (eg: in villages along the river Niger) with piles of assorted beads to choose from.

All ethnic groups wear traditional robes for special occasions, and some of these garments are beautifully made from carefully manufactured **fabric**. The Tuareg prefer to use a specific kind of indigo, cotton fabric. Narrow strips of around 1cm-wide fine cotton tissue are sewn together to a chosen width. The delicate fabric is then dyed with indigo, the deep-blue pigment that produces a particular, almost metallic shine. When worn, indigo garments heavily stain the skin, and this earned the Tuareg the epithet of 'blue men'. Some cheaper fabrics are clearly intended to mimic this fabric, but the 'real thing' is easy to distinguish, if only because it is very expensive. Many ethnies use embroidered robes and blouses, all in very distinct styles and colours. Nowadays, the decorations are often machine-embroidered, but the better qualities are still handmade. Look for elaborate Hausa *boubous* for men, Tuareg and Peul blouses, tunics and long wraparound skirts.

There are plenty of **other items**, such as small soapstone statues and boxes; knives, daggers and swords; wooden boxes and trunks covered in decorated leather. Leave some space in your luggage to carry it all home!

ARTISAN COOPERATIVES In 1995, the Coopération Nigero-Luxembourgeoise started a programme for the **Développement de l'Artisanat au Niger**, or **DANI** for short. Since then, the programme has founded 13 cooperatives in many urban areas to promote and support the work of the craftsmen. Most of these cooperatives now have their own workshops, where members can use tools, machines and space in return for nominal contributions. In this way, they can improve their skills and apprentices can be introduced to the different techniques. At the same time the centre doubles as a selling point for the products. It is one of the few places where prices are more or less fixed, and they are reasonable prices as items are sold straight from the workshop. In 2003, in order to improve working conditions of the artisans and to perfect their trade initiatives within the philosophy of fair trade, the Groupement d'Intérêt Economique or GIE was created by the cooperatives. DANI and the GIE have just under 3,000 members (almost one-third of them women), and the whole programme has stimulated the sector tremendously. The workshops are open to visitors, where they can see the craftsmen at work and buy from the shops. No entrance fee is payable. For more details on the various villages artisanals supported by DANI; see the relevant sections in different chapters.

DANI BP 13254, Niamey; ☏ 72 51 53; f 72 51 73; e luxdev@intnet.ne

GIE BP 11277, 5181, Bd Mali Béro, Niamey; ☏ 74 02 83; f 74 07 83; e gie-dani@intnet.ne; www.artisanat-equitable.niger.com

While DANI represents an impressive number of craftsmen in Niger, there are thousands more. Many are organised in one way or another, and there is a growing tendency to join forces for social, practical and economic reasons. Some of these smaller initiatives are also mentioned in the relevant sections.

TO BUY OR NOT TO BUY By buying handicrafts, you support artisans and vendors who offer their products. Sometimes vendors can be persistent to a degree that is off-putting, but bear with them: they are only trying to make a living. In little-visited areas, your purchase is even more appreciated, as the people are fully dependent on the few visitors they receive. In some villages in the Aïr Massif, I witnessed women who sat by the side of the *piste*, waiting for days to sell their beautifully made baskets and leather bags. Buying directly from these and other artisans helps and encourages them.

There are objects you should refuse to buy, and these are not the usual craftworks; I am referring to the work that has descended from ancient times: archaeological artefacts (mortars, arrow points, etc). Often, these items are removed from archaeological sites, then end up as oddities in craft displays, as local people have realised that foreigners show an interest in these items. It is illegal to buy any such item, and by doing so you would encourage people to continue to loot precious sites that need to be left undisturbed. The same warning applies to any item that is made of or with parts of endangered animal species. Horns or skulls, any kind of hide from gazelles, and ostrich eggs – do not be tempted to buy them.

 ## COMMUNICATIONS AND MEDIA

POST The mail service is reasonably efficient and provided you mail your letters in Niamey, they will get to European destinations in around a week's time. Add time if you mail your letters in one of the major towns. Letters to other overseas destinations take longer; count on two weeks. Stamps for letters to France cost CFA225, to other European destinations CFA395–515 (5–10g), while postage to the USA costs CFA415–545 (5–10g). A poste restante service is available from major post offices. Collecting letters costs CFA300 per item, while collecting parcels will cost CFA1,000. Opening times vary slightly between towns and branches, but are roughly Monday–Friday 07.45–12.15 and 15.00–17.45, Saturday 08.00–12.00, Sunday closed.

TELEPHONE AND FAX Niger now has two telephone systems: land lines and the mobile network. The land lines (*lignes fixes*) are provided by Sonitel and have reached only urban areas. Land lines are cheaper to use for calls than cellphones, especially for international phone calls. Check the rate per time unit first, and remember that a *cabine téléphonique* charges far less than any hotel. Timing is usually done through a stopwatch. In some places (like Agadez) land lines hardly work at all, and you may have to wait a long time to get connected. You could ask someone whether you can make your phone call using their cellphone (*le portable*). Have the other person check the balance first (which can be done free of charge), make your phone call and pay the difference and some more for the service. As the balance always seems to be running low, you may have to buy a card first. Where there are land lines, you will also find a fax machine.

The introduction of the mobile network has brought about big changes, as already networks reach beyond the scope of land lines, and more antennas are being installed all the time. For this reason, information about networks will outdate quickly, but at the time of research, most urban areas had networks already. The two biggest companies are Celtel (*www.msi-cellular.com*) and Telecel. It seemed as if Celtel was doing better than the competition as they had installed more antennas throughout the country than Telecel. However, Telecel is striking back with the introduction of a SIM card that should work in six countries: Niger, Benin, Burkina Faso, Ivory Coast, Gabon and Togo. It is therefore well worth considering buying a local SIM card. Local calls are still relatively costly, but sending messages within Niger costs next to nothing. To send international SMS messages would still work out cheaper than when you would use either your European or US SIM card. Cards are available from CFA1,000–10,000 and can be purchased from Celtel or Telecel selling points (often a kiosk in the street), and these are well signposted.

If you are heading out to remote areas and you want to be able to stay in touch, the only option is a satellite telephone. Some of the better travel agencies include the use of a satellite phone in their package as a matter of course.

EMAIL AND INTERNET Internet access still very much depends on land lines, which is not always good news. It may affect both the speed and the rate for getting online, so check first before you log in. Internet cafés (*cybercafé*) are popping up in most towns, but the speed of connection to the web can be either excellent or frustratingly slow, in which case downloading attachments can be problematic. Some of the better options are listed in the relevant chapters, but bear in mind that this information is likely to outdate quickly.

MEDIA Though Niger has many – mostly weekly – newspapers, there are some major obstacles resulting in newspapers being accessible to only a limited part of the population. One problem is how to get the news to potential readers before it outdates. Most newspapers are printed in and distributed from Niamey. In the capital and bigger towns along the main tarred axes, newspapers are available from certain bookshops, kiosks and street vendors. However, further away from the printers, newspapers are hard to come by, while off the main roads you would be looking in vain to find a recent, unread copy. The other problem is illiteracy. Statistics show that 80% of the population cannot read or write at all, and many more will have difficulties reading a news story. Add to that the cost of a newspaper (typically CFA300) in relation to the level of poverty, and that rules out a big proportion of the population as potential readers.

Nevertheless, many Nigériens show a deep interest in national and regional politics, and general news. The answer to their hunger for news comes from numerous radio stations scattered all over the country, covering main stories and local news items. Therefore, if you as a traveller have an interest in keeping yourself posted on the latest news and if your French is good enough, consider bringing a pocket radio, or buy one locally. You could then join the army of listeners who walk around with a small transistor glued to one ear.

Newspapers The *Sahel Dimanche* and *Sahel Quotidien* are both state operated. Other newspapers from the private press reflecting governmental opinions are *La Hache*, *Le Canard Déchaîné* and *Libération*. Some newspapers reflecting views of the opposition are *Le Républicain*, *La Roue de l'Histoire*, *L'Evénement*, *La Griffe*, *Alternative* and *Le Témoin*. *Aïr-Info* is a regional opposition newspaper, printed and distributed from Agadez.

Radio Broadcast from Niamey and the only radio station that can be received in many corners of the country, La Voix du Sahel (5020.72 SW) is the national radio representing the governmental point of view. Also based in Niamey are ten private radio stations, some of which are clearly siding with the opposition. All of them broadcast on the FM band. The biggest ones are Saraounia (102.1 FM), Anfani (100 FM), Ténéré (98 FM) and REM (104.5 FM). The frequencies for local radio stations are signposted at the entrance of the town where they are based.

For international news in English, try the BBC World Service or the Voice of America. In Niamey, the BBC can be received on 100.4 FM, while you could also tune in on their short wave lengths for their service to west Africa. Frequencies used are 6,005, 7,120, 7,160, 9,860, 11,765, 15,400, 17,830 and 51,105 kHz, but these are liable to change from year to year. Check the current frequencies and scheduled programmes on www.bbc.co.uk/worldservice.

For frequencies of the Voice of America, check www.voa.gov.

Television When there is electricity, there is television. The national (governmental) channel is Tele Sahel, but often there is a wider choice of channels. Most of these are in French (like TV5) but sometimes CNN and even the BBC can also be received.

CULTURAL SENSITIVITY

Having the following characteristics, responsible tourism:

- minimises negative economic, environmental and social impacts
- generates greater economic benefits for local people and enhances the well-being of host communities, improving working conditions and access to industry
- involves local people in decisions that affect their lives and life chances
- makes positive contributions to the conservation of natural and cultural heritage, to the maintenance of the world's diversity
- provides more enjoyable experiences for tourists through more meaningful connections with local people, and a greater understanding of local cultural, social and environmental issues
- provides access for physically challenged people
- is culturally sensitive, engenders respect between tourists and hosts, and builds local pride and confidence

(Source: the Cape Town Declaration; International Centre for Responsible Tourism 2002; for more information: www.icrtourism.org/capetown.html)

DRESS CODE In a country that is predominantly Muslim, the way people dress is partly influenced by religion. Partly, because all ethnic groups had their traditional costumes before Islam was introduced, and guidelines to dress in a certain way according to the new religion have been interpreted in different ways. Consequently, the personal appearance of the people of Niger is like a colourful, visually very attractive parade. While you observe all the different modes of how to wear a wraparound or turban, remember that you will be looked at too, for your appearance may be just as striking to the local people. In urban areas, the sight of a foreigner attracts less attention, and the tolerance for foreign habits is usually considerable. This changes when you venture to rural areas or to places that are strictly Muslim. The general rule to sufficiently adapt, is to cover what they cover. Females should be more comprehensive about this than men, as women are often more restricted in their ways of dressing. This definitely rules out shorts for females, but often also for men.

When I was invited to the annual animist gathering in Massalata (see box *Arwa: ceremony of the Azna*, page 150) I was more aware than ever of the implications of that fine soundbite 'cultural sensitivity'. That day, I was living it, as I trod on very fragile cultural ground in many ways. The setting: a rural village that sees very few tourists. The occasion: a traditional ceremony of the Azna, where foreigners are a rare sight and where women are kept out of range. Yet permission for my presence was granted by the *chef* of Dagarka, who presided over the ceremony. I was very relieved to be in the company of two local radio journalists, who doubled as guides and translators for me. I tried my best to keep a low profile; I was geared to blend in as much as I could, as I was clearly the outsider at this highly important annual event. After some initial procedures, seven fetishists began their ritual 'turning of the soil' to allow the *génies* or spirits to speak. One by one, the fetishists determined whether the conditions to really start the ceremony were right. After the third fetishist had spoken, all eyes turned on me. One of the journalists translated: 'You are wearing sunglasses and your head is covered. The *génies* will only speak in front of people whose heads and eyes are naked.' No-one else was wearing glasses or a headdress, and I had missed it.

In a country like Niger, so poor in the material sense of the word, but so rich in cultural diversity, it is all too easy to go wrong without ever knowing it. People are polite and respectful, they are forgiving. Yet, as we are the visitors in their 'house', we should at least try our best not to embarrass our hosts.

The following suggestions are more female-specific: a long skirt – preferably covering the knees and part of the calves – is more acceptable than trousers, but wide, non-revealing long trousers are generally fine too. In many places, a short, tight T-shirt is not appropriate, and sometimes armpits and shoulders are best covered, while a low neckline is also something to be conscious of. But then again, in some areas women go bare-breasted even in the presence of men, which shows that really there are no clear rules that apply everywhere. When visiting a mosque, on certain Muslim holidays, or on formal occasions (eg: when you greet a traditional *chef*), it will be appreciated if you loosely cover your hair with a scarf. Do not use a turban 'the male way'. It may feel like the best way to cover your head, but traditional Nigériens would not understand your wish to dress like a man. When you are out in the desert, with guides and camel drivers who have travelled with tourists before, it is a different issue.

BEGGARS In urban zones, beggars are a common sight. More often than not they have a good reason to ask for handouts, either because they are extremely poor with no income whatsoever, or they are handicapped in one way or another. Blind people, guided by a young child, often walk the streets to ask for alms. Giving alms is totally acceptable in a Muslim country. In fact, it is one of the pillars of Islam (see *Religion*, page 33), and local people will often keep some coins to hand if they can afford it. However, in some urban zones beggars have learnt to single out (white) tourists, and while it is not difficult to see why, it can become quite overwhelming. Some beggars are very persistent and put up a real show to make you feel bad about your wealth and the fact that you never have to skip a meal. It even happens that a perfectly healthy person who had a humble job gave up work simply because begging is financially more rewarding than working. There is no easy answer to questions triggered by these situations, but consider this: giving alms is an act of free will, not an obligation, and no matter how willing you are to give to beggars, you couldn't possibly please all the poor. Draw a line where you think it is fair, and then stick to it for your peace of mind. Also bear in mind that CFA100 is enough to buy a plate of rice and sauce or some meat skewers. If you want to help in a more substantial manner, there are other options (see *Giving something back*, page 87 and also see the box, pages 86–7).

CULTURAL ETIQUETTE Niger is a colourful melting pot of ethnies and cultures, and all of them have their own behavioural patterns. It is impossible to fully describe what you should or shouldn't do to avoid offensive behaviour, as there are just too many subtleties and differences between ethnic groups, but also in the communication between men and women. When you are on an organised tour and in a well visited region, local people will have become used to other ways of doing things and they are more accommodating. However, the further you stray from the beaten track and the more you are in direct contact with local people, the more you should try and adapt. The golden rule is to keep your eyes open and make observations, then copy what you see. Some suggestions may serve as a guideline.

- Preferably use your right hand to greet people and hand over objects, as the right hand is considered the clean hand, while the left hand is used for hygiene purposes. When you are sharing a meal from a communal bowl, never use your left hand to eat or touch food! Too bad for left-handers, but this is an important rule.
- Familiarise yourself with the art of greeting in different regions. It is rude not to greet a person before starting a conversation. Greetings are lengthy and often formal, in the sense that queries about health and the family need to be answered positively at first. Eventual bad news can only be revealed after the initial dialogue. For an example of such a greeting ritual, see box *The old woman of Fariz*, pages 192–3. Gestures and handshakes are at least as important as the words chosen. Do not squeeze a hand tight and do not shake, as we are used to. Just very loosely squeeze the other hand, and this contact may continue throughout the formal greetings. To lightly touch your right underarm with your left hand shows respect. Consider making this gesture when you greet an elder or a traditional *chef*. In the Aïr Massif, handshaking takes on a different dimension, with repeated gentle touches and gestures. Some traditional Muslim men do not shake hands with women.
- Try to learn a few words in the local languages Hausa, Djerma or Tamashek, depending on where you are travelling. If you master as little as a few greetings, this demonstrates your willingness to adapt.
- Avoid prolonged eye contact, especially between different genders. It is considered impolite and provocative. Only people of equal social standing can keep prolonged eye contact.
- Should you be introduced to a traditional *chef*, a sultan, a marabout or any other dignitary, a special protocol applies. Usually you will have to take off your shoes, but you may have to kneel, while a handshake is not always appropriate. A gift of some kola nuts is often appreciated. Ask advice from a local guide.
- Do not show affection in public, even when you are a married couple. You may see two males holding hands as a token of friendship, but male/female couples should not do this. Nor should they hug or kiss, stroke an arm, etc, so be patient and make up for it in private.
- Homosexuality is not allowed, and should not be openly discussed. It is considered offensive and unlawful, and homosexual behaviour can cause a

Walking between villages along the river Niger with French travellers I had met, we were sometimes followed by dozens and dozens of villagers, mostly children. We sang with them, held hands, played games, talked with those who could speak some French and learnt how to greet in Djerma. In some places, that is where the encounter would end: sharing some delightful time and stories. These were villages that had not seen many visitors. Other villages were more frequently visited, and the attention we received was still overwhelming, but different. Many children and adults alike asked for presents, often without greeting first when greetings are such an important social act in Niger. Some were even more impolite, fumbling our pockets and bags, trying to figure out what we were carrying.

'Why are you all expecting gifts from us?' I asked. 'Can't you see that you are so many and we are only five? How could we possibly put a small present in each and every hand?'

One child persisted: 'But you can give to some of us, maybe ten or so, and then the next time somebody else may be lucky too. So why don't you just start with me, and give me a pen or some money or your watch perhaps?'

The difference between villages was striking, though not so surprising for those who have travelled before. These villagers had learnt to ask for handouts by the actions of previous visitors who thought they were doing good, regardless of the long-term effect it triggered or possibly out of ignorance of the consequences. Is it fair to judge the children who have learnt to bluntly ask for presents, and is it fair to judge those who feel it is rewarding to put a smile on an child's face? Probably not, but I do feel there are different, much better ways to help people who have so little in terms of material goods, or even the basic necessities of life. Leaving a gift at a local school or with a village elder is one example. It means that your gift will be more evenly distributed, even to the shy ones who did not dare to ask you directly. Consider the following suggestions as possible gifts to a school or community.

real stir. Two males or two women are usually not allowed to share a room with one double bed only, and if that is the rule of the house, do not try to argue.

- When you are visiting someone, clap your hands when you approach the door or the yard. As most of the time there are no doorbells, this is the Nigérien equivalent of announcing your arrival. Calling out *Salem aleikum!* (peace to you) is a respectful greeting that will be replied with *Aleikum asalaam* (come in peace). It is often custom to take off your shoes before entering a house. When you are offered a drink, it is impolite to refuse.

- It is unusual to eat in front of another person without offering to share. Men and women do not eat from the same bowl or even in the same room as a matter of course. In more visited areas, foreigners are often exempt from this rule. When you share a meal, observe the rules for the right and left hand. Tuareg use a spoon to eat, and traditionally they carry their own wooden spoon.

- Burping, clearing one's throat and spitting in the company of others is generally acceptable. However, farting in public is considered an impolite and disrespectful act. Nigériens do not use handkerchiefs to blow their noses, but the nose is cleared 'straight into the sand'. Do not attempt this in public unless you master the art! If you consider this dirty behaviour, consider this also: some Nigériens wonder why we first pay money for a handkerchief, then blow our nose in it to safekeep the harvest in our pocket.

A gift of children's clothes does not have to be expensive. You could bring some from your home country, or buy them locally. On bigger markets you will usually find both new and used clothing, or sandals and slippers at very reasonable prices. Certain toys will be very much appreciated. A sturdy ball that is not likely to pop at the first contact with thorns is better than an inflatable one or than balloons. Colouring books and colour pencils are a nice luxury item, but felt pens are of little use in the dry climate; they wouldn't last very long. If you want to bring sweets, buy a bagful and hand it to an adult for distribution. They will be *anasara's* sweets all the same (*anasara* is the Hausa word for European or white foreigner), but children are less likely to pick up the habit to beg for goodies directly from foreigners.

Schools in rural areas are almost without exception badly equipped. They are often little more than an empty shell with way too few desks to seat all the pupils, and a pitiful collection of tattered schoolbooks that have to be shared by all. Many new classrooms have been constructed as part of the Programme Spécial du Président de la Republique (see *Poverty reduction*, page 23), but the school materials did not come with the building. So if you plan to travel to little-visited rural areas, you could make a difference there. Leaving a gift of money is risky; someone could be tempted to use it for private purposes. Instead, bring items that are not available in the area. Posters from home (and something to fix them onto the walls) to brighten up the dull classrooms will go a long way, as well as picture books. Exercise books and pens are useful items, but these can often be obtained locally. The most essential gift would be that of schoolbooks. In Niamey and most of the regional towns these are widely available from bookshops or even from bookstalls. All schoolbooks that are published by Institut National de Documentation de Recherche et d'Animation Pédagogiques (INDRAP) in Niamey are used throughout Niger. They are inexpensive by our standards, and a dozen copies will cost less than most travellers' daily budget for food and accommodation.

- A gift is never refused, nor will a gift be elaborately praised as is customary in the West, but it will just be quietly laid aside with a well-meant 'thank you'. A wrapped gift is not opened in front of the giver.
- Bargaining is common, and in fact unless you are in a shop where prices are clearly marked, anything is open to bargaining. It is a serious game, but it should not be exaggerated and it is best done with a smile. Do not pay more than what you want to spend, but be fair.
- When you want to take pictures of people or their private homesteads, always ask permission first. Many people will refuse for different reasons, and they have the right to do so. It is unusual for people to ask for money to be photographed, but if that happens, agree on a price first and do not offend people by taking pictures anyway. When you promise to send a picture, make sure to keep that promise. All too often this is forgotten once the journey is over, while someone somewhere in Niger may not get another opportunity to have a picture of themselves or their family.

GIVING SOMETHING BACK

There are various ways to make a contribution to the people of Niger. While you are travelling around, you can buy crafts directly from the artisans, which helps them to support their families. Various cooperatives throughout the country produce high-quality and affordable products (see *Handicrafts and what to buy*, page 79). You can supply schoolbooks and other materials to rural schools that often have to make do with the little equipment they have (see box *Giving presents*, pages 86–7). You can also buy medical supplies for rural health centres. Most medicines are available without prescription from pharmacies in regional towns, and pharmacists can advise you on what is mostly needed. If you have a heart for streetkids, there are a few projects running in Niamey. One of these is located on the premises of the National Museum, with workshops to teach the children a few skills. Enquire at the entrance gate to the museum near the Centre Culturel Franco-Nigérien to see someone from the workshops. You can also contact Gilles Akakpo, a devoted individual whose live revolves around streetkids, and who badly wants to set up some structural help for them. For more information, see the following section.

After you have returned home, you can contact NGOs and organisations who are active in Niger. Some of them are listed below, and we would like to hear about more charities that work for Niger. If you are an American citizen, you could enrol as a Peace Corps volunteer and spend some time working for and with local communities.

Projects in Niger

SOS Faune du Niger BP 13578, Niamey; ↘ 92 77 16/98 13; f 73 36 02: e infos@sosfauneduniger.org. This non-profit association was created in 2003 as a cry-out for the Nigérien natural and cultural heritage in general, and endangered animal species in particular. A long list of objectives includes the battle against poaching; informing the population about the necessity to preserve wildlife; developing sustainable strategies to exploit nature reserves and protected areas; promoting captive-breeding programmes of endangered species and enable scientific research on wildlife and different habitats. The association initiated a thorough wildlife survey in the Termit and Tin N'Tessoumt regions in 2004 (see box *SOS Faune du Niger: addax survey*, page 226). For as little as CFA10,000 you can become a member of the association, while more substantive donations are highly appreciated.

SYRENE Niamey; ↘ 73 21 16; f 73 20 92; e profor@intnet.ne; www.niger-eu.net. SYRENE is a project run by the Nigérien Ministry of Tourism and Artisanat and is financed by the European Union. In the battle against poverty, SYRENE helps to set up small private enterprises and programmes that go side-by-side with the agro-pastoral sector. Projects focus on developing new technology to produce household energy. The use of recyclable by-products and waste from all sectors is one of the strong points of this programme. Some examples are the recycling of car batteries, and the recycling of plastic waste (polythene bags etc) for the manufacture of synthetic bricks and tiles suitable for paving.

Club International 'Enfants du Niger' BP 12113, Niamey; ↘ 99 46 52; e desmomesauxenfants@yahoo.fr. This private project is entirely run by Gilles Akakpo, an individual who dedicates his life to streetkids. Through the 'Enfants du Niger', Gilles mobilises children from better-off families to help and assist streetkids in a very direct approach. The club collects clothes throughout the year, and these are distributed on 16 June, the International Day of the Child. Just before Christmas, the club organises a street festival for the kids. The festival is a mix of theatre, music and play, and free food for all. Apart from these two annual gatherings, the 'better-off' children help to monitor the well-being of groups of streetkids. They provide medical care when one is ill, as well as some extra care when needed. Apart from the work with the club, Gilles personally looks after a few children at a time, providing daily meals and shelter, and eventually an apprenticeship if he feels a child is ready for that big step. Gilles is a teacher by profession, and he works in the evenings to earn a basic salary. The day is spent for and with the streetkids. Gilles is very eager to set up more structural support for larger groups of children, but he is lacking the finances. Visitors with a heart for this touching project are welcome to contact Gilles. Do not hesitate to donate cash, as all donations will go towards the children.

NGOs and other organisations with representations in Niger

Africare BP 10534, Niamey; ↘/f 75 44 00; e afrniger@intnet.ne; www.africare.org. Africare is a non-profit organisation that addresses needs in the principal areas of food security and agriculture; health and HIV/AIDS; water resource and environmental management; basic education; micro-enterprise development; governance initiatives; and emergency humanitarian aid. Africare was founded by 17 volunteers who provided medical aid to a Nigérien hospital during the food crisis of 1970. Since then Africare has developed numerous rural development programmes throughout Africa, over 50 of which are in Niger.

CARE International
www.careinternational.org.uk/cares_work/where/niger/. CARE International opened operations in Niger in 1973, following the drought and subsequent famine in the Sahel region. In the 1980s, CARE International added reproductive health, small economic activity development and primary health care to its project roster. More recently, CARE International is helping government health workers in northern Niger to strengthen local government capacity to provide basic mother–child health services to a very beleaguered and isolated population.

Eirene BP 1322, D-56503 Neuwied, Germany; tel: +49 02631 83 790; f +49 02631 31 160; e eirene-int@eirene.org; www.eirene.org/eng. Eirene is a German ecumenical peace and development organisation, working to improve human living conditions in different countries. In Niger, Eirene has employees and volunteers working from different regional towns, and one of their objectives is the promotion of intercultural dialogue. Amongst other projects, Eirene mediates between groups of pastoralists and agriculturalists to find peaceful solutions to the problems that have often led to violent clashes between these groups (see box *Agro–pastoral clashes*, page 33).

Food and Agriculture Organisation of the United Nations BP 11246, PL040, Plateau 1, Niamey; e FAO-NE@fao.org; www.fao.org. FAO leads international efforts to defeat hunger, acting as a neutral forum to negotiate agreements and debate policy. FAO also helps developing countries like Niger to improve agriculture, forestry and fisheries practices and ensure good nutrition for all.

International Refugee Rights Initiative MNDHP BP 13847, Niamey; \/f 73 37 39; e abdou_r_manzo@yahoo.fr; www.refugee-rights.org. MNDHP helps refugees from Congo, Liberia and Chad living in Niger, but also helps to reintegrate those displaced within Niger, typically rural populations fleeing famine who come to live in the capital.

SNV BP 10110, Av Zarmakoye, Niamey; \ 75 36 33; f 75 35 06; e snvniger@snv.ne; www.snv.org/niger. SNV Netherlands is a multi-cultural development agency with support organisations in 28 countries worldwide. SNV mobilises expertise in marginal areas, aiming to structurally alleviate poverty through capacity building and improved governance. SNV has built effective partnerships with government institutions and civil society organisations on both national and local levels. Through these partnerships, SNV has been able to assist in the process of transferring central authority to the local elected councils as a crucial step in decentralisation.

UNICEF BP 12481, 2 Rue des Oasis, Niamey; \ 72 37 24/72 50 87; f 73 34 68; e niamey@unicef.org; www.unicef.org/infobycountry/niger.html. UNICEF exists to protect the rights of children all over the world; to promote girls' education; to immunise children against childhood diseases; to prevent the spread of HIV/AIDS among young people; and to create protective environments for children. UNICEF has 3 bases in Niger: Niamey, Agadez and Maradi.

US Peace Corps www.peacecorps.gov. Peace Corps volunteers work in areas like education, youth outreach and community development, the environment and information technology.

NGOs and other organisations active for Niger

Islamic Relief www.irw.org. Based in the USA, Islamic Relief is a non-profit organisation and a member of the Islamic Relief Worldwide family. Islamic Relief operates emergency relief and long-term development projects including health clinics; water and sanitation projects; orphan support; education; and microcredit.

OXFAM www.oxfam.org/eng; OXFAM International is a confederation of 12 organisations, operating in over 100 countries worldwide to find lasting solutions to poverty, suffering and injustice.

Rain for Sahel and Sahara PO Box 545, Newmarket, NH 03857, USA; e info@rain4sahara.org; www.rain4sahara.org. Rain develops programmes in education and health to promote a sustainable and vital Tuareg society. This registered non-profit organisation works with communities of Tuareg people creating profitable gardens and other enterprises to support boarding schools for their children, and sponsors an AIDS prevention campaign. Rain responded to the drought of 2004 by founding a store to sell animal feed to nomads. In addition to this, Rain formed a women's cooperative to operate the store on a permanent basis. The website provides extensive information on activities (and they are many!) through reports and newsletters. You can help by sending donations and goods, or enrol as a volunteer.

RESEARCH Half of the pleasure and excitement lies in the preparation of a trip. Your choice to travel to Niger may stem from a specialist background, or maybe you just like to read more about a certain topic. In *Appendix 2* (see page 214) will find a list of books for further reading, while a selection of websites will certainly keep you browsing for a while.

For particular queries, consider contacting the **Friends of Niger** (**FON**), a registered non-profit corporation that was founded in 1985. Their purpose is to initiate and support activities related to Niger and its people, and for the benefit of its membership, eg: through a newsletter, a website with plenty of information and links to other interesting sites, as well as forums. For more information and to find out how you can join the Friends of Niger, go to www.friendsofniger.org.

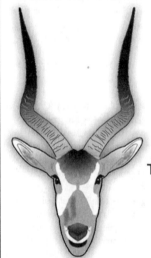

Part Two

THE SOUTHWEST

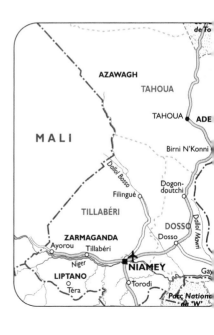

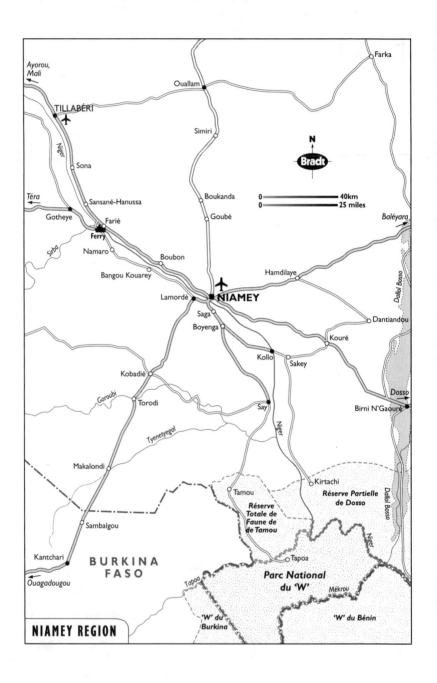

NIAMEY REGION

3

Niamey

Most visitors to Niger arrive at the Hamani Diori International Airport, which is situated around 12km southeast of Niamey. Ample boulevards and avenues leading into the city may come as a surprise to those newcomers who are familiar with the more chaotic capitals of west Africa. Indeed, Niamey is not excessively busy or crowded, built-up areas are generally quite spacious and – apart from a few bottlenecks – traffic can circulate unobstructed. On a clear day, when there are no dust clouds, one could even go for a leisurely stroll along wide lanes and breathe in relatively unspoilt air. During rush hour, Niamey presents itself in a different way. All at once streets become busier, roundabouts and junctions get clogged for a while, causing agitated taxi drivers to hoot repeatedly. Yet, it is all relative.

The picture changes in those places where human activity is most concentrated: markets, *taxi-brousse* stations and stretches of road with an abundance of vendors and stalls. Streets and alleys become a noisy whirlpool, crawling with life and a hotchpotch of vehicles, wheelbarrows and push carts, motorbikes and pedestrians carrying goods on their heads. With the colourful bustle come the odours, all senses are stirred: this is truly Africa after all!

HISTORY

When the Europeans came to the zone now known as Niamey, they found five sectors: Gaweye, Kalley, Maourey, Foulani Koira and Zongo. As they had successively been founded by settlers originating from various directions, it was more like a cluster of villages. Various stories referring back to these founders claim to explain the origin of the name Niamey. One such story tells of an old woman who would take water from a particular place along the river Niger. Later, it is said, this was to be the site of the first permanent dwelling, and the site was named 'Nya-me', which means 'mother's water's edge'.

The name pops up in history for the first time around 1898, in written reports on the French-led Hourst Mission. It is in this era that 'Niamey' was chosen as a military base, thus radically changing the fate of this village. In 1905, Niamey became the provisional capital of the *Territoire Militaire du Niger* or the Military Territory of Niger, which then spread from Timbuktu and Gao all the way to N'Guigmi near Lake Chad. Not all the French were happy with this choice of location, but as they had only just laid claims on the territory, and with whole regions still struggling with insecurity and resistance from the original population, the location of Niamey seemed like a reasonable solution for the time being. Its population was estimated at around 1,800 individuals only, a mixture of mainly Djerma, Songhay and Peul.

By 1911, the territory had been significantly reduced to its current proportions, and the dust had settled enough for a significant move: the capital was shifted to Zinder, capital of the Damagaram (see map, page 214), a crossroads of trade and of recognised social and political importance. However, complications soon arose. The French and British conquerors were still in conflict over territorial and economic issues, and Zinder was too close to Nigeria, by then heavily under British influence. At the same time, Zinder was too far from Cotonou, the nearest seaport under French control. For this reason, it proved both difficult and costly to supply Zinder with provisions. Moreover, there just wasn't enough easily accessible water for the growing population. In 1926, just four years after Niger had become a French colony, the capital was shifted back to Niamey. By then its population had almost doubled to 3,100 inhabitants, but barely enough to call the capital a town.

Much of that population had migrated to Niamey in an attempt to run away from famine, which was the result of consecutive serious droughts (1901–03). A second wave of migrants arrived after the droughts in 1913 and 1914. These migrations were to be only the beginning, as the development of Niamey would repeatedly be determined by the effects of droughts and famine. After Niamey had become the capital of Niger in 1926, and at the same time as it was developing and expanding to provide the necessary facilities for its growing population, a third and massive wave of migrants temporarily fled to Niamey. In 1931–32, locusts had destroyed harvests in a wide region around the capital, forcing tens of thousands to live off food aid supplied by the colonisers. New quarters like Boukoki and Deizebon mushroomed to house these growing numbers of migrants. Most of them left again in better times, but the number of sedentary inhabitants grew steadily to around 8,000 in 1945.

It was in the years that followed that Niamey started rapidly evolving into a metropolitan city. The French attracted scholars from surrounding countries to fill the void in their administration that Nigériens could not yet fill though lack of education. Others came to try their luck and set up businesses. Simultaneously, more famines in the 1960s and 1970s forced ever growing numbers of people to seek permanent refuge in Niamey, causing the city to expand at a startling rate. When Niger became independent in 1960, the population amounted to 30,000. By 1975, this number exceeded 135,000. In 2000, Niamey counted an estimated 700,000 inhabitants.

ORIENTATION

Niamey is spread out along the two banks of the river Niger, connected by the Kennedy Bridge. The southern side (*rive droite*), consists mainly of residential areas and the University Abdoul-Moumouni Dioffo. There are no hotels or renowned restaurants, and on average there is very little to detain tourists on this side. The northern bank (*rive gauche*) is where most activities are concentrated. Crossing the bridge to the northern bank towards the Kennedy Roundabout (Rond Point Kennedy), some striking buildings catch the eye: the Palais de Congrès, Hotel Gaweye and the Grand Hotel.

From the roundabout to the left, the Avenue François Mitterand leads to Yantala and Plateau, Issa Béri and the area widely known as Château 1 (named after the first water tower to be built). These are the quarters with the most governmental buildings like ministries, embassies and consulates and the presidential residence. Not surprisingly, the residential areas in this part of Niamey are among the most prestigious of all, while some of the best primary and grammar schools are found here. These quarters are cleaved by the Boulevard de l'Indépendance, more often called the Route du Tillabéri, leading there when leaving Niamey to the northwest.

When following this thoroughfare towards the east, past the Stade Général Seyni Kountché, the prominent sports stadium, it changes names a few times and then hits the Avenue de l'Islam, another main artery of the city. Outbound, the avenue passes the Big Mosque (Grande Mosquée) to the eastern quarters. Sooner or later, independent travellers will find their way here for onward transport into the interior of the country, as most major bus companies are based here. The biggest *taxi-brousse* station Ecogare de Wadata, as well as the handicraft centre Wadata and the Centre Culturel Oumarou Ganda are all located in the same area.

Turning back along the Avenue de l'Islam, in the direction of the river Niger, the road leads through some of the oldest city quarters and towards what could be described as 'the centre'. It is not so much the heart of the city because it is the most ancient, nor has it many buildings or monuments of great beauty and historical importance, but it is the buzzing, commercial centre of the capital. Both the big market (*grand marché*) and the small market (*petit marché*) are found here, it has a higher concentration of shops, hotels and restaurants than anywhere else in the city, most banks are represented here, and some administrative buildings are located in the area as well. On a spacious location not far from the Kennedy Roundabout, are the National Museum and the Centre Culturel Franco-Nigérien.

Leaving this centre to the southeast, in the direction of Gamkallé, two thoroughfares embrace a military and industrial zone. Boulevards and avenues are often cut into sections with different names, which can cause confusion if you are not familiar with the layout of the city. To add to the confusion, like the Route de Tillabéri above, some roads are known by yet another, more logical name. And so the northern artery of the two said thoroughfares, the Avenue de l'Amitié, passes the fire brigade and some military barracks, before changing its name to Boulevard du 15 Avril. It then passes the race course (*hippodrome*), before heading towards Hamani Diori International Airport. No wonder most people refer to this boulevard by its unofficial name: Route de l'Aeroport.

GETTING THERE AND AWAY

BY AIR For **international arrivals and departures** see *Getting there and away*, page 43. Remember that flight schedules are liable to change, so always check for the latest information.

There are no scheduled **domestic flights**, which means that all travelling (other than the limited river options) has to be done by road, and distances are huge. The only alternative to reduce the travelling time is a very expensive one: chartered plane. Nigeravia SA (✆ 73 30 64/35 90; f 74 18 42; e nigavia@intnet.ne; www.nigeravia.com) has one six-seater and two ten-seater aircraft available at CFA1,500,000 per hour. As the plane often returns to its base empty, the return flight is payable as well; for example, the journey from Niamey to Arlit takes just over two hours, and will thus cost around CFA6,500,000 in total.

The aircraft are mostly used by bankers and mine employees, working in Arlit and other out-of-the-way destinations. Even if they do not fill up a chartered aircraft, it is not possible to pay a share and book one of the available seats, which makes this option barely feasible unless there are many of you. In case of an emergency, the planes are used for evacuations, even to Europe if necessary.

BY RIVER Though the formidable river Niger flows through Niamey, there is no regular passenger transport along it. Pirogues occasionally leave for local upstream and downstream destinations, but these services are erratic and there is no port or harbour serving as a fixed departure point. Chartering a pirogue is always a possibility, but then you should regard this as a way to explore the beauty of the riverine area rather than as an efficient means of travelling. See *Excursions from Niamey*, page 111 for options to navigate the river Niger with Niamey as a starting point.

BY ROAD Until not too long ago, travel options by road were rather limited. Fortunately, passenger transport along the main axes has become a regular and relatively comfortable affair. Four Nigérien companies using big coaches shuttle between Niamey, Agadez and Arlit in the north, and Maradi, Zinder and Diffa in the south and east. Some companies also cross the various borders into Mali, Burkina Faso and Benin. Remember to book your ticket a day in advance and preferably pay and collect your ticket a day in advance as well, especially on busy days, like around Tabaski and other Muslim holidays. Always check the time you have to report before departure (*rendez-vous* or *temps de convocation*), which is usually half an hour before the actual departure time. The four bus companies are **Aïr Transport** (📞 74 36 50/98 93 13); **Maïssagé** or **EHGM** (📞 74 37 16); **Rimbo Transport** (📞 74 14 13); and **SNTV** (📞 72 30 20). Aïr Transport is located near the Wadata Ecogare (*gare routière*); Rimbo Transport is located in the town district to the north of the Big Mosque along the Avenue du Gober; Maïssagé is located near the Wadata market; SNTV is just off the road to the airport in the Gamkallé quarter.

Bear in mind that the following information is liable to change and that travel times are no more than rough estimates. You are advised to always check with the bus company you choose to travel with. In the listing of the Nigérien destinations below, scheduled journeys and reporting times are the same for all, unless specified otherwise. Fares, however, are only indicative as they may differ slightly between companies. See *Getting around,* opposite.

Agadez–Arlit Daily; reporting time 04.30; 11–12 hours to Agadez, 14–15 hours to Arlit; Dosso (CFA3,400); Birni N'Konni (CFA6,800); Tahoua (CFA9,000); Agadez (CFA12,000); Arlit (CFA17,000). SNTV has no departure for Agadez–Arlit on Mon.
Zinder Daily; reporting time 04.30; 8–10 hours; Birni N'Konni (CFA6,800); Maradi (CFA9,000); Zinder (CFA11,800). The reporting time for SNTV is at 05.00; their rates are higher, eg: Zinder (CFA14,725). Diffa on Wed and Sat, Maïssagé has buses going to Zinder and onwards to Diffa (overnight stop in Zinder, hence arrival in Diffa on Thu and Sun); reporting time 04.30; Diffa (CFA17,200).
Cotonou–Lomé Maïssagé: Tue, Thu, Sun; reporting time 04.30; Cotonou (CFA18,700); Lomé (CFA22,300). SNTV: Tue, Thu, Sat, Sun to Cotonou

only (15 hours); Mon and Fri to Lomé (18 hours); reporting time 04.30; Cotonou (CFA22,850); Lomé (CFA26,200). Rimbo Transport: Wed, Fri, Sun; reporting time 04.00; Gaya (CFA5,500); Parakou (CFA11,900); Cotonou (CFA19,700).
Ouagadougou Rimbo Transport: Wed; reporting time 05.30; 10 hours; Ouagadougou (CFA10,000). SNTV: Tue–Sun; reporting time 06.00; Ouagadougou (CFA10,000).
Ouagadougou–Bobodioulasso–Bamako Maïssagé: this is a new service, and the schedule was not known at the time of research; overnight stop in Bobodioulasso; price indication: Bamako (CFA28,000).
Ayorou–Ansongo–Gao SNTV: Mon, Thu; reporting time 06.30; overnight stop along the way (CFA11,500). Askia Tours: Fri; no details were given.

For nearby destinations, Peugeot 504s (9 seats) and minibuses (19 seats) leave from different *autogares* or *taxi-brousse* stations. The Peugeots are usually somewhat faster than minibuses, while they charge only marginally more. Vehicles leave when full on any given day, but especially to meet local markets.

Minibus and *taxi-brousse* services from the **Autogare Wadata**:

Baleyara–Filingué 9-seater (CFA2,750): **Dosso–Gaya–Kamba** (Nigeria) 9-seater CFA2,100–4,100–5,500; **Harikanassou** (CFA1,900); **Kaygolo** (CFA2,200); **Bocko** (CFA7,600). At Wadata, some big buses with 50–70 seats leave for international long-haul journeys to **Parakou**

(CFA7,350), **Lomé** (CFA10,850), **Cotonou** (CFA10,850) and **Accra** (CFA12,350). For the same destinations but in a minibus, pay around CFA2,000 less. Another itinerary is **Ouagadougou** (CFA7,600), **Bobodioulasso** (CFA12,100) and **Abidjan** (CFA17,100).

Minibus and *taxi-brousse* services from the **Autogare Route du Tillabéri** (near Pharmacy Deyzeibon):

Ayorou Boubon (CFA600); Farjé (CFA1,250); Tillabéri (CFA1,800); Famalé (CFA3,000); Ayorou (CFA3,000); tarred all the way. **Téra–Yatakala** Boubon (CFA600); Farjé ferry (CFA1,250); Tera (CFA3,000); Dolbel and Yatakala (CFA6,000); tarred up to Tera, then rough dirt road. **Ouallam** (CFA1,800); 3–4 hours. **Mangaizé** (CFA2,300); dirt road all the way. **Kollo, Say, Torodi** (no exact fares were given)

GETTING AROUND

There are some public buses in Niamey, but they are a rare sight and can simply be ignored, since there is a much better alternative: the **taxi**. They are easily recognisable, inexpensive and plentiful. Taxi drivers have no fixed routes, but they will decide where to go next as they pick up and drop off passengers along the way. Before looking for a taxi, familiarise yourself with the city map and find a point of reference near your final destination. Points of reference can be a market, a roundabout (*rond point*), a 'building with a name' (like Palais de Congres), a water tower (eg: Château 1), a pharmacy or simply the name of a city quarter (Yantala, Boukoki, etc).

There are only very few places (*petit marché* and *grand marché* amongst others) where taxis line up and wait for passengers. Otherwise, it shouldn't take too long before one passes by on the main thoroughfares. Just casually stretch out your arm to indicate you are looking for a taxi. A firm '*Taximan!*' will also attract a driver's attention. Name your destination and point of reference through the open window to allow the driver to decide whether he is going the right way. If so, a barely visible nod of the head will invite you on board. If not, he will just drive off without much ado.

While a ride typically costs CFA200 per person in a shared taxi (which takes up to four adults and as many children as can fit in between), the taxi driver may ask for CFA300 or CFA400 (*deux courses*) for longer distances. The fare will rarely exceed CFA400 within Niamey during the daytime, but fares may double and even triple during the late night and early morning, eg: to get to a bus station at 04.30. Any fare other than CFA200 should be discussed beforehand, so if your driver failed to do so, you may safely assume that you have to pay no more than CFA200. If you have any excess luggage, you may be asked to pay something extra, but again, this has to be discussed beforehand with the driver. Have your money – preferably the exact amount – ready.

Should you wish the taxi driver to take you straight from A to B without stopping for other passengers, ask for a *location*. In that case you need to discuss the fare beforehand, but for an average distance this should not exceed CFA1,000 during the daytime. Taxis that are waiting outside the more expensive hotels are without exception *locations*. They will, however, usually charge more than CFA1,000 even for a short distance. You may also rent a taxi for any length of time. Expect to pay CFA1,500–3,000 per hour, depending on the time and distance (hence fuel) required.

Car hire with or without a driver is another option. The rates vary according to your destination. For a small car to take you around town and nearby destinations along tarred roads, expect to pay at least CFA30,000–40,000 without fuel. However, when you plan to venture well outside the city and off the main roads, you will have to rent a 4x4. Prices start from CFA60,000–80,000, fuel not included. Make sure it is specified in your contract when the price does include fuel. For car rental, try **Nigercar Voyages** (↘ *73 23 31*) or **Satguru Voyages** (↘ *73 69 31/32*).

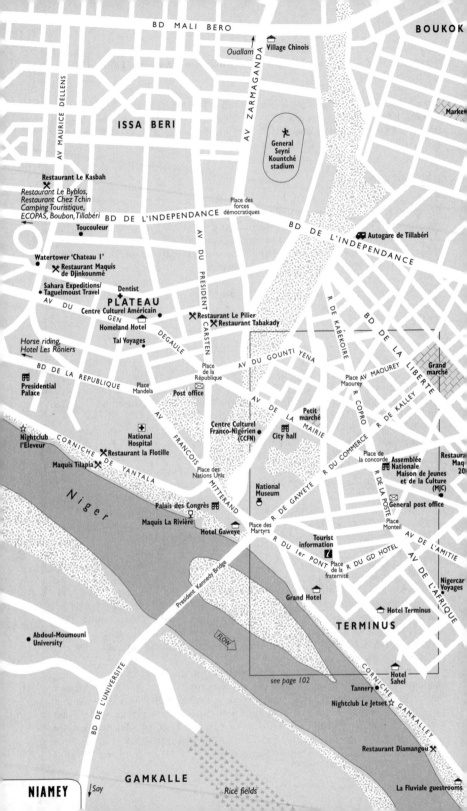

BD MALI BERO

BOUKOK

Ouallam

Village Chinois

AV ZARMAGANDA

ISSA BERI

General
Seyni
Kountché
stadium

Market

AV MAURICE DELLENS

Restaurant Le Kasbah

Restaurant Le Byblos,
Restaurant Chez Tchin
Camping Touristique,
ECOPAS, Boubon, Tillabéri

Place des
forces
démocratiques

BD DE L'INDEPENDANCE

Toucouleur

BD DE L'INDEPENDANCE

Autogare de Tillabéri

Watertower 'Chateau 1'

Restaurant Maquis
de Djinkounmé

AV DU PRESIDENT CARSTEN

Sahara Expeditions/
Taguelmoust Travel

Dentist

PLATEAU

Centre Culturel Américain

GEN

Homeland Hotel

Restaurant Le Pilier

Restaurant Tabakady

AV DU

DEGAULE

Horse riding,
Hotel Les Rôniers

Tal Voyages

R DE KABEKOIRE

BD DE LA LIBERTE

BD DE LA REPUBLIQUE

Place
Mandela

Place
de la
République

AV DU GOUNTI YENA

Place AV MAOUREY
Maourey

AV MAOUREY

Grand
marché

R DE KALLEY

Presidential
Palace

Post office

R COPRO

Nightclub
l'Eleveur

CORNICHE DE YANTALA

AV

National
Hospital

Restaurant la Flotille

AV FRANCOIS

Centre Culturel
Franco-Nigérien
(CCFN)

AV DE LA MAIRIE

City hall

Petit
marché

R DU COMMERCE

Place de
la concorde

Assemblée
Nationale

Restaurant
Maq
20

Maquis Tilapia

MITTERAND

Place des
Nations Unis

National
Museum

R DE GAWEYE

Maison de Jeunes
et de la Culture
(MJC)

R DE LA POSTE

General post office

Niger

Palais des Congrès

Maquis La Rivière

Hotel Gaweye

Place des
Martyrs

Place
Monteil

AV DE L'AMITIE

Tourist
information

R DU 1er PONT

Place
de la
fraternité

R DU GD HOTEL

AV DE L'AFRIQUE

Président Kennedy Bridge

FLOW

Grand Hotel

Nigercar
Voyages

Abdoul-Moumouni
University

Hotel Terminus

TERMINUS

BD DE L'UNIVERSITE

see page 102

CORNICHE GAMKALLEY

Hotel
Sahel

Tannery

Nightclub Le Jetset

Restaurant Diamangou

NIAMEY

Say

GAMKALLE

Rice fields

La Fluviale guestrooms

MADINA

BD MALI BERO

AV DU GOBER

🚐 Rimbo Transport

DAN GAO

AV DE AMENOKAL

ABIDJAN

☪ **Grande Mosquée**
Place de la
Grande Prière

Market

Police

Centre Culturel
Oumarou Ganda ●

AV KASSAI

BD DE L'INDEPENDANCE

R DE L'EGYPTE

AV SONNI ALI BER

AV DE L'ISLAM

🚐 Air Transport

AV DU GOBER

🎬 Jangorzo
cinema

Place
Mammanet

Hotel Moustache 🏠

BD MALI BERO

Ecogare
Wadata

R DE TCHAD

AV DU NIGER

**Muslim
burial ground**

AV DU CANADA

Wadata
handicrafts centre ●

Maissagé
(buses)

BD DE L'INDEPENDANCE

AV DU CANADA

Auberge Chez Tatayi 🏠

L'ENTENTE

SABON GARI

POUDRIERE

🎬 Zabarkan cinema

Restaurant Chez Kady ✕🍴 Patisserie Salon
de thé Les Lilas

AV DE

Ecobank 💲

Hotel Ténéré 🏠

BD DE LA LIBERTE

R DE LA LIBYE

Nouveau
Marché

AV POMPIERS

**NOUVEAU
MARCHE**

AV DE L'OUA

AV DE L'AMITIE

Place de la
Bienvenue

AV DE L'OUA

N

🅱 Bradt

0 ————— 500m
0 ————— 500yds

R DE L'AEROPO

AV DE L'AFRIQUE

🚐 SNTV

Gamkalley Clinic ✚

La Pillule,
Kollo

GAMKALLE SEBANGAYE

Race course

Airport

Top end

🏠 **Hotel Gaweye** (164 rooms, 36 suites) ☎ 72 27 10/11; **f** 72 33 47; **e** gaweye@intnet.ne. The Gaweye has an excellent reputation. Rooms (all with internet access) and facilities are immaculate and meet international standards. The setting on the river Niger is stunning, the terrace by the swimming pool has one of the best views in Niamey. *All 164 dbl rooms cost CFA70,000 (view to the National Museum) and CFA75,000 (river view), while junior and presidential suites cost CFA100,000 and CFA150,000.*

🏠 **Le Grand Hotel du Niger** (94 rooms) ☎ 73 26 41/42; **f** 73 26 43; **e** grandhotelniger@yahoo.fr; www.grandhotelniger.com. The Grand Hotel is beautifully located high on the riverbank. Rooms and bungalows are spotless and very comfortable. Extras like a swimming pool, terrace with superb views to the river Niger, internet access, shops and hairdresser justify the rates that *start at CFA45,000/50,000 (sgl/dbl room or bungalow) up to CFA70,000/80,000 (sgl/dbl senior suite). An extra bed costs CFA10,000.*

🏠 **Homeland Hotel** (9 rooms, 2 suites) ☎ 73 26 06/32 82; **f** 72 29 67; **e** homeland@intnet.ne. A new and upmarket hotel, well hidden in the government administration area. The immaculate rooms are very well equipped (including internet access), while the sheltered garden has a small swimming pool. *Rooms with dbl bed cost CFA45,000, or CFA55,000 with an extra bed, while suites cost CFA75,000.*

🏠 **Hotel Ténéré** (52 rooms) ☎ 73 20 20/30 55; **f** 73 30 45; **e** hotenere@intnet.ne. Another good hotel with many amenities, such as a small business centre with internet access, and a swimming pool. A bit musty here and there, this hotel could do with some upgrading, but all in all a comfortable place to stay. The rooms are well equipped – with bathrooms in a striking blue – and start from *CFA35,000–43,000 (sgl–dbl) to CFA52,500 for a suite.*

🏠 **Hotel Terminus** (36 bungalows) ☎ 73 26 92/93; **f** 73 39 74; **e** hotermi@intnet.ne. The Terminus has very comfortable and clean bungalows, centred around a yard, while 12 more rooms were under construction at the time of writing. To the back is a secluded garden and terrace with swimming pool. By comparison, this is good value for money, hence the listing under the top-end hotels. This hotel is regularly used to accommodate participants in conferences, in which case the hotel may well be fully booked, so booking in advance is recommended. Of the existing bungalows, some have fridge and TV and *they cost CFA37,500 or CFA45,000.*

Mid-range

🏠 **Hotel Maourey** (19 rooms, 1 suite) ☎ 73 28 50/20 54; **f** 73 35 69. Conveniently located between the *petit marché* and the *grand marché*, near to shops, internet and the CCFN. It is a friendly place with a family atmosphere. The s/c AC rooms are a bit dark and musty, and therefore *overpriced at CFA21,000/26,000 (sgl/dbl), or CFA32,000 for the suite.*

🏠 **Hotel les Rôniers** (20 rooms) ☎ 72 31 38; **f** 72 31 33; **e** horonier@intnet.ne. This hotel first opened its doors in 1969, and you would have probably guessed so from the interior design of the bungalows. Once a top-class hotel, this is still a comfortable place in quiet surroundings. The amenities include a swimming pool (CFA2,500 for non-guests), 3 somewhat neglected tennis courts (CFA1,500 for non-guests) and a spacious, green garden leading down to the river. *Self-contained AC rooms cost CFA23,000/26,500 (sgl/dbl).*

🏠 **Hotel Sahel** (35 rooms & apartments) ☎ 73 24 31; **f** 73 20 98. Though clean and basically OK, some beds are saggy, the interior décor isn't very interesting, nor is the view to the parking. However, many rooms have panoramic views over the river Niger. Not to worry if you have been given a room at the wrong side of the hall, as there is always the huge garden-cum-terrace with a bar. A new wing and restaurant were being constructed at the time of writing. Just next door is Piscine Olympique. *AC rooms with TV at CFA25,000/27,500 (sgl/dbl) and some apts at CFA38,500.*

Budget

🏠 **Auberge Chez Tatayi** ☎ 74 12 81; **e** auberge@tatayi.com; www.tatayi.com. A delightful backpackers' place that opened its doors at the end of 2003. It can accommodate up to 30 people in rooms of various sizes and standard. A covered terrace and the reception area that feels like a living room give this auberge a homely feel. There is no restaurant, but there is a dining area and you can make use of the fridge, cutlery and crockery from the kitchen. Some good nearby restaurants as well as food stalls also make up for the lack of an indoor restaurant. *Rates start from CFA5,000 for a dorm bed up to CFA19,000 for a large s/c AC room with 2 dbl beds. The location is not far from Autogare Wadata and Cinéma Zabarkan.*

⌂ **La Fluviale** (8 rooms) ☏ 73 22 82. This place belongs to the Gendarmerie Nationale and is not really a hotel. In fact, it looks more like a sports club with a sandy basketball field; there is a small bar-cum-restaurant and some barracks with rooms. Tourists are welcome when there is a vacancy, but those who work for or with the gendarmerie will get priority. The quiet riverside location is pretty, but the area between La Fluviale and the city is unsafe after dark, while taxis will be hard to find. On the other hand you may use the sports grounds, river trips by pirogue can be organised from La Fluviale (CFA5,000 per person/hour, less if more people join in), while the military swimming pool is just next door. *On balance rooms are somewhat overpriced at CFA10,000 for a room with shared facilities, while s/c AC rooms with TV cost CFA20,000.*

⌂ **Hotel Moustache** (33 rooms) ☏ 73 33 78. A lively, dingy, sometimes noisy and basic place to stay. The rooms come in 3 categories and *cost between CFA5,000 for a dbl with fan to CFA10,000 for a s/c AC dbl.*

⌂ **Village Chinois** (40 rooms) ☏ 72 33 98. This place is among the cheapest accommodation in town. It has basic rooms, most of which share 1 bathroom between 2 rooms. There is ample parking space and camping is allowed at negotiable rates, though it is questionable whether it is safe to leave any valuables in your tent. A small restaurant and bar are on the premises. The location is just to the north of the Seyni Kountché Stadium, at the junction of Bd Mali Béro and Bd du Zarmaganda. This place hardly ever sees tourists, but *at CFA5,000 for a room with a fan or CFA7,000 for an AC room, it is worth giving it a try.*

⚑ **Camping Touristique** ☏ 75 44 89. Once a popular place for overlanders, this site along the Route de Tillabéri has been very quiet for many years now. The spacious and tranquil garden is now mainly used by local businessmen for lunch, with a bar and basic restaurant — playing loud music — catering for African meals. *Camping is allowed at CFA2,000 per person, there is an extra charge of CFA1,000 for vehicles.*

WHERE TO EAT AND DRINK

Niamey has a surprising number of restaurants, some of them really good. The following list is only a selection, and you may well stumble upon another interesting alternative.

All top end hotels have a restaurant serving mainly European and some African food, with **Hotel Gaweye** and the **Grand Hotel** being among the best, while the restauration at **Hotel Terminus** is another very good choice. Food at the mid-range hotels ranges from the usual steak-and-fries to more surprising, sometimes very succulent meals. The settings of **Hotel les Rôniers** and **Hotel Sahel** are winners, with spacious gardens and delightful views, while at **Hotel Maourey** guests are confined to a basic indoor dining room or a small patio. Of the budget range, only **La Fluviale** and the **Camping Touristique** can provide (stodgy) meals with a beer or soft drink.

✘ **Bar Guiguignya** ☏ 74 11 02. On the Bd de L'Oua, the atmosphere in the spacious yet intimate garden is very relaxed and the chilled draught beers are unmatched.

✘ **Chez Kady** A simple friendly Malian restaurant.

✘ **Chez T'Chin** ☏ 72 25 28. Also worth a visit, preferably during the daytime when you can sit outside in a very lush and green garden to enjoy fresh salads, *nems* (spring rolls) and plenty of other dishes. The crocodiles in small enclosures are

a pitiful sight, though.

✘ **Exot'ic** ☏ 73 40 50. Opens for both lunch and dinner and serves mostly European and some African food, while live music (rock, R&B) is played every Fri and Sat.

✘ **La Cascade** ☏ 73 26 06. A Lebanese restaurant, with an indoor waterfall and altogether pleasant décor, with exquisite and well-presented dishes.

✘ **La Flotille** ☏ 73 32 54. Serves African specialities. Closed Mon.

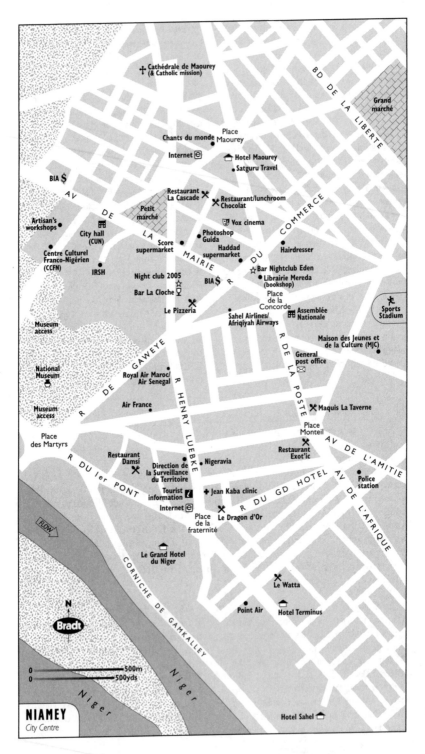

Cathédrale de Maourey
(& Catholic mission)

Grand marché

BD DE LA LIBERTÉ

Place Maourey

Chants du monde

Internet

Hotel Maourey

Satguru Travel

BIA $

AV DE LA MAIRIE

Restaurant La Cascade

Restaurant/lunchroom Chocolat

Petit marché

Vox cinema

DU COMMERCE

Artisan's workshops

City hall (CUN)

Photoshop Guida

Score supermarket

Haddad supermarket

Hairdresser

Centre Culturel Franco-Nigérien (CCFN)

IRSH

Night club 2005

Bar La Cloche

BIA $

Bar Nightclub Eden

Librairie Mereda (bookshop)

Le Pizzeria

Place de la Concorde

Sahel Airlines/ Afriqiyah Airways

Assemblée Nationale

Sports Stadium

Museum access

R DE GAWEYE

R DE LA POSTE

Maison des Jeunes et de la Culture (MJC)

General post office

National Museum

Royal Air Maroc/ Air Senegal

Air France

R HENRY LUEBKE

Maquis La Taverne

Museum access

Place Monteil

Place des Martyrs

R DU 1er PONT

Restaurant Damsi

Direction de la Surveillance du Territoire

Nigeravia

Restaurant Exot'ic

AV DE L'AMITIE

Tourist information

Jean Kaba clinic

Internet

Police station

AV DE L'AFRIQUE

Place de la fraternité

Le Dragon d'Or

R DU GD HOTEL

FLOW

Le Grand Hotel du Niger

CORNICHE DE GAMKALLEY

Le Watta

N

Point Air

Hotel Terminus

Bradt

0 ——— 500m
0 ——— 500yds

Niger

Hotel Sahel

NIAMEY
City Centre

102

✘ **La Pizzeria** ✆ 74 12 40/73 40 50. Open in the evenings only, serving very good pizzas (around CFA4,000), and also does take-aways. Unfortunately, this restaurant is in an unsafe area after dark, so it is best to take a taxi to get there and away.

✘ **Le Byblos** ✆ 72 44 05. Another establishment catering for Lebanese food lovers.

✘ **Le Dragon d'Or** ✆ 73 41 23. Has an excellent reputation for its Chinese food, but is also known for its karaoke evenings (every Fri) and Buffet Asiatique (every Sat; CFA8,000), where you can have a taste of a variety of dishes you would perhaps otherwise dare not order.

✘ **Le Maquis 2000** ✆ 73 55 54. Popular with groups, this is a casual restaurant where some very good African dishes and juices are served either indoors or on a terrace.

✘ **Le Shanghaï** ✆ 75 38 29. Owned by the same Chinese–Tuareg couple as Le Dragon d'Or.

✘ **Le Watta** ✆ 73 24 23. Another restaurant with African specialities, mostly from Ivory Coast.

✘ **Maquis la Taverne** A friendly and airy place, serving basic food like spaghetti and brochettes, unfortunately with the downside of noisy traffic passing just the other side of the green hedges.

✘ **Maquis Tilapia** Just across the road from La Flotille and overlooking the river Niger, serving grilled fish and meat dishes.

✘ **Patisserie Salon de Thé les Lilas** Near the Chez Kady, and serving sweet and sticky cakes accompanied by hot or cold drinks.

✘ **Restaurant Damsi** Has a garden-like terrace with nice views towards the river, with fine international cuisine.

✘ **Restaurant Diamangou** ✆ 73 51 43. Le Bateau is an excellent spot for lunch. Meals and drinks are served on a boat, and if that wasn't riverine enough, from Oct–Jan you can even book the boat for a sunset trip along the river Niger. Don't forget to bring insect repellent after sunset.

✘ **Restaurant le Kasbah** ✆ 75 26 02. Serves Moroccan and other north African dishes.

✘ **Restaurant Le Pilier** ✆ 72 24 86/49 85. The Le Pilier has a downstairs cave or cellar for pizzas, while in a very different, tasteful setting on the ground floor you have a wide choice of other Italian specialities. Pricey, but well worth the expense.

✘ **Restaurant Maquis de Djinkounmé** ✆ 72 72 86/96 51 32. A friendly restaurant with African cuisine near Château 1. Occasionally live music is staged here, and it is worth checking their programme.

✘ **Restaurant Tabakady** ✆ 73 58 18. Also expensive, but outstanding, with mostly French dishes, the Tabakady is one of the best restaurants in town.

ENTERTAINMENT AND NIGHTLIFE

NIGHTCLUBS AND BARS Nightclub le Ryan at Hotel Gaweye and **Fofo Nightclub** at Hotel Sahel play all sorts of music. The latter is open on Fridays and Saturdays from 23.00 onwards, entrance fee usually CFA2,500, but up to CFA5,000 for special occasions. **Bar la Cloche** (✆ 73 24 62) doubles as a restaurant for snacks and a bar which stays open until well into the night. On the ground floor in the same building is **Nightclub 2005**, open on weekdays until 04.00 and on weekends until 05.00. Opposite Haddad supermarket is **Bar Nightclub Eden**, where live music is played regularly.

Formerly known as Le Hippopotame Bleu and under new ownership, this bar-cum-nightclub will now probably be renamed **L'Eleveur**. It is beautifully located on the riverbank, but the area (Corniche du Yantala) must be considered unsafe after sunset. If you don't have your own transport, make firm arrangements to be picked up from here. The same applies to **Nightclub le JetSet** at Corniche du Gamkalley, a popular open-air club by the riverside.

CINEMA AND THEATRE Two places that regularly show films and stage theatrical productions are the **Centre Culturel Franco-Nigérien** (CCFN) and the **Centre Culturel Oumarou Ganda** (CCOG). To find out what their programmes are, it is best to enquire at the cultural centres directly, though you may be able to pick up a booklet from the CCFN at some hotels and bookshops. The programme is also printed in the *Niameyze*, a monthly bulletin with practical information on the capital. Look for a free copy at hotel reception desks, in shops and some restaurants.

The **Centre Culturel Américain** shows a film every Wednesday. Though usually in English, they are sometimes dubbed in French. Enquire at the Centre for their programme. Also check for other cultural events, but most of these you will be able to visit by invitation only. For opening times see *Practicalities* below.

Not too long ago, Niamey had about a dozen popular cinemas. Then came television and video, spiking the cinemas' right to exist. Only one or two are functional now, but even those are struggling to survive as their former audience has diverted to video clubs scattered all over town. At the time of research, **Cinéma Jangorzo** was still functional, featuring mostly Hindu and violent films. Check out the posters at the entrance and bear in mind that it doesn't matter that the film will probably be dubbed into French: it's the whole setting that makes an African cinema an experience, while the film itself is a kind of bonus if you manage to follow the storyline. Tickets cost only a few hundred CFA.

PRACTICALITIES

TOURIST INFORMATION The tourist office (*Avenue du President H Luebke; BP 612;* ↘ *73 24 47;* f *73 39 40*) near the Grand Hotel is of very little use, if any at all. This place is as sleepy as the guard who spends his days with his eyes closed on a bench just outside the premises. There are no maps, leaflets or books to be handed out. Should you wish to contact the **ECOPAS** office (↘ *72 53 48/59 34 03;* e *ecopas@intnet.ne*), they are located on the outskirts of Niamey, not far from the Malian consulate. Bear in mind that this is not a tourist facility, but the seat of a project (see *'W' National Park* on page 124). However, staff are willing to help if you need additional information concerning the 'W' National Park.

VISA EXTENSIONS Next to the Telecentre du Passeport on Rue Heinrich Luebke, at the **Direction de la Surveillance du Territoire**, is where you can have your visa extended. Bring CFA20,000 (for up to another 30 days) or CFA50,000 (for one to six months' extension), two photographs and a submissive attitude. If you hand in your passport in the morning, you can pick it up again next morning. It could probably be done the same day, but it may cost you more than a friendly smile to get the machine going.

MONEY There are many banks, most of them with more than one branch. Banking hours vary slightly between banks, but it is fair to assume that most are open Monday–Friday 08.30–11.30 and 15.45–17.00; Saturday 08.30–11.30.

The **Bank of Africa** or **BOA** (↘ *73 36 20*) changes most hard currencies, but cash only. At the **BIA** (↘ *73 31 01*) you can get cash advances with Visa, Mastercard and Carte Bleue. Changing travellers' cheques is possible, but you need to bring the receipt. Buying travellers' cheques is also possible, and you can pay with Visa and American Express cards. **BINCI** (↘ *73 27 40*) changes euro and US dollars – cash or travellers' cheques – only. **BCEAO** (↘ *72 24 91*) takes cash euro only, while **Ecobank** (↘ *73 71 81*) takes most cash currencies. **Sonibank** (↘ *73 45 69*) takes travellers' cheques. Most banks and post offices have a **Western Union** branch for international cash transfers.

LOCAL TOUR OPERATORS
Agence Songay Voyage Navigation Fluviale or **ASVNF** ↘ 91 40 54/55 13 12; e asvnf2000@yahoo.fr.

This company started off as an agency specialising in river trips. After many years of experience, ASVNF

now claims to be specialised in all tourist destinations, even outside the regular tourist itineraries eg: Filingué, Oualam and Tera.
Nigercar Voyages ☎ 73 23 31; f 73 64 83; e nicarvoy@intnet.ne; www.gsi-niger.com/nigercar. In business since 1970, when they used to rent out cars only, then gradually expanded to a full-blown travel agency. By now, they have a great deal of experience in organising trips along the river Niger as well as in 'W' National Park, where they run their own *campement*. And, of course, they still have a whole fleet of vehicles to rent out.
Sahara Expeditions ☎ 72 38 82/98 58 71; f 72 38 82; e sahara_expeditions2000@yahoo.fr; www.sahara-expeditions-niger.com. A new travel agency run by a Tuareg with many years of experience in the tourist industry. This agency can organise trips into the desert regions and 'W' Park starting from Niamey.
Satguru Travel and Tours Service ☎ 73 69 31/32/33; f 73 69 34; e stts-nim@intnet.ne.

Satguru specialise in ticketing, car hire, hotel reservations and foreign exchange. A small car and a driver for use around town will cost approximately CFA40,000 (fuel not included); a 4x4 costs CFA100,000 (fuel not included). Satguru Travel represents Air Burkina.
Taguelmoust Travels and Services ☎ 75 38 82/98 58 71; f 72 38 82; e tts@intnet.ne. Their main office is in Agadez, but in recent years they have also achieved a great deal of experience with river trips – both upstream and downstream – and excursions to 'W' National Park and Kouré. In Niamey they are represented by Sahara Expeditions (see above).
Ténéré Voyages ☎ 73 47 10; f 73 47 55; e atv@intnet.ne. Ténéré are mainly in business as a ticketing office. However, they can provide some information on the main tourist destinations, and put you in touch with an agency in Agadez for instance. Some programmes for river trips and excursions into 'W' National Park are being developed.

Other travel agencies in Niamey include:

Croix du Sud ☎ 96 03 17
Megacontact ☎ 96 32 08

Tal Voyages ☎ 72 52 92
Zenacom Voyages ☎ 98 77 43

COMMUNICATIONS AND INTERNET There are various post offices in Niamey. The main **post office** (*Rue de la Poste/Place Monteil*) is open Monday–Friday 07.30–12.15 and 15.30–18.00, and 08.00–12.00 on Saturdays. Poste restante service charges CFA300 per letter. **DHL Express** (☎ 73 33 59) is at Boulevard de la Liberté.

For the **internet**, do not feel tempted to use the internet at the Centre Culturel Franco-Nigérien (CCFN), as connection is very, very slow. In the centre around the *petit marché*, there are two much better options. At Cyber S@tguru (*open Mon–Sat 08.00–22.00*), you pay for a minimum of 45 minutes (CFA500) up to eight hours (CFA5,000). In return, your own PIN code allows you to use the time whenever you like in as many sessions as you like. CyberADC (☎ 73 36 39; open Mon–Fri 09.00–21.30 and Sun 10.30–19.00) is located between the *petit marché* and *rond point Maourey*. The charge is CFA200 for ten minutes or CFA1,000 per hour. At Cyber Bebeto, near Pharmacie Yantala, computers are old and worn out. Do not attempt anything other than checking your email – forget about opening attachments – to avoid frustration (CFA500 per hour).

MEDIA AND BOOKS If you are craving for something to read in English, the place to be is the **Centre Culturel Américain** (☎ 73 31 69 41 07; open Mon 09.00–12.00, Wed 09.00–12.00 and 15.00–18.00, Thu 09.00–12.00; Sun and Tue closed). They have a selection of around 20 different magazines and sometimes newspapers. The books are mostly about the USA, with only very little about Niger. Books and magazines can be consulted only in the library. Across the yard is a small library with novels and other books. These are used by Nigériens who take English lessons at the Centre. However, if you have a novel you would like to swap, ask the librarian if he agrees.

3

The library at the **Centre Culturel Franco-Nigérien** (*open Tue 15.30–18.30, Wed–Sat 09.00–12.30 and 15.30–18.30, Sun 09.00–12.00*) has plenty of books, but all are in French. Only a couple of magazines are in English. Meanwhile, books about Niger (*le fonds Niger*) are in the **Centre de Resources Documentaires** (*opening times are the same as the library but closed on Sun, open on Tue morning*), also part of the CCFN. The collection is truly impressive, but again just about all are in French.

Another library is at the **Centre Culturel Oumarou Ganda** (↘ *74 09 03; open Mon 16.00–18.30, Tue–Sat 08.30–12.00 and 16.00–18.30*).

If you are planning to do some serious research on Niger, two libraries are worth a visit. One is at the **Institut des Récherches des Sciences Humaines** or **IRSH** (↘ *73 51 41*). While the library has approximately 18,000 titles, they are only accessible through the librarians, so this is not a place to go browsing as a pastime. Next door, on the same premises, is the **Centre d'Etudes Linguistiques et Historiques par Tradition Orale** or **CELHTO** (Centre for Linguistic and Historical Studies through Oral Tradition; ↘ *73 54 14*). The same rules apply here, and in both cases, books can be consulted only in the library.

Of the many bookshops in town, the following two are among the best. **Photoshop Guida** has some interesting and quality books on Niger (the wildlife in particular), many of them published by internationally known publishers. This is also the right place to be looking for a good selection of postcards, magazines – some in English – and French and Nigérien newspapers. **Librairie Mereda** focuses more on the local market, with schoolbooks and some African and French literature. Schoolbooks are worth having a look at, as not only can they be informative, they also reflect the way young Nigériens are being educated about their country and the rest of the world.

SHOPPING AND MISCELLANEOUS Most supermarkets have a very limited choice of produce, but in Niamey there are a few good exceptions to this rule. Near the *petit marché* are two supermarkets run by the same family, called **Haddad supermarché** and **Le Score**. Both have a good selection of the ordinary, as well as plenty of items that are considered a luxury by Nigérien standards. Another well-stocked supermarket is along the road to the airport.

While it is recommended that you bring all the film material you think you will be using during your stay, you can buy some extra supplies from **Photo Guida**, again not far from the *petit marché*. The owner is a professional photographer who will sell quality films only. When in stock, you may even get slide films there.

There are numerous tailors in Niamey, where you can hand in the fabric of your choice and order clothes to be made within a few days. One interesting address is **Tou'couleur** (↘ *72 26 53*), a workshop run by an enterprising female designer from Senegal. You can buy original clothes, bed covers, bags and scarves directly from her shop, or choose from a large selection of fabrics and batiks, and have any design made to a perfect fit. Open Monday–Saturday, by appointment only.

An excellent hairdresser with an international clientele, is **Mona Lisa** (↘ *73 29 23*), between the *petit marché* and the *grand marché*. By appointment only.

HEALTH Niamey has a number of good **private clinics** for first aid, consultations, lab analysis and treatment. Usually, these clinics are also equipped for X-rays, echography and even surgery. **Clinique Jean Kaba** (↘ *73 21 08/26 52*) is open day and night for emergencies. If the front door is closed, try the side entrance. A regular consultation costs CFA3,000; CFA5,000 for specialists, during evenings and holidays; and if a specialist has to be called in, it will cost CFA10,000. Another

During the daytime, Niamey presents itself as a friendly town, which in certain areas feels like a regional town rather than a capital city. It is generally safe to explore the city on foot, even when you are just by yourself. Make sure you do not become an easy target, though, by following these simple rules: do not carry any (visible) valuables, like jewellery or a camera; do not expose your moneybelt at any time, but keep it well hidden under your clothes or leave it in your hotel room; carry as little as possible when visiting busy places – like markets and bus yards – and carry your daypack in front of you. After dark, you should be vigilant wherever you go, while walking in a group is better than walking alone. Do not panic for no reason though, and do enjoy the streets as they come alive in the evenings; just stay on the alert.

Having said all that, some specific warnings do apply. In a country so poor, and in a city with so many unemployed people, there are always those who have taken to criminal behaviour. Certain areas are definitely notorious for petty theft, muggings and even violent robberies. Criminals tend to operate during the evenings, especially where a hiding place is nearby. One such hiding place is the undeveloped area fringed by the National Museum, the CCFN, the *petit marché* and the Rue Heinrich Luebke (between the Grand Hotel and the *petit marché*). These streets and the marketplace are best avoided after dark, as violent robberies – some with knife stabbing – occur regularly. The same applies for the Kennedy Bridge and the whole stretch along the riverside, the Corniche de Gamkalley and the Corniche du Yantala. When venturing to and from one of these areas, always take a taxi and make prior arrangements to be picked up. If you should end up being cornered, hand over your belongings without hesitation.

Beware of conmen (and women) who have developed cunning ways to convince foreigners you are the only one who can help them out in a desperate situation. I almost fell for the heartbreaking story of a baby with serious burns, who supposedly had been admitted to a nearby clinic and was in urgent need of special ointment from the pharmacy. I decided to see the child first, and the sobbing mother didn't think that was a smart idea: she suddenly ran away. One month later, not having recognised me, she tried exactly the same again.

clinic which is recommended by embassies and expats, is **Clinique Gamkalley** (🔍 73 20 33/73 46 39) for all medical services but surgery. Opening hours are Monday–Saturday 08.30–12.30 and Monday–Friday 15.30–18.30, but day and night for emergencies.

For **eye problems**, try Clinique Opthalmo opposite Hotel Terminus, or call Doctor Amza (🔍 73 47 27) for a consultation. If you need a **dentist**, contact Cabinet Tafadeck (🔍 73 20 34), which is not far from the Grand Hotel, or Doctor Janine Kobéret (🔍 72 40 29), who works in a clinic opposite the *Lycée Fontaine*.

FOREIGN REPRESENTATION IN NIAMEY
Embassies

🇪 **Algeria** Bd des Ambassades, BP 142; 🔍 72 35 83

🇪 **Benin** Rue des Dallols, BP 11544; 🔍 72 28 60

🇪 **Canada** Bd Mali Béro, BP 362; 🔍 75 36 86/ 87; f 75 31 07; e niamy@dfait-maeci.gc.ca

🇪 **Chad** Av du Général Charles de Gaulle, BP 12820; 🔍 75 34 64

🇪 **France** Route de Tondibia (Yantala), BP 10660; 🔍 72 24 31/ 32; f 72 25 18;

e ambafrance@intnet.ne; www.ambafrance.ne

🇪 **Germany** Rue du Général Charles de Gaulle, BP 629; 🔍 72 35 10

🇪 **Italy** BP 10388; 🔍 73 20 00

🇪 **Libya** BP 683; 🔍 72 40 19

🇪 **Nigeria** Bd des Ambassades, BP 617; 🔍 73 24 10

USA Bd des Ambassades, BP 11201; 🔍 73 31 69/72 39 41; f 73 55 60; e niameyPASN@state.gov

❸ Belgium Route du 1er pont, BP 10192; ✆ 73 34 47/40 07; **f** 73 37 56; **e** niamay@diplobel.org

❸ Mali Koira Kano, opposite the IGNN; BP 10115; ✆ 75 42 90/41 88; **e** consmali@intnet.ne; www.gsi-niger.com/consulat-mali

❸ Netherlands Sonicar, BP 685; ✆ 72 27 31; **f** 73

35 69; **e** hensten@intnet.ne

❸ Spain BP 10272; ✆ 74 26 24

❸ Switzerland Behind Rue Maurice Dellens, BP 728; ✆ 73 38 39 16

❸ UK Vice-consulate (for limited services), BP 11926; ✆ 72 46 76/ 75 24 51; **f** 72 46 76

For visas to Burkina Faso and Ivory Coast, go to the French consulate.

WHAT TO SEE AND DO

NATIONAL MUSEUM Formerly known as L'Institut Français d'Afrique Noire, the museum was inaugurated in December 1959. Since then, the museum has had its ups and downs, with the lowest ebb being a huge fire which wreaked havoc in 1980. Despite difficulties, the National Museum emerged from the ashes and deservedly has become one of Niger's major attractions. The spacious layout of the premises includes different pavilions, traditionally built houses and dwellings, a zoo, a handicraft training centre for handicapped people, workshops and a shady bar.

The pavilions are built in decorative Hausa style and are dedicated to aspects of Nigérien history and traditions, with exhibitions on palaeontology, archaeology, uranium mining, objects and costumes from different ethnic groups, and traditional instruments. While these pavilions accommodate very well-presented displays, the zoo leaves much to be desired; some of the cages and enclosures are a pitiful sight. The captive lions, hippo and many smaller mammals, as well as birds and reptiles, do serve a worthy purpose, though. The museum as a whole is an important educational centre, regularly visited by groups of pupils, whose chances of ever seeing these animals in their natural surroundings are very meagre. An oddity on display is the remains of the famous *Arbre du Ténéré* or Ténéré tree (see *The Ténéré Desert*, page 198).

The National Museum has two entrances: on the Rue du Musée and opposite the Palais du Congrès (✆ 73 43 21; **f** 73 35 91; *open Mon–Fri 08.00–18.30 for the open-air exhibits, the zoo and the handicraft workshops, while the pavilions are open from 09.00–12.00 and 15.30–17.30. Entrance fee is CFA1,000; guided tours are CFA2,500; a photography permit is CFA1,000).*

CENTRE CULTUREL FRANCO-NIGÉRIEN Opposite the National Museum is the Centre Culturel Franco-Nigérien or CCFN, which hosts a whole range of cultural activities, including theatre, cinema, live concerts and temporary exhibitions. Major events are staged in the amphitheatre-cum-cinema with 400 seats. These usually take place on weekends, with rap concerts being one of the most popular of all. While you are staying in Niamey, it is well worth picking up a programme to find out what events are scheduled. Even when nothing much is going on, the open-air bar is still a good place for a drink as well as a meeting point for students and a colourful array of people with an interest in French and Nigérien culture. The CCFN also accommodates a public library and a documentation centre, both with almost exclusively French titles. Ignore the cybercafé unless you have strong nerves and plenty of time to waste.

CCFN (✆ 73 48 34/42 40; **f** 73 47 68; **e** ccfndir@intnet.ne; *www.ccfn.ne*; *opening times for the temporary exhibition and general information: Tue–Sat 09.00–12.30 and 15.30–18.30. Library: Tue 15.30–19.00, Wed–Sat 09.00–12.30 and 16.00–19.00, Sun 09.00–12.00. Documentation centre: Tue 10.30–12.30 and 15.30–18.30, Wed–Sat 09.00–12.30 and 15.30–18.30).*

CENTRE CULTUREL OUMAROU GANDA In 1980, the Centre Culturel Oumarou Ganda or CCOG (↘ 74 09 03) was created to host the 5th *Festival National des Jeunes des Sports et de la Culture*. It is named after Oumarou Ganda, an important Nigérien film director (see *The arts*, page 37). Most of all, the CCOG is a recreational centre with an emphasis on cultural expressions, very much like the CCFN (see above). The CCOG is located in the vicinity of the Wadata market and the Ecogare, the biggest *taxi-brousse* station in Niamey.

One entrance leads to the amphitheatre. This sizeable arena can receive as many as 5,000 spectators. It is an awesome experience to be part of such a huge and generally enthusiastic crowd for any event. Check at the centre for scheduled performances and films. Another entrance leads to an open-air bar and the library. Like most libraries in Niger, almost all books and magazines are in French. (*Library open Mon 16.00–18.30; Tue–Sat 08.30–12.00 and 16.00–18.30.*)

BIG MOSQUE The Big Mosque (Grande Mosquée) along the Avenue de l'Islam is the biggest mosque in Niamey. Impressive crowds gather here for prayer on special occasions like Tabaski. In between hours of prayer, the mosque is open to visitors – non-Muslim and women included. There is no fixed fee to be guided around, which means that you are entirely at the mercy of the warden, who has developed a greedy habit. He expects you to pay some money (several hundred CFA francs) towards the mosque, and some more towards his own expenses (several thousand CFA francs), while refusing to take you further or to give any kind of explanation if you are not generous enough for his liking. The best part of the tour is to climb the endless stairs in the minaret. If the warden will let you, of course.

CATHEDRAL DE MAOUREY This cathedral combines local and European architecture and decoration in a modest way. It is a place of worship, prayer and joyous celebrations for the Christian minority. When attending mass, people tend to dress up meticuously. While the Muslim sermons and prayers are more introvert, in this cathedral mass can be very lively and expressive. Enquire at the Catholic Mission (↘ 73 32 59) for scheduled sermons in French or Hausa.

MARKETS The best market on any given day is the *grande marché* or big market, rebuilt after the market was destroyed by a fire in 1980 in a style that is quite bizarre and hard to miss. This labyrinth hides all you can think of in terms of enamel pots and pans, plastic bowls and buckets, clothes and different styles of African textiles, locally produced tools, transistors, and calabashes, while food stalls and food merchants line the main street. A visit to this sprawling place is an adventure for all the senses.

The *petit marché* or small market is more about fruit and vegetables, spices, bundles of tied hens and guinea fowl, and new and second-hand clothing. With many people pushing their way through the narrow alleys between stalls, this is a place to watch out for pickpockets and bag-slashers. However, if you carry nothing or very little at all, there is no reason not to explore this lively market. Outside the area filled with stalls, vendors, pedestrians, cars, motorbikes and taxis all compete for the same, limited amount of space.

When walking from the small market towards the Place de la République, the pottery market is to your left. Huge decorated terracotta jars are called *canaries*; these are used to store water, and as it gradually evaporates through the faintly porous skin, the water cools down to a surprisingly refreshing temperature.

In Niamey there is no shortage of markets, varying from big, designated areas to small and informal concentrations of vendors. Each quarter of the city hides at least one aptly named marketplace, like the *nouveau marché* or new market in the quarter called Nouveau Marché, and the *marché de Wadata* or Wadata market in Wadata.

HANDICRAFTS Le Village Artisanal de Wadata (✆ *74 02 83;* f *74 07 83*) is a training centre as well as a huge complex of workshops, where artisans with expertise in many different fields try to make a living. All techniques you could find anywhere in Niger amalgamate in this centre, and it will be hard to resist the temptation to buy anything from the shop. Prices are fixed and more than reasonable. Also on the premises is a workshop or garage, run by a much respected female mechanic since 1997. This centre of handicrafts is the biggest of a whole chain of *villages artisanals* financed and founded with the *Coopération Nigero-Luxembourgeoise* (see *Handicrafts and what to buy,* page 80).

Founded by the same *cooperation* is the **Tannery of Corniche de Gamkalley**. Tanning needs a lot of water, as the skins and hides have to be drenched and left to soak for days, hence the location near water. Along one section of the Corniche de Gamkalley, leather skins are spread out to dry. Ask around to find someone to show you around and give some explanation.

The **Cooperative des Métiers d'Arts** (✆ *73 77 78*), just opposite the National Museum, is another collective with a structure similar to the one from Wadata. Around 100 members have been trained here so far, and you can see some of them at work daily, even on Sundays. The shop is open Monday–Saturday from 09.00–12.00 and 16.00–18.00, Sunday closed. Just outside the museum are more craftsmen trying to persuade every white pedestrian into buying from them.

A high concentration of – mostly Tuareg – handicraft shops is found around Château 1, along the Avenue du Château d'Eau.

ACTIVITIES

Swimming pools Most hotels with swimming pools allow non-residents to make use of the pool at a charge that is very much in accordance with the standard of the hotel. Prices vary from CFA1,000 to CFA3,000 per day. Hotel Terminus accepts only clients from the hotel and clients who have taken a subscription. The swimming pools at Hotel Gaweye and Grand Hotel are very attractive, if only for the fact that they overlook the river Niger. At GAMAT, the military swimming pool next to Hotel la Fluviale, the charge is CFA1,000 per person. Next to Hotel Sahel is the Piscine Olympique, where the entrance fee is also CFA1,000.

Tennis If you feel energetic enough, even when it is hot and sunny (which is most of the year), you could play a game of tennis at Hotel les Rôniers or Hotel Gaweye. The Tennis Club (✆ *73 25 34; open daily*) is near the Stade Municipal.

Horseriding Not too long ago, Niamey boasted at least three riding schools, but only one survived the declining interest. The **Club Equestre de Niamey** (✆ *72 28 30*) was founded in 1963 and has over 50 horses, more than half of which are private horses. The riding school takes most of its members mainly from the expat circuit, but anyone with some experience with horses can join for a ride along the river. As a non-member, you pay CFA5,000 insurance fee and CFA10,000 for the ride.

Jogging The **Hash** or **HHH** (**Hash House Harriers**) was invented by British colonisers in Malaysia in 1938. It is an international informal club that organises social and sporting activities, and more than 150 Hash clubs exist globally. In Niamey, members meet every Sunday afternoon at an out-of-town location where a jogging route is plotted. It is a pleasant way to discover beautiful and surprising locations, and to meet some expats. Most people need one to two hours to either jog or walk the route. Participating costs CFA500. For more information, call Mr Yacine Saad (✆ *73 38 34* or *73 21 37*).

Golf Golf Club Rio Bravo (✆ *72 51 29; open daily*) is an 18-hole golf course, located 15km from Niamey along the Route de Tillabéri. See also below.

EXCURSIONS FROM NIAMEY

ALONG THE RIVER NIGER A most relaxing way to observe different aspects of the river Niger is taking a trip in a **pirogue**, small dugout canoes or their larger cousins made from curved planks. Starting from Niamey, you will see a lot of human activity: fishermen trying to catch a meal, both men and women slapping their laundry over the rocks, people watering their riverside gardens from buckets and calabashes. Even with Niamey still well in sight, nature will be all around you and it is a good opportunity for birdwatching. Ask around for a pirogue near Pont Kennedy (both sides) or at one of the bars and restaurants along the river (Corniche du Gamkalley and Corniche de Yantala). Expect to pay around CFA5,000 for an hour, but this hourly rate should drop considerably if you take a pirogue for a full day, in which case CFA20,000 would be reasonable. Obviously, when the boat is motorised, the cost of fuel will be part of the bargaining.

To see hippo, the option nearest to Niamey is upstream, just 15km along the Route du Tillabéri near the Golf Club Rio Bravo and Relais Kanazi VSD. For this road section, pay around CFA200 tollage at the barrier when leaving Niamey. Follow the signposts leading to **Golf Club Rio Bravo** (see above). If you do not mind the greens being anything but green, this is your chance to hit some balls in Niger. The golf club is located just at the top of a plateau with panoramic views over the river Niger.

Only a stone's throw away from the golf club and beautifully located on the northern riverbank is **Relais Kanazi VSD** (✆ *73 26 52/97 62 99*). VSD stands for Vendredi-Samedi-Dimanche which means Friday-Saturday-Sunday, the only days you can pop in for a drink and a meal without a special booking. The Relais Kanazi is a lovely place for a day's outing or a picnic in the shade of the mango trees, but if you wish you can stay the night in one of the four air-conditioned bungalows. Down near the river, local guides will propose to take you for a pirogue ride (approximately CFA5,000 per hour in a motorised pirogue), and you may well see some **hippo** as they are frequently spotted in the vicinity of the small islands in the river.

Another riverine option – though without a pirogue – is a **camel ride** along the opposite riverbank, *la rive droite*. Sahel Accueil is a small company who organise this kind of excursion. The starting point is ten minutes away from Niamey and the ride takes around two hours. Booking one day in advance is required (✆ *85 33 93*; **e** *sahelaccueil@yahoo.fr*).

A relaxing place, frequented by expats, is **La Pilule**, a sheltered beach area 5km downstream from Niamey. This was the location of the second FIMA fashion event in 2000 (see *Public holidays and festivals*, page 78).

For other river trip options, see box *River trips between Ayorou and Gaya*, pages 118–19.

BOUBON Around 25km from Niamey along the same Route du Tillabéri, is the village of Boubon. Wednesday (market day) is when Boubon is at its liveliest, but on any other day the village is worth a visit if only to admire the pottery, for which Boubon is perhaps best known.

As Boubon is only 5km from Relais Kanazi VSD, you could opt to take a taxi to the Relais, find a pirogue to take you upstream to Boubon (one hour by motorised pirogue), visit Boubon and take public transport back to Niamey. Finding a minibus or *taxi-brousse* leaving in this direction should be no problem until early in the evening. However, finding public transport from the Relais is more

Joost Brouwer

The irrigation areas around Niamey are good for birdwatching. You can take the road to Kollo and on a bit to Sibéri and turn to the irrigation areas along the river anywhere. Especially good is the Saga irrigation area, only 7km from the centre of Niamey. Take the Kollo road and 1–2km past Saga, turn right where you see a canal with a large pumping station at the other end or take a bush taxi to this point. Just drive or walk around. There are lovely little wetlands in various low-lying places, although these are being reclaimed little by little. More than 110 species have been recorded here, including purple swamp-hen *Porphyrio porphyrio* and Allen's gallinule *P. alleni*, greater painted-snipe *Rostratula benghalensis* and great snipe *Gallinago media*, as well as bee-eaters, rollers and kingfishers.

You can also go to the Goudel irrigation area on the western side of town. Drive or take a taxi to Goudel and turn left into the irrigation area either just before or a bit after Hotel les Rôniers. The irrigation area on the right bank (*rive droite*) immediately to the south of the Kennedy Bridge in Niamey is also quite nice and within walking distance from the hotels in the centre of town. Just check about walking back to your hotel after dark (see box *Dangers and annoyances*, page 107).

Good bush and tigerbush habitat (see box *Tigerbush*, page 6) can be found along the sealed road to Torodi and Ouagadougou. On the Torodi road there are three small hills just beyond the checkpoint outside Niamey, not rich in species but they may provide fox kestrel *Falco alopex*, spotted eagle owl *Bubo africanus*, plain nightjar *Caprimulgus inornatus* and blackstart *Cercomela melanura*. Further along the same road 15km out of town, there is excellent tigerbush with a good chance of seeing eg: Saville's bustard *Eupodotis savilei*. During the rainy season you will no doubt hear this species' piping call long before you see it. You may also see quail-plover *Ortyxelos meiffreni* or bronze-winged courser *Rhinoptilus chalcopterus*.

Just before Kobadié there is a lovely wetland a couple of hundred metres off the road on the west side. Park your car or hop off a bush taxi before the bridge just north of the town. Keep in mind that the wetland is not permanent.

At 100km from Niamey, centred on the border village of Makalondi along the main road to Ouagadougou (Burkina Faso), there are a number of wetlands and temporary watercourses: the wetlands of the Goroubi River, Balla Foulbé wetland (25km to the northeast along the road to Tamou) and the Koulbou wetlands (10km southeast of Makalondi). Some 310 species have been recorded in the Makalondi district alone. The area is not really in the vicinity of Niamey, but as the sealed road is good, the Makalondi district is still within fairly easy reach from the capital. It is frequented by public transport, but distances between wetland areas are considerable, so it is best to hire a vehicle. During the dry season, most roads are accessible without the use of a 4x4.

complicated as you'd have to walk back to the mainroad first. See also *Chapter 4, Boubon,* page 115.

BALEYARA Sunday is market day in **Baleyara**, approximately 100km to the east of Niamey along the Route de Filingué. There are no facilities, but you will always find a bite to eat and public transport to and from Niamey should be no problem (see *Getting there and away,* page 96).

KOURE A day trip to **Kouré**, where the last herds of giraffe in west Africa can be spotted, is another highly recommended excursion. For more information on this option, see *Kouré and the Dallol Bosso Partial Reserve,* page 133.

'W' NATIONAL PARK Though this national park definitely merits a multiple-day visit, at only 150km from the capital, the **Parc National du W** provides an extraordinary opportunity to go on a game drive, see some elephants and even lions, and return to the capital to go nightclubbing, all on the same day. For more information, see *'W' National Park,* page 122.

Sodom apple, Calotropis procera

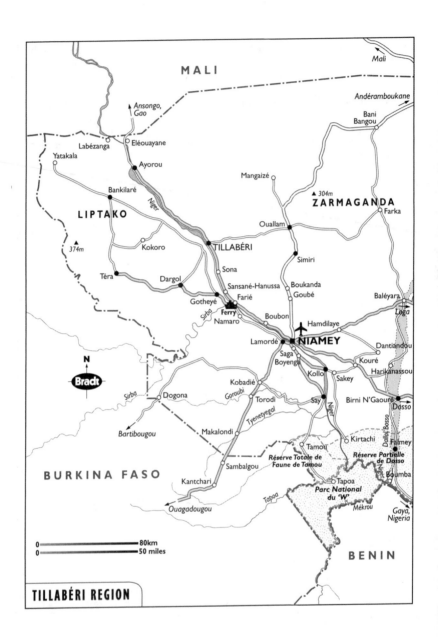

TILLABÉRI REGION

4

Tillabéri

The region of Tillabéri is the westernmost of Niger, wedged in between Mali to the north and Burkina Faso to the southwest and girding the capital Niamey. Two main traffic arteries run parallel through this region: the first is the RN1 – the tarred road leading to the Malian border – and the second is the river Niger. Different ethnic groups have settled down here, the majority of them Djerma-Songhay (see *Ethnic groups,* page 27), while nomadic people like the Peul, Bellah and also Tuareg and their livestock migrate from the arid northern side – the Zermaganda Plateau – to the river during the dry season. Not only is human life abundant along the river, but the water also attracts many aquatic birds, while hippo are frequently seen on certain sections of the river Niger.

To the south of the river Niger, in the Torodi and Tera regions, are many wetlands. In a country where arid landscape prevails, these wetlands are unsuspected jewels of great environmental importance. For visitors, the attraction of the wetlands lies in the presence of many bird species (see *Chapter 1,* pages 6–8 for information on wetlands, IBAs and birds).

Continuing east, the river Niger soon diverts from the RN1 towards the extreme south of the region. Before reaching the Beninese border, the waterway meanders in the shape of the letter 'W', and it is this particular shape that gave the 'W' National Park in this southern corner its name. In the whole of west Africa, there is no natural environment as densely inhabited by wildlife as this park, which straddles the borders of and spreads out deep into both Benin and Burkina Faso.

All these destinations lie within easy reach of Niamey, and some could be visited as multiple-day trips with the capital as a home base. In reality, one could spend weeks exploring the beauty of the region and still not see it all. Strangely enough, this far west of Niger sees very few visitors every year, though their numbers are on the rise.

BOUBON

At only 25km from Niamey, the village of Boubon is easily accessible both by road (see *Niamey,* page 97) and by river (see *Excursions from Niamey,* page 111). The riverine location is very appealing, but the real attraction that has earned Boubon a solid reputation, is pottery.

Traditionally, this is uniquely a female affair, performed by Bouzou and Djerma women. The rough material is taken from the river's edge, then kneaded and moulded by hand into various household objects. When the women have produced enough jars, pots and bowls, the dried objects are collectively baked in enormous open pits. The most striking products are the *canaries*: huge, pot-bellied water containers with white decorations. As the baked terracotta is slightly porous, the water inside these bulky jars slowly evaporates through the skin of the *canarie*, cooling the water down to a refreshing temperature.

A Swiss woman, who moved to Boubon in the early 1990s, has developed new interpretations of this craft. Through a combination of the traditional and modern techniques and shapes, she has introduced an original style that fits well within the existing elements.

The potters, their meticulously decorated utensils and works of art are omnipresent in Boubon. The best day to visit Boubon is Wednesday when the weekly market attracts people from the whole region.

TILLABERI

With just over 16,000 inhabitants (2001), Tillabéri is the smallest regional capital in Niger. Most activity of this friendly town is centred along the thoroughfare and the riverbank, and the market street connecting the two. While it is not a striking place, the charming and hospitable people make up for this. Conveniently located along the main road, Tillabéri makes a good halting place especially on Sundays, when the regional market brings the town alive. It could also be a starting point for a four–five-day journey along the river, as the section between Tillabéri and Ayorou is particularly beautiful.

GETTING THERE AND AWAY Vehicles from Niamey to Tillabéri leave from the **Autogare de Wadata** along the Route du Tillabéri (CFA1,500–1,800). From Tillabéri, public transport to Niamey and Ayarou is frequent until late in the afternoon. Vehicles shuttle up and down the main road, looking for passengers, but you could also go to the **Autogare de Tillabéri** and wait there. The journey to Niamey takes 2½–3 hours.

For onward transport to **Ansongo** and **Gao** (Mali), a converted SNTV truck passes every Monday and Friday between 09.00–10.00 (see *Ayorou*, page 118). It is not a bad idea to make a booking through the Niamey office to ensure not all seats are taken. The truck stops not far from the junction to the city hall and the fare to Gao is CFA7,500.

Transport by public pirogue is another option. The fare to Niamey is CFA2,500. Public pirogues are often very fully laden so do not expect this journey to be comfortable. You will find compensation, though, in the pleasure of travelling with Nigériens. The journey will take up most of the day.

WHERE TO STAY, EAT AND DRINK The only accommodation in Tillabéri is **Hotel Restaurant Bar la Girafe** (❄ 71 13 20). At the time of research it was being thoroughly upgraded and extended to a total of 15 rooms. The first results looked promising and it should be a comfortable hotel by the time you read this. The self-contained air-conditioned rooms cost CFA15,000 for a single and CFA17,500 for a double. The restaurant and bar are open daily. Meals are best ordered in advance, though some basic meals can always be arranged when the cook is around.

Restaurant Koubeini is a simple, friendly open-air restaurant – serving African food – near the city hall.

OTHER PRACTICALITIES There is a **post office**, but Tillabéri has no banks.

WHAT TO SEE AND DO

Market Sunday is market day, and apart from the food market, there is a cattle market past Hotel la Girafe and the *autogare*.

Festival de l'Eau The second **Festival de l'Eau** took place in March 2005. This festival – a sporting and cultural *rencontre* with participants of many west African

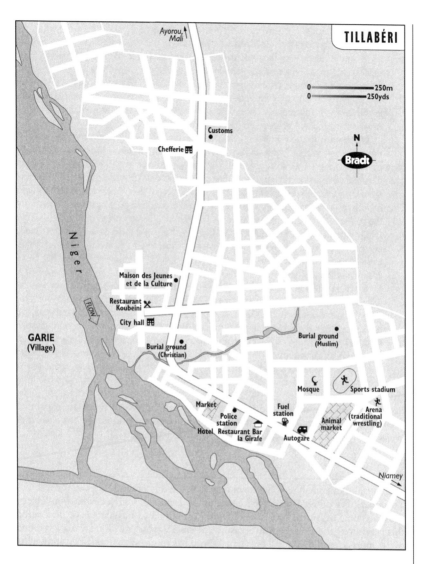

TILLABÉRI

Ayorou, Mali

0 — 250m
0 — 250yds

N

Brandt

Customs

Chefferie

N i g e r

FLOW

GARIE
(Village)

Maison des Jeunes
et de la Culture

Restaurant
Koubeini

City hall

Burial ground
(Christian)

Burial ground
(Muslim)

Mosque

Sports stadium

Market

Police
station

Fuel
station

Hotel Restaurant Bar
la Girafe

Autogare

Animal
market

Arena
(traditional
wrestling)

Niamey

countries – stages theatre, storytelling, music, ritual performances, conferences and watersports. Enquire at the Centre Culturel Franco-Nigérien, as they should be able to inform you about future stagings. See also *Public holidays and festivals,* page 74.

River Niger Along the waterfront it is possible to find a pirogue to take you across the river or to go for a longer trip. This is not the place to be looking for hippo, but the riverine landscape has plenty of other things to offer, like many different bird species (see *Ayorou*, page 118), rice paddies, cattle wading or crossing, small villages and hamlets. These are always attractive to visit, but especially on market days. **Ialouali** is just across the river, market day is Saturday and the fare by public pirogue is just CFA200. The villages of **Sakoré** (Monday market day) and **Mehana** (Wednesday market day) are within reach of a day trip. In some villages – eg: Tchoungalmé, Mousayekeré, Kandadji – some women have tastefully

As life in this region is so much dominated by the river Niger, some of the liveliest travel destinations are to be found along the banks of the river. It would be a real shame not to spend some time here, and the most comfortable way to travel is by pirogue. It means being able to cross to the other side, but also to approach the wildlife quietly while taking in the whole landscape in a most relaxing manner. Meanwhile, it isn't complicated to organise a combined boating and hiking trip.

Upstream to the northwest from Niamey, the main road follows the river while at the other bank a good dirt road also sees frequent transport to and from the capital. This means there is always a way out and you could even plan as you go along. Just do not expect to find any accommodation in any of the villages, so you would have to be fully self-supporting and put up with a total lack of luxury. There are no toilets, no showers and no restaurants in between towns. For more information on this part of the river, see the relevant sections of *Tillabéri* (page 117) and *Ayorou* (pages 119–20).

Downstream to the southeast of Niamey, the river soon bends towards Benin, away from the road. Therefore, the above also applies here. However, once you reach the 'W' National Park, there are a few good options to spend the night. For more information on this part of the river, see *'W' National Park*, page 122.

Travelling with a **guide** makes absolute sense in either direction, especially if you wish to visit some of the numerous villages along the river or if you wish to hike in the 'W' National Park. Certain towns and villages have seen a good number of tourists through the years, but the further away you get from these, the more likely it is you enter fairly untrodden ground. As the villagers – especially the children – have not yet seen that many foreigners, they will follow you, touch you, try to communicate with you in words or pantomime. This is a very touching experience, and an overwhelming one, too. With so many people around you in

decorated both the inside and the outside of their houses in relief, then painted them in bold colours. For more information on riverine options, see box *River trips between Ayorou and Gaya* above and *Ayorou* below, pages 119–20.

AYOROU

At first sight, this small regional town may look like any other. However, it combines a number of favourable factors that make this an attractive tourist destination. Expats, the occasional organised tour and a handful of individual travellers have discovered this pearl along the river. Ayorou is easily accessible by road, the Sunday market is one of the most colourful you will ever see, Ayorou has accommodation (albeit somewhat derelict), it is a good starting point for trips along one of the prettiest stretches of the river Niger, and chances to see hippo are almost guaranteed.

GETTING THERE AND AWAY At the *autogare* minibuses (19 seats) and station wagons (9 seats) leave daily for **Niamey**. The fare to Tillabéri (85km) is CFA1,500 while the journey to Niamey (190km) costs CFA3,000.

From Ayorou, it is also possible to travel to **Ansongo** and **Gao** (Mali). For this journey you need stamina as it is a two-day and at times very rough journey. The least uncomfortable option is with SNTV. Every Monday and Thursday a converted truck leaves from Niamey to attempt the crossing, and it will pass through Ayorou mid-morning. The lesser option is to find a Land-Rover or truck heading the same way. Your best chances to find a place on board any of the vehicles are to look for the driver on a Sunday. It is basically a matter of asking around, as there is no fixed schedule. When you are lucky, you will get a seat in the

an unfamiliar, traditional environment, a guide would keep you from making unintended mistakes, while he would also be able to be your interpreter and to introduce you to the *chef du village* or a teacher at the local school. See also box *Giving presents*, pages 86–7. When you travel downstream and intend to visit the 'W' National Park, it should need no explanation why a trained guide and even an official ranger would be useful.

To **organise a trip**, there are countless possibilities, as you can opt for a public pirogue or a private one, in which case you can make up your own programme, whether it be one-way or a return trip. You could start from Niamey and go all the way upstream or downstream, then come back by public or arranged transport. Or you could start from a village or town along the main road, taking a boat for the day only. If your French is good enough or if your guide is a reliable chap who can make all arrangements, it is quite possible to organise a tailor-made trip yourself. The price you would have to pay for a pirogue, a boatman and a guide depends on many factors: Is the pirogue motorised or not? Are fuel and food included? Is the pirogue returning empty? How many clients are travelling? Distance? Time? As an indication, prices for a pirogue often start from CFA5,000 per person per hour for a short trip, and should not exceed CFA40,000 per day for the whole pirogue, unless you are many. Some boatmen, however, will boldly ask double or triple that. The fee for the guide is not included, and fuel needs to be discussed and is always a sensitive item.

While experienced travellers will find organising this kind of journey reasonably easy, if you feel unsure about venturing out on your own, there is another way: have a travel agency take care of all the logistics, even buying the supplies and organising the cooking. Several travel agencies in Niamey have experience in this relatively underdeveloped sector of the tourist market. Booking through one of them ensures that you can really lie back, enjoy the view, and leave the work to the crew. See *Niamey*, page 105.

cabin of a Land Rover (CFA8,500), because the alternative is usually a place at the back on top of the merchandise (CFA7,500). Yet, it could still be worse, as most passengers opt for the cheapest: a place amongst 40 to 60 fellow travellers at the back of a lorry. This means holding on for dear life and putting up with the sun, the wind and the dust for as long as it takes – and of course the cold of the night in the cooler months and a couple of hours of sleep somewhere along the road. The price: a mere CFA2,500–3,000 for Ansongo and CFA4,000 for Gao. Departure of these vehicles is usually early on Monday morning.

Travelling to Mali by **pirogue** is also possible, again especially after the market. Some boats leave on Sunday afternoon straight after the market, the last ones no later than early Monday morning. It is essential to enquire well beforehand, and this is best done directly in the port. Your chances of getting ripped off are very realistic when you use a mediator who is used to dealing with tourists. It would help if you can speak some French or find a reliable person to translate for you. The fare for a seat aqueezed into one of the huge *barques* should not exceed CFA5,000 for the few days' journey to Gao. The fare will increase when you choose a smaller pirogue with fewer bales and livestock on board.

Thomas and Bethany Eberle, two adventurous travellers I met in Niger, took the journey in the opposite direction from Gao to Ayorou:

> There is another, more rickety possibility once weekly by two private Gao companies with truck buses with no glass in the window openings (± two days and not for the faint hearted), feasible probably only in the dry season since at two of the wadi crossings bridges were completely down. Don't forget to bring lots of water. We wanted a quicker and more

comfortable option by renting a 4x4 with driver through a local priest, but finally ended up with a vehicle without licence plates and proper insurance which was then impounded at the Nigérien border. Not finding any other vehicle there, we rented a cheap pirogue with three paddlers down the Niger that took three hours, saw a bunch of hippo on the way (with a baby hippo resting on her mother's nose) and arrived right at sunset on the shores of the nice Hotel Amenokal in Ayorou.

Thomas and Bethany do not fail to remark that 'the area might still be troubled by bandits, so get information beforehand'. Indeed the section between the border and Ansongo has seen some 'incidents' over the years, quieter times alternating with troubled times. See *Safety*, page 59.

WHERE TO STAY, EAT AND DRINK The entrance of **Hotel Amenokal** (↘ 71 14 24) is rather plain, but the beauty of this establishment lies around the back: a shady garden by the waterside, a lovely place for a drink while watching pirogues go by. What a shame that this hotel has been left to degrade to a pitiful state, though there is always hope that plans to improve it may materialise. Of the 25 rooms, those without air conditioning cost CFA8,000–10,000 for a single/double, and air-conditioned rooms are CFA12,000–14,000. Camping costs CFA3,000 per person. Meals are available for CFA3,500 or CFA5,000 for a three-course menu. You are allowed to bring your own picnic, in which case you pay CFA2,500 for a table for four on the waterfront. As there are no real alternatives in Ayorou, the restaurant and terrace are sometimes booked for groups or seminars. Should you wish to make a booking, call the above number and ask for the *gérant de l'hotel*, as the number belongs to the neighbours.

Most of all on market days, there will be plenty of freshly cooked streetfood to choose from. Consider Ayorou a testing ground to try local titbits.

WHAT TO SEE AND DO
Market Along the waterfront, hidden on small squares behind houses and shops along the main street, at open places all around the small town, Ayorou transforms into one big market every Sunday. It is almost like a funfair, as you have to wind your way between people, beasts and stalls to gradually discover the many corners, odours, colours and faces of this market.

River trips Upstream or downstream from Ayorou, this must be one of the prettiest stretches of the river Niger in the whole country. Downstream, islets and huge granite boulders split up the waterway into smaller channels and mild rapids. Temporary dwellings are put up on the small islands and cattle are left to graze there in the dry season, while human activity along the riverbanks announces the next semi-permanent settlement or village. Some of these villages are very pretty with banco architecture (sometimes with extravagant and colourful decorations) and bulbous granaries that seem to play a trick on our sense of proportion. Upstream, the river widens and deepens, allowing bigger boats or *barques* to navigate here. Towards the village of Firgoun, around 10km from Ayorou, big groups of hippo reside throughout the year. Your chances of actually spotting the animals are very good indeed. Should you continue towards the Malian border, the village of Koutougou is worth a visit to admire the beautifully decorated houses.

River trips can be organised through travel agencies in Niamey (see page 105) but it is possible to just find a *piroguier* in the port of Ayorou. There are no fixed rates, but note that local people are very much aware that foreigners are keen on taking a river trip, resulting in much-inflated fares. It is difficult to give an indication, though, as much depends on the number of your party, the size of the boat, whether or not it is motorised, the time and distance you are bargaining for. For around four people, an average-sized motorised pirogue including the fuel, for at least half a day, expect to pay anything from CFA20,000 to CFA40,000.

Look for a guide at Hotel Amenokal; at least one of them speaks a fair bit of English. However, many of them do overcharge, and even if you manage to cut down the price, it is not a very good start to any trip. On the other hand, travelling with a guide does make sense in the area (see box *Giving presents,* pages 86–7). Organising the boat through the guides at Hotel Amenokal obviously also boosts the fare. The fare for a four-day return trip to Gao (Mali) they quoted me, was CFA700,000 (guide's fee included, but food not included) which is way over the top. In the port, the first asking price for the same journey in a very small, wobbly pirogue, was CFA260,000 one-way, all inclusive (but no guide). I declined further negotiations. I was then asked an outrageous CFA40,000 for a couple of square inches on a huge *barque*, heavily laden with dozens of other passengers, who paid a mere CFA3,500 for the same journey. Finally someone proposed CFA80,000 one-way, all inclusive in a medium-sized, comfortable, motorised pirogue with far more space than people but no guide. A reasonable price at last.

Birding There are at least 33 recorded waterbird species along this section of the river Niger, but most likely that number will rise after more structured counts. Species include knob-billed ducks, *Sarkidiornis melanotos*; white-faced whistling ducks, *Dendrocygna viduata*; black crowned cranes, *Balearica pavonina*; river prinia *Prinia fluviatitlis*; as well as different heron species, plovers, kingfishers, cormorants and the African jacana.

TERA

Not many people travel as far as Téra, and the rough stretch of road from the junction off the Route de Tillabéri to Téra certainly didn't encourage travellers. In recent years, this section of road has been tarred all the way, improving the accessibilty of the town. Wies Buysrogge from the Netherlands provided the following information on Téra:

Téra is a small town of about 20,000 inhabitants (2001) 170 km northwest of Niamey. It is a typical Nigérien village, with a calm, pleasant and friendly atmosphere. It is situated on one of the tributaries of the Niger, while a perennial dam turns Téra into a beautiful lakeside town. The dam receives a fresh water supply during and after the rains. Lake views are great, especially at sunset, with many different species of birds flying over.

GETTING THERE AND AWAY Téra is easily reached by a very good tarred road; the toll to Téra is CFA500. The *Bac Farié* (ferry at Farié, 70km from Niamey) crossing the river Niger could however cause some delay. The ferry runs every day at hourly intervals from 07.00–12.00 and 14.00–20.00 and costs CFA1,000 for a small vehicle. Minibuses leave daily from the **Autogare Route du Tillabéri** in Niamey (CFA3,000).

WHERE TO STAY, EAT AND DRINK The best option is to stay with the Morey family. Their **air-conditioned rooms** with fridge (CFA9,000) were newly built in 2004 and were of high standard at the time. Ask for directions at the petrol station near the *grand marché*. At the *campement* the **bungalows** (CFA3,500 with fan) are a bit run down. You can order simple meals for around CFA1,500; soft drinks and beer are also available.

Restaurant L'amitié has an extensive menu, though in reality the choice is probably limited to various combinations of pasta, rice, chicken, beef or eggs. Vegetables, other than canned peas, are a rare commodity. Meals cost between CFA500 and CFA1,500.

For some freshly prepared **streetfood**, go to the small market (*petit marché*), where you can have a full plate of rice, beans or pasta with sauce for as little as CFA100 in the evenings.

There are two **bars**: Le Jardin which has a nice green setting, and the bar at the *campement* which can be a bit noisy.

PRACTICALITIES For food and drinks (including bottled water), there is a small but well-stocked **supermarket**. Fresh bread is available all morning. To get directions for this shop, ask for the owner Alzuma.

WHAT TO SEE AND DO Thursday is **market day** and the town is packed with people, donkeys and a whole array of goods (pottery, leather, wooden furniture). While people start trickling in during the morning, the market is at its busiest from around noon onwards. The town offers no great entertainment at night. At the Maison de Jeunesse et de la Culture (MJC) videos are played several nights a week.

If you want to explore the lake, birdlife and activities along the shores, it is possible to rent a pirogue. Just ask any of the fishermen, and expect to pay around CFA1,000 for one to two hours.

EXCURSIONS FROM TERA There are many small **villages** well worth a visit: Bankilaré (60km) which has mainly a Tuareg population; Mehana on the banks of the river Niger; or Diagourou at just 15km from Téra with its Peul population. In Doumba (last small village before Tera on tarred road) you can buy great wooden furniture for CFA500–2,000 (small tables, chairs, etc).

'W' NATIONAL PARK

Though less than a century ago many parts of west Africa were teeming with wildlife, nowadays this part of the African continent isn't much associated with the presence of game. It is a sad and largely irreversible reality that, because of various factors, most of the larger animals have been wiped out. Pockets where wildlife roams free still exist, but these are usually small, fragile ecosystems under constant threat of further degradation.

One area that stands out for its relatively well-balanced ecosystem, including many large mammals, is the Parc National du W or **'W' National Park**. This park takes its name from the local W-shaped bend in the river Niger and covers 220,000ha or 2,200km². The 'W' National Park is actually the northernmost section of the **'W' Regional Transboundary Park**, an exceptionally large conglomerate of three national parks that straddles the borders of Niger, Burkina Faso and Benin and covers a total of 10,242km². Beyond any doubt, this vast area is the largest natural haven for a rich diversity of wildlife in the whole of west Africa. It is therefore encouraging to see how crucial efforts are made here to try and beat the odds, and preserve these parks and their wildlife for future generations.

HISTORY When European cartographers first put the region roughly covering what is now known as **'W' Regional Transboundary Park** on the map, they labelled it 'vast, uninhabited spaces'. The fact that they found so little human presence was linked to certain diseases that kill both human beings and their cattle.

Joost Brouwer

The Kokoro and Namga wetlands are located halfway between the River Niger and Téra, 40km from the latter. To reach these wetlands, turn north just before Téra (RN4) towards Bankilaré. After about 25km, near Foneko, turn right onto the road going east to Kokoro. Kokoro wetland is a further 20km on the right, while Namga wetland is another 12km further east.

Kokoro wetland is a large, shallow wetland occupying part of an ancient valley surrounded by orange sand dunes, some granite outcrops of Pre-cambrian age and flat-topped hills carved from Tertiary sediments. It is a semi-permanent wetland, containing water seven to 12 months of the year. At its greatest extent it is 13km long and occupies 2,100ha. It is a lush, brilliant green flooded pasture, studded with birds and surrounded by palm trees, fields and bush vegetation. Towards the end of the dry season, it is heavily used by cattle, which affects the vegetation through overgrazing and trampling. Kokoro wetland is used for fishing using cast nets and fixed lines, but not too extensively. The sand dunes threaten the wetland at its northern border and have been the target of a dune-fixation programme. **Namga wetland** is much smaller in size, and has an abundant aquatic vegetation, including water lilies. To the southern edge, there are areas of woodland containing several species including acacia and desert date. Both wetlands are owned by the government and may be used by the population under supervision. A total of 54 species of waterbird have been recorded, and these include large numbers of purple swamp hen, *Porphyrio porphyrio*; fulvous whistling ducks, *Dendrocygna bicolor*; white-faced whistling ducks, *Dendrocygna viduata*; spur-winged geese, *Plectropterus gambensis* and the glossy ibis, *Plegadis falcinellus*.

Onchocercosis or river blindness, a disease caused by a parasite that first blinds and then kills people, was commonplace. At the same time tsetse flies, which can transfer different forms of trypanosomiasis or sleeping sickness to cattle and people, kept the nomadic cattle herders well away from this zone. Because health conditions were unfavourable to people and their livestock, wildlife could thrive, as its natural habitat was left almost untouched and hunting was done only on a relatively low scale.

Recognising the uniqueness of the ecosystem, the colonisers classified the zone Parc Réfuge as early as 1926. It marked the beginning of a whole chain of classifications, and in 1954, still well before independence of the three countries concerned, the three areas involved were classified as Parcs Nationaux du W du Niger – with 'du Niger' referring to the river rather than to the country. Various measures to reduce the impact of the use, and abuse, of natural resources were taken. The most intrusive measure, causing a terrible stir but put to effect all the same, was to remove the sparse population from the zone. Within a couple of years the last remaining villages in the area had been forcefully relocated to the outskirts of the national park, thus creating a 'vast, uninhabited space' indeed.

Through various other reserves, these Parcs Nationaux du W du Niger are connected towards the south to the Arli National Park in Burkina Faso and Pendjari National Park in Benin. The whole complex of reserves and their immediate surroundings is now referred to as the **Complexe Ecologique du WAP** (Ecological Complex of 'W', Arli and Pendjari) and covers approximately 50,000km. In Niger this ecosystem is protected through the following reserves: 'W' National Park (220,000ha, as mentioned), the Tamou Total Fauna Reserve (77,000ha, a buffer zone with land use restrictions), the Dosso Partial Reserve

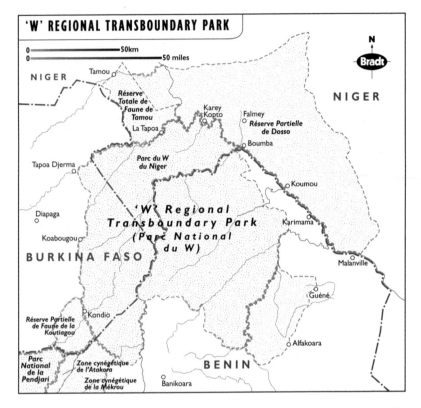

(306,000ha, a transition area with few land use restrictions) and, furthest from 'W' National Park, the giraffe area of approximately 107,000ha (see *Kouré and the Dallol Bosso Partial Reserve*, page 133). The 'W' National Park has been designated both a UNESCO World Heritage Site and a Ramsar Wetland of International Importance. All four reserves together form the UNESCO 'W Man and Biosphere Reserve'. There are no fences around any of these areas.

ACTIVE CONSERVATION MEASURES/ECOPAS As all over west Africa ecosystems are rapidly degrading and wildlife is being reduced in numbers or even wiped out, this WAP patchwork of national parks and reserves must be considered the largest refuge with an abundance of wildlife in the whole of west Africa. This doesn't mean, however, that this Noah's Ark can now happily continue to exist without further human intervention. Active conservation measures were, and continue to be, very necessary.

Despite the fact that the population had been settled in the periphery of the park in the mid-1950s, the pressure on the natural resources was still on. Firstly because of the explosive growth of the population at some 3% per year, which meant that from the edges of the park poaching and clearing vegetation for agriculture were still commonplace. In addition, the serious droughts of the 1970s and 1080s urged the nomadic Peul and their cattle to move deeper into the park, despite the dangers that lurked behind every bush: tsetse flies they had to put up with, but predators they could hunt down and kill.

Since the beginning of the 1990s, Niger, Benin and Burkina Faso have been looking at ways to join forces in the battle against further degradation of the Parcs

Nationaux du W du Niger. Naming these parks World Heritage Sites and signing the *'Déclaration de la Tapoa'* in 2000 were two of what were many important steps showing at least the will to preserve the three parks. The real action started when the ECOPAS project was initiated in 2001 (ECOPAS stands for Ecosystèmes Protégés en Afrique Sahélienne). At that time, the three parks were united under their current name: Parc Régional Transfrontalier du W or **'W' Regional Park**. The project, supported and monitored by the European Union, was created to conserve this park in all three countries. Not only does this programme intend to stop further degradation, but ECOPAS actually aims to reverse the damaging effects of the past in ways that are beneficial to the population living in areas close to the transboundary park. Simultaneously, ECOPAS plans to improve the infrastructure of the park to attract a higher number of visitors, taking into account the need to minimise the long-term effects on the environment and, again, trying to involve the local population.

A few years into the ECOPAS project, some of the goals stipulated for the park have already been achieved on the Nigérien side, while many more plans are in the process of implementation or lie anxiously waiting to be executed. These future plans include improvement and expansion of the road system; more picnic facilities and accommodation within the boundaries of the park; options to explore the park by mountain bike or on horseback; 4x4 rental from La Tapoa; and training of more local guides. In addition to this, it will be made possible to cross the borders between Niger, Benin and Burkina Faso within the boundaries of the 'W' Regional Park.

ARCHAEOLOGICAL SITES Throughout the 'W' Regional Park, traces of ancient human presence have been discovered. In the Nigérien part of the park alone, over 100 archaeological sites have been identified, and these are being researched by the Institut des Récherches et Sciences Humaines (IRSH) in Niamey. Thus far, the research has revealed that certain zones – like the Mékrou Valley – were inhabited as early as 200,000 years ago, during the early Stone Age. Many objects, such as bolas, bifacial stone tools and polyhedrons indicate the presence of *Homo ergaster*. Other finds, related to the presence of our direct ancestors, *Homo sapiens*, include polished stone arrow heads and axe heads, as well as pottery fragments. A very striking find was that of a terracotta figurine statue, affectionately baptised 'the Venus of W'.

The archaeological sites are not indicated in the park, nor are they open to the public. In fact, the location of the sites is known only to those involved in the research because it is feared that the sites will be destroyed by looters, as has been the fate of many archaeological sites in the northern regions of Niger.

GEOLOGY, FLORA AND FAUNA
Joost Brouwer

Landscape and vegetation The Nigérien part of the park lies within the northern Sudan zone, and usually receives 500–800mm of rainfall per year. The rain generally falls in 30–50 rain events in the period May–October, with a marked peak in August. Virtually no rain falls at all during the rest of the year. This rainfall pattern and the underlying geology largely determine vegetation patterns in the park. The altitude of the park varies between 180m (along the Niger River) and 338m (Yeriyombou). Average altitude is about 250m. Large parts of the park are quite rocky, caused by the outcropping of metamorphic Pre-cambrian rocks such as quartzites, schists and gneisses, rocks more than 500 million years old that form the greatly eroded northern end of the Atakora range that starts in Togo. These rocky areas mostly have a wooded savanna vegetation.

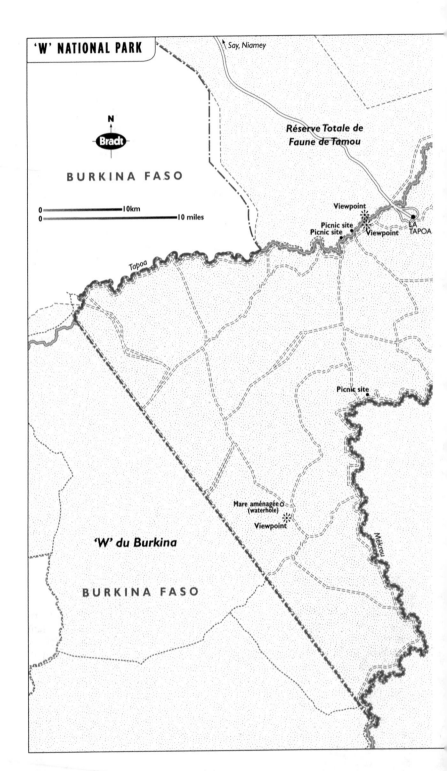

'W' NATIONAL PARK

Say, Niamey

N
Bradt

BURKINA FASO

0 ——————10km
0 ——————10 miles

Réserve Totale de
Faune de Tamou

Tapoa

Viewpoint
Picnic site
Picnic site   Viewpoint   LA
                                    TAPOA

Picnic site

Mare aménagée
(waterhole)
Viewpoint

Mékrou

'W' du Burkina

BURKINA FASO

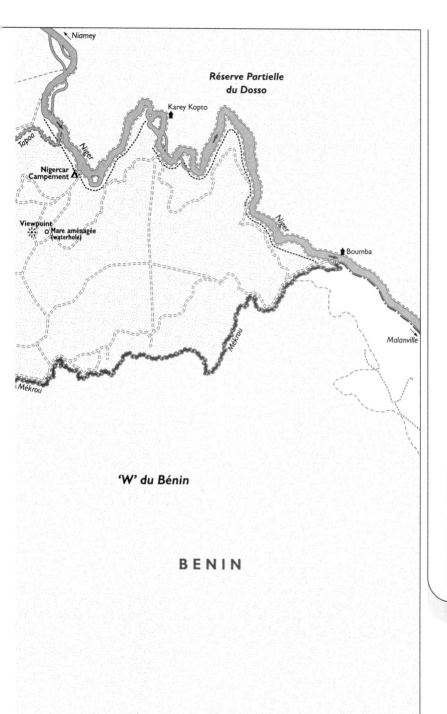

Réserve Partielle
du Dosso

Karey Kopto

Niger

Topoa

Nigercar
Campement

Viewpoint
Mare aménagée
(waterhole)

Niger

Boumba

Mékrou

Malanville

Mékrou

'W' du Bénin

BENIN

Source: ECOPAS – Niamey

In certain areas the Pre-cambrian rocks are overlain by Tertiary sediments, which give rise to the quite widespread, flat, laterite-capped plateaux in the park. On these plateaux the vegetation is mostly tall shrubs and short trees, up to about 6m in height, mostly deciduous but with a few (thorny) evergreens. There is also a small amount of grassland. Along the three rivers there are Quaternary alluvial floodplains. Along the river Niger these contain some stands of palm trees, while along the Mékrou and Tapoa there are nice gallery forests. There are also a number of ephemeral pools and wetlands in the upland areas.

Close to 500 species of plant have been found in the park to date. Many, many more remain to be discovered without doubt. Common tree species include the baobab *Adansonia digitata,* a tree with a very bulky trunk and which looks as if it has been turned upside down, with its roots sticking up in the air; the desert date *Balanites aegyptiaca,* a very thorny tree you should never park your car under; the camel's foot *Ptiliostigma reticulatum,* named after the shape of its leaves; the deleb palm *Borassus aethiopum* along the river, on whose leaves palm swifts make their nests; and the kapok tree *Bombax costatum* which has lovely orange flowers on the bare tree during the middle of the dry season, from December through February.

Although the park gives a flattish impression overall, there are a number of nice lookout points, especially along the rivers Tapoa and Niger.

Wildlife

Mammals When you plan a visit to 'W' National Park, don't expect vast grassy plains teeming with large herbivores like you might see in east Africa. Because the vegetation of 'W' is much more shrubby, you have to look harder to find your species. Many visitors feel, however, that having to really search for game is very rewarding in its own way. There is little doubt that you will indeed be satisfied: 'W' has an amazing variety of large mammals, and controlled burning at the start of the dry season ensures that you will see quite a few of them.

More than 80 species of mammal have been recorded in the park, including a population of some 300 African elephants that wander down as far as northern Togo. There are also good numbers of African buffalo and species of antelope, ranging from small duikers and the very common kob and red-fronted gazelles to the very impressive roan antelope with its swept-back horns. Large carnivores include lion, leopard, cheetah and wild dog, but you have to be quite lucky to see any of these. You have a much better chance of seeing golden or side-striped jackals. In the river there are hippo, especially visible during the dry season, as well as all-but-invisible manatees. With only little effort you are likely to see three species of monkeys: vervet monkey, patas monkey and olive baboon. If you can arrange a night game drive using spotlights, you have a good chance to see bushbabies near La Tapoa, while there is a 50/50 chance of seeing a porcupine. You would be exceptionally lucky to spot an aardvark though.

For more information on the mammals of 'W' National Park, see the excellent illustrated book published by ECOPAS. It provides background information as well as a comprehensive description of 51 larger mammals. The book is available through ECOPAS in Niamey. For details, see pages 105 and 130.

Birds Birding in 'W' National Park is excellent. Majestic Rüppell's vultures and marabou storks, tiny black-faced firefinches and sunbirds; vocal helmeted guineafowl and vinaceous doves, secretive ground hornbills and Pell's fishing owls; colourful African bee-eaters and drab European warblers all these species and many more can be found in the park.

Of the 352 species of bird recorded up until 2000, 319 have been observed during the dry season and 252 during the wet season. The best months are

November and December, with over 230 species each. Even the quietest months, September and October, still boast a very worthwhile 180 species. Water adds considerably to species' richness: the Niger River habitat has the most species (263), the shrubland (88) and woodland (194) the fewest. In total, 82 species have been found breeding in the park, with a clear peak in June–July/August and a secondary peak in December–January.

The species you may see in the park vary from month to month: 32 species show wet-season, intra-African migration (from further south in Africa), 68 show dry-season, intra-African migration (from nearer the Sahara or waterbirds dispersing after breeding elsewhere), and 64 are at least partially dry-season migrants from both Europe and Asia. Certain northern migrants apparently oversummer in small numbers in the park as well, or arrive early and/or depart late.

The park forms the main Important Bird Area (IBA) in Niger for the Sudano-Guinean ecological zone, with 21 out of 25 key species recorded. These include violet turaco, red-throated bee-eater, white-winged swallow, white-fronted black chat, red-winged pytelia and black-faced firefinch. A number of Sahelian species, including Arabian and red-crested bustards and black scrub robin, can also be found, mostly during the dry season. In addition, there are quite large colonies of egrets in the interior of the park, which have never been properly censused.

For more information on the birds of the park, including a full species' list and references to relevant articles, see www.africanbirdclub.org/countries/Niger/ibas.html.

Other In addition to mammals and birds, the park also harbours many other animals. Success is not guaranteed, but you can search for Nile crocodiles (best chance at the dam in the Tapon River, just west of the entrance); Nile monitors (lizards that can reach 2m in length in the gorge below the hotel at Tapoa and also along the Mékrou); African spurred tortoises (anywhere in the park); and pythons (generally close to water). Only the tortoises you might approach, with care. Very little is known of other reptiles and amphibians. You must assume that any snake you come across is poisonous; these include puff adders and spitting cobras. However, the chances you will see any snake are small. The fish species found are typical of the river Niger and include various catfish, tilapia and carp, lungfish and Nile perch. As yet, very little is known of butterflies, dragonflies and other invertebrates in the park.

WHEN TO VISIT The 'W' National Park is open to visitors throughout the year. The beginning of December coincides with the start of the cooler months when temperatures are more moderate, which is deep into the dry season. In certain sections of the park some tall grasses will have been burnt (see opposite), thus creating open spaces as a side effect. However, the best game viewing is done when temperatures start soaring by the end of February, and when the lack of open water drives the animals to the rivers and the few watering holes around the park. A game park is no zoo and never provides any guarantees of spotting animals, but this is the time of the year when the whereabouts of the game get increasingly more predictable, as the animals roam in ever smaller circles near water.

With the start of the rainy season at some point in April or May, the park sees some significant changes. Many roads become inaccessible, so itineraries are of a more limited kind, while high numbers of insects can have an unpleasant effect on a journey into the park. The vegetation is at its lushest in the months following the rains, but it also means that game viewing becomes more of a lottery as the dense vegetation may obstruct clear views in places. On the plus side, big tortoises are often spotted during the rainy months as they move along the roads at a gentle pace.

ORGANISING YOUR TRIP The best way to explore the 'W' National Park is by **4x4 vehicle**. As the entrance to the park in La Tapoa is only 150km from Niamey (tarred as far as Say; count on roughly three hours driving), theoretically the visit could be considered a day trip. Many animals, including elephants, are regularly spotted not far inside the game park even during the daytime. However, you would miss out on the cooler early-morning hours when life in the bush switches from nocturnal to diurnal; often a good time to spot animals. Therefore it is preferable to spend at least one night in or near the park, allowing more time to explore the different zones of vegetation and at the same time increasing your chances of seeing a good diversity of game.

When you are driving your own vehicle, you can pick up a guide – which is compulsory – at the entrance gate and pay the entrance fees. Unless you are staying at one of the *campements* (where meals and drinks are available on request), you should bring a picnic. Always bring plenty of water, and take some extra in case you should have a serious breakdown. Meanwhile, several travel agencies in Niamey offer all-inclusive trips to the 'W' National Park.

Another option to visit the edge of the park is by **pirogue**. Starting from Niamey, it is possible to travel down the river Niger, following the W-shaped bends after which the park is named, and make use of the *campements* to spend the night. The river itself is not part of the game park, so no entrance fee is payable while you stay on the pirogue and disembark only at the opposite riverbank or at the Campement Nigercar. Birdlife along the river is very abundant and you may even spot some hippo, but overall you would be lucky to see any of the bigger animals. It is possible, though, to go for a gamewalk, usually starting from the Campement Nigercar in which case entrance fees would be payable. Even then chances to see lots of animals are limited, as the distance covered by foot is relatively short. Since a guide and an armed ranger are compulsory for a walk along one of the routes, a game walk has to be booked in advance. Therefore, a trip along the river is best organised through an agency (see *Niamey*, page 105).

The entrance fee is CFA8,000 for the first 24 hours for adults and CFA4,000 for each following day. Foreign residents and Nigériens pay CFA6,000/3,000 and CFA3,000/1,500 respectively. No fee is charged for the use of photographic equipment. For more information, check with the ECOPAS office in Niamey (✆ 72 53 48/59 34 03; e ecopas@intnet.ne).

WHERE TO STAY, EAT AND DRINK

⌂ **Relais Hotel La Tapoa** (35 rooms)
e hoteltapoa@hotmail.com. This is the only hotel in the vicinity of the park. While it is owned by the state, it has been run by the French travel agency Point Afrique since the end of 2005. This is good news, as Point Afrique intends to bring the dormant, dusty hotel back to life. According to reports in March 2006, the hotel has been upgraded to meet luxury standards, while the swimming pool overlooking the gorge of the River Tapoa is again filled with water. Views to the gorge are beautiful, even when the river stands dry (as is the case most of the year). All rooms are s/c, and those with fans cost CFA25,000 for a dbl, while the AC studios (bedroom, spacious sitting area and private terrace) cost CFA38,500. For more information and bookings, contact the above email address or enquire at Point

Afrique in Niamey (✆ 73 40 26/96 44 78/93 35 31).

⋀ **Campement Nigercar** This campsite with large, pitched tents with beds and mosquito nets is inside the park. The campsite is basic but adequate. Cold drinks are available and amenities include clean showers and flush toilets. From the campsite, river trips can be organised at CFA1,500 pp per hour in a motorised pirogue, or CFA500 pp per hour for a small pirogue. If you have the time, do not turn down this opportunity to enjoy the beauty, the quiet and the wildlife of the river Niger. Do not expect to see big mammals from the water, though you might be lucky. However, birds are plentiful and the vegetation is lush along the riverbanks. is at CFA12,500 pp HB (bed, breakfast and dinner). Note that this rate does not include the entrance fee to the park.

Across the river, hence outside the boundaries of the park, accommodation can be found in two villages, where two campements have been established in close co-operation with ECOPAS and the European Community (see pages 124–5). Visitors are urged to make bookings through a travel agency or at the gate in La Tapoa. The staff of the *campements* will then be informed through radio contact, the only means of communication available. This is essential when you are coming from the 'W' National Park, since you will have to cross the river and pirogues are stationed near to the villages. This would be the wrong side of the river and out of sight or hearing distance from where you would embark. However, when informed, a pirogue will be waiting for you at an agreed time. When you are travelling by car at the eastern side of the river or by pirogue and you have not made a booking, the *campement* may not be staffed on arrival, in which case you will have to report to the village first. For obvious reasons, meals have to be ordered in advance as well.

Å **Campement de Boumba** This *campement* is at the southern tip of the park, bordering Benin. The rooms have been constructed a little higher up the riverbank where the view is truly panoramic. Even the village of Boumba, some 3km away is visible. Facilities are similar to those in Karey Kopto, and the rates are the same. Most visitors prefer *pension complet* (FB) at CFA8,000 pp, which includes bed, breakfast, lunch and dinner. However, if you wish you can cook your own meals and pay CFA3,000 for accommodation only. *Pay CFA1,500 pp for a place to pitch your own tent.*

Å **Campement de Karey Kopto** Less than 1km away from the village, on a quiet and beautiful, secluded location on the riverbank, this was the first to be established. 7 huts with thatched roofs, dbl beds and mosquito netting have been prepared for visitors. Amenities are limited but do include refrigeration for cold soft drinks and beers, flush toilets and showers. On request, villagers will come over to perform traditional music, dances and storytelling. No price is fixed, but spectators are expected not to let the performers leave empty handed. Meanwhile, it is also possible to visit the village, meet the villagers and their plentiful offspring, visit the school and buy some souvenirs from the local artisans.

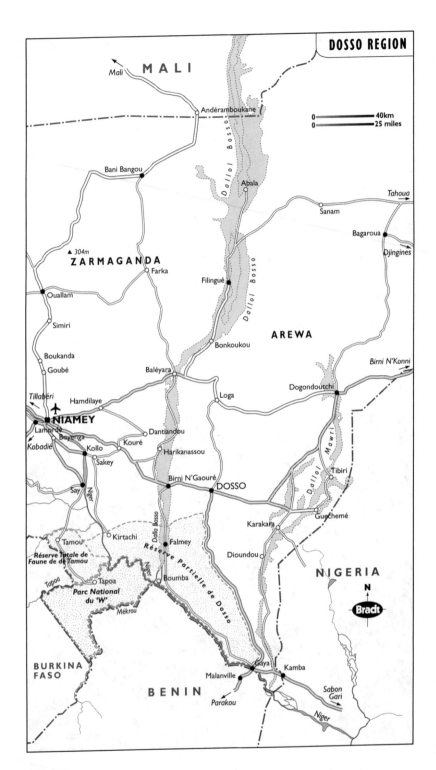

5

Dosso

Only 60km from Niamey, along the Route Nationale to the east and north, is Kouré. This small town is located just before the boundary of the region of Dosso, to the west of the Dallol Bosso Partial Reserve. This zone hides a treasure: the last viable herds of giraffe in west Africa. Kouré is frequented by visitors for this reason only, as it is the starting point to search for these free-roaming animals.

At Dosso, the regional capital, the road turning right leads to Gaya, Niger's southernmost town located at the Beninese border, and not far from Kamba at the Nigerian border. Meanwhile, the main highway continues from Dosso to the east, then bends towards Dogondoutchi. It marks the boundary between the range of influence of the Djerma-Songhay and the Hausa, who dominate the southern regions of Niger along the Nigerian border all the way to Zinder. It holds a special position within the Hausa territory, though, as the district of Dogondoutchi is a stronghold of indigenous animist beliefs. While conversion rates to Islam are high, animist rituals and ceremonies of the Bori cult still take place, and two key figures in the tradition of the animists – the Sarauniya of Lougou and the Baura of Bagaji – live in villages in the region.

KOURÉ AND THE DALLOL BOSSO PARTIAL RESERVE

The west African subspecies of the giraffe, *Giraffa camelopardalis peralta*, is different from the seven subspecies elsewhere in Africa. Various rock engravings in and around the Aïr Mountains are testimony that once upon a time this sub-species of giraffe was common all over Niger. In fact, 10,000 years ago, at the end of the last ice age when the Sahara was still green, the giraffe could be found in many west and north African countries, from Senegal, Mauritania and Morocco to Cameroon, Chad and Libya (and also Egypt and Sudan). Only a century ago, they were still present in Senegal, Mali, Niger and northern Nigeria. However, since the beginning of the 20th century, numbers of giraffe have dwindled dramatically. By 1960, it was estimated that only a few hundred individuals could still be found in the belt stretching from Dakar to Bamako and along the north bank of the river Niger all the way to Gaya, with some animals wandering as far as Zinder and Agadez. During the 1980s, because of intensive poaching in combination with the serious drought of 1984, a serious blow was dealt to the existence of the giraffe in west Africa. Apart from a few survivors in Mali, the only remaining viable herds are to be found in Niger.

GIRAFFE AND THE HUMAN POPULATION According to the season, the giraffe migrate between the regions around Kouré and the Dallol Bosso, 60–80km southeast of Niamey (see map, page 92). The area around Kouré, the Fakara Plateau, is a rocky area with excellent tigerbush vegetation for the giraffe to eat, but with very little water (see box *Tigerbush,* page 6). This is where they forage during the rainy season. But as soon as the water in the stagnant rain-fed pools evaporates, the animals migrate either towards Harikanassou or towards Niabéré, on the western edge of the Dallol Bosso, where groundwater is much closer to the surface and there are pools to drink from all year round. In these dry-season areas the giraffe often feed on *Acacia albida* trees.

Until not too long ago, the giraffe shared their habitat with the local population without many complications, and fodder was abundant. The giraffe population grew to around 120 individuals, who seemed to happily coexist with the local villagers. In recent years, however, the situation has changed dramatically.

In an attempt to provide the human population with a means of living, in 1993 an NGO proposed to exploit the woodlands of the region, including the tigerbush. A programme for sustainable cutting of dead wood, to provide the people in the capital Niamey with fuel for cooking, was implemented. Though in theory the ecosystem should not have degraded, in practice this proved otherwise as more and more people took to the economically rewarding tree cutting. Savanna woodland and tigerbush degraded to ecosystems of only a few tree species and eroding topsoil. As a result, the giraffe started including other foods in their diets, such as cultivated cowpeas and fruit trees, a turn of affairs not appreciated by affected locals. Simultaneously, some of the giraffe seemed to be looking for greener pastures well outside their usual habitat. This latter fact threatened to lead to a dispersal of the last groups. In January 1995, no more than 65 individuals were counted, leaving *Giraffa camelopardis peralta* on the brink of extinction. Add to this that poaching was still taking place, and it will be clear that something had to be done in order to safeguard this sub-species of giraffe.

Thanks to the policy of decentralisation (see pages 24–5), local authorities can now take matters into their own hands, provided they can find funds. In Kouré, a promising conservation programme was launched in 2005. The first step to be taken is a ban on wood cutting, which of course will only be successful if the affected timber merchants are offered an alternative source of income. Next, agriculture will have to be banned from those areas where the soil is poor and eroded already, and pastoralists will have to limit their flock to goats and sheep, which forage on different food sources from the giraffe. More positive measures include the restoration of the woodland, installation of water holes, and an active programme to boost eco-tourism and to train more local guides and rangers. In order to attract higher numbers of visitors, various facilities – such as an information centre and a hotel – are planned, while options to search for the giraffe by mountain bike or on camel back are being considered.

HOW TO VISIT THE GIRAFFE At the time of research, options to visit the Kouré giraffe were of a more limited kind. You definitely need your own 4x4 vehicle and a local guide to get anywhere near them. A signpost not far from Bangou Kouarey (hard to miss after some 60km when you are coming from Niamey, but a rather insignificant *'guides des girafes'* signpost when coming from the east) will lead you to the very modest shack where guides await clients. These guides track the giraffe throughout the year, and are therefore well informed about the whereabouts of groups of animals. A guide will direct you to one or more groups of giraffe, and though no guarantee of success is given, the chances are always good. Visitors are allowed to approach the animals on foot and observe them at very close range, though care must be taken not to scare them away. As the giraffe are used to human presence, they are surprisingly tolerant and probably as curious as you are.

Entrance fee to the *Réserve Partielle du Dallol Bosso* where the giraffe can be found is CFA2,000 per person, while an additional local tax may be charged (see *Tourist information* page 40). The guides have no fixed rates, but they expect a fee of at least

CFA5,000 per vehicle or convoy when you are satisfied with their services. One of the guides speaks basic English.

DOSSO

The regional capital of Dosso has 43,000 inhabitants (2001), and the town is quite sizeable but with an open and spacious layout. Most quarters are either residential or administrative areas, but all the amenities are concentrated around the main thoroughfare. The best place to explore is the market area, where the daily market is stretched out alongside the road and spreads out through the alleys behind there. In the same quarter you will find the beautiful *chefferie* of the *Zermakoye*, the traditional leader of the Djerma.

GETTING THERE The main road from **Niamey** to **Agadez** or **Zinder** traverses Dosso, 136km from Niamey. At least eight big buses pass through each day, while minibuses and other vehicles also ply the route to Niamey on a regular basis, so there are plenty of options to travel to other destinations. The bus yards of the four major bus companies are a bit spread out over the town and especially buses coming from Niamey could be full. They arrive in Dosso around not long after 06.00 (reporting times are 05.30 and 06.00); not a convenient time to discover there are no seats left on the bus of your choice. Do therefore collect your ticket the day before travelling if you have the opportunity. Buses travelling to the capital arrive very early in the afternoon when coming from Maradi, and a few hours later when coming from Agadez or Zinder.

When you are travelling to Dosso, bear in mind that SNTV and especially Rimbo Transport are located away from the centre, while Maissagé is most conveniently located just near Hotel Djerma. There will be taxis waiting at the bus yards, though.

For off-the-mainroad destinations, vehicles leave when full from the **autogare**. A ticket to **Loga** costs CFA1,500, the journey taking around two hours. For **Guechemé**: CFA1,500, two hours; **Gorou-Bankassame**: CFA1,500, 1½ hours; **Tassa**: CFA1,200, 1½ hours.

To travel to the Beninese border and onwards, also look for regular transport leaving from the same autogare. The 150km to **Gaya** are covered in less than two hours and the journey costs CFA2,000. You will find ongoing vehicles to **Malanville** (Benin) in Gaya for CFA500. Alternatively, SNTV, Maissagé and Rimbo Transport run coaches from Niamey through Dosso to Benin. See *Niamey*, page 96.

There do not seem to be any vehicles heading directly to **Nigeria**, but in Gaya there are vehicles to the border post of Kamba and Sabon Gari in Nigeria. Travelling into Nigeria is more convenient from Birni N'Konni, with good connections to Sokoto.

GETTING AROUND There are taxis in Dosso; they charge the usual CFA200 per person for an average distance.

WHERE TO STAY

⌂ **Centre d'Artisanat** (4 rooms) The immaculate rooms easily provide the best accommodation in Dosso. At CFA18,000 for a s/c dbl with fridge and TV, these rooms are a good deal.

⌂ **Hotel Djerma** (19 rooms) ☎ 65 02 06. This is one of those hotels where you can imagine what it must have looked like in its heyday. It is still OK, though furniture and fittings seem to be gradually falling apart. The rooms at the back are the more quiet ones, but when going there make sure you do not trip and fall into the empty swimming pool. The rooms come in 3 categories, with fan; s/c with fan; s/c AC and cost CFA12,500/14,500/16,500 respectively.

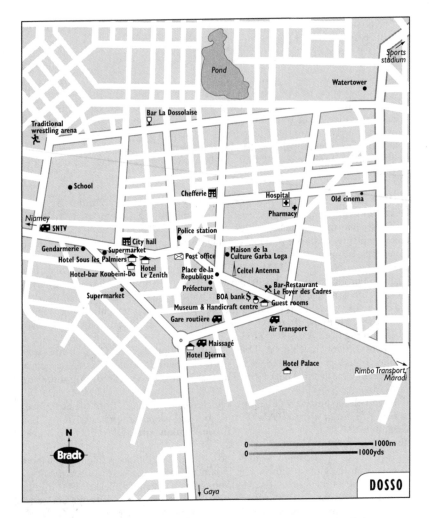

DOSSO

Hotel Koubeïni-Do (6 rooms) You can take a room to 'rest' for a few hours for CFA1,500, and if you didn't bring a female to rest by your side, some are patiently waiting in the yard. *Otherwise has dirt-cheap rooms at CFA2,500.*

Hotel le Zenith (8 rooms) Has rooms around a yard, which is used as a *boite de nuit* and where loud music is played from early afternoon until well after midnight. Forget about having a quiet moment to yourself while staying at this hotel.

Rooms are somewhat dark, with cold showers tucked in a corner of the room, king-size beds and shared, dirty toilets. *CFA6,300.*

Hotel Palace At the time of research, this was in a dormant state, though it was supposed to open up again as soon as the Belgian owner returned from his home country.

Hotel Sous les Palmiers (6 rooms) Fits a similar description to the Koubeïni-Do.

WHERE TO EAT AND DRINK For breakfast, the usual menu and drinks, try the airy bar at the **Centre d'Artisanat**. The garden of the **Foyer des Cadres** is not too bad, but indoors it looks like a run-down cantina and a real drinking place. But if it's a drink you're looking for, that could do just fine. At the **Arène de la Lutte Traditionelle** are two bars (*buvettes*) where you can have a bite to eat as well as cold drinks.

ENTERTAINMENT AND NIGHTLIFE Hidden behind a tailor's workshop is **Bar Restaurant la Dossolaise**, which is no longer a restaurant but rather a bar-cum-nightclub. The interior is fairly plain, but outside, where the dancing is done, the walls are decorated with Disney figures. **Hotel Sous les Palmiers** stages live music every evening, but it's a dubious joint.

PRACTICALITIES The **Bank of Africa** (*open Mon–Fri 08.30–11.30 and 15.45–17.00*) is located on the same premises as the museum and the Centre d'Artisanat. This bank changes cash euro only. The **post office** is open between 07.30 and 12.15 and 15.00 and 17.45. Not far from the **city hall**, past Hotel Koubeïni-Do, is a small **supermarket**, while fresh **dairy produce** can be bought straight from a wholesale shop nearby.

WHAT TO SEE AND DO

Museum The museum tries very hard to be taken seriously as an ethnical exhibition, though it clearly needs some encouragement, cash and clients. The concept is well understood, but most of the display cases stand virtually empty. However, entrance is free so why not pop in while you are here anyway to visit the handicraft workshops? (*Open seven days a week 08.00–12.30 and 15.00–18.00.*)

Handicrafts Like the other **Centres d'Artisanat** set up and supported by the *Cooperation Luxembourgoise* (see *Handicrafts and what to buy,* page 79), this is a place of work in progress. Visit the various artisans and see how they make leather sandals, embroidered *boubous* (the wide garment mostly worn by men) and painted calabashes. In the museum, you can sometimes see a weaver at work, while upholsterers have their workshop behind the shop. This is also where you can see how the omnipresent *marmite* is cast from recycled metal. In the shop, everything has a fixed price. On Sunday the shop is normally closed, but the keeper of the key is always willing to open doors for visitors.

Market In Dosso, every day is market day. The shops and stalls are spread out and somewhat hidden behind and between banco shops and houses.

Chefferie Unfortunately a wall is blocking the view of the *chef*'s residence which is strikingly decorated in cream, light blue and red.

Maison de la Culture Garba Loga Formerly known as the Maison des Jeunes et de la Culture, this cultural centre sometimes stages concerts and theatre, and it also doubles as a cinema (the ancient cinema is no longer functional). Check the programme at the centre.

DOGONDOUTCHI

The district of Dogondoutchi is considered the boundary between the regions that are dominated by the Djerma (to west of this region) and the Hausa culture and language (to the east and including the district of Dogondoutchi). Most of the population are Mawri people, a name comprising the two main ethnic groups: the Gubawa and the Arewa. Their Hausa ancestry is not the only factor linking the two; both groups passionately rejected Islam, even when the *jihad* launched by the Peul (see *Chapter 1, History,* page 17) led to the conversion of most of the southern regions bordering present-day Nigeria. Instead, the Azna or animist cosmology continued to determine life in the region. Dogondoutchi – or 'Doutchi' for short – remains a stronghold of animism, with the two neighbouring villages of Lougou

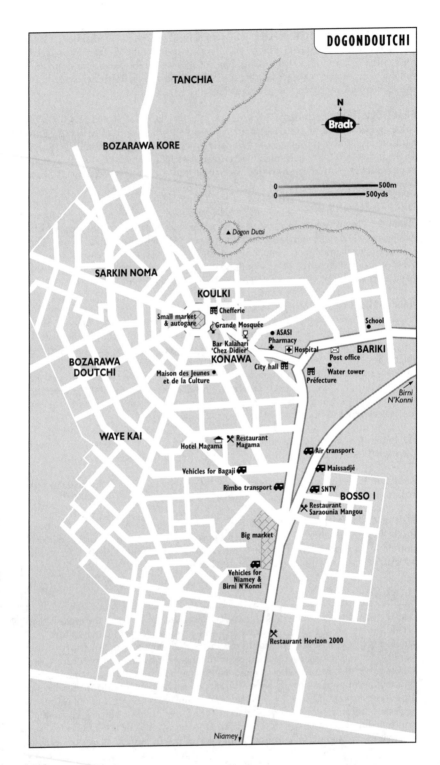

DOGONDOUTCHI

TANCHIA

BOZARAWA KORE

N

Bradt

0 ————— 500m
0 ————— 500yds

▲ Dogon Dutsi

SARKIN NOMA

KOULKI

Chefferie

Small market
& autogare

Grande Mosquée

ASASI
Pharmacy

School

BOZARAWA
DOUTCHI

Bar Kalahari
'Chez Didier'
KONAWA

Hospital

Post office

BARIKI

City hall

Water tower

Maison des Jeunes
et de la Culture

Préfecture

Birni
N'Konni

WAYE KAI

Restaurant
Magama

Hotel Magama

Air transport

Vehicles for Bagaji

Maissadjé

Rimbo transport

SNTV

BOSSO I

Restaurant
Saraounia Mangou

Big market

Vehicles for
Niamey &
Birni N'Konni

Restaurant Horizon 2000

Niamey

and Bagaji still being the seats of powerful traditional leaders. The indigenous belief is centred around the existence of *génies* or spirits. While certain sub-groups of Azna recognise two important spirits only, the cult of the Bori assumes the existence of large groups of spirits, all individuals with names, characters and peculiarities. These spirits reveal their presence through mediums, mostly women, who are susceptible to trance and possession by the spirits. The Bori cult is typical for the Azna of the district of Dogondoutchi.

Yet, while the core of animist practitioners hold on to their ways, a growing number of Mawri have embraced Islam in recent decades. Some say that conversion to Islam is no more than a gesture, while animist practice is continued in a more private manner. By the same token, antagonists claim that Islam now has deeply penetrated the community of Dogondoutchi, and the rituals of animism will soon be no more than folkloric assets, a cultural heritage. While the discussion lingers on, mosques and Koranic schools are visibly present in most quarters of the town. The Big Mosque is situated just opposite the *chefferie*, court of the traditional leader, the Sarkin Arewa.

HISTORY According to oral history, the first people to move into the region were the Gubawa (see box below *Sarauniya,* page 140), followed by the Arewa. The Sarkin Arewa, *chef* of all Arewa, was based in the community of Matankari, some 20km to the north of Dogondoutchi. By the end of the 18th century, a sub-group of the Arewa, the Konawa (under traditional leadership of their *chef* or *kona*) moved to the northern side of what is now Dogondoutchi. They probably found some other settlements already there, and the agro-pastoral communities lived side by side, as independent *chefferies*. Then came the Europeans, shaking the foundation of all these villages.

In 1899, the destructive Voulet–Chanoine Mission passed the area (see *Chapter 1, History,* page 18). In 1903, the French set up a military post in Matankari. Meanwhile, the British still laid claims on the territory (see *Chapter 1, History,* pages 18–19), and they in turn opened a military post in Dogondoutchi in 1906. Not much later, the French took over from the British and they shifted their regional colonial administration from Matankari to the military post in Dogondoutchi. The Sarkin Arewa was forced to follow suit, and his *chefferie* was shifted to Dogondoutchi. Though the French acknowledged his importance as a traditional leader, the Sarkin's ruling power was redefined by the French as they incorporated the *chefferie* in the colonial administration. Other *chefferies* did not cease to exist either, but like all over the French Military Territory of Niger, their political influence became highly restricted (see *Nigérien society,* page 31). Yet to this day, the Konawa are still unified under their Kona of Dogondoutchi, while the Sarkin Arewa continues to hold court at his residence.

The Konawa and other Arewa, all part of the Mawri people, form the vast majority of the population of just under 30,000 inhabitants (2001). They share the town with a small community of Djerma, and some groups of semi-nomadic Tuareg and Peul.

GETTING THERE All buses running between the capital (277km) and Maradi (384km) or Agadez (664km) pass through Dogondoutchi; there are at least eight going to or coming from Niamey. Therefore you should have no problem finding transport to any of these destinations. All four bus companies are located in each other's vicinity, which makes it easy to shop around for a ticket and check the reporting times.

For nearby destinations, check out the **autogare** behind the *grand marché* or big market. There do not seem to be any direct vehicles to **Lougou** (38km), the village

According to oral history, the first people to settle in the region of Dogondoutchi originated from Daura, the first of the seven Hausa city-states (see *Chapter 1, History*, page 17). At one time, probably in the 16th century, the *Chef* du Daura had one child only, a girl, and her name was Sarauniya. When her father died, she should have been installed in his place, but the *chef*'s younger brothers refused to accept this and threatened to kill Sarauniya. However, she was informed about the conspiracy, after which Sarauniya made her escape in the night. On horseback, she made it all the way to a place now known as Lougou, and it is said that she found the area uninhabited.

Sarauniya was soon joined by two brothers, Dagogé and Gijé. All Gubawa, the name for this first group of habitants, claim to be descendants of Dagogé and Gijé. Sarauniya never produced any offspring, but her position as the first occupant and founder of the new settlement earned her immortality in name; sarauniya became a title, symbol of magical powers connecting living humans to their ancestors, symbol of fertility of the soil the Gubawa had made their territory. When Sarauniya died, a new sarauniya was chosen from the descendants of Dagogé and Gijé. Or rather, when Sarauniya's corpse was carried around the settlement on a bier, the corpse itself guided the bearers to the woman who was to be the next sarauniya. To this day, this is how the title of sarauniya is passed on.

History has shown that the sarauniya does not merely possess magical powers in words alone. The consecutive sarauniya managed to withstand invasions from the Tuareg, the Djerma and most of all the Peul (see *Chapter 1, History*, page 17). Moreover, in 1899 the sarauniya effectively scared off the notorious mission, Voulet–Chanoine (see *Chapter 1, History*, page 18), an outstanding achievement given the relentlessness of the mission.

However, immortality and a fierce, though highly respected reputation come at a price. The life of a sarauniya is a solitary one, to say the least. She lives in Lougou, alone in a secluded, confined space, with all social ties – even family ties – completely severed. She is allowed to communicate, but through a curtain or hanging only, as the sarauniya must remain invisible. Twice weekly, she will administer justice using her divine knowledge. For this occasion, she will sit on a sacred stone, *tunguma*, the stone that was carried all the way from Daura by the first sarauniya, Sarauniya of Daura.

where the sarauniya lives. A journey to **Bagaji** (56km) costs CFA500. The **autogare de la brousse**, for more off-the-road destinations, is at the *petit marché* or small market.

GETTING AROUND There are no taxis in Dogondoutchi, but *kabou-kabous* will take you around for CFA200 per ride.

WHERE TO STAY, EAT AND DRINK The only hotel is **Hotel Magama** (✆ 81 43 51), a walled yard where space is filled out with rows of rooms and rondavels. The design is not particularly attractive but very efficient. Just across the road are the bar and restaurant, laid out in a pleasant garden: a much better place to sit down and relax while having a meal or a cold drink. The choice of food is limited and may take some time to prepare, and if you want something out of the ordinary you should order in advance. Service is very friendly. The 24 rooms come in three categories and start at CFA4,300–5,000 (for a single/double with fan and shower but a shared toilet) up to CFA17,000–20,000 (for an air-conditioned, self-contained double/family room with fridge and TV).

A convenient location for travellers who are just passing through, **Restaurant Saraounia Mangou** is situated right at the thoroughfare. It does not have a lot of charm, but service is efficient and the meals are good value for tasty, stodgy meals between CFA500 and CFSA3,000. Its location makes it suitable to sit here and wait for your bus to arrive, as most bus stops are centred around the triangular open space. **Restaurant Horizon 2000** is a bit further down the road, and is a simple but welcoming place to sit and have a meal.

A friendly bar with a pleasant garden to the back is **Bar Kalahari**, also known as **Chez Didier**. It is well hidden in the dry riverbed that cuts across town. In the rainy season the bar sometimes becomes inaccessible, while the water may even flood it.

PRACTICALITIES The **post office** is located at the tarred road near the water tower. There are no banks in Dogondoutchi.

WHAT TO SEE AND DO

Market The small market always sees some merchants every day, but the big marketplace comes alive on Fridays. It then becomes a colourful chaos of people from different ethnic groups, their cattle and rickety vehicles being loaded until their height almost doubles.

Chefferie When arriving at the centre of the old town, the Big Mosque stands out. The *chefferie*, on the other hand, needs some tender loving care, as the façade and part of the roof gave way some time ago. One day it will be repaired, but in Dogondoutchi no-one seems to be in a hurry. Walking past the *chef* and his court feels like walking into a different era. Yet, this is living history. A big change at the *chefferie* must be the fact that most dignitaries have converted to Islam, despite the profound animist history of the town. Protocol remains strict, and if you want an audience with the *chef*, remember to take off your shoes and kneel before the Sarkin Arewa, who is seated in his chair in a shaded area in front of the *chefferie* most of the day. This is still the place where community issues are discussed and where weighty decisions are taken.

CULTURAL FESTIVAL JESIPA Dogondoutchi is the seat of the Association d'Action contre le SIDA (ASASI), an NGO dedicated to educating people about HIV/AIDS. This association is especially active for and with the younger generation through activities and demonstrations. February 2004 saw the first edition of the cultural festival JESIPA. This musical event was a combination of young rappers and traditional musicians. Obviously, the festival is worthwhile for the music only, but moreover it is an excellent occasion to witness the enthusiastic input of a group of young people believing in the urgency of their mission. They will be more than willing to share their ideas with you. Contacting ASASI through email or telephone may prove difficult, but enquiries about future stagings of the festival can be made at the Centre Culturel France-Nigérien in Niamey (see *Niamey*, page 108).

LOUGOU

This village – approximately 40km to the northeast of Dogondoutchi – is the seat of the *sarauniya*, a both feared and respected female leader within the traditional belief of the Gubawa, one of the groups of the Mawri people (see box *Sarauniya*, opposite).

BAGAJI

Not long after Sarauniya of Daura had settled in Lougou, some other groups arrived in the area. Among one of these was a blacksmith. Sarauniya commanded him to give up his profession and to stay at the location of present-day Bagaji. As he buried his anvil (*baura* in Hausa) at the site, he obtained supernatural knowledge and power, most of all about matters related to the uncultivated soil. Since then, Baura is the title of the village *chef* of Bagaji, and one of the most important figures in the animist cult of the Gubawa.

The first Baura is also the ancestral link between the Gubawa and the Arewa people: Ari, son of the Sultan of Bornou, is considered to be the founding father of the Arewa or 'people of Ari'. He had children with a Gubawa woman, who was the daughter of the Baura of Bagaji.

Part Three

THE CENTRE AND NORTH

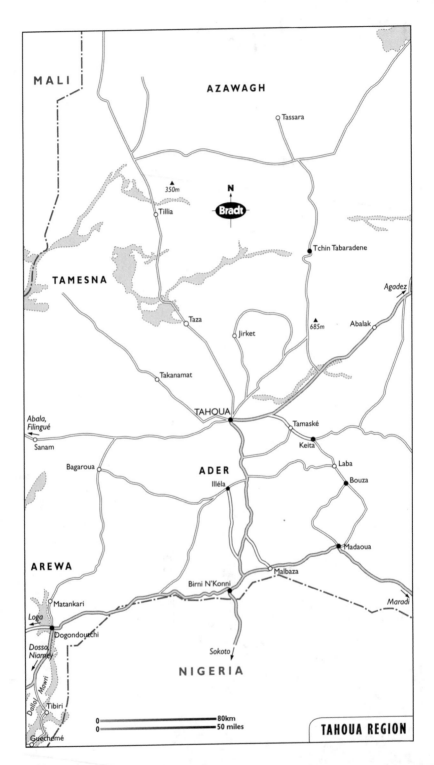

MALI

AZAWAGH

Tassara

▲ 350m

N

Bradt

Tillia

Tchin Tabaradene

TAMESNA

Agadez

Taza

Jirket

▲ 685m

Abalak

Takanamat

TAHOUA

Tamaské

Abala,
Filingué

Sanam

Keita

Bagaroua

ADER

Laba

Illéla

Bouza

AREWA

Madaoua

Malbaza

Birni N'Konni

Maradi

Matankari

Loga

Dogondoutchi

Dosso,
Niamey

Sokoto

NIGERIA

Tibiri

Guechemé

0 ────────── 80km
0 ────────── 50 miles

TAHOUA REGION

6

Tahoua

A remarkable section of the RN25 that connects Niamey to Agadez is the section that traverses the region of Tahoua: from Birni N'Konni to the boundary of the region of Agadez – just north of Abalak – the road passes through different vegetation zones (see map *Vegetation and rainfall,* page 5), and the eye will see how in the course of only a few hundred kilometres, vegetation and land use change dramatically. Around Birni N'Konni, the landscape is visually dominated by millet fields and the impressively sized gaos or apple ring trees, while the bulky, onion-shaped granaries are a typical sight in villages inhabited by sedentary farmers. Azawak cattle are common around these villages. They are a fairly small breed with short horns, suitable as 'sedentary cattle' and good milk and meat producers.

The vegetation becomes increasingly thin and thorny, while bigger trees are found only in – usually dry – riverbeds where groundwater is found at shallow depths. Millet fields look different: the distance between stalks increases as plants compete for water until the soil dries and breaks. Where the soil has badly degraded, the sodom apple thrives.

North of Tahoua, villages are few and far between, while agriculture is hardly possible. Peul Bororo appear in a cloud of dust, as they herd their Bororo cattle. The Bororo cattle are a striking breed, with long, lyre-shaped horns, long legs and a humped neck. The Peul prefer this breed as the animals have strong characters and they form ties with their owners. More importantly, though they produce less milk than the Azawak, the Bororo cattle are better adapted to covering huge distances in search for fodder and water. The view of the landscape leaves no doubt: grazing is sparse, and so is water. You have entered the land of the nomadic pastoralists.

BIRNI N'KONNI

HISTORY
The name Birni N'Konni means 'the citadel of Kanni', a name which leads us back to its founder. Though often mistakenly recorded as a 'prince of Gobir', he was a member of the 'Kanni' dynasty, which originates from the region of present-day Birni N'Kebbi in Nigeria. Around the 15th century, he founded the state of Kanni, which had no permanent capital yet. Centuries later, when the Peul and Muslim cleric Ousman Dan Fodio launched a *jihad* or holy war against the Hausa animists, many people sought refuge in fortified villages. In 1823, the settlement which was then the capital of the state of Kanni was also fenced in by a thick wall, a *birni* in the Hausa language. Since then 'Birni N'Konni' has been the official name.

The majority of the Hausa that lived here were either Azna or Anna, descendants of one of the founders of the seven Hausa city-states. According to one version of the legend of the Queen of Daura (see box *The Queen of Daura,* page 146), these are in fact the descendants of a bastard son, child of the Queen of

Different myths describe the origins of the founders of the seven Hausa city-states, and most of them lead back to a central figure: the Queen of Daura, and her descendants.

One myth tells of a terrible monster or snake that lived in a well near the city of Daura. The monster did not allow the inhabitants of Daura to take water from the well. The reigning Queen of Daura therefore made a vow: she would marry the brave one who would kill the animal.

Many years went by, and many men perished in fruitless attempts to stand up to this monster. But then one young man succeeded, and he married the Queen. By then she was an old woman and no longer able to have children. She therefore allowed her young husband to have a child with a concubine: a slave serving the queen. A bastard son was born, and he was given the name 'Karba-gari' ('I took the city'), as he was to inherit the Queen's power and possessions. The Queen of Daura, however, became so jealous of this bastard son that miraculously she bore a child after all. The child was named 'Bawo Abuna' ('Return what is mine').

Bawo Abuna later had six sons of his own, and the Queen's heritage was divided between these six and the bastard son Karba-gari. These were the founders of the seven Hausa city-states. The latter also became the religious leader, the *chef des Azna* or *Sarkin Ana*, a title that is still used for the leader of the Azna animists.

Daura's spouse and his slave concubine. In this legend, the Azna are considered the spiritual leaders of all Hausa, the safekeepers of the animist culture. True or not, nowadays the term 'Azna' or 'Anna' refers to those groups of Hausa that still practise animist rituals and ceremonies (see *Religion*, page 34 and also box *Arwa: ceremony of the Azna*, page 150).

Birni N'Konni – Konni for short – is a kind of crossroads, as tarred roads lead to important towns at all points of the compass: Niamey to the west, Tahoua and Agadez to the north, Maradi and Zinder to the east and Sokoto (Nigeria) to the south. Over the centuries, the Hausa have always shown their talent for commercial activities, and today that is no different. The Hausa, still very much the majority of the population of Konni, made perfect use of the combination of geographical location and easy access, and thus Konni has developed into a buzzing commercial centre. The main street leading from the Carrefour de l'Unité to the Nigerian border is a chain of countless shops, vendors, small and big enterprises competing for space, while traffic shuttles up and down until late at night. This street is one of the liveliest in the country; it never sleeps. Also, it is one of the few streets in the whole of Niger where crossing to the other side can be hazardous.

GETTING THERE As Birni N'Konni is along the main road not far from the junction to the north and east, there are plenty of buses – from all four big bus companies – going north, east or west every day. Enquire about the reporting time and preferably book your ticket in advance. For **Niamey**, reporting times vary between 08.00 and 13.00 and the fare is around CFA7,000. For **Agadez** and **Arlit**, reporting times are 09.00 and 10.00 (CFA7,500 and CFA11,000). For **Maradi** and **Zinder**, reporting times are 09.00 and 10.00 (CFA3,500 and CFA6,300).

For nearby destinations, check out the **autogare**. These are some of the villages on the itinerary: **Dagarka** and **Massalata** (CFA100); **Dossey** (CFA350); **Galmi** (CFA750); **Carrefour Sarnawa** (CFA200). You could also travel to bigger towns like **Madaoua** (CFA1,250) or **Dogondoutchi** (CFA1,500, or CFA2,100 for a nine seater). As Birni N'Konni is only 5km from Nigeria, this is also where you will find

RN 1 - Maradi

Fuel station

Gendarmerie
Hotel Le Motel

Carrefour de l'Unité
Préfecture

Maissagé

Air Transport
Rimbo Transport

Auberge Les Routiers
Restaurant Le Fleur
Bar-supermarket
Le Relax

Internet
Alkara

Gardens

Gardens

Internet Olympique
Relais
Touristique

SNTV

City hall

Pharmacy

Post office

Gardens

RN1 - Dagarka,
Massalata, Niamey

Kan Kowa
Shi Wave Centre

Hospital

Celtel Antenna

Gardens

Hotel Kado
Bar Maquis 2001
Hotel Wadata

Maison
des Jeunes

Evangelical mission

Prison

SABON GARI

Gardens

Gardens

Market
Elhadj supermarket

OLD TOWN

Gardens

Tchilankom
Gardens

Traditional
Chefferie

Ancienne
Grande Mosquée

Gardens

MOUNWADATA I

Grande Mosquée

Autogare

Burial
ground

MOUNWADATA II

OLD TOWN

Customs

Police
station

Gardens

N

Bradt

0 ──── 500m
0 ──── 500yds

Nigerian border,
Sokoto

Mageia (seasonal river)

BIRNI N'KONNI

transport to towns and villages across the border. Drivers prefer to be paid in naira, the Nigerian currency, but CFA francs are also accepted. For **Illela** (in Nigeria, not to be confused with Illela in Niger, 80km north of Birni N'Konni), pay around 40 naira or CFA150; the fare to **Sokoto** (90km) is around 400 naira or CFA1,300.

GETTING AROUND Since there are no taxis in town, you'll have to walk or hop on the back of a *kabou-kabou* (CFA150 per ride). Do have a quick look at the state of the motorbike first, as some are really rusty models with weary suspension or worse.

WHERE TO STAY The water in Birni N'Konni comes from a thermal source. Therefore tap water is neither hot nor cold, but lukewarm.

⌂ **Camping Relais Touristique** (6 rooms) ☎ 64 06 00/29 55 15. This place has a choice of accommodation in a huge yard just off the thoroughfare. Spacious s/c AC rooms cost CFA12,500 or CFA10,000, depending on the degree of convenience and the furnishings. One room with fan costs CFA7,000, while an extra bed costs CFA1,000. Camping is also allowed at CFA1,500 pp. The charge for a vehicle is also CFA1,500.

⌂ **Hotel Kado** (24 rooms) ☎ 64 03 64/87 91 21. Here the furniture is *un peu fatigué*, a little tired. The bold-coloured wall decorations, however, do freshen up this hotel and you may want to see a few rooms before deciding which décor suits you best: a landscape, chunky fruit, or do you prefer flower power? Altogether this is a very friendly hotel with a pleasant yard, and right in the middle of the buzzing town. The s/c rooms cost CFA6,800 for a dbl with fan and CFA9,800 for an AC dbl.

⌂ **Hotel le Motel** (8 rooms) ☎ 87 65 05. This hotel opened its doors to the public at the beginning of 2005. The small restaurant, open-air bar and rooms are all very bright and clean. The downside is that while the upstairs gallery is ample, the rooms are small and some of the bathrooms hardly big enough to squeeze into. 6 rooms at CFA22,500, 1 room at CFA27,500, 1 suite at CFA37,500.

⌂ **Hotel Wadata** (26 rooms) Very simple and unpretentious, this is a welcoming place with some charm. Facilities, however, are limited to shared bucket showers and a seatless toilet, while the only water comes from a tap in the yard. Though this hotel is signposted at the main road, the entrance is well hidden in a narrow street: look for the first gate to your right. There are 20 rooms – each with 1 bed only – at CFA2,000, while the 6 rooms with fan are CFA3,500. An extra bed can be supplied at no extra charge.

WHERE TO EAT AND DRINK The restaurant at **Hotel le Motel** hadn't opened at the time of research, but it is worth checking out as everything seemed to be of a good standard.

The **Camping Relais Touristique** serves excellent meals, including succulent fish dishes and salads, but you will have to take your time as the cook does exactly the same.

The restaurant in **Hotel Kado** serves basic meals that are sometimes bought from street stalls if the cook has left to run some errands. You can choose to have your meal in the dining room-cum-bar, in the yard or – if you are staying here – at your front porch.

Auberge les Routiers is Chinese owned, but the meals are pretty much what you will find anywhere and cost around CFA1,000–1,500 per meal. The speciality of the house is a variety of *capitaine* dishes. Open seven days a week.

Restaurant le Fleur doesn't look very striking, but it is a hospitable place with very good meals, mostly well under CFA2,000. Try a salad or *hors d'oeuvre* (cold platter with eggs and vegetables) or the succulent *pintade en sauce* (guinea fowl in sauce). Open every day. Conveniently located opposite the Maissajé bus yard.

Bar le Relax is both a bar and supermarket, where you can have chilled drinks while watching out for your bus to arrive.

PRACTICALITIES There are no banks in Birni N'Konni, but if you need some naira – the currency of Nigeria – there is a thriving **black market** at the autogare. Changing money here is fairly safe and is done openly. Rates are more or less fixed and not much different from the official rate. If possible, check the latest rate just to be sure. See also *Money,* page 66.

For the **internet** there are a few options, but connection is erratic and very slow. Try Internet Olympique along the Route Nationale or Internet Alkara along the main road cutting through the town. Both charge CFA125 per minute.

Opposite the big market is the fairly well stocked **Elhadj supermarket**.

WHAT TO SEE AND DO

Market The enclosed market area shows some activity every day, but on market day (Wednesday), it stretches out along a few dusty roads as well. It is well visited by many different ethnic groups, predominantly Hausa (note the different facial scarifications), but also Peul, Tuareg, Djerma and others.

Walk around town Start at the **market** and walk west. Hidden behind houses and yards, the garden area called **Tchilankom** with small vegetable plots comes as a green surprise. It is a bit of a maze, and finding an entrance or exit is a matter of trial and error. Walk back to the main street and cross to the other side. The **old town** is made up of different quarters, labyrinths of winding streets and alleys that are often too narrow even for donkey carts. These quarters are divided by some wide lanes. One of these leads past a school and the **Big Mosque**, and then you are not far from the traditional *chefferie* in the quarter called Kangouri. This is the residence of the *chef du canton* or *sarki*, and around this court you will often see some of the dignitaries in colourful garments. It is not a matter of course to visit the *sarki* or his residence, but if you are interested, you can ask for an audience through a guide or one of the court members and respect the prescribed protocol (see *Cultural sensitivity,* page 85). The old town or *ancien noyau*, is surrounded by a small seasonal stream, the **Maggia**, which stands dry most of the year. What a shame that waste and plastic are dumped just where the building area ends, as all along the dry riverbed are **gardens** in an altogether lush scenery. Try to look beyond the dirt if you can. Follow the Maggia a while, then cross back to the main street. Refreshments are never far away!

Centre Kan Kowa Shi Waye This place of meetings and learning belongs to the Catholic mission. The adult literacy project – focusing on both Hausa and French – attracts a lot of people, many of them women. If you have affinity with this kind of project, you are welcome to see what is going on and meet some teachers and students. If your French is good enough, you can also browse through the many books from the library (*open Wed 16.00–18.00, Sat–Sun 10.00–12.00 and 16.00–18.00*).

Maison Kondo Maison Kondo is the name of the local Maison des Jeunes et de la Culture (MJC). Together with a few local video clubs, this centre provides just about the only entertainment for Konni's youth. It occasionally stages concerts and other events like *la lutte traditionelle* (traditional wrestling, see *Public holidays and festivals,* page 77). The only way to find out about the programme is by asking around or by checking at the MJC, but often the place looks pretty abandoned.

Excursion to villages While Birni N'Konni is teeming with life, the nearby villages reveal the other side of life in this region: the quiet life where the days revolve around agriculture, harvesting enough food to feed the family, fetching

The cosmology and rituals of the Azna animists revolve around the belief in the existence of *génies* or spirits. These spirits are often connected to certain natural objects or places (a tree, a lake, a rock or hill) or natural phenomena (water, wind, thunder), and they are known to have human characteristics: they can be shy, bold, bad-tempered, witty, etc. Earthlings can communicate with spirits through a medium, usually a fetishist who has developed skills to perform rituals in which the spirits are invited to 'speak'. It is then up to the fetishist to interpret the message or signals. Meanwhile, any other person who is receptive to the potency of the invisible can temporarily be the 'voice' of the spirits through trance and possession. The spirits are said to have knowledge beyond the boundaries of time and beyond what humans can see. Therefore they play an important role in understanding existing situations, in foretelling what lies ahead, and in prescribing possible ways to alter one's fate. The spirits are even capable of causing visible and tangible effects, as a warning, a punishment or token of appraisal. Thus, for the Azna, life is an ever-fragile balance in which good fortune heavily depends on natural factors and the benevolence of the spirits. The *Arwa* ceremony is all about this balance and the hope to benefit from prior knowledge.

The timing of the ceremony – also called *l'ouverture de la brousse* – is calculated according to the lunar calendar: four lunar months and 14 days after the last rains is the most important day of a multiple-day gathering. It marks the start of the agricultural season (when farmers have to plan work in the fields) and the beginning of the hunting season. The French term *'l'ouverture de la brousse'* refers to the fact that after the ceremony, the Azna are once more allowed to make use of the natural resources. But first they have to ask the spirits what to expect of the new season: will there be enough rain? What will be the best time to plant seeds? Will the harvest be good or will locusts

water and preparing and sharing meals. Some nearby villages – Dagarka and Massalata – are not just very pretty, they are also the scene of the yearly ceremony of the Azna. These villages and the *Fête des Aznas* are described below.

Getting to these villages is usually no problem at all, especially on market days when vehicles leave early in the morning to take vendors and merchants there. It's getting back that may be a problem, and the best thing to do is arrange the return transport before leaving, or be sure you leave the village well before the last vehicle heads back to Konni. Alternatively, rent a *kabou-kabou* for the day, or make arrangements for one to collect you at some point.

DAGARKA

The village of Dagarka is truly picturesque, with its *banco* architecture and the pot-bellied granaries. Enormous gao trees add green, while the inhabitants offer just about every colour of a painter's palette to the otherwise pale background. To understand the proportions of such a village, you just have to walk between the walls and houses. Moreover, as villages like Dagarka receive very few visitors, you will be overwhelmed by their hospitality and friendly response.

When you are here (preferably with a guide), present yourself to the *chef du village* as a matter of courtesy. Very often, a *chef* fits the image of a wise, old man. In Dagarka, however, you'll be surprised to find this *chef* is wise indeed, but he has not yet turned 40. His late father was the previous *chef*, but it doesn't mean that the position of *chef du village* is heridatary. In accordance with tradition, the corpse of the deceased *chef* was carried around on a stretcher until the body 'sat upright' in front

devour the fruits of their labour? Will hunters be successful and will mothers bring forth healthy children?

Days prior to the fixed date, those groups of Azna that are related to the Arwa ceremony travel to Massalata and nearby Dagarka for ritual sacrifices, drumming and trance dancing. In the mean time, seven fetishists start consulting the spirits. On the big day, one by one the representatives of all groups gather in Massalata under a huge gao tree, while the crowd keeps a certain distance from the whole scene or disperses in the village.

The ceremony involves a lot of protocol, culminating in the 'turning of the soil': all seven fetishists routinely make rows of little holes or dents in the soil. Each rhythmic pattern leads to one of four symbols, and each set of six symbols is then discussed in front of all bystanders. Surprisingly enough, while the discussion is an earnest matter leading to the revelations for the coming year, the atmosphere is not only tense; there is also room for jokes and laughter. When finally consensus is reached about the interpretation of the spirits' message, the sandy surface is flattened once more, the next question is asked, and the whole sequence is repeated again and again until all answers are known.

For the remainder of the day, the village of Massalata turns into a spectacular stage for the *dance des Gardawas*, the dance of the invulnerables. These are members of the different villages' courts, all dressed in brightly coloured costumes and each carrying a long sword. The long metal blades slice through the air during dust-stirring dances, accompanied by loud drumming and whistling. Spectators gather at every open space and square, climbing on walls and carts for a better view of the performance. Most of them haven't yet heard what the spirits have foretold through the mediation of the fetishists, but the tension that has built up prior to the ceremony finds an outlet in the late afternoon of the day of the Arwa.

of a house, indicating who should be his successor. In this case, it was his own son who was thus appointed.

The current *chef* of Dagarka also happens to be the one elected to preside over the *Fête des Aznas* or *Arwa* in Massalata. The night prior to the ceremony, the yard behind his house is crowded with people, dancing and playing stringed instruments, drums and calabashes. Music is played all night long until dawn, and the whole atmosphere is very tense, almost electric. Women dance until they reach a trance-like state, and sometimes one of them falls to the ground, shaking all over and uttering barely audible words: the spirits have answered the call and speak through the people of Dagarka.

MASSALATA

After the state of Kanni was founded, the many animists in the region were divided in independent entities or *groupements*. It is believed that these groups held a special annual ceremony, the *Fête des Aznas* or *Arwa,* even before the state of Kanni was founded. Since these groups have settled in the region of Birni N'Konni, the fixed location of the ceremony is the village of Massalata, some 15km to the west of Birni N'Konni. Because of many conversions to Islam in recent years, the number of Azna is dwindling, but still a few thousand Azna from the different groups attend the ceremony each year.

Most of the people disperse into the village, as the ceremony itself is meant for the representatives of each of the groups present. It is a male-only event, and although it is not strictly for Hausa only, Peul are most definitely not welcome.

Given the historical background, this is not surprising (see *History,* page 17). Muslims, or rather non-animists, are very much discouraged to join in, though official delegations from the regional governmental authorities are always invited as a matter of courtesy. All in all, being white, female and non-animist I didn't expect to be allowed to attend the ceremony, but I was. I was the only white person around, and felt very priveliged. Provided you take some necessary steps first, you may be so lucky, too. However, *never* consider this ceremony a shallow opportunity to take a few snapshots.

In short, this is the way to go: present yourself to the local, traditional authority first (eg: the *sarki* in Birni N'Konni or the *chef du village* in Dagarka) and ask permission. Do not leave it until the big day, as everyone will be focused on the event rather than on visitors. Find a local guide who will stay with you at all times to explain the dos and don'ts. You could embarrass a whole crowd of much-respected traditional leaders without being aware. Some knowledge of the French language is required, as finding a guide who speaks English is very unlikely. Try to blend in as much as possible and dress properly without overdoing it. (See also box, *Cultural sensitivity,* page 84.)

Of course the chances are very slim that you will be in the area at the right time. All other days of the year, however, Massalata is still very much worth a visit. The scenery is just beautiful, and the huge, bulbous granaries you may have seen only through a bus window, are something you have to stand next to in order to understand their scale. And while you are there, ask around for a *cabaret*, a kind of bar where you can try the local millet brew, called *boulkoutou* or *tchapalu*.

TAHOUA

HISTORY Various groups of Azna or animists were among the first people to settle in the environs of present-day Tahoua. They had come from the Aïr region, ousted by Berber Arabs and Tuareg but also to flee the Muslim conqueror Askia Mohamed (see *Chapter 1, History,* page 16). As the Gobirawa and Katsinawa Hausa blocked their way in the south, they descended in the forests of the Ader region, often in the vicinity of hills and ravines where they could seek refuge if necessary. The Azna were hunters, farmers, and also kept cattle. From the 16th century onwards, more groups of Azna and other ethnies came trickling in. Among them were the first waves of Tuareg (like the Kel Gress, page 179), coming from the Aïr region, but gradually migrants from all directions moved in and scattered all over the area, often oblivious to the presence of others at first.

Around 1700, the site of present-day Tahoua consisted of two hamlets: Bilbis and Fakaoua. Every new wave of migrants settled next to the existing hamlets, initially forming two larger villages, but eventually the clusters merged to form the conglomerate of Tahoua. To this day, the different quarters carry names that refer to the first inhabitants of each additional settlement, and their early history – jam-packed with legends – was passed on through the generations. As seen on the map of Tahoua below (note that to avoid clogging the map, only some of the more than 15 quarters are marked), the old town – between the airstrip and the big market – now has a regular, uniform street pattern. However, a walk through the old town reveals that different clusters of streets have preserved characters of their own.

The administrative quarter is situated to the north of the old town, while Sabon Gari ('new village') is constructed to the east, in the bend of the Route Nationale. Tahoua has 73,000 inhabitants (2001), and is a true melting pot of ethnies with a Hausa majority, Tuareg, Peul, Arabs and Djerma. Animism has steadily lost ground over the centuries, and Islam is now the prevailing religion.

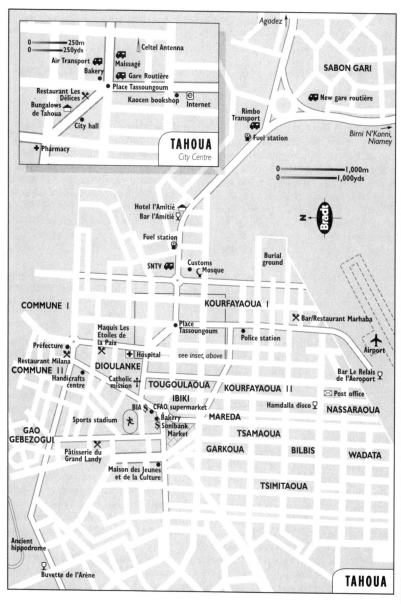

TAHOUA
City Centre

TAHOUA

GETTING THERE Tahoua is situated along the RN25, the main road between Niamey and Agadez. All four major bus companies have their own bus yards and four buses run in both directions daily. All reporting times are around 12.00–13.00 for **Niamey**; the fare hovers between CFA8,200 and CFA9,000. For **Agadez** the reporting time is 10.00 or 11.00 while the fare varies from CFA6,000 to CFA7,000.

Though most travellers will only stop over in Tahoua and then continue their journey to Niamey or Agadez, there are vehicles venturing off the tar to small villages and hamlets. The **autogare** is not far from the market. On Sundays, it is a very chaotic place with ramshackle pick-ups so heavily laden with merchandise and passengers that they almost seem to give way. Think twice before heading out with one of these, and if you do, enjoy the jolly company of fellow travellers who will welcome you on board.

GETTING AROUND Taxis and some *kabou-kabous* are available and cost CFA200 per ride.

WHERE TO STAY

🏠 **Bungalows de Tahoua** (13 rooms) ☎ 61 05 53. These are the only other option. While these detached, run-down rooms are more centrally located, guests have to put up with broken windows, leaking taps and creaky beds. Staff are very friendly, though. The 13 s/c dbl rooms cost CFA7,500 (with fan) or CFA9,500 (with AC).

🏠 **Hotel l'Amitié** (18 rooms) ☎ 61 04 83. This hotel is owned by the famous Nigérien cineast Moustapha Allasane (see *The arts*, page 36). It is

sometimes referred to as 'La Girafe', as 2 hard-to-miss giraffe statues are positioned under the trees just outside the gate. While this hotel must have seen better days, it is still reasonably comfortable and has rooms of different categories. Only some of the s/c rooms have extras like AC, TV and fridge, and therefore prices vary considerably from CFA8,500 for a dbl with fan, up to CFA25,300 for a suite that sleeps 3–4 people.

Showers in both hotels are equipped with one tap only, but the water is quite warm as it comes directly from a thermal source. This is definitely an advantage in the cold season, but you would be waiting in vain for a refreshing shower when the sun is scorching hot.

WHERE TO EAT AND DRINK The bar and restaurant at **Hotel l'Amitié** are simple but friendly, with a menu that holds no surprises. The restaurant sometimes fills up with groups, and if you are staying at the hotel, you can opt for room service.

Restaurant les Délices is conveniently located when you are staying at the Bungalows de Tahoua. This open-air restaurant serves good and affordable dishes in a pleasant garden.

Restaurant Milana (☎ 29 46 72) may look like a humble shack at first, but the food is really excellent and very reasonably priced. The Nigérien cook has had extensive training in Italian cuisine, and the menu really reflects this. Choose from home made tagliatelli or cannelloni, homemade cheese, osso bucco or nine different guinea fowl dishes. Certain dishes are best ordered in advance, as stock is kept down to a minimum to ensure fresh ingredients. When you are craving for a fresh cup of coffee instead of the usual Nescafé, you have one more reason to visit this restaurant. Based on comments from other travellers, **Maquis les Etoiles de la Paix** is another small restaurant worth checking out. However, it was temporarily closed at the time of research.

Just off the road to the airport is **Bar Restaurant Marhaba**, which stages live music on certain days (see below). Open seven days a week. The garden of the **Bar le Relais de l'aeroport** enjoys a view of the airstrip, but very few planes actually touch down in Tahoua. During the day this is primarily a bar, but in the evenings some basic meals can be served. This location is popular for parties and special occasions, in which case there may be live music and a cover charge.

On the same premises as the Arène de la lutte traditionelle is the **Buvette de l'Arène**, a lively bar, but well away from the Centre of town.

ENTERTAINMENT AND NIGHTLIFE Live music – mostly rap – is played in **Bar Restaurant Marhaba** on Tuesdays, Wednesdays and Saturdays (CFA500 entrance fee). The occasional party at **Bar de l'Aeroport le Relais** adds some spice to Tahoua by night. A **discobar** (the Handalla) that attracts Tahoua's youth above all, is hiding away not far from the post office. The nightclub adjacent to **Hotel l'Amitié** is open on Fridays and Saturdays.

The **Maison des Jeunes et de la Culture** occasionally stages live music (mostly rap) and theatre. Enquire at the Centre for the programme.

SHOPPING The best **bookshop** in town is Librairie Kaocen, while the biggest **supermarket**, called CFAO, is next door to the BIA bank. A good place to buy pastry is **Pâtisserie du Grand Landy** at the northern side of town.

OTHER PRACTICALITIES There are two **banks** in Tahoua. BIA Bank (*open Mon–Fri 07.45–11.30 and 15.45–17.30, Sat 08.30–12.00*) changes most hard currencies and travellers' cheques. Bring your passport and the receipt and allow plenty of time. Sonibank (*open Mon–Fri 07.45–11.00 and 15.45–17.00, Sat 08.30–12.00*) does change cash, but employees would be surprised if you wanted to change money at the bank rather than on the black market. Moneychangers can be found at the market.

Try to get connected to the **internet** only if you really have to and check if the computers are in working condition before heading there. At Moutalé Consult (↘ *61 00 58/98 86 30*) next to the bookshop, the price per minute is CFA150, but you could bargain it down a bit. The best time to give it a go would be between 19.00 and 20.00.

The **post office** is not far from the airport.

WHAT TO SEE

Handicrafts At the **Centre Artisanal**, founded by the Cooperation Luxembourgoise, you can visit various workshops to see the craftsmen at work (*open daily 09.00–17.00*).

Market On Sunday the big market is swarming with Hausa, Peul, Tuareg, Djerma and Arabs, making this market as colourful as it can get. Look for *tchoukou*, the flat pieces of cheese, as this region produces a lot of the thin, almost crispy and slightly sweet variety made from cow's milk. When you are travelling between Tahoua to Agadez by bus, a special stop (between Tahoua and Abalak) is sometimes made just to allow passengers to buy *tchoukou* directly from the Peul women who prepare this cheese (see *Food and drink*, page 73).

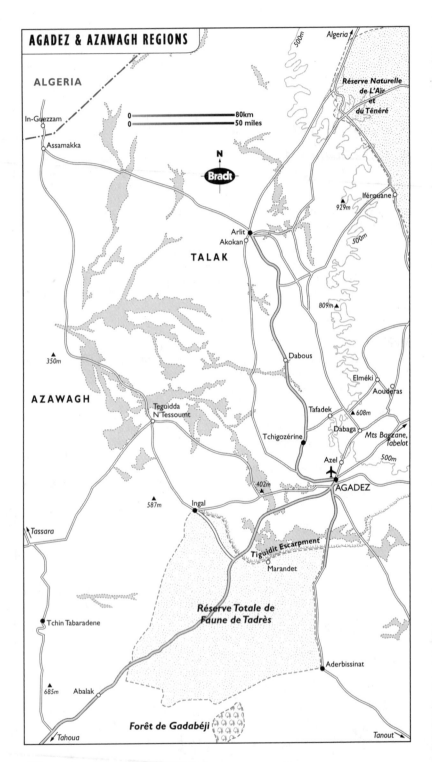

AGADEZ & AZAWAGH REGIONS

7

Agadez

The region of Agadez is the largest in Niger by far. It boasts some of the most spectacular and highly contrasting landscapes in the country. The western plains of Azawagh, Tamesna and Talak are inhabited by semi-nomadic and nomadic Peul and Tuareg pastoralists, who migrate between wells in search of suitable pastures for their livestock. Arlit is the northernmost town of Niger, and was created only a few decades ago when uranium deposits were discovered in the area. The historical town of Agadez is the buzzing heart of the region, as a centre of trade, a tourist destination in its own right and the gateway to the Aïr Mountains and the Ténéré Desert. In the far northeast – the Kawar and Djado regions where Toubou and Kanouri dominate – oases are dotted along the ancient trans-Saharan trade routes.

Traces of prehistoric civilisations can be found throughout this vast zone, but its history goes back even further, to the days when dinosaurs roamed the lower parts of the region. Some of the most important dinosaur graveyards were discovered along the Tiguidit Escarpment – 100km south of Agadez.

TIGUIDIT ESCARPMENT

Just to the north of the junction to Ingal, the main road traverses the Falaise de Tiguidit. The faint bend of this escarpment stretches out over 200km east–west and is the northern natural boundary of the Réserve Totale de Faune du Tadrès.

In 1906, the French geologist Chudeau was the first to identify some skeleton remains he found in the region as being dinosaur bones. During the colonial period, some more sites were recognised as 'dinosaur graveyards', but it would take until 1964 before serious research began. Phillipe Taquet led many expeditions to Gadoufawa, east of the Tiguidit Escarpment, where he unearthed many fossils and several complete skeletons. One of the finest examples, the herbivore *Ouransaurus nigériensis* is now on display in the National Museum of Niamey. In the 1990s, the American Paul Sereno started his extensive research in the environs of Ingal, Gadoufawa and Marandet, located halfway along the cliffs of Tiguidit. He identified many dinosaur species, mostly dating back to the Cretaceous period.

Whilst many of the skeleton remains were removed by researchers (as was the case in Gadoufawa), and looters and irresponsible tourists carried out more bones as souvenirs, a number of the sites are still intact and even preserved: some of the exposed bones are covered with a resin to minimise erosion and degrading. The population of the village of Marandet is dedicated to protecting the fossil finds as best as they can, and exploit the zone as a tourist destination. This guarded zone to the east of the village is known as Tawachi, and visits are payable. The site can be reached by 4x4 only, by turning off the main Agadez–Niamey or Agadez–Zinder roads and following the *piste* at the bottom of the cliffs.

Along the road from Agadez to Zinder, at 60km from Agadez is a Texaco signpost. The other side indicates that this is also the place to turn off the road towards the east, to get to the location of the first FIMA fashion event, which was held 20km off the road amidst dunes and rocks (see *Public holidays and festivals,* page 78).

INGAL

The small town of Ingal used to be on the trans-Saharan highway. Overlanders and expeditions descended from Algeria into Niger, and Ingal was the place where they would hit the tar after days, possibly weeks on a dusty *piste*. After spending this long in the desert, Ingal must have felt like quite a considerable town. When uranium was discovered further to the north, this led to the construction of the *route de l'uranium*, the highway from Agadez to Arlit. Overlanders soon preferred to drive from the Algerian border at Assamaka to the tar at Arlit, cutting the distance over Nigérien *pistes* and tracks by half, and most overlanders have bypassed Ingal since. Owing to the insecurity in the region during the Tuareg rebellion (see page 182), the new trans-Saharan route turned quiet altogether, but that was long after Ingal had become a dusty outpost once again.

Most of the year, Ingal is a quiet town inhabited by people of Songhay origin and sedentary Tuareg. However, towards the end of the rainy season in August and September, when the grazing in the region is good and when seasonal *mares* or ponds are filled with water, a massive transhumance of Tuareg and Peul pastoralists from all over the Azawagh region gravitates towards Ingal and environs for the yearly cure salée or salt cure. As the region between Ingal, Teguidda N'Tessoumt and Agadez is rich in salt and minerals, the nomads cover huge distances to allow their cattle to feed on the grasses and drink the saline water, which has a purgative action and which kills parasites and worms in their intestines. However, the cure salée is not just about salt; it is a multi-purpose event, one of the rare occasions for different confederacies or *groupements* to reunite for meetings, marriages and other festivities, and to stay in touch with the central administration in Niamey.

Many of the activities are centred around Ingal, which also serves as a stepping stone for travellers who want to witness the cultural manifestations of the cure salée, or who want to look for groups of Peul Bororo who organise their striking Geerewol festivities in the same region, usually just after the Cure Salée. For more information on both events, see *Public holidays and festivals*, page 76.

TEGUIDDA N'TESSOUMT

To the north of Ingal, across reddish plains, are the salines of Teguidda N'Tessoumt, meaning 'source of salt'. It is an almost lunar landscape: huge pits surrounded by mounds of soil hide the many basins in which the salt is obtained. This is an arduous process which begins with the collection of grubby, saline sand. Certain basins are used to mix the sand with water, and remove all impurities. The saline water is then transferred to other basins and left to evaporate. Every day, a thin crust of salt that has sealed the surface, needs to be broken to allow further evaporation. When at last the salt is crisp and dry, women carry it to the village, where they put the crystals in moulds to form bricks of salt. These are then ready to be bartered or sold.

AGADEZ

In days gone by, when travelling was done at a camel's pace, the first glimpses of Agadez, shimmering in the distance, must have caused many hearts to beat faster.

The skyline of the town of Agadez was dominated by its highest construction: the magnificent minaret of the ancient mosque with wooden sticks protruding on all four sides. Adjacent to the mosque is the Sultan's Palace and the old town with its irregular maze of alleys and squares. While all of this has been preserved, through the years it has been thoroughly hemmed-in by structures that are much less appealing to the eye and the imagination. Nowadays, in all fairness, arriving at the gate of Agadez in one of the big buses coming from Niamey may be a bit of a disappointment. The most striking structure must now be the brand-new water tower, standing solitary just outside the built-up area. The outskirts of Agadez, littered with waste plastic bags, are a patchwork of plain walls to fence off square plots of land, many of them with box-like, unattractive buildings. Though the ancient minaret may still be visible from certain angles, the skyline is now dominated by the Celtel antenna, providing the network for cellphones.

Yet, allow Agadez some time to show its beauty, as is evident in the heart of the town. Not just around the famous mosque or in the old quarter, where every corner and view to a courtyard are real still lifes, but the beauty also lies within the fact that life in Agadez is an embrace of both ancient and modern, and it breathes an almost metropolitan way of life.

HISTORY In the 11th century, the Gobirawa Hausa were pushed from the Aïr Mountains by the first wave of Tuareg tribes. They descended on the southern edge of the Aïr and created a permanent settlement just kilometres to the south. Until the 15th century, this settlement called Agadez was a small place of trade, not much different from other settlements. It was also a place for Tuareg to temporarily descend between journeys into the desert. All that changed with the arrival of one of the first sultans of the Aïr – Sultan Ilisawan (1430–49) – who had first resided in other local areas, and then decided to construct a palace in Agadez, turning it into the political capital of the region (see *The Aïr Mountains,* page 179). Meanwhile, its location on the southern fringes of the Aïr Mountains proved a favourable and easily accessible one: caravans or *azalaïs* halted frequently, causing trade to thrive.

The days of splendour The rising prosperity of Agadez did not escape Askia Mohamed, ruler of the Songhay empire in the west (see *Chapter 1, History,* page 16). On his pilgrimage to Mecca in 1498, he had crossed the region and had liked what he saw. On his return, he set out to conquer Agadez and environs, and succeeded. Agadez was now forced to pay taxes to the Songhay sovereign (a plight that continued until the collapse of the empire in 1591). During these early days of prosperity in Agadez, the Aïr region was not a secure place. Internal conflicts between confederacies as well as conflicts between ethnies regularly led to destructive campaigns during which entire villages were ravaged. The sultan and other aristocrats would not venture out in the mountains without an army of servants and slaves.

For protection against such violence, Agadez was fortified by a 4.5m-high wall with ramparts with four gates and a total length of 4.5km. Meanwhile, Askia Mohamed had installed two Songhay outposts in the region – one in Agadez and one in Ingal – to maintain the security and safe passage of the trade caravans. This proved successful, and for a century Agadez flourished. The cosmopolitan town attracted Songhay and Hausa craftsmen of all types, traders in gold, salt, cereals, dates, spices, textiles, leatherware and perfumes. More quarters had to be built outside the ramparts to house all these newcomers. Besides the economic importance of the town, Agadez also became a religious stronghold: in the 16th century alone, around 70 Muslim scholars of Peul and Arab origin descended on Agadez and profoundly marked its spiritual heritage. One of these scholars was Zakarya, who constructed the famous mosque of Agadez.

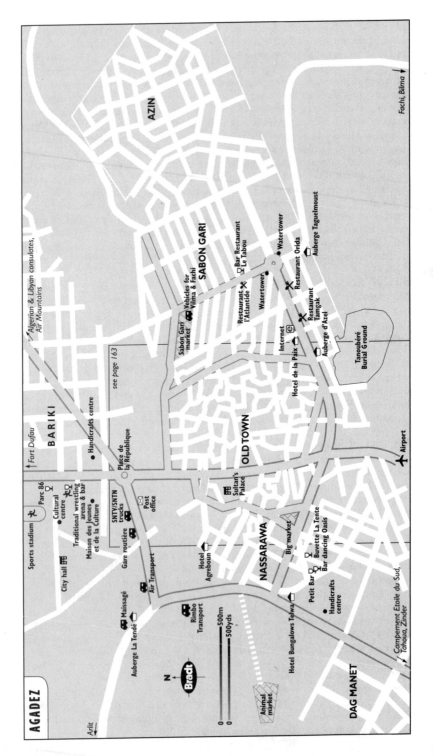

AGADEZ

BARIKI

AZIN

SABON GARI

OLD TOWN

NASSARAWA

DAG MANET

Arlit

↑ Fort Dufau

Algerian & Libyan consulates,
Air Mountains

Fachi, Bilma →

Sports stadium

Parc 86

City hall

Cultural centre

Traditional wrestling
arena & bar

Maison des Jeunes
et de la Culture

Handicrafts centre

see page 163

Place de
la République

SNTV/SNTN
trucks

Post
office

Air Transport

Gare routière

Maïssagé

Auberge La Tendé

Rimbo
Transport

Hotel
Agreboun

Sultan's
Palace

Big market

Petit Bar

Buvette La Tente
Bar dancing Oasis

Handicrafts
centre

Hotel Bungalows Telwa

Campement Etoile du Sud,
Tahoua, Zinder

Animal
market

0   500m
0   500yds

N

Bradt

Vehicles for
Vlima & Fachi

Sabon Gari
market

Restaurant
l'Atlantide

Bar Restaurant
Le Tabou

Watertower

Watertower

Restaurant Orida

Restaurant
Tamgak

Internet

Hotel de la Paix

Auberge d'Azel

Auberge Taguelmoust

Tanoubéré
Burial Ground

Airport ✈

The decline In the centuries that followed, more Tuareg confederacies migrated from the north to settle in the Aïr region. Some merged with the already present groups of Tuareg, others moved on southwards to the Ader region. It was an era of growing unrest and sometimes fierce battles, revolving around the conflicts between the three dominant confederacies: the Kel Owey, the Kel Gress and the Kel Ferwan. Life was troubled, Agadez suffered tremendously, and if peace was restored, it was only temporarily. In addition to the internal conflicts, there were droughts, epidemics and a torrential rainstorm which destroyed over 300 houses in Agadez. By the end of the 18th century, the Kel Gress – outnumbered by the Kel Owey – were ousted from the region and pushed further south. Conflicts between confederacies continued, and so did the north–south migrations. Meanwhile, hefty disputes of a different kind took place within the walls of Agadez, as the succession of sultans was marked by fratricide, dethroning and the seizure of power. When the first Europeans arrived on the scene, Agadez was heavily scarred.

Heinrich Barth, the German explorer who travelled extensively in west Africa in the 19th century, visited Agadez in 1850. He described the town as 'a shadow of its past', a ghost town with many houses and mosques in ruins, and only some parts of the town intact and inhabited. The Mission Saharienne, led by Lamy and Foureau (see *History*, page 18) passed the Aïr region in 1899, adding substantially to the unrest and violence. Foureau confirmed what Barth had seen: a withering town, with three-quarters of its dwellings crumbled to a ruinous state, and even the once–invincible ramparts had been reduced to isolated, useless obstacles.

The French penetration and the siege of the French garrison in Agadez In the first years of the 20th century, while the French gained a foothold in the southern regions of Niger, the north put up strong resistence. Some unsuccessful and unconvincing attempts were made to penetrate the Aïr region, and it took until 1906 to set up a military post in Agadez. Though the French now seemed to have control over the Sultan of Agadez, recurring Tuareg revolts and raids in the region meant that the instability steadily increased.

In 1916, a turn of events took place. Sultan Tegama, thought to be an ally of the French, and Kaocen, an Izkazkazen Tuareg from Damergou, conspired against the French. At the beginning of the French penetration, Kaocen had left the Aïr to join the Tuareg forces who had continually revolted against the French. This army of rebels had fought their way through the Damagaram and onwards to the east, to the region of Lake Chad. There, they teamed up with the Sanusi forces of the Kanem and Bornou empires (see *History*, page 17). This army, under the command of Kaocen, was now en route to Agadez. Tegama was awaiting his arrival, and had even constructed a house for Kaocen, adjacent to the sultan's palace.

The plan was to disperse the French garrisons on various missions, and attack the units one by one as they returned to Agadez. One suspicious captain foresaw trouble, and ordered his troops to return to Agadez before the arrival of Kaocen. Most units arrived in time to retreat to Fort Dufau, a fortified storage building with ammunition and food supplies. Those who didn't arrive in time awaited a terrible fate. On 13 December 1916, the French who had retreated the fort were besieged by Kaocen and his army. The siege lasted 81 days, until French reinforcements sent in from the south came to their rescue. Kaocen and Sultan Tegama and many of his allies had fled the region by then, but hundreds of conspirators and marabouts were brutally slaughtered by the French troops. Agadez was now back in the hands of the French, but the massacre left the town with a decimated population.

The sultanate under a new administration It would take some decades for the French to subjugate the Tuareg who had retreated to the Aïr Mountains. In the mean time, both Agadez and the surrounding region were more or less paralysed: many people had lost their livestock and left the region, a malaria epidemic had taken many lives and the trans-Saharan trade had virtually come to a standstill. Agadez had become little more than a desolate military outpost.

The French started to reorganise their military administration. As the local population was reluctant to deal directly with the French military, it was necessary to re-establish the sultanate. In May 1917, ex-sultan Ibrahim was called back to Agadez by the French. He had been dethroned and expelled by the first French occupants in 1907, who had considered him too little compliant. Now he was needed to act as an intermediary between the population and the French administration. However, the sultan's power was heavily restricted under the new administration, as he now had to obey the imposed French rule. All matters concerning justice, customs (eg: taxes on merchandise) and the organisation and security of the salt caravans now rested with the military authorities (see also *Nigérien society*, page 31).

The region of Agadez remained under the French military administration until Niger's independence in 1960. The military quarters and barracks were located in the quarter that is still aptly named 'Bariki'. This quarter symbolises the shift in power, from traditional to colonial. Demographic statistics reveal the recovery of Agadez: in 1941 the population comprised no more than 3,500 persons, and this number gradually increased to 6,720 in 1963, then to 77,000 in 2001. However, these figures also include the many victims of recent droughts, who settled along the outskirts of Agadez after losing their livestock.

GETTING THERE AND AWAY

By air In recent years, the heavily eroded airstrip of Mano Dayak Airport in Agadez has been largely improved, and direct flights from France to Agadez by **Point Afrique** and **Go Voyages** have been resumed. Timetables change every year, and furthermore these air companies have a tendency to alter schedules even at the last minute. Therefore, always check and double check the most up-to-date information on their websites. Even if you have purchased a ticket already, stay informed on the latest changes as flights may be cancelled, postponed or rerouted at will. This is a definite downside, especially if you have paid for a ticket to Paris or Marseille, only to find out your connecting flight to Agadez has been rescheduled to the day prior to your flight to France. Situations like this have occurred in the past, and while the companies do try to provide a reliable service, they reject all liability for missed flights and extra expenses. Having said all that, these companies fill a niche with very competitive fares, and even more attractive special offers. Read the conditions carefully before planning and booking your trip and allow plenty of time between connecting flights (think in terms of days rather than hours) to avoid disappointment, and you won't easily find a cheaper or faster way to get to Agadez.

At the time of writing, **Point Afrique** (✆ 28 99 89) has weekly flights from Paris to Marseille and onwards to Agadez on Saturdays from October through March. Occasionally a second stop is made in Tripoli. The flight arrives in Agadez around midday and leaves again for Marseille and Paris only hours later. Normal fares are CFA188,000 (€280) for a one-way ticket and CFA248,000 (€380) for a return ticket. An extra CFA50,000 is charged if you want to change the flight date, and CFA70,000 if you want to alter the place of departure.

Go Voyages (✆ 44 03 72/98 45 85) has weekly flights to and from Paris on Saturdays from October through March. Rates vary from CFA170,000 to CFA240,000 for a one-way ticket, though occasionally there are special offers at lower rates. Go Voyages is represented by the travel agency Dunes Voyages, so you can contact them for more information (see page 167).

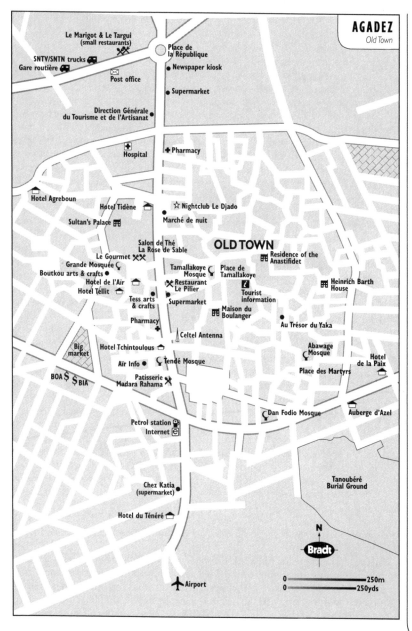

AGADEZ
Old Town

Le Marigot & Le Targui
(small restaurants)

Place de
la République

SNTV/SNTN trucks
Gare routière

Newspaper kiosk

Post office

Supermarket

Direction Générale
du Tourisme et de l'Artisanat

Hospital

Pharmacy

Hotel Agreboun

Hotel Tidène

☆ Nightclub Le Djado

Sultan's Palace

Marché de nuit

Salon de Thé
La Rose de Sable

OLD TOWN

Le Gourmet

Residence of the
Anastifidet

Grande Mosquée

Tamallakoye
Mosque

Place de
Tamallakoye

Boutkou arts & crafts

Heinrich Barth
House

Hotel de l'Aïr

Restaurant
Le Pilier

Hotel Téllit

Tourist
information

Tess arts
& crafts

Supermarket

Maison du
Boulanger

Pharmacy

Au Trésor du Yaka

Celtel Antenna

Big
market

Hotel Tchintoulous

Abawage
Mosque

Aïr Info

Tendé Mosque

Place des Martyrs

Hotel
de la Paix

BOA $ $ BIA

Patisserie
Madara Rahama

Dan Fodio Mosque

Auberge d'Azel

Petrol station
Internet

Tanoubéré
Burial Ground

N

Chez Katia
(supermarket)

Bradt

Hotel du Ténéré

0 ———— 250m
0 ———— 250yds

✈ Airport

By road All four bus companies (*SNTV,* ↘ *44 02 07, Rimbo Transport,* ↘ *74 14 13; Aïr Transport,* ↘ *99 37 31;* and *Maissagé,* ↘ *44 03 11/99 24 75*) have regular services between Niamey and Arlit, with a stop in Agadez. Getting to Agadez, or finding a seat to get from Agadez to Arlit will hardly ever be a problem. On the other hand, while you may have purchased your ticket to Niamey well beforehand, it does occasionally happen that buses coming from Arlit are full. With breakdowns being the other cause for delays, don't take your chances: travel to

Unless you have a few months to explore the Aïr and Ténéré regions, you will have to choose from many possible itineraries. Your mode of travel obviously determines how far and how fast – or slowly – you can move around, while it also significantly influences the nature of your experience. The large majority of travellers organise their trip through an agency, and with good reason. The most apparent one is the fact that public transport is very limited, very uncomfortable and time consuming (see page 69). Even if you manage to find your way to Iférouane or Timia, options for further travel become even more limited. You will probably find someone willing to act as a guide and to provide camels for transport, but there are no organised guides, agencies or contact addresses. Finding provisions is another issue, unless you are willing to restrict yourself to the local diet of bread, noodles, takomért (see *Food and drink*, page 73), dates, tea, some vegetables and occasionally meat. Forget about finding a guide who understands English, but there are guides who speak very good French. Therefore, while it is not entirely impossible to venture out on your own, you would be throwing yourself into the deep end and you would have no back-up in case of any problem.

WHEELS, HIKING BOOTS OR THE SHIP OF THE DESERT Organising a trip through an agency invariably involves the use of a 4x4 vehicle. Even if you decide to go trekking (a walking trip with camels or sometimes donkeys to carry your luggage), or to set out on a *méharee* (a combination of walking and riding a camel), you need to get to the point of departure first. More often than not, this means at least one day travelling by 4x4. Walking or riding a camel (with saddle) is a magnificent way to discover parts of the Aïr and the Ténéré. It allows plenty of time to zoom in on the beauty of the landscape and all the life it hides, at a harmonious pace, in accordance with the local way of life. Unless you have opted for an ambitious itinerary where finding water becomes relevant, it also means that you are flexible in the distance you want to cover. Without any doubt it is the best way to make you feel part of the surrounding landscape, and to experience what it takes to adapt to a life out in the open desert.

If you are especially interested in the Ténéré, a *grand raid* or grand tour by 4x4 is a possibility. This long-distance round trip takes you to the remote oases of Bilma and the Djado Plateau, while you will see much of the Aïr Mountains in the process. For safety reasons (car breakdowns or getting stuck in soft sand), a minimum of two cars is required for this option, so unless you are many or if you can find fellow travellers, this is an expensive option. A trip specifically to the Aïr Mountains and its fringes – *la bordure de l'Aïr* – leaves many options open.

Niamey at least a day before you need to catch a plane. Tickets are sold from 07.00 to 19.00.

Maissagé Transport (or EHGM), Rimbo Transport and SNTV have daily buses going to **Niamey** (reporting time 07.00, 06.30 for Rimbo Transport only; ten hours), while Aïr Transport has buses leaving on Tuesdays-Thursdays-Fridays-Sundays (reporting time 07.00). Prices vary from CFA12,000 (Maissagé) to CFA14,300 (SNTV). On certain days SNTV has air-conditioned buses, costing CFA15,550. If you want to get off in towns along the way, expect to pay around the following fares: **Tahoua** (CFA7,000); **Birni N'Konni** (CFA8,800); **Dogondoutchi** (CFA10,000); **Dosso** (CFA11,000).

For daily buses to **Arlit**, reporting time is 15.00 (15.30 for Rimbo Transport), the journey takes around two hours and costs between CFA3,200 (Maissagé) and CFA3,400 (SNTV; with air conditioning: CFA3,560).

An interesting route by Maissagé and SNTV is the direct connection between Agadez and **Zinder** (via Aderbissinat and Tanout). Since a stretch of road is not

Many travellers opt for a combined trip, with some exploration by 4x4, and a shorter méharee in those areas that are more suitable for camels than for cars. It offers the best of both worlds, with a wider travel range as well as the experience of walking the dunes at a camel's pace, with no disturbing sounds of an engine. When the 4x4s stay with you during the méharee (as some agencies propose), you will only meet the cars again at an agreed lunch or camping spot (see also *Local tour operators: examples of itineraries and rates*, page 167).

ROUTE APPROVAL The authorities stress the importance of travelling with a licensed travel agency or tour operator if you intend to head out to the Ténéré Desert or the Aïr Mountains. First of all because the environment is extremely hostile, and inexperienced travellers often underestimate the travel conditions and circumstances. Secondly, security has been an issue in the northern region for many years. Though the situation has calmed down, efforts are made to minimise risks, and encouraging tourists to book with a licensed agency is one protective measure.

Licensed tour operators register all clients through a *feuille de route* or 'route approval', a document that includes all relevant details of a journey (personal details, name of the agency, guides and drivers, itinerary, etc), and this form is copied to the local authorities. In case of any problem, these authorities will assist if necessary. This document is delivered free of charge through the agency.

Unlicensed agencies or independent (mostly unlicensed) guides are not entitled to get this piece of paper. The only way for them to purchase one is through a licensed agency, willing to act as an umbrella. They usually charge money to get the paperwork done, and these costs will be passes on to you. So, if you are told you have to pay for the route approval, you know the score. Asking to see the licence is another way of figuring out the status of the agency you are dealing with.

Though the authorities will say it is compulsory to travel with a guide in the northern zone, this is not the case. Nor is it compulsory to travel with a *feuille de route*, though in places you may be asked to produce your copy. Regardless of your mode of travel, and whether it be independent or with an agency, it always makes sense to register and fill out that form. If you fail to get one in Agadez (at the police station or at the Direction Régional du Tourisme (DRT), see above), you could report at the police station at the larger oases like Iférouane or Timia.

tarred, the already not–so–new buses take a heavy beating. The weather and road conditions determine how much this section will slow down the bus. Expect the journey to take at least seven, but more likely eight to ten hours. Along the way, there will be three short stops only. Female travellers should be aware that the only toilets with doors are in Tanout, while the landscape between towns is barren, with very few bushes to squat behind. Both companies have two weekly departures, on Tuesdays and Saturdays (reporting time for Maissagé 08.00; CFA7,600, reporting time for SNTV is 07.30; CFA6,700).

Another option between Agadez and Zinder is provided by SNTN. This is the older counterpart of SNTV, and generally deals with the transport of merchandise. Occasionally, SNTN provides passenger transport as well, especially on rougher sections. On some Tuesdays, SNTN sends out converted passenger trucks from Agadez to Zinder. Reporting time is at 06.00 and the journey costs around CFA6,000. Inquire at the SNTN station next to the *autogare* or *gare routière*.

Two or three times a week, battered medium-sized SNTN buses leave for **Ingal** (CFA3,000). SNTN is also considering a transport service to Arlit and onwards to **Assamakka** near the Algerian border. Again, enquire at the SNTN station for more details.

For adventurous travellers with stamina, SNTN has converted trucks for passenger transport (*camion voyageurs*) leaving for **Dirkou** and **Bilma** three or four times a month at CFA20,000 per person. Though it should be less demanding than travelling amongst dozens of passengers on top of a truck primarily meant for the transport of merchandise, do not take this option lightly. The journey takes at least 30 hours of driving; allow extra time for breakdowns, getting stuck and unstuck, and stops. There will be at least one overnight stop somewhere along the *piste*, and you should be fully self-supporting for food and water. These trucks take the northerly *piste* past the Falaise d'Achegour, thus bypassing Fachi. For security reasons, a military escort is provided by the Force FNIS.

At the *gare routière* you will find all sorts of vehicles (usually leaving when full) to nearby and long-haul destinations. Smaller buses leave daily for **Tchighozérine** (CFA1,000) and **Arlit** (CFA2,600), as well as for **Ingal** (CFA1,850). There are almost daily departures by minibus or truck for **Zinder**. These vehicles are less comfortable than the SNTV and Maïssagé buses, but if you need to cut down the expenses, travelling by truck is cheaper at CFA3,600 (at least ten hours to Zinder), while the minibuses still charge CFA7,100 (eight–nine hours). Ask around for trucks leaving for the oases of **Iférouane** and **Timia** and expect the journey to both destinations to take at least a full day, with a possible overnight stop along the *piste*. Trucks leave for **Dirkou** (CFA15,000) once every four days, and take three to four days to reach their final destination. More trucks heading for **Bilma** (CFA25,000) and **Fachi** (CFA45,000) leave from town near the *Marché de l'Est* or *Sabon Gari*, the daily vegetable market to the east of the centre. Ask around for departure dates and fares. Read the travel advice on pages 68–70 to have a realistic idea of what's involved.

GETTING AROUND While everything in Agadez is well within walking distance, when the sun stands high in the sky you could always opt for a taxi or *kabou-kabou*. While taxis are less abundant, young *kabou-kabou* drivers are everywhere. They seem to pass the time sitting on their stationary motorbikes, chatting with friends and taking a nap every now and then, while waiting for clients. The fare for *kabou-kabou* is CFA150 or 200 per person, which are fixed rates for shorter/longer distances within town. Agree the price beforehand. For taxis, the fixed rate is CFA200 per person within town during the daytime.

TOURIST INFORMATION In Agadez, the governmental body concerned with the executive side of tourism is the **Direction Regionale du Tourisme** (DRT). They monitor the quality of facilities and services provided, and see to it that regulations are being followed. To the public, the DRT is of limited use. Though they will assist travellers who find themselves stranded because of serious problems such as an accident, loss of passport, theft or robbery, the DRT is not a tourist office. As growing numbers of tourists find their way to this part of the country and facilities and travel agencies mushroomed, some travel agencies decided to pool their knowledge in order to to promote sustainable tourism and to improve the quality of all services provided in the tourist sector in the region.

In 2001, these agencies founded the **Syndicat du Tourisme du Niger**. The lack of a public tourist counter is one of the issues they intend to tackle. To fill that void, the Syndicat founded the **Centre d'Information Touristique** (*CIT; open Fri–Tue, mornings and afternoons, closed for lunch*) based in the old town. Opening hours are somewhat erratic, as only one person is running the office, and when he is running errands he simply closes the door. Even on an administrative level it is not yet a smoothly functioning information centre, though. The Syndicat is struggling to get all its members – with diverse and sometimes rigid ideas based on years of experience in the profession – looking in the same direction. So while the Syndicat is trying to make the 'marriage' work, their baby – the information centre – is left somewhat neglected. Still, while there is room for improvement, this is one place where you could find some folders, maps, books and someone to inform you about the numerous tourist sites in the region. Information about travel agencies will for obvious reasons be limited to the members of the Syndicat, while there are several more agencies to choose from in Agadez.

LOCAL TOUR OPERATORS Around 50 tour operators sell trips into the desert or the Aïr Massif from Agadez. Sometimes the agency is little more than an office in France with a representative in Agadez; others not only have an office in Agadez, but also a workshop with mechanics to maintain their vehicles, as well as trained drivers and guides, and plenty of camping materials (including tents and mattresses). The following selection – of the larger tour operators with many years of experience – is by no means complete, nor does it do justice to those relatively new or smaller agencies who work well but who do not appear in the list. One exception to this rule is Tafadek Voyages, a young agency run exclusively by Tuareg women: a courageous initiative and I wish these women well!

To avoid clogging the map, these tour operators are not indicated on it. If asking around does not do the trick, enquire at the Centre d'Information Touristique for directions.

Abal Voyages BP 75; ☎ 44 03 25/98 31 35; satellite phone: 00 88 216 212 26 71; f 44 03 25; e abal_voyages@yahoo.fr
Adrar Madet BP 223; ☎ 44 03 72; f 44 02 72; www.saharatravel.com
Agadez Expeditions BP 277; ☎ 44 01 70/96 66 55/96 27 00; f 44 01 70; e agadezexpeditions@yahoo.com; www.agadez-tourisme.com
Agharous ☎ 44 03 09
Azalaï ☎ 44 04 38
Dunes Voyages BP 279; ☎ 44 03 72; Jun–Aug ☎/f 00 33 (0)4 74 62 36 27; f 44 02 72; e dunes@dunes-voyages.com; www.dunes-voyages.com
Ewaden Voyages BP 61; ☎ 44 01 83
Expéditions Ténéré BP 246; ☎ 44 01 54/98 32 60; f 44 01 54; e expeditionstenere@yahoo.fr; www.expeditionstenere.fr.fm

Planète Sable BP 98; ☎ 49 79 16/28 38 44; e info@voyages-touaregs.com; www.voyages-touaregs.com
Pléiades Voyages BP 254; ☎ 44 05 41/98 32 50; e sidi@pleiades-agadez.com; www.pleiades-agadez.com
Sahara Découverte BP 127; ☎ 44 05 43/99 45 20; f 44 05 44; www.saharadecouverte.com
SVS (Société de Voyages Sahariennes) BP 272; ☎ 44 04 77/96 64 26
Tafadek Voyages BP 102; ☎ 44 04 16/97 62 22; f 44 04 16
Taguelmoust BP 69; ☎ 44 01 48; f 44 01 48; e tts@intnet.ne/dissoufa@libero.it
Tidène Expeditions BP 270; ☎ 44 05 68/98 30 65; f 44 05 78; e tidenexp@intnet.ne; www.tidene-expeditions.com
Touareg Tours ☎ 44 05 26/98 12 13

Examples of itineraries and rates The price tag for any kind of journey to the Aïr and Ténéré regions is considerable. Prices vary between tour operators, so does the standard of luxury and the content, and there are many other variables to take into account. As most organised trips are tailor-made, it is very difficult to indicate how much a day out in the Aïr or Ténéré would cost. To not leave you completely in the dark, the rates mentioned below are realistic, but not necessarily the same for all tour operators. Consider them guidelines only, and no guarantee whatsoever. For details on the given destinations, see the *Aïr Mountains* and the *Ténéré Desert* sections, pages 177–9.

Price indications are per person for a party of seven or more and starting from Agadez, and generally include vehicle and fuel; driver, guide and cook; all meals; foam mattress; local taxes. Travel agencies will only head out to certain remote or sandy destinations (like Arakao, Temet, Bilma and Orida) with at least two vehicles. As transport is the most expensive factor in the total cost, the rate for a trip to any of these places will be very costly if you are travelling on your own or with one companion only. Try to team up with other travellers to reduce the cost.

Trekking through the Aïr Mountains by foot Elméki – Tchintoulous – Kogo (start eight-day trekking, camels for luggage only) – Arakao – Adrar Chiriet – Tezirzek (end trekking) – Iférouane – Timia – Agadez; 12 days; €840.

Méharée in the Aïr Mountains Elméki – Tchintoulous – Kogo (start eight-day camel trek, riding possible) – Arakao – Adrar Chiriet – Kogo (end camel trek) – Timia – Agadez; 12 days; €820 (€1,585 per person for a party of two persons).

Aïr Mountains by 4x4 Elméki – Timia – Assodé – Tchintoulous – Kogo – Arakao – Adrar Chiriet – Tezirzek – Temet – Iférouane – Agadez; seven days; €565 (€1,645 per person for a party of two persons).

Grand tour Arbre du Ténéré – Bilma – Orida – Tafassâsset – Temet – Adrar Chiriet – Arakao – Timia – Agadez; 12 days; €970.

WHERE TO STAY

🏠 **Auberge Taguelmoust** (12 rooms) 📞 44 04 50/97 31 39; f 44 01 48; e tts@intnet.ne. Located next to Taguelmoust Voyages, this hotel is due to open in 2006. It has been recently built in traditional style. The comfortable s/c rooms with fan and the option to use AC have up to 4 beds and are pleasantly laid out around a spacious courtyard. *Expect prices around CFA22,000.*

🏠 **Hotel Agrebou** (10 rooms) The hotel is run by a lady with abrupt manners, but otherwise staff are very helpful. No meals are available. *Provides budget accommodation, with very basic rooms with fan at CFA4,000/6,000 (sgl/dbl) and rooms with fan and shower at CFA5,000/7,000.*

🏠 **Hotel Auberge d'Azel** (10 rooms) 📞 44 01 70/ 96 66 55/96 27 00; e agadezexpeditions@yahoo.com; www.agadez-tourisme.com. This place has a beautiful layout with a secluded garden and a homely setting. The auberge is run by a knowledgeable French–Tuareg couple who also run the travel agency Agadez Expeditions and who will be able to supply plenty of information. Rooms are very tastefully decorated and immaculately kept. Excellent international and traditional meals can be enjoyed inside or outside. *Rates for the s/c AC rooms vary between CFA30,000 and CFA40,000.*

🏠 **Hotel Auberge La Tendé** (15 rooms and 6 traditional *cases*) 📞 44 00 75/99 25 09; f 44 00 75; e tende@free.fr; http://tende.free.fr. A very friendly place situated at the edge of town. The owners also run a travel agency and will gladly inform you about options to explore the region. The hotel has a pleasant restaurant for grilled meat, international and traditional meals. *The premises hold many different types of accommodation, like a campsite (CFA2,500 pp); a mattress on the roof or in a case Tuareg or hut made from woven mats (CFA3,500 pp); rooms with fan (CFA10,000/12,500 sgl/dbl); or AC rooms for CFA21,000/25,000/30,000 (sgl/dbl/triple). Two rooms share 1 bathroom.*

🏠 **Hotel Bungalows Telwa** (19 rooms) 📞 44 02 64/97 14 41. Has comfortable s/c rooms in 3 price categories around a pleasant garden. While maybe lacking in character, the rooms are clean and well kept, and not overpriced. Breakfast is available at CFA2,000, as well as a limited menu or diner complet (CFA4,000). *The least expensive and middle categories of room cost CFA18,000 and CFA28,000 per dbl respectively (18 rooms). One room (CFA37,000) has all the luxuries such as AC, a fridge and TV.*

🏠 **Hotel de l'Aïr** (16 rooms) 📞 44 02 47/96 91 23. This hotel was constructed by order of Sultan Tegama of Agadez, to be the temporary residence of Kaocen (see page 161). Rich history has now been covered with a layer of dust, as the hotel reflects little of its former glory. The rooms are basic and not so well maintained, but all have shower, though some rooms share toilets. The food is filling but uninteresting, but the view from the terrace, opposite the minaret of the famous mosque, couldn't be any better. *The prices are fair, starting from CFA10,000 for a room with fan up to CFA15,000 for an AC room.*

🏠 **Hotel de la Paix** (48 rooms) ↘ 44 02 34/45 22 13/96 12 92; f 45 21 10; e hotel@intnet.ne. This is the largest and most expensive hotel in town, suitable to cater for larger groups and conferences. While the outside of the large building is trying to copy some aspects of the local architecture, the interior design lacks character. Management is struggling to keep the number of guests up, which is not surprising with the current rates and plenty of other options. The swimming pool is open to non-clients at CFA1,500. A daily menu can be served for CFA7,000. *Comfortable s/c AC rooms start from CFA30,000/35,000 (sgl/dbl) to CFA60,000 for a dbl de luxe.*

🏠 **Hotel du Ténéré** (12 rooms) This Italian-owned hotel is conveniently located just opposite the airport. It is built in traditional style, and is reasonably priced and straightforward. So far there are 6 rooms with fan starting at CFA10,000, and 6 s/c AC dbls at CFA20,000. There is also talk of constructing some more rooms during the course of 2006. You may also pitch your tent in the yard, where you can have the use of basic facilities. Meals available on site.

🏠 **Hotel Tchintoulous** (12 rooms) ↘ 44 04 59. Another hotel with interesting architecture and original banco decorations is the friendly and somewhat sleepy. The combination of gravel floors, traditional Tuareg beds and fridge-like AC installations in the rooms must be unique. The state of the bathrooms leaves much to be desired, though. Indoors is the office for Caravane Voyages,

one of the many travel agencies in town. The restaurant is barely functional, but if you order in advance, you can have a meal for CFA4,500. *Rooms with fan cost CFA10,000, while s/c AC rooms cost CFA15,000.*

🏠 **Hotel Tellit** (5 rooms, 3 suites) ↘ 44 02 31/98 33 08. The Tellit is owned by the same Italian who runs Restaurant Le Pilier, and the architecture is similar in style: a playful combination of the traditional and the practical. *This small hotel has 5 rooms only, the cheapest of which is a s/c AC dbl with hot water and fridge (CFA18,000). The suites are well furnished, and some rooms enjoy a wonderful view of the mosque, but then the price of these suites is set accordingly at CFA38,000. An annexe well out of the centre of Agadez has 4 more rooms (↘ 44 03 59).*

🏠 **Hotel Tidène** (15 rooms) ↘ 44 04 06/98 33 84. The Tidène is nestled against the Sultan's Palace, and its architecture fits well within this setting. Through the main building is a yard with many corners and corridors, hiding more rooms than you would have thought. Breakfast is served at CFA2,500, and a daily menu (CFA4,500) is available on request. It is a friendly and welcoming place, *with s/c rooms starting from CFA9,500 for a sgl with fan to CFA20,000 for an AC dbl. Add CFA2,500 for a supplementary bed.*

🏠 **Restaurant Orida** (3 rooms) ↘ 98 34 32. The Orida has basic rooms with saggy beds at *CFA5,000 per person.*

🏠 **Restaurant Tamgak** (4 rooms and 4 *cases traditionelles*) ↘ 89 92 62/29 10 37. Rather small and basic, but adequate s/c rooms with cold water only. Besides the rooms (*CFA10,000*), 4 *cases traditionelles* (CFA7,000) will be put up in the courtyard.

Out of town

🏕 **Camping l'Escale** 4km out of town in the direction of Arlit. This camping has seen its heyday during the years when overlanders used to cross the desert from Algeria into Niger. Since then it

has gradually become dormant, but staff are there to welcome anyone looking for a shady place to pitch a tent (*CFA2,000 per person, CFA1,500 extra for a 4x4*). Order in advance for a basic meal.

Ignore signposts and white painted rocks leading to the out-of-town Hotel de la Plage, as this hotel has shut down. It is unlikely that this hotel will open up again soon.

WHERE TO EAT Most hotels have restaurants. For some details, see the listing above.

✗ **Buvette La Tente** A small bar near the *marché de tôles* serves basic meals, but more interesting

are the fresh juices, including *jus de mille* and bissap (see *Food and drink*, page 74).

✕ Le Gourmet Just next to the Salon de Thé is this local restaurant where you can have a filling meal of spaghetti or rice-and-something straight from the cooking pot.

✕ Marché de nuit Not far from the Sultan's Palace. If you like to try local food you can choose from a wide variety of very cheap, stodgy meals (*a plate of pâte de mille and sauce de gombo – sauce made of okra or lady's fingers – for CFA150*), brochettes, grilled chicken and different *beignets* and *galettes* (different types of fritter made from wheat, millet or rice).

✕ Restaurant l'Atlantide ☏ 88 88 92. The straightforward interior with long tables makes this a suitable place for groups. The tasty, inexpensive local dishes are best ordered in advance. Another good reason to have a meal here is to meet the owner Bibi, a lady Tuareg with a strong, enchanting character. She has been catering for big events very successfully, and Bibi is one of the driving forces behind lots of activities run by women.

✕ Restaurant le Marigot A small local restaurant. *Enjoy a basic meal for around CFA1,000–1,500.*

✕ Restaurant Le Pilier ☏ 44 03 31. The same Italian who also owns Restaurant Le Pilier in Niamey converted a former house into the highly original, labyrinth-like Restaurant Le Pilier. In the busiest months you can choose between a cosy indoors room or the airy courtyard. The mostly Italian dishes are reasonably priced, considering the

fine quality of the food, the friendly service and the setting as a whole. *The restaurant closes Apr–Sep.*

✕ Restaurant le Targui Like le Marigot, this restaurant is near the SNTV bus station. *Basic meals cost CFA1,000–1,500.*

✕ Restaurant Orida ☏ 98 34 32. Near the Tamgak, this serves inexpensive meals in a clean but rather barren interior.

✕ Restaurant Tamgak ☏ 89 92 62/29 10 37. While you could order steak and chips if you wish this place is more renowned for its excellent and very affordable local food. Choose from a variety of dishes like *tanderou* (deliciously spiced mutton cooked in a traditional oven), *alfitate* or *gourrassa* (2 kinds of traditional pancake with vegetables and sauce) or homemade couscous. Certain dishes, like *mechoui* (see *Food and drink*, page 74), have to be ordered in advance. To add to the local flavour, enjoy the pre-recorded or occasionally live Peul and Tuareg music (see pages 34–5).

✕ Salon de Thé La Rose de Sables ☏ 44 02 18/99 57 55. If you grow tired of having French bread and jam for breakfast every morning, try this place near the Place de la Grande Mosque. Choose from a mouthwatering selection of pancakes, muffins, cinnamon pastry, cakes and fruit pies from only a few coins each. *Open 08.00–12.00 and 16.30–20.00, closed Sun. (But opening times vary according to the season.)*

ENTERTAINMENT, BARS AND NIGHTLIFE Hotel du Ténéré doubles as a bar-restaurant, and is frequented by local people. The location is especially good for those waiting to depart with one of the two weekly charter flights: you can check in your luggage in the morning, then have a meal or drink at Hotel du Ténéré. Once the airplane has touched down, you can walk to the airport and be there well in time to proceed to the gate.

A music lover and connoisseur, the owner of **Restaurant Tamgak** regularly invites Tuareg and Peul musicians to perform in the evenings, especially at weekends but also on request. Groupe Oyiwane, a group of local musicians, often play traditional Tuareg music at this restaurant.

The open-air **Bar de l'Arène** could be described as a Tuareg disco, that stages live music on most Fridays and Saturdays, mostly 'tradi-moderne' Tuareg music. It becomes a rather noisy drinking place late at night.

Open since the beginning of 2005, **Parc 86** is a very spacious open-air bar. It became very popular with local people in a short time, a meeting place where you can have a cold beer and a snack.

Formerly a hotel, now **Petit Bar**, this bar is frequented mostly by Agadez's youth. A lively place where modern local music is played. Next dor to the Petit Bar is **Bar dancing Oasis**. For some deafening discomusic, go to the **Djado Nightclub** near the *Marché de nuit*. Entrance fee is CFA500.

The **Maison des Jeunes et de la Culture** or MJC (☏ 44 00 27) regularly stages live concerts and theatre plays in the amphitheatre. Their programme is badly advertised though, so it could be a matter of pot luck to find out what is going on. Posters are sometimes spread around town, or otherwise cars with loudspeakers drive around the town to invite people to join the show. Asking around or calling the above telephone number are the only other options. A brand-new **Cultural Centre** financed by the Alliance Française was under construction at the time of research.

SHOPPING Pâtisserie **Madara Rahama** (open daily) sell fresh milk and sweetened yoghurt in plastic sachets (like Solani and Kossam, see *Food and drink*, page 74). The choice of pastry is limited to a modest selection of sweet cakes and croissants with cream. Next to Restaurant Le Pilier is a small, but well-stocked **supermarket**. Another supermarket is along the same road, but towards the administrative quarters of Agadez. Between the petrol station La Concorde and the airport is '*Le Libanais*' also known as '*Chez Katia*', a well-stocked supermarket and the only place to buy alcoholic drinks like whisky and wine. Note that shops usually close for lunch.

ARTS AND CRAFTS Across the road from Restaurant le Pilier is the new shop **Tess** (✆ *89 24 11*) selling good-quality, rather pricey arts and crafts from Niger and neighbouring countries. The mixture of old and new objects is pleasantly displayed and worth having a look at even if you are not sure you need anything. In the labyrinth of the old town, a new shop called **Au Trésor de Yaka** sells beads and necklaces, as well as some other souvenirs. The traditional beads are the best, though. The **Village Artisanal d'Agadez** not far from the main route to Niamey and Arlit is a cooperative with workshops and items for direct sale. Another cooperative is the **Service Artisanat d'Agadez**. This centre was founded by women after the drought of 1984, in an attempt to help out their families after they had lost most of their cattle (*open Mon–Fri 08.00–12.30 and 15.00–18.00, Sat and Sun 10.00–12.00*). **Boutkou** is a shop at the foot of the ancient mosque. It has a good choice of clothing, fabric, silverware and other items. Fixed prices are reasonable.

OTHER PRACTICALITIES
Tourist office Centre d'Information Touristique (*open Fri–Tue 08.30–12.30 and 15.00–18.00, closed for lunch*). See also *Tourist information*, page 166.

Communications and media The **post office** is located not far from the Place de la Republique, almost opposite the SNTN bus yard.
The best options for **internet access** are the Cybercafé next to the petrol station at the junction from the Route de Bilma and the Route de l'Aeroport and the internet café Desertelecom not far from the SNTV bus yard. Connection (by satellite) is fast and costs CFA500 per 20 minutes. The telephone connection at Alher Net opposite Hotel de la Paix, on the other hand, is a lot slower yet more expensive at CFA100 per minute.
Newspapers are available from a small kiosk near the Place de la République. Look out for the monthly newspaper *Air Info*. This local newspaper is run by young and dedicated journalists. Their office is signposted not far from Hotel Tchintoulous.

Banks The two **banks** are near the market, just next to each other. The BIA changes cash euro and US dollars and gives cash advances on Visa or MasterCard. Commission on credit card transactions is fixed at CFA10,000. The BIA will also change most travellers' cheques at a 2–5% commission, depending on the currency.

The bank opens from 08.00–11.30 and 16.00–17.30 on weekdays, and from 08.00–12.00 on Saturdays. The BOA changes cash euro and US dollars. Open on weekdays from 08.30–11.30 and 15.45–17.00, and on Saturdays from 08.30–11.45. Both banks are closed on Sundays.

Other In theory, you could apply for a visa at the **Algerian consulate** (↘ 44 02 95/01 17) and the **Libyan consulate** (↘ 44 02 92), but the request for a visa has to be approved by the authorities based in these countries and it will in all likelihood take well over a month to get a reply. Therefore, if you are planning an onward journey to either of these countries, it is advisable to obtain your visa before travelling to Niger. For travel advice and information regarding the security of the border regions and as to whether or not the border is open for travellers, the consulates are best contacted in the mornings.

The **Institut de Récherches des Sciences Humaines** or IRSH is part of the *Faculté des Lettres* of the University of Niamey. If you are interested in the history of Agadez and other towns, books and documents from the modest library can be consulted on site.

WHAT TO SEE AND DO
Sultan's Palace The two-storey palace was constructed in the 15th century. The *banco* structure includes various courtyards, a reception hall, living quarters and a prison. Through a special exit from the premises, the sultan has almost direct access to the adjacent Grande Mosquée. The sultan is surrounded by an extensive court, and court members are well recognisable through their traditional costumes. The palace can not be visited, but it is possible to cross one of the courtyards to get an impression of the size and beauty of the building.

Tendé Mosque Like the Big Mosque, this mosque was also built by Zakarya, in the part of town where he used to live in celibacy. Though much smaller in size, this mosque plays an important role in the celebration of Mouloud – the celebration of the birthday of the prophet Mohammed – and the Tendé – seven days after Mouloud, the day when Mohammed was baptised (see also page 174).

Abawage Mosque After the siege of the French garrisons of the fort in 1916–17, the French massacred the conspirators. This mosque is one of the sites that is strongly linked with these brutal events, as many marabouts were decapitated here. The square where this mosque is located is named the Place des martyrs.

Dan Fodio Mosque This ancient mosque has sheltered many Muslim scholars, one of whom was the Peul leader Ousman Dan Fodio (see *History*, page 17).

Special houses in the old town The old town hides many treasures. There are some houses that stand out from the rest for one reason or another. A very peculiar house is the **maison du boulanger** or 'baker's house'. In 1917, the baker Sidi Ka, a Peul from Senegal, must have had a smashing time when he converted all rooms and every corner into fairytale-like grottoes. Bulky monsters, mischievous creatures and burlesque details on pillars, walls and ceilings alternate in this two-storey house. An entrance fee is payable, and starts from CFA1,000 per person depending on the mood of the guide. You will have to add to this if you want to take pictures. The **house of the Anastifidet** is the residence of the Anastifidet, the leader of the Kel Owey *groupement*. The house where **Heinrich Barth** resided in 1850 has been turned into a small museum. Very little of what is there is original, and the old couple who look after the place

In the heyday of Agadez, one of many Muslim saints who came to the town was Zakarya. His origins are not known, though two theories trace him back to either Fezzan (Libya) or the Songhay empire (Mali). Zakarya became a legendary person, who constructed the Grande Mosquée and other mosques in town. According to legend, the big mosque was first built on another location, but it soon collapsed. Another site, just to the north of the previous mosque, was chosen for a second attempt. Again the minaret crumbled to pieces. Zakarya then requested the sultan not to use any forced labour, nor anything taken from the poor, as this must have been the reason for the two minarets collapsing. The third attempt succeeded, and the mosque exists to this day.

The Big Mosque can be visited by men and women alike. You will have to take off your shoes, and appropriate dress is required. To the side, opposite Hotel de l'Aïr, is an entrance gate. Find the warden, who will lead you to the staircase in the minaret. The 27m-high tower can be ascended all the way, in an increasingly narrow stairway. The view from the top is magnificent, with all the different quarters of Agadez neatly laid out before you. There is no entrance fee, though you will be expected to leave a donation.

make an effort to explain what is 'real' and what is 'just a good example of what Heinrich Barth may have had'. It's a charming curiosity that is being kept with the best of intentions, but altogether not too exciting. There is no fixed charge, but you are expected to leave some money.

Place de Tamallakoye Until the big market was established on its present location, the Place de Tamallakoye was the economic centre of Agadez. One of the reasons why the market was relocated was because the narrow streets did not provide ample passage for lorries. With most of the trading now done elsewhere, the ancient square has acquired a sense of tranquillity. It is not devoid of activity, however, as there are still small shops and stalls, while the central location guarantees a lot of pedestrians, donkeys, motorbikes – but no big trucks. Place de Tamallakoye has become a friendly meeting place, and a wonderful site to just sit down in the shade and watch the pace of life in the old town.

Big market The big market is also known as the *marché de tôles* (with *tôles* referring to the omnipresent corrugated-iron) or the *marché moderne* (as opposed to the ancient Tamallakoye market). It is the place to look for anything from fruit and vegetables, spices and sweets, to shoes, turbans, tools and buckets. If from the outside this market looks lively, enter one of many small alleys to the interior for an overdose of odours and colours!

Sabon Gari market Stretched along the roads in the 'new quarter', this market is primarily for the sale of food and provisions.

Animal market Away from the centre of town and in a very lively commercial quarter, is the animal market, where camels, cattle, goats and sheep are bought and sold.

Muslim events One of the pillars of Islam is the month of fasting, or Ramadan, and the **Id al Fitr** is the last day of this month. It is a happy day, when everyone dresses up in preparation for the evening's festivities. After sunset, when the fasting (*le carême*) is finally over, an evening of joy and feasting begins. Early next morning, all believers gather at the Tanibère cemetrey, the open-air site for the prayer that officially marks the end of Ramadan.

Seven days after Tabashi begins the **Bianou** (see box above).

Mouloud is the celebration of the birth of the prophet Mohammed. It is mostly a day (or rather night) of prayer and reciting of Koran verses. It also is an occasion to see the sultan and his court, as well as many marabouts in full regalia on the way to sites that remain significant to this day, and to the mosque. The same can be said for the **Tendé**, which is seven days after Mouloud and the day that the Prophet was baptised. The sultan and his court, marabouts and butchers walk in procession to the Tendé Mosque for the ritual sacrifice of sheep – just in front of the mosque – and for prayer. If you are lucky, one of the marabouts will bless you with a touch of blood on your forehead.

ARLIT

The only link between the towns of Agadez and Arlit is a physical one: a pot-holed ribbon of tar. In every other sense, these towns couldn't be more different from each other. The history of Agadez goes back to the 11th century, a time when written records were scarce. Despite many missing pieces, historians managed to reconstruct a patchwork of events that shaped the town to what it is today.

How different is Arlit! Its entire history can be traced from newspapers alone. Half a century ago it was a barren desert and the territory of the Tuareg only. Then the discovery of uranium in the 1960s gave this new mining town a purpose in life. Within decades Arlit attracted an international and intercultural population of tens of thousands of people. Arlit was constructed for the future, or at least for the years the mines can meet the demand for uranium. When the demand halts, or when the supplies are exhausted, the future for Arlit will look bleak.

HISTORY Just before Niger's independence in 1960, the first uranium deposits were discovered 1,200km north of Niamey, 240km north of Agadez, in a desert region that was inhabited by (semi-)nomadic pastoral Tuareg. In the 1960s, more deposits were discovered in the area, leading to the establishment of Niger's first uranium mining company SOMAIR (Société des Mines de l'Aïr) in 1968. The first open-air mining pits became operative in 1971.

Solely for the benefit of the mining industry, in 1969 SOMAIR created a brand-new town and named it Arlit. It was a purpose-built town, highly adapted to suit the hundreds of expats from France who were employed by the new industry. Apart from the French, thousands of other Nigérien SOMAIR employees from the south moved to Arlit, while townships mushroomed to house the people who served those working in the industry. Arlit became known as '*petit Paris*', or 'little Paris', and it boasted modern facilities like supermarkets that received supplies directly from France, restaurants, a swimming pool, banks, a modern hospital and an airstrip. Given its desolate location in a landlocked country, transport of the uranium was problematic. To achieve a road link to the south, the tarred road from Niamey to Agadez was extended to Arlit, and this section was nicknamed '*la route de l'uranium*'. Most uranium could then be exported through Benin to the coast and then onwards by ship.

As the global demand for uranium was high initially, the industry blossomed for a decade. In 1975, a second mining company COMINAK (Compagnie des Mines d'Akouta) started exploiting other uranium deposits from a closed, 250m-deep mine 6km from Arlit, in the newly developed town of Akokan. Each company extracted around 2,000 tonnes of uranium annually, and the export revenues amounted to well over 80% of the total national exports over a number of years. The trans-Saharan route to Algeria had shifted eastward to Arlit, allowing other economic activities to develop in the region. The town became a regular stopping place for both traders and trans-Saharan travellers.

However, in the 1980s the demand for uranium plummeted, with depressing consequences for the industry. At the same time, serious droughts forced many Tuareg – who had lost most of their livestock – to seek refuge in the expanding shanty towns of Arlit. When insecurity in the region reigned as a result of the Tuareg rebellion in the early 1990s and the border to Algeria was closed, life in Arlit deteriorated. This resulted in the exodus of most expats and many others, and a high rate of unemployment for those who remained behind. While the security in the region is now largely restored, Arlit is not the booming town it used to be for a short period of time. The environment has suffered deeply from the presence of so many inhabitants who need firewood and grazing for their livestock. In a wide circle around Arlit, all timber has been cleared, which in turn led to the decimation

THE GIANT GIRAFFES OF DABOUS

At 110km to the north of Agadez along the road to Arlit is a site with the most extraordinary rock engravings. The site is 8km off the road along a rough track, where an ancient lake was fed by an ancient river, the Dabous. The water evaporated 4,000 years ago, leaving behind a sea of sand with some exposed rocks. These rocks hide over 800 engravings depicting antelopes, ostriches, predators, rhinoceros, horses, camels and people. The engravings that this site is most famed for, however, are two giant giraffe. Both giraffe are found on a large faintly inclining slope and the biggest one measures 5.4m. It is difficult to put an exact date to the age of these engravings, but the appearance of the different domesticated animals has made it possible to at least determine the chronology of these and other engravings. This way, it is estimated that the giraffe have been there for at least 6,000 years.

The sites are fragile and prone to damage, as has been proved in the past. Therefore, when visiting this site, visitors are requested to leave their car in the marked parking area, and explore the site on foot, while considering a few simple guidelines to avoid further deterioration (see box *A code of conduct at archaeological sites*, page 179, and box *Archaeological sites in the Aïr region*, pages 180–1).

Agadez ARLIT

7

PAST The indigenous people of the region were the (semi-)nomadic Tuareg. At the time the mines started operating, already they were very frustrated by the central administration in the south. They had been overlooked for a long time, as very little was being done to develop the northern rural regions and to assist them in their struggle to secure their means of subsistence. The Tuareg even felt slighted by the southern 'black' administration, and the overal situation became increasingly inflammatory (see *The Aïr Mountains*, page 182).

Then, with so much economic interest going on, all seemed possible after all: an extremely inaccessible zone was opened up and transformed into a cosmopolitan centre with high living standards for a happy few. Those who benefited were French expats and contractors drawn from the south; not the Tuareg. To make matters worse, the revenues seeped away from them and their zone, and were not used to improve their conditions of life, health, education, nutrition and so on. The Tuareg felt seriously bypassed once again, which created an even wider gap between them and the administrators. While uranium mining provided a badly needed boost to the national economy, it also lit a fuse in the impoverished Tuareg community and significantly added to the problems that eventually led to the Tuareg rebellion.

PRESENT Uranium is a highly dense metal, which is used to fuel nuclear power stations. When extracting the ore, radioactive gases and dust are released into the environment. The mining has to be done in carefully controlled circumstances to avoid contamination. In recent years, when high numbers of residents of Arlit suffered from serious illnesses (including lung cancer, tuberculosis and many skin diseases), they questioned whether the safety regulations had been sufficient to avoid overexposure to radiation. In other words: was there a direct relationship between the uranium mining and the outbreak of diseases?

Different NGOs have started to investigate the issue, and they analysed samples of water, air, soil and scrap metal. Some of the results showed that water samples contained levels of contamination 10 to 110 times higher than is considered acceptable by the World Health Organisation, while lack of waste management meant that contaminated scrap metal was sometimes re-used for construction in town. However tempting it may be to jump to conclusions, it cannot yet be established beyond doubt whether there is indeed a direct link as many of the miners who worked in the industry over the past 35 years have moved away from the area, some of the occurring diseases can be attributed to the harsh desert circumstances alone, and reliable statistics have been lacking. Yet, the alarm has been raised and there seems enough reason for further investigation. For more up-to-date information, see www.criirad.org.

of the fauna. The number of overland travellers that pass by and halt in Arlit remains very low, and even smaller numbers of visitors find their way to Arlit as a travel destination in its own right.

The mining industry now produces 3,200 tonnes of uranium annually between the two companies, and uranium deposits are estimated to last for another ten–13 years. In 2004, Niger was ranked fourth of all uranium producing countries in the world, after Canada, Australia and Kazakhstan. Despite the collapse in uranium prices, the industry still provides a significant 31% of Niger's export revenues. Out of an urban population of around 70,000, a total of 1,600 are employed by the two mining companies.

GETTING THERE AND AWAY All four big bus companies have buses leaving to and from Agadez and Niamey. From **Agadez**, the reporting time is 15.00 (15.30 for Rimbo Transport) and the fare is around CFA3,400. The reporting time for the return journey to the south is at 05.00 (04.30 for Rimbo Transport). The fare to Niamey is CFA17,000. Smaller vehicles leave from the *gare routière* to and from **Iférouane**.

THE AÏR MOUNTAINS

In the accounts of his journey through Niger in the mid-19th century, the German explorer Heinrich Barth called the Aïr Mountains 'the Switzerland of the desert'. The Aïr Mountains are like an elevated island, with a much more comfortable Sahelian climate than its Saharan surroundings (see *Climate, vegetation and land use,* page 3). Rains are rare, but the water is dispersed from the mountains to the lower levels, to the valleys and *oueds* or *koris*. *Oued* is the Arab word used by the Tuareg, *kori* the *Hausa* name for a mostly dry riverbed. While these dry riverbeds indeed stand dry for most of the year, water may flow for a few hours after the rains, causing brief inundations of lower parts for the valleys or pans before the water seeps through the sand or evaporates. It feeds and replenishes the groundwater, and fills up *gueltas* or rock pools. Flora and fauna are much more abundant along the *koris*, and there are green pockets of trees and shrubs, giving away the presence of groundwater at shallow depths. Indeed, coming from the arid and Saharan zones all around, the Aïr Mountains are pleasantly refreshing.

The mountains stretch out over 400km towards the north, and are the southernmost tail-end of the Hoggar Mountains in Algeria. It is a vast plateau of around 80,000km and an average altitude of 700–800m, with various volcanoes, mountain ridges, isolated cone-shaped peaks and eroded fields with rocks and boulders. Some of the flatter areas are like a lunar, almost surreal landscape. Towards the east, about 15 separate massifs can be distinguished, as they rise from the plateau along a north–south axis. The most important ones are the Monts Bagzane (2,022m), Adrar Tamgak (1,988m) and Taghmert (1,813m). Further north, from Mont Greboun (1,944m) onwards, the plateau gradually fades into the sand. Adrar Bous (1,123m) emerges from the sand in isolation.

The Aïr Mountains are the dominion of the Tuareg people, traders, nomadic pastoralists and cultivators. While some communities have settled on the most elevated plateau of the Monts Bagzane, the majority of the population live along the *koris*. These are the more accessible and most fertile parts of the Aïr, where wells provide water for consumption and for the irrigation of garden plots and *palmeraies* or palm gardens. Some of the inhabited *koris* are fringed with green, cultivated ribbons, with a surprising variety of cereals, fruits and vegetables. While at the eastern side of the Aïr Mountains the *koris* plunge into the sand at a steeper angle, the western side shows a very different face. This part is characterised by wide *koris* and valleys, gradually opening up to the Tamesna, Talek and Azawagh plains. One such *kori* is the Kori de Téloua, and Agadez is located where the *kori* fans out into the plains. It is the main gateway into the Aïr Mountains for those coming from Agadez.

There are several good reasons for travellers to venture into this part of Niger, primarily to visit the many oases and villages, and witness a lifestyle that has changed very little over the centuries. The close-knit communities are open to visitors, and proudly allow them to catch a glimpse of the richness of the Tuareg culture. But the nature and wildlife alone are worth the effort too. The ever-changing landscape is at its most dramatic where the mountains meet the sand, where breathtaking panoramic views over endless sand dune fields leave even the

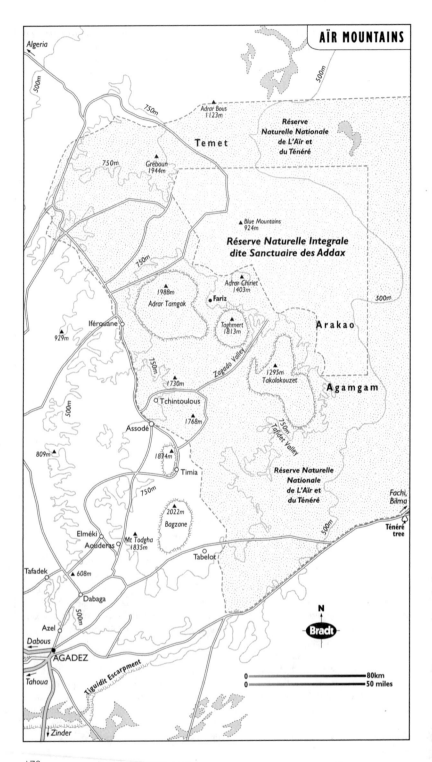

AÏR MOUNTAINS

Algeria

500m

750m

Adrar Bous
1123m

Temet

Réserve
Naturelle Nationale
de L'Aïr et
du Ténéré

500m

750m

Gréboun
1944m

500m

Blue Mountains
924m

Réserve Naturelle Integrale
dite Sanctuaire des Addax

750m

1988m

Adrar Chiriet
1403m

Adrar Tamgak

Fariz

500m

Iférouane

Taghmert
1813m

Arakao

929m

750m

Zagado Valley

1295m
Takolokouzet

1730m

Agamgam

Tchintoulous

1768m

Tafidet Valley

750m

Assodé

500m

1874m

809m

Timia

Réserve Naturelle
Nationale
de L'Aïr et
du Ténéré

Fachi,
Bilma

750m

2022m

Bagzane

500m

Ténéré
tree

Elméki

Aouderas

Mt Todgha
1835m

Tabelot

N

Tafadek

608m

Bradt

Dabaga

500m

Azel

Dabous

AGADEZ

0   80km
0   50 miles

Tahoua

Tiguidit Escarpment

Zinder

most spoilt desert travellers in awe. Scattered all over the region are many sites that tell the story of the Aïr: abandoned villages, now in ruins, or prehistoric sites with rock engravings or archaeological finds, the silent witnesses of a more distant past.

HISTORY

Prehistory Archaeological sites have shown that the Aïr region has been settled for at least 300,000 years, from the prehistoric Palaeolithic and through the Neolithic periods. Research of these sites by foreign scientists and the Nigérien IRSH (Institut de Récherches des Sciences Humaines) in Agadez and Niamey has created a fragmented image of these early settlers. The prehistory is characterised by dramatic climatic changes with a significant fluctuation in temperatures and rainfall. Lakes and rivers contained water until 4,000 years ago, but these rivers have since been transformed to fossil riverbeds or *koris*. This is where most archaeological sites are found. In the Neolithic period, the climate became too dry to support the abundant fauna, and animals in need of a wetter habitat vanished from the region. The first Neolithic civilisations were based on hunting and pastoralism, while agriculture was introduced at a later stage. See also *Chapter 1, History,* page 15.

The arrival of the Tuareg The Tuareg are a people of Berber origin who fled the northern parts of Africa in waves to escape Arab domination. When the first Tuareg groups descended on the Aïr in the mid-8th century, they found a population of Gobirawa Hausa. The first Tuareg to arrive in the region assimilated with the Gobirawa. Migrations from the north continued for centuries and different groups scattered over the immense plateau. Among the many confederacies were the Isandalan, the Kel Gress, the Kel Owey and the Kel Ferwan. The Kel Ferwan settled in the region of Iférouane, where they prospered for centuries. The Kel Owey reigned over the central parts of the Aïr, while the Kel

A CODE OF CONDUCT AT ARCHAEOLOGICAL SITES

One could describe the region of Agadez as an open-air museum, a sanctuary where the rich natural and cultural heritage is embedded in the environment. Many archaeological sites of great importance are omnipresent and have been subject to intensive research. Sadly, what has been there for numerous millennia, or even millions of years, can be destroyed by men within decades. Many objects have already been removed from sites, and sometimes entire sites have been so badly destroyed that their scientific value has been lost for ever. Unfortunately, some guides set a bad example as they pick up items to later sell them through souvenir shops. Do not follow their example, and better still discourage them from selling off their national heritage for a few CFA francs.

When you visit a site of archaeological importance, you are urged to respect a few simple rules:

- do not touch or destroy anything
- do not remove anything from the site: it is illegal to carry archaeological artefacts home with you
- do not use water to clean a rock engraving or painting or to enhance visibility
- do not walk over rock engravings on flat surfaces
- do not litter the site

For more information on the preservation of archaeological sites, and rock paintings and rock engravings in particular, see www.tara.org.uk.

Agadez **THE AÏR MOUNTAINS**

7

ARCHAEOLOGICAL SITES IN THE AIR REGION

DINOSAUR GRAVEYARDS Entire dinosaur skeletons, mostly from the Cretaceous period, have been discovered at different locations. Sadly, most of these sites have been looted and destroyed, as was the fate of the site near Gadoufawa, 160km to the southeast of Agadez. Almost complete skeletons have been found near Tawachi and Marandet, along the Tiguidit Escarpment to the south of Agadez. These locations are among the most important dinosaur sites in Niger. See also *Tiguidit Escarpment*, page 157.

PETRIFIED TREES All over the Aïr region are sites where fossilised wood can be found. An accessible area is along the Tiguidit Escarpment.

STONE TOOLS AND POTTERY FRAGMENTS The history of the first human civilisations in the Aïr region goes back to the Early Palaeolithic period, to more than 300,000 years ago. Over the immense period of time that separates us from these populations, the climate fluctuated time and again, and the human civilisations moved in and out of the region as circumstances demanded. Among the remains they left are countless stone tools, such as spear points, scrapers, arrow heads, axes and grinding stones, as well as objects made from bone (needles and piercers) and ostrich shell, but also pottery fragments and metal objects. Many sites with an abundance of these objects have been discovered, sometimes through excavation or sometimes the objects were exposed at the surface.

One striking site for pottery is at Tagalagal at the extreme north of the Monts Bagzane. This site was discovered in 1978 at an altitude of 1,850m, and holds the oldest pottery known in the Sahara. Access is extremely difficult, which is probably why it has been so well preserved over the approximately 10,000 years of its existence. Other important pottery sites are found near Temet, Adrar Bous and Tin Ouaffadene.

Near Takadda-Azelik (150km northeast of Agadez) remnants of ancient copper metallurgy have been found. Among the finds were blocks of ore, piles of scoria, small copper objects, as well as different types of furnaces where the ore was smelted. More metallurgic sites can be found in Marandet along the Tiguidit Escarpment.

ROCK ENGRAVINGS From around 4,000BC onwards, the inhabitants of the Aïr left not only tools and utensils, but also rock engravings. There are different theories trying to explain

Gress were more concentrated in the southern zones. Because of its geographically favourable position, the Aïr region became a centre of trade. Two important trade routes crossed through the Aïr Mountains: the east–west route from Fezzan (Libya) and Egypt to the Mali empire, and the north–south route from Algeria to the Hausa city-states of Kano and Katsina. Caravans transported gold, ivory, cotton, tanned hides, blankets and also slaves.

While trade prospered, the region was the scene of repeated battles and violent internal and external conflicts. These fierce disputes led the Isandalan to take measures. According to legend, they invited an outsider – Younous, a bastard son of the Sultan of Istanbul – to intervene. This theory is the subject of debate, and some historians believe that a dignitary from within the Isandalan confederacy was appointed to settle the disputes. The historical outcome is unquestioned: in the beginning of the 15th century the sultanate of the Aïr was created, and peace was temporarily restored. One by one the different Tuareg confederacies recognised the authority of the sultan, and their own traditional leaders agreed to pay tribute to the sultan. The first sultans had no permanent residence, and they lived in Assodé, then Tadeliza, and later in Tin Chamane. When Sultan Ilasawan (1430–49)

what might have urged these people to leave an engraved message in the rocks. Was it to capture the spirit of the animals and figures depicted? Was it part of a cult or worship? Was it art for its own sake, for the pleasure of creating an image? While these questions are difficult to answer, the rock engravings left us with a profound cultural heritage that allows us to at least get some idea of what these early civilisations saw.

Unless some kind of organic colouring agent is used, it is very hard to date the engravings. Archaeologists have managed, however, to determine a plausible, overlapping sequence of different styles and images. The oldest period is the **Chasseur Primitif** or the Primitive Hunter. It dates back to the time when wildlife was abundant, and the engravings show realistically depicted elephants, rhinoceros, giraffe, donkeys, ostriches and various herds. This style is widely found all over the Saharan zone in Algeria, Libya, Chad and Niger, and the engravings are sometimes estimated to be older than 12,000 years. In Niger, this style is little represented, but some probable examples are the rhinoceros and the giraffe of Dabous (see box *The giant giraffes of Dabous*, page 175).

The **Pastoral Period** overlaps with the Primitive Hunter period and is estimated to be 5,000 years old. The engravings show schematic outlines of animals – including cattle – with little detail inside the contours. Some images show humans and their cattle, together with herds of wild animals. The humans may hold bows and arrows, but no spears. Most engravings of this era are found on vertical rock faces.

The majority by far of all engravings in the Aïr stem from the tradition of the **Libyan Warrior**. Different styles are recognised within this period that date back to 3,000–1,000 years ago. It shows a big diversity of both human figures and animals, such as giraffe and ostriches, as well as cattle and horses. The style is somewhat rudimentary, and scenes are often repeated. Human figures may carry spears, but no bows and arrows. Images of horse-drawn carriages are attributed to the Garamantes warriors, a Berber people from Libya who are thought to have taken control over the northern caravan routes through the Aïr Mountains. Inscriptions in primitive tifinagh, the Tamashek script (see box *Tifinagh*, page 31), also appear.

Some of the best rock engravings are found at Iwelene (25km southwest of Mont Greboun); Arakao; Tamakon; Tazerzait (sometimes also spelt 'Tezirzet'); Mammanet (west of the Aïr Mountains, 60km to the north of Arlit); Azélik (160km to the east of Agadez); Iférouane; and Adrar Bous.

had a palace constructed in Agadez, the seat of the sultanate permanently left the Aïr Mountains.

Peace in the region was short lived. Internal conflicts flared once more, while Askia Mohamed conquered Agadez and important parts of the Aïr Mountains in the beginning of the 16th century (see *Chapter 1, History*, page 16). The Gobirawa, who were the founders of Agadez, eventually left the region and migrated south, while the Kel Gress – outnumbered by the Kel Owey and other confederacies – were ousted from the Aïr region and they too moved south, to the northern fringes of the Hausa city-states, the Adar Doutchi and the Gobir. The Kel Owey, Kel Ferwan and other confederacies, meanwhile, remained in the north. They are collectively known as the Kel Aïr.

The arrival of the French More difficult times dawned in the 20th century. The arrival of the French military coincided with long periods of drought, and the combination of violence and famine had devastating effects in the Aïr region. An all-time low was the episode of the siege of the French garrison in Agadez, when the Tegama–Kaocen conspiracy and the subsequent Tuareg revolt was broken by the French military (see page 161). Not only did the Tuareg suffer many deaths and casualties, but they also lost most of their livestock and pastures. To make matters worse, trade in the drought-stricken and insecure zones had virtually come to a standstill.

While the population in the Aïr Mountains gradually recovered, they did not benefit from the new French, centralised regime. The seat of colonial authority was in the south, and became dominated by the second-largest group in the territory, the Djerma-Songay. This group enjoyed better access to education, jobs and the political apparatus than any other ethnie, including the Tuareg. This tendency continued after independence in 1960, and the north of Niger had become a politically ignored outpost. In the 1970s, when the uranium industry started booming on their territory, the Tuareg were not properly compensated. Meanwhile, the droughts of the 1970s and 1980s hit hard and once again many cattle were lost, causing tens of thousands of Tuareg to cross borders and seek refuge in Algeria and Libya.

The Tuareg rebellion To give the growing dissatisfaction a voice, in 1985, the Tuareg who had left for Libya created the Popular Front for the Liberation of Niger (FPLN). This political party in exile launched an attack on the prison of Tchin-Tabaradene (500km north of Niamey). In order to suppress the growing unrest that came from the Tuareg in Libya, the Nigérien government started a major repatriation operation and around 18,000 people – most of them Tuareg – returned to Niger. By then, recession had set in as a result of the decline in demand for uranium, and few of the promises that had lured the Tuareg back to their country materialised. This made the whole situation even more inflammatory. The Tuareg were put under close surveillance and many arrests were made.

In May 1990, the prison of Tchin-Tabaradene was attacked again in an attempt to free Tuareg prisoners. The Nigérien government responded with ferocious repressions, resulting in many hundreds of deaths among the Tuareg including women and children. This sparked the beginning of the Tuareg rebellion that would last for five years. More Tuareg parties were created, one of these being the Liberation Front of the Aïr and Azawagh (FLAA) headed by Rhissa ag Boula, and another the Temoust Liberation Front (FLT) led by Mano Dayak. The objectives of different parties ranged from the demand to create a Tuareg federal state to the demand for decentralised administration and Tuareg representation in the Nigérien government. Armed resistance became a fragmented and violent conflict, characterised by attacks from rebel groups and counter attacks from the Nigérien military, and resulting in an overall state of insecurity in the Aïr region. As the Tuareg had the advantage of being familiar with the terrain, the Nigérien army did not succeed in oppressing the rebels by force.

Meanwhile, negotiations had begun on neutral ground, but the peace process would take many years. Mano Dayak and Rhissa ag Boula managed to unite most rebel parties and thus became the leading figures in the negotiations that first led to a truce, then to a peace accord, signed in Ouagadougou on 15 April 1995. The terms of the agreement included: decentralisation; a new division of the territory; the disarming of the armed rebel forces; Tuareg integration in the national military, administration and paramilitary; an elaborate programme to reintegrate refugees; and measurements to enclose the northern region.

Recent years After the peace accord was signed, tranquillity was largely restored in the Aïr region. Isolated incidents that occurred were criticised even from within Tuareg circles, as both the population and Tuareg leaders now strived for peaceful ways to achieve the goals as mentioned in the agreement. A temporary, precarious situation arose after Rhissa ag Boula, who had been appointed Minister of Tourism in 1996, was arrested in 2004, but the stalemate was broken in a remarkable way (see box *A Tuareg's pardon,* page 60). One of the crucial objectives of the peace accord was achieved in July 2005, when the first municipal elections in the history of Niger were held. This major step in the long process of decentralisation means that for the first time in post-colonial history, the local authorities are elected members from within the community.

Meanwhile, tourism in the Aïr region flourishes like never before, and tourism has become one of the pillars of the local economy. With the regional capital Agadez as a starting point, many travellers find their way to the magnificent region once again. Below are some of the destinations that are often included in itineraries. For information on how to organise your trip to the Aïr region, see box *How to organise your trip to the Aïr and Ténéré regions,* pages 164–5.

TAFADEK The village of Tafadek is famed for its thermal springs. The water, with a temperature between 60°C and 70°C is renowned for its healing powers. People with various skin diseases or rheumatic afflictions seek the benefit of the hot water.

AOUDERAS While on the IGN map the main route into the centre of the Aïr Mountains passes Elméki, the route via Aouderas is often the preferred one. After Dabaga (where the *forêt classée* or classified forest is degraded and no longer distinguishable from its environs), the track branches to the east. The terrain is fairly flat with some isolated cone-shaped gravel hills. The panoramic view from any of these tops is stunning, so this is one good opportunity to stretch your legs. After the plain and just across a dry riverbed is Aouderas. It was one of the first settlements of importance in the Aïr, and in the beginning of the 20th century the biggest inhabited conglomerate after Agadez. Aouderas has extensive *palmeraies* and gardens, aligned along the riverbed to the west of the village. These gardens were badly affected by the locust invasion in 2004.

After Aouderas the landscape becomes more eroded and uneven. Views to the massif of Monts Bagzane are no longer blocked by Todgha Mountain (1,835m), and wonderful vistas unfold. Colours seem to change every minute as the rocks and boulders catch the light at different angles.

MONTS BAGZANE The Bagzane is a vast, elevated plateau of 600km and with an average altitude of 1,500m. The Idoukal-en-Taghès (2,022m) is the highest peak in the whole of Niger, and if the night temperatures at the plateau reach freezing point in the coldest months, the summit is even colder. The rocky plateau is littered with granite rocks and boulders, heavily eroded to almost perfect giant marbles. In between the rocks on sandy depressions and *koris* live the Kel Bagzane, cultivators, pastoralists and *caravaniers*. It hardly ever rains on the plateau, but when it does – usually by the end of July, beginning of August – the heavens open. The downpour fills basins and increases groundwater that will last for the whole year for consumption and irrigation. At this altitude, the gardens and *palmeraies* do surprisingly well, and the Kel Bagzane grow a whole variety of produce, including some cash crops (onion, tomato, potato, garlic and peppers). Meanwhile, subsistence crops (wheat, millet and sorghum) are not sufficient for the population to be fully independent, and therefore the caravan trade plays an essential role in the life of the Kel Bagzane.

The only way up the Monts Bagzane is by foot. There are a few passages to the plateau, but many of them are too steep and rocky for camels. Therefore, donkeys are commonly used as beasts of burden. A trek of several days across the plateau is a excellent way to explore the Monts Bagzane, and it contrasts sharply with trekking through the dunes along the fringes of the Aïr region.

TABELOT One track leading down from the plateau starts near Ighalabélabene and it leads to the green valley of Akréreb and Tabelot. Gardens and cultivated plots stretch out over a length of 20km, and this must be one of the most heavily exploited agricultural zones in the Aïr. Onions are an important cash crop, and trucks loaded with big sacks filled with onions frequent the route south of Monts Bagzane via Dabaga to Agadez.

KREB-KREB AND ABAKARAN Continuing north from Aouderas, the track passes through some wide *koris*, then forks. The track that continues north leads to Assodé, while the eastern track leads to Timia. After the village of Kreb–kreb (sometimes written Krb–krb), you pass the small hamlet of Abarakan, where you can visit another Centre Artisanal as well as a Centre des Arts et Métiers. The latter has workshops on the premises where you can see artisans at work. Since good-quality argil can be found nearby, you will find a lot of pottery here.

The *piste* changes from flat and sandy to a rocky ascent, a hurdle that in places resembles a giant staircase. Only 5km before Timia is the *guelta de Timia*, a natural basin or rockpool fed by a waterfall. Even well into the dry season water trickles down from the gorge above, but during the rainy season it becomes an imposing waterfall. After a narrow passage cut out through the rocks, the track opens up into the *kori* that leads to Timia.

TIMIA The oasis of Timia (230km from Agadez) is located at the foot of the Adrar Egalah (1,874m) along the wide dry *kori* that winds along the mountain base. Where the built-up area ends, gardens and *palmeraies* continue for many kilometres. The favourable microclimate in this zone allows the Kel Owey population to cultivate wheat, tomatoes, dates, figs, grapes and pomegranates, as well as the sweetest and juiciest oranges and grapefruits you'll ever find. A view from Fort Massu, nestled on top of a hillock across the *kori*, reveals that the gardens stretch out to the southeastern side of Timia as well. The community of Timia counts around 6,000 inhabitants, including those who live outside the village proper. The school has 250 pupils, 110 of whom are girls, and 10 Koran schools with 20–30 pupils each.

Timia is one of few places where you may find your way independently, so if you do, introduce yourself to the village chief as a matter of courtesy. He can often be found near the coopérative, which is also the point of departure for trucks (see below). This is also a good place to ask around for a guide, if you need one. Timia is a good starting point for treks into the mountainous area or to the fringes of the Aïr Mountains. Around ten days are needed for a round trip to the beautiful valley of Tafidet, to name just one option.

Getting there and away The only public transport you will find to and from Timia are trucks. There are no fixed departure days, but trucks leave almost weekly, sometimes even more often. Try your luck and ask around at the *gare routière* and at the SNTN bus yard in Agadez, or (to get away) at the square in the heart of Timia, where the coopérative is also located. Ask for the *camions de la coopérative*. Some trucks carry passengers only, in which case you will be travelling with dozens of travel companions, packed together like canned sardines. The alternative is hardly better: when the truck is primarily meant to transport goods, passengers may take their place on top of the goods, whether they be oranges, onions or anything else. The experience costs only CFA3,000 for a physically very demanding two-day journey. Not for the faint-hearted. Bring plenty of fluids and do not forget to keep warm clothes to hand in the cold season.

Where to stay, eat and drink Only a few years ago there was no official accommodation in Timia, then someone constructed a few *cases* (huts made from woven mats) and ablution facilities, and proudly called it a *campement*. Since then this first *campement* has been washed away after heavy rains, but as Timia is included in most itineraries to the Aïr Mountains, new options fill this niche.

⌂ **Auberge de Timia** (6 suites + *cases*) ↘ (satellite): 00 882 165 020 32 41; ↘ Agadez: 89 63 53; e mopassan@club-internet.fr. The auberge has been open since March 2005, and is beautifully located halfway up the hill at the eastern side of the village, at the opposite end of the built-up area coming from Fort Massu. The s/c suites are built with local materials in a rustic style. While you will appreciate the hot showers in the cold months (CFA1,300 for non-guests), you may also enjoy a cold beer on a hot day. When it comes to paying the bill, remember that all drinks (including wine and mineral water) have to be transported by road. Meals from CFA2,000–3,000 are available on request, and there are 3 separate open-air places for campfires. *Views from the comfortable rooms are magnificent, but the price is set accordingly at CFA18,250 per suite. For budget travellers, some cases (1 bed, 1 mattress on the floor) are available at CFA5,000.*

⌂ **Auberge Taguelmoust** (6 rooms) Open since the beginning of 2006, this beautifully located auberge is about 1km to the south of the village, along the *oued* Amerig past fort Massu. The s/c rooms are comfortable, while camping is also allowed. Anything other than basic meals has to be ordered in advance. Cold refreshments, beers and some other alcoholic drinks are available. On request, local people will play traditional music and perform dances. In fair-sized enclosures on the premises are 2 ostriches, 3 barbary sheep and around a dozen Dorcas gazelles. When it becomes fair to assume that they will not be poached, the animals will be

released, but for now they are better off in a secluded area. *Enquiries and bookings can be made through Taguelmoust Voyages in Agadez:* ↘ 44 01 48/97 31 39 *or book directly through satellite phone: 0088 216 213 33 808. CFA14,000.*

⌂ **Fort Massu** (see below) Though it has not been (re)constructed to house visitors, the fort is sometimes used for this purpose on request. As the fort is often locked, you will have to find the warden first. There are some beds inside, but sleeping on the terrace in the warm season is another attractive option. On cold evenings, on the other hand, the huge fireplace will provide the necessary warmth. *The rate is CFA3,000 pp, meals are available on request.*

Å **Campement de Tasselot** About 3km further along the *kori*, past Auberge de Timia, is a small hamlet called Tasselot, the location of this *campement*. You can sleep in a *case* or pitch your tent for CFA2,500 per person. Pay another CFA2,000 for a vehicle. Meals are available only on request.

Å **Campement de Timia** The new *campement* so far has 3 rooms (construction *sans bois* or woodless constructions) at CFA2,000 pp. Camping is allowed, and pay an extra CFA2,000 for parking a vehicle. Though there is a dining room, meals are only available on request.

✗ **Restaurant de Timia** This is just at the foot of the hill where Fort Massu overlooks the *kori*, near to the pharmacy. Fruits and vegetables are freshly taken from the gardens, so you can have crispy salads and juicy fruit. The only problem is that it is often closed.

What to see and do

Fort Massu The fort was built by the French General Massu in 1952. It was never used for military purposes, though, and it is more a historical curiosity. It has been restored recently, and is sometimes used to shelter travellers. In the cold months, a fire can be lit in the huge fireplace. The fort is usually locked, but ask around before scrambling up the hillock to have it opened for you. If that doesn't work, the view is still glorious and well worth the effort of the short, steep walk.

Waterfall and rockpool The *guelta* and waterfall are 5km west of Timia. It looks and feels like a spot for a Sunday picnic, or even a swim if you don't mind the freezing water. Numerous craftsmen hang out near the rockpool to sell their goods, but no food or drinks are available.

Gardens Many gardens are open to visitors for a tour or a shady place for a picnic. You can buy fruit and vegetables directly from the gardens, and often there is someone willing to prepare you a meal. There are no fixed rates for a visit, but expect to pay around CFA1,000 per person; food, food preparation and tip not included.

Handicrafts More handicrafts can be seen and bought in the Centre Artisanal at the foot of the hill where the Auberge de Timia is situated. Craftsmen will be more than pleased if you ask them to show you their workshop at home. Often this leads to an invitation to have tea first, then see how silverware, carvings or leatherwork are being made. Though an invitation does not imply any obligation to buy from your host, the artisan will certainly hope that you will. Bear this in mind before accepting the invitation and remember that bargaining is part of the game and can be done with a smile.

Mouloud The day after the Prophet's birthday (see *Agadez*, page 75) is a day of festivity in Timia. Everyone looks their absolute best, with new indigo costumes and *taguelmousts*. In the morning all the inhabitants gather a few kilometres to the east and proceed in slow procession to the village. Two groups of women, representing the east and the west of Timia, sing and play hand-held drums in the middle of the *kori*, while camel riders circle around them with a critical eye and ear. The group that eventually is cheered on by most camel riders, wins.

ASSODE To the north of the Adrar Egalah, at around 35km from Timia, is the abandoned town of Assodé. A short scramble on a rock is rewarded by a panoramic view of the ruins: piles of rocks lie scattered over a wide area; only a few walls are still standing. The narrow tracks between the rubble are used by goats and sheep, and sometimes by tourists who wander around the site. It is still marked on the map as if it were a large settlement, yet the only inhabitants are craftsmen, patiently waiting for clients to buy from them. Despite the ruined state of Assodé, it is apparent that this must once have been a place of importance.

Based on carbon dating it has been concluded that Assodé was founded in the 14th century. Assodé was well placed in the centre of the Aïr Mountains and the capital of the Kel Owey and their traditional leader, the Anastifidet. It was also the first seat of the sultan of the Aïr in the 15th century, if only for a short period of time. When the sultanate was shifted to Agadez, so was the centre of trade and the town lost its dominant position. Nevertheless, in its heyday Assodé consisted of around 1,000 houses and dwellings and could harbour as many as 10,000 inhabitants. Narrow streets converged to an impressive mosque – with multiple parallel corridors – in the middle of the town.

At some point, decline set in. It is not clear what caused the population to gradually leave Assodé. Maybe water became a scarce commodity, or continuous insecurity pushed both the population and trade caravans out of the centre of the Aïr. When the German explorer Heinrich Barth visited the town in 1850, only around 80 houses were in use. The Anastifidet of the Kel Owey and his court were among the last to leave Assodé in 1917, and by 1920 Assodé was completely abandoned.

TCHINTOULOUS Just below Agueraguer Mountain (1,730m) is the village of Tchintoulous. Travellers spend little or no time here, yet it is worth a visit, if only to stop by the Centre Artisanal and buy a beautifully made leather bag or cushion cover. When you have more time, ask to be taken around and see the gardens, where fruits and vegetables grow thanks to intensive irrigation.

Near Tchintoulous are the ruinous remnants of the village of Tadenak. Heinrich Barth stayed here for a few weeks under the protection of the local *chef* Anour Ouandara, who claimed he would kill anyone who touched Heinrich Barth. According to oral tradition, Heinrich Barth engraved a rock and buried it in the vicinity, but the rock was never found. Tadenak was abandoned in 1917.

The track from Tchintoulous towards the northeast leads to the *oued* of Zagado, a valley that is kilometres wide in places and rich in wildlife. Dorcas gazelle, patas monkeys and birds of prey are regularly spotted here. The Zagado *oued* eventually fans out into the Ténéré at Kogo. This location is remarkable for the high dunes and mountains of white marble (see *Kogo*, page 194).

IFEROUANE To the north of Assodé, another 90km along the *piste* lead to Iférouane. It was one of the first Tuareg settlements in the Aïr, and was dominated for a long time by the Kel Ferwan or Kel Eghazer. They came from the direction of Fezzan and Tripoli, and were probably reponsible for the introduction of agriculture, animal traction, irrigation and other techniques related to agriculture. Their knowledge spread through the Aïr, especially after periods of drought – as in the first decades of the 20th century – when the population dispersed from the area in search of a better life further south.

The French military administration was installed in Iférouane in 1947, and Iférouane is still an administrative post of importance. The mixed Tuareg population are agriculturalists, pastoralists, traders and craftsmen. The wide valley is beautiful and tranquil, with many gardens a few kilometres distant, mostly to the eastern side of the village. In the background, again to the east, is the massif of Adrar Tamgak.

When you are travelling independently, make sure to report at the military post at the entrance to Iférouane. To find a guide, enquire at the hotel, auberge or *campement*.

Getting there and away There is no public transport on the route as described above (from Timia via Assodé), but occasionally small trucks do ply this route. The only way to find out is by asking around. However, the *piste* leading to the southwest heads directly for the *route de l'uranium*, the tarred road from Agadez to Arlit. Public transport of some sort is more regular here, and sturdy vehicles leave for either of these destinations. Again, you need to ask around to find out about departures. Count on a full day from Iférouane to Arlit, while the journey between Agadez and Iférouane may involve a night spent somewhere along the *piste*. See also *Agadez*, page 166.

Within Iférouane, all is within walking distance. There are no official *kaboukabous*, but if you need a ride, eg:to the gardens or the *campement*, just ask around and someone will be happy to earn CFA200 for one ride.

Where to stay, eat and drink
There are a couple of small and **informal restaurants** serving simple meals like spaghetti or couscous.

🏠 **Auberge Tidargo** or **Chez Sidi** Basic but very hospitable. Facilities are no different from what local people use. Meals are not available, though it is always possible to discuss options with Sidi, a remarkable and energetic character. On request, he will invite local musicians, dancers or poets to perform for his guests. The yard has plenty of space for 5 cases *(huts made from woven mats) that sleep up to 4 people and cost CFA7,500, but you may bargain. You can also pitch your tent at CFA2,000 pp.* Discuss a price in advance.

In the heart of the Tuareg dominion of the Aïr Mountains, yet relatively easily accessible from Agadez, is Iférouane. It is the location for the Festival de l'Aïr, a Tuareg festival that is held every year during 27–29 December. The setting is magnificent, in the wide and green valley just outside the built-up area, with views to the massif of Adrar Tamgak to the east. There were different reasons to organise a festival of this kind, one being to promote the Tuareg culture and this particular area for tourism. Besides that, an event that attracts many Tuareg – who easily outnumber foreign visitors – provides an ideal occasion to combine the festivities and the practical. The first stagings of this event have proven a good opportunity for the many Tuareg confederacies and their leaders to meet and discuss matters of importance to the Tuareg community.

The festival has become a huge success for both Tuareg and visitors alike. The three-day programme includes a colourful presentation of all the delegations; different *tendés* (traditional dances for men or camel riders); various very attractive beauty contests to win the title of 'best turban', 'best harnessed camel', 'best traditional costume', etc; poetry and music; and a dust-stirring camel race. The whole of Iférouane comes alive and people look their best, with plenty of indigo and other colourful garments, women with special make-up to emphasise their beauty and elaborate traditional turbans. If you are planning a trip into the Aïr Mountains at the end of December, it is absolutely worthwhile to include this festival in your itinerary.

For practical information, see *Public holidays and festivals*, page 76.

🏠 **Hotel Tellit** (6 rooms) 📞 44 02 31/98 33 08 (reservations). A small hotel with lots of charm. The building as such is tastefully designed and constructed with banco, while the interior decorations complete the picture. The restaurant is rather expensive – alcoholic drinks especially – but given the fact that everything has to come by road from Agadez or Niamey, this is just the way it is. The hotel is open Oct–Mar. *The rooms are very comfortable at CFA20,000 for a dbl and CFA24,000 for a s/c dbl.*

🏕 **Camping Oasis les Arbres** 📞 (satellite) 00 88 216 212 77 439; e agalheroasis@yahoo.pr. To get here you need some kind of transport as it is about 2km away from the built-up area. If you are without a car, look for someone with a motorbike. The campsite is spacious and has lots of shade. Water is pumped up from a well and used to irrigate the lush gardens where crops like maize, millet, onions and wheat are cultivated. Toilets are very basic but the showers are fine. *Choose to stay in a case (CFA5,000 per case) or pitch your tent for less.* You may even camp for free, provided that you make use of the bar and restaurant, which is almost automatic anyway. Special dishes like *toguella* or *mechoui* (see *Food and drink*, page 73) have to be ordered in advance.

What to see and do

Museum and handicrafts There is no shortage of skilful craftsmen in Iférouane. Most of them work at home, but many finished items are brought to the **Centre Artisanal** to be displayed and hopefully sold to visitors. At the shop you will find nickel and silver jewellery, steatite carvings, carefully decorated leatherwork – cushions, bags of all sizes and even saddles – as well as basketry. If you are interested, it is possible to arrange a visit to one or more craftsmen in their workshops.

To see how much these crafts are still based on tradition, pay a visit to the adjacent **CAMI the Artisanal Centre and Museum of Iférouane** (*open daily 08.00–12.00 and 15.00–18.00*) The idea to open up a museum goes back to 2001, but it took until 2004 before the museum was ready to open its doors to visitors.

There is a display of traditional objects and some archaeological artefacts, but the emphasis lies on the explanations about the natural environment. Written explanations are in French only, but at least one of the artisans and wardens speaks some English. The entrance fee is only CFA500, and the revenues are used to purchase more items to exhibit, as well as to pay for the training of guides who could run the museum and Centre Artisanal. In the low season, when visitors are scarce, the museum may be closed, in which case you can ask around to locate the keeper of the key. If you have a special interest in the flora and fauna of the region, ask to see anyone from the project supporting the **Réserve Nationale de l'Aïr et du Ténéré**, as it is based in Iférouane. Iférouane is also the seat of **Projet Faune Iférouane**.

Wildlife in captivity While you can learn about the natural environment in the museum, there is some wildlife in captivity to be seen in Iférouane. As the number of ostriches was dwindling rapidly, in 1996 a couple were caught and taken to a back yard in Iférouane. Though their enclosure is fairly small, the birds seem to be doing well. They hatched their first batch of eggs in 2002, and three of the four chicks survived. These youngsters have now started reproducing as well, but it is obvious that this happy family's gene pool is far too limited to be healthy. Donations are welcome and will be used to buy fodder and to implement plans to breed more ostriches in captivity. Ideally, at some point in the future, these animals should be released. However, it will take a while to ensure that an eventual release would not end in poaching and ostrich stew.

Three Barbary sheep that used to live in a depressingly small enclosure just next to the ostriches have been moved to Auberge Taguelmoust in Timia (see page 185).

Tifinagh Tamashek is the language of the Tuareg but few people know that originally this language had its own script: the tifinagh. Sidi Moumounia, the friendly chap who runs the Auberge Tidargo, is most of all an idealist and sometimes even a fanatic in defending and promoting the culture of the Tuareg. Making sure that not only today's youth but even visitors will at least know about tifinagh, is one of his goals. Through the association Tidargo ('mirror' in Tamashek) he is trying to reach many young Tuareg to teach them to write in tifinagh. Sidi is a very ambitious and proud Tuareg who will be pleased to receive visitors with an interest in tifinagh. When you visit the Festival de l'Aïr, you will see him excel as a dancer at the *tendé des hommes*. See also box *Tifinagh*, page 31.

Gardens All around Iférouane are gardens, where fresh water from wells brings the barren soil alive. Cattle and goats are kept out of these gardens at all costs, as they would undo weeks, even months of hard labour within hours. Spending some time in any of these gardens will make you appreciate the fresh local produce even more.

ADRAR TAMGAK The Adrar Tamgak is the largest elevated massif in the Aïr Mountains. Different peaks tower above the uneven and rocky terrain, where many gorges cut through the mountains. The only reasonably accessible area is the narrow Kori de Tamgak, but the only way out at the eastern end is a rough scramble to high altitudes, then down again along rocky tracks. A small population of olive baboon *Papio anubis* lives in this massif. Before heading out into this massif, enquire about the security of this zone, as this inaccessible area was closed for visitors after the 2004 incidents (see *A Tuareg's pardon*, page 60).

In January 1988, after almost two decades of preparation, the Réserve Naturelle Nationale de l'Aïr et du Ténéré or RNNAT was created with the help of the IUCN and WWF. The boundaries of the RNNAT partly coincide with existing roads and tracks through the Aïr Mountains, and where this is not the case, straight lines were drawn on maps, crossing the Ténéré Desert from Adrar Bous to the isolated Grein Mountain, then southward until the boundary meets the salt route to Bilma. The total area measures 7,736,000ha (6% of Nigérien territory), with a total perimeter of 1,218km, and includes the eastern part of the Aïr (including nine important and some smaller massifs); the whole zone where the Aïr Mountains meet the sand of the Ténéré; and a section of the desolate Ténéré Desert. The physical characteristics are very diverse, and include features from the Cambrian, Tertiary and Quaternary periods – including volcanic remnants, granite rocks, conglomerate rocks and marble. The massifs emerge from low rocky plateaus, and both are intersected by seasonal drainage systems koris or oueds. The Ténéré Desert consists of several ergs or sand dune fields and some areas of high sand dunes, especially where the prevailing winds send the sand piling up against mountain walls. The ergs and dunes are surrounded by reg or flat plains of coarse sand, gravel and stones. In some areas, different types of shifting sand dunes occur. Completely within the boundaries of the RNNAT is the Sanctuaire des Addax or Strict Reserve for the Addax. It is located in the lower Ténéré area and covers 1,280,000ha. The RNNAT shelters many archaeological sites of great historic and cultural importance.

FLORA Despite the low annual rainfall (less than 100mm per year), 350 different plant species have been identified, most of which occur in the more elevated parts of the RNNAT. Thanks to the cooler climate, many species are more characteristic of the Sahelian vegetation zone (see Climate, vegetation and land use, page 3), like the Balanites aegyptiaca, Salvadora persica, Ziziphus mauritania, Boscia senegalensis and some acacia species. Above 1,000m and in sheltered corners of the massifs, some Sudanian species occur, including several species of Grewia and Ficus, and Cordia sinensis. Above 1,500m even some Mediterranean species, like the wild olive Olea laperrini, occur. In the lower, Saharan areas just below the mountains (average altitude 400–500m), various grasses and herbs are important elements of the scarce vegetation, as they provide fodder for both wild and domesticated animals. Important wild crop species that grow in the region include wild olive, millet and sorghum.

FAUNA Over 40 mammal species have been identified, though some are now believed to be extinct in this region, like the oryx Oryx damma, the slender-horned gazelle Gazella leptoceros, and most larger carnivores. Among the endangered species are the Addax gazelle Addax nasomaculatus, the Dama gazelle Gazella dama and the Barbary sheep Ammotragus lervia. With a population of around 12,000, the Dorcas gazelle Gazella dorcas seems to be doing relatively well, but is also listed as endangered. While hunting is prohibited throughout the RNNAT, some gazelle species have suffered greatly from tourist disturbance. Vehicles sometimes pursue animals in open areas just for the fun of it, and while the animals do not seem physically hurt in the process, they may later die from heat exhaustion.

THE FRINGES OF THE AIR AND TENERE

All along the fringes of the Aïr Mountains (la bordure de l'Aïr et du Ténéré) are stunning landscapes with high sand dunes, piled up against the mountains by the prevailing northeasterly winds; isolated mountains; mountains of marble; and

Smaller carnivores occur in healthier numbers, and include golden jackal *Canis aureus*; fennec fox *Fennecus zerda*; Rüppells sand fox *Vulpes rüpelli*; caracal *Felis caracal*; and sand cat *Felis margarita*. An estimated 70 olive baboons *Papio anubis* survive in the Tamgak Massif, while some 500 patas monkeys *Erythrocebus patas* live in small groups in the lower mountains and on plateaux. Colonies of rock hyrax *Procavia rucifeps* are found in rocky areas.

BIRDS A total of 165 bird species have so far been identified. Resident birds that are commonly seen are the sand grouse *Pteroclididae*; doves *Columbidae*; barbets *Capidonidae*; larks *Alaudidae*; crows and ravens *Corvidae*; buntings *Emberizadae*; and weavers *Ploceidae*. The population of ostrich *Struthio camelus camelus* is believed to have been wiped out in this zone (the latest sightings of a single male were years ago), while the Nubian bustard *Neotis nuba* is considered very rare. Many migratory species pass or overwinter in the RNNAT, including herons *Ardeidae*; birds of prey *Accipitrdae* and *Falconidae*; waders *Charadriidae*; thrushes *Turidae*; and warblers *Sylviidae*.

OTHER Among the 18 reptile species are the desert monitor lizard *Varanus griseus*; sand viper *Cerastes cerastes*; and various species of sand boa and gecko. Outside of Antarctica, the Aïr region is the only mountain system in the world that does not harbour fish species.

CONSERVATION CONCERNS The region covered by the RNNAT offers a high level of biodiversity and includes some endangered animal species. Hunting and the exploitation of certain tree species is prohibited, while commercial wood cutting and collection of firewood are banned. In an attempt to protect the highly endangered Addax, the Strict Reserve for the Addax was created. All human access in this area is officially banned, though in reality tourist excursions to certain parts are tolerated.

Despite these restrictions and efforts to inform the local population on the importance of nature conservation, management and control are extremely difficult, if only for the size of the RNNAT. Illegal hunting – often by military and mining personnel – has continued in many parts of the zone. During the years of the Tuareg rebellion, management practices came to a standstill, while hunting practices became more commonplace. Surveys that have taken place in recent years have shown that wildlife populations have declined during these years. Ironically, it seems that most Addax gazelle have either perished or abandoned the region, and the only viable Addax population now lives in the region of the Termit Massif (see *SOS Faune du Niger: addax survey*, page 226).

In 2005, a renewed conservation programme was initiated. The programme involves different stages: first of all extensive survey and evaluation of the current state of the wildlife and vegetation of the RNNAT, followed by implementation of active measures to better protect the total assemblage of landscapes, vegetation and wildlife. The emphasis lies on creating an atmosphere of willingness of the local population and the tourist sector, as their co-operation is essential for any conservation programme to succeed.

(*Source: UNEP-WCMC*)

endless seas of sand. Even for those who have travelled to desert destinations before, this zone holds many treasures of extreme beauty, unseen elsewhere. From Adrar Bous in the north, to the salt caravan *route du Bilma* in the south is almost 300km as the crow flies. By car, this can be done in a matter of days, but to really appreciate the stillness and the variety of the landscape, hiking or cameltrekking is

THE OLD WOMAN OF FARIZ

When I was travelling along the fringes of the Aïr Massif, my guide Achmed Tcholli, a wonderful and very knowledgeable Tuareg decided to make a detour to the small hamlet of Fariz to fill our jerrycans from the well. The next one would be too far away. We parked the car behind some boulders, out of sight from the few dwellings at the other side of the well. As we sat down to prepare a meal, an old, frail woman approached. She was dressed in black, barefooted. Achmed adjusted his turban to make sure his mouth was properly covered. It was over a year since he had last passed Fariz, and he was very pleased to see her. But he said nothing, did not even look up while the woman sat down, facing slightly away from us and covering her face. I could see only her leathery hands as Achmed and the woman greeted each other the Tuareg way: handpalms barely touching, sliding until only the fingertips touch, letting go swiftly, then the same motions again. A gracious duet of hands. Achmed spoke first, very gently and still without looking up.

How are you?	I am fine.
How is your family?	The whole family is fine.
How is your health?	Thanks to God, it is fine for now.
How is your weakness?	Thanks to God, I manage fine.
How is the neighbourhood?	Everyone is fine.
How is the cold?	The cold has struck us with force this year.
Is the cold worse than last year?	Yes, without any doubt the cold is fiercer than last year.
How is the lack of grazing after the drought?	It is not so bad now, but all the same there is some weakness amongst the young goats, and some are dying through lack of milk.
How was the wind, did you get a lot of wind?	Yes, during the whole of last week we had very strong winds but now it is better.

the preferred mode of travel. It would then take at least a month to cover the whole distance. From north to south, below are short descriptions of some of the most remarkable areas.

ADRAR BOUS In 1960, the Mission Berliet discovered rock paintings and other remnants of ancient civilisations in the Adrar Bous. The location of the mountain means that few travellers get here by foot or camel, but the Adrar Bous is invariably included in the itinerary for a *grand raid* or grand tour (see box *How to organise your trip to the Aïr and Ténéré regions,* pages 164–5).

TEMET At the foot of Greboun Mountain, the awesome dunes of Temet reach altitudes of 300m. One of the most impressive dune fields in Niger, even in the world.

IWELENE Between 3500BC and 1250BC, the Kori of Iwelene was inhabited by a large population of probably semi-nomadic civilisations. Iwelene is now one of the richest archaeological sites in Niger, as the valley is littered with traces of human

The parents are fine, but they have become weak. My mother has been bedridden for over a year now.

Yes, she manages with a stick.

Thanks to God, he can still see and walk without any help.

How are your parents?

Ah, I have heard news about her, I was informed about her illness. Is she able to get up at all?

How is your father's vision?

You know that your parents and I, we have lived through a lot together. We used to live in the same area. Since then I have left the environment. It has now been 40 years since I last saw them. I am here. I am caught by the situation. Now even my grandchildren have grown up in this zone and I stay with them so they can look after me.

Forty years earlier, the woman – known to all who have met her as *la vieille de Fariz* – was married and she moved to Fariz with her husband and son. It was a good area in which to be living, with many trees, good shade and plenty of grazing most of the year. After generous rains, the area would even flood temporarily, a shallow lake in the desert. Then there were years of serious droughts and many trees withered and died. All the families who lived in Fariz had to migrate to find good grazing for their livestock. The woman stayed behind to look after the youngest children and the youngest goats. This was to be her fate: year after year she saw her family leaving, and returning after some months. Other families moved away, to places where the trees hadn't died. But she stayed in Fariz. Only a few years before, her husband had died, soon followed by her only son. Since then, the old woman of Fariz has lived with her daughter-in-law and her grandchildren. Her only belongings are hung from wooden poles: a woven mat, a blanket, a few baskets and bags, a cooking pot. That is where she sleeps; her house has neither roof nor walls.

After the initial greetings, the old woman moved her headcloth back and turned towards Achmed. A pleasant conversation ensued. Some laughter, recalling of memories, gestures, a face that spoke of years in a quiet corner in the desert. Her only contact with the outside world is when somebody stops to take water from the well.

presence. Among the finds are over 60 tombs and countless pottery fragments ('iwelen' means 'potsherd' in Tamashek), but most of all the valley is one of the best sites for rock engravings. Many of these show human figures, often in conjunction with wild animals (elephants, giraffe, rhinoceros, lions, Barbary sheep, gazelles…) and domesticated animals (horses – used to draw chariots – and cattle). The majority of human figures are depicted frontally, with a short tunic and one spear. Some figures have a big head with three points on top, a design that vaguely resembles a tulip. The meaning of this peculiarly shaped head or headdress is not understood.

BLUE MOUNTAINS To get to the Blue Mountains or *Montagnes Bleues*, you first have to cross a vast zone of sand dunes. The dunes suddenly switch to a flat gravel plain with no landmarks whatsoever. From a distance, the Blue Mountains look like a ship lost in the wrong environment. The mountains got their name because of the presence of cipoline, an impure marble in which minerals such as mica and serpentine are embedded. When the sun reflects on a cipoline surface, it gives a bluish appearance.

TEZIRZEK Sometimes spelt 'Tazerzait', this is a permanently inhabited oasis at the base of Adrar Tamgak. It is an important stopping point for water, and a good place to wander around and explore the area for rock engravings. Tuareg children will lead you to the best sites with frontal, symmetrical figurines with big, round heads, and to some engravings in the tifinagh script (see box *Tifinagh*, page 31).

ADRAR CHIRIET If from the nearby dunes the Adrar Chiriet Mountains look imposing, walking or driving through the cluster of volcanic mountains is a humbling experience. A few passages only give access to the massif, which consists of different basins. In between the rock formations, one could imagine these natural structures are the ruins of a giant fortress.

FARIZ Nestled in the corner of a wide plain with a dead forest, in the shadow of Taghmert Mountain (1,813m), is the small settlement of Fariz. See box, pages 192–3.

KOGO High sand dunes are alternated by white marble mountains, which from a distance look like reflecting snowfields. The zone is very picturesque and varies from wide, flat fields to narrow passages between dunes and rocks.

ARAKAO In the 1960s and early 1970s, the fringes of the Aïr Mountains were being thoroughly explored and opened up for motorised research, and later tourism. All the manageable passages are now known, but in these years it was by no means obvious how vehicles could penetrate the areas of shifting dunes and rocky ridges. One of the pioneers to chart and uncover this region was the Frenchman Louis-Henri Mouren. In 1972, he and his team explored the region by plane, taking aerial pictures along the way. One day, Mouren flew over an area that was known only to the Tuareg living in nearby *oueds*, and which they called 'Arakao': an immense circular valley surrounded by a dark-coloured rocky ridge, with an opening to the eastern side. Fom the air Mouren saw what he described as, 'an enormous shape with two arms that look like the pincers of a crab'. Since then the immense circular valley has been known as *la pince de crabe*. The dunes that engulf the valley – an extinct caldera – stretch out over 15km and are up to 200m high. Along the flanks of the surrounding hills are some slightly elevated circular stone tumuli, and these are tombs dating back to the Neolithic period.

AGAMGAM Agamgam is an area of high sand dunes, while the Kori of Agamgam leads to a *guelta* or rock pool.

TAFIDET VALLEY In the beautiful valley of Tafidet wildlife is still relatively abundant. Apart from Dama and Dorcas gazelle, Barbary sheep still roam free in this area. Also look out for patas monkeys and rock hyraxes, and if you are lucky you might see the rare porcupine. In the valley are sites with rock engravings.

THE TENERE DESERT

Ténéré means 'the desert behind the desert', and in a very compact way, it describes just what it is. The extremely inaccessible area stretches north–south over 1,500km (including the Erg du Ténéré), and over 500km from the Aïr Mountains in the west to the Djado and Kawar regions in the east. With very little vegetation and water, the heart of the Ténéré mainly consists of plains of coarse sand and gravel, and shifting sand dunes, making it one of the most hostile environments on our planet. The most important traffic route is the one the salt caravans have used for centuries, the 600km-long route from Agadez via Fachi to

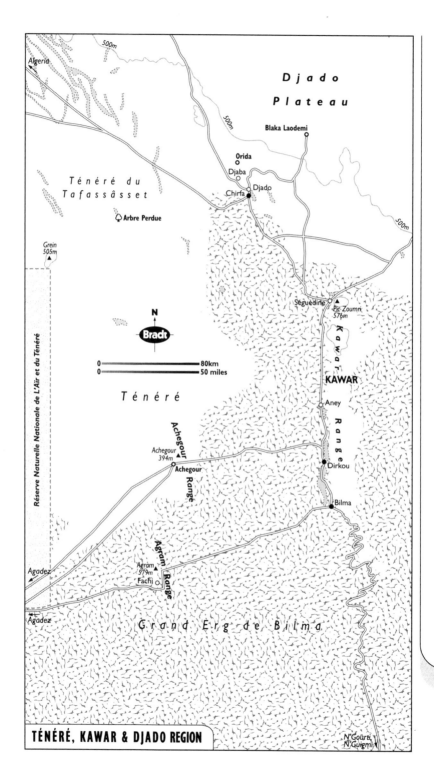

TÉNÉRÉ, KAWAR & DJADO REGION

Bilma. A more northerly branch of this route – used for motoring traffic (mostly big trucks) – leads from Agadez to Bilma via the oasis of Achegour. The route to Fachi marks the invisible boundaries of the Réserve Naturelle Nationale de l'Aïr et du Ténéré, the natural reserve that has been created to protect the ecological and archaeological richness of the region (see box *Aïr and Ténéré National Reserves,* pages 190–1).

To the extreme northeast of Niger, the landscape changes dramatically as the sand meets the southern edge of the Djado Plateau. Ancient rivers that have ceased to flow long ago, cut deep canyons in the red-coloured rocky surface. The many archaeological sites and rock engravings on the now largely uninhabitable plateau are testiment to the fact that favourable climatic circumstances allowed human presence in the region over 50,000 years ago. At the southern edge of the plateau are the stunningly beautiful abandoned desert cities – like Djado and Djaba – remnants of a more recent history when the region was frequented by caravans consisting of tens of thousands of camels. They were following another important trade route, situated in the east of Niger, north-south from Libya to Chad.

Further south, 200km from the Djado Plateau, the caravans crossed the Kawar region, which is dominated by a 150km-long mountain range. It rises from the sand to an altitude of 150m, and its orientation is almost perfectly North–south, with Bilma at the southern tip of the mountains. The caravans then had to cross the Grand Erg de Bilma before reaching Agadem, N'Gourti and Lake Chad.

AZALAÏS: THE SALT CARAVANS

Trans-Saharan trade has been transformed tremendously since big trucks have entered the scene. The equation is simple: camels cannot compete with trucks for speed, efficiency and capacity. While the *azalaïs* are restricted to making use of the cooler months, plying a certain route only once a year, trucks can come and go as they like. Since Bilma became accessible to trucks, most of the salt trade is done on wheels and *azalaïs* have become a rare sight.

Nevertheless, smaller caravans from the Aïr region still leave for Fachi and Bilma to acquire salt and dates, then proceed to the southern regions of Niger or to Nigeria to sell their load at a profit. They prepare and leave around October, sometimes November, after the rains when the camels have been able to feed well and gain strength. It is essential for the camels to be in good shape, not just because of the long distance that is walked each day (60km without stopping is not unusual) and the load they have to carry. On top of that the camels' ability to stay without water is stretched to the limit, as they will not drink for days, even up to a week – depending on their point of departure – until they reach Fachi. The camels carry their own fodder, the provisions and water for the camel drivers, as well as produce from the Aïr Mountains, like dried vegetables and wheat. As the Kawar region lacks firewood for cooking, caravans often also carry dry wood to sell or barter.

After leaving the mountain region, the terrain becomes extremely difficult. Fachi is surrounded by hundreds of kilometres of shifting dunes, where the camel drivers have to find the best possible passage to avoid deep, soft sand and steep slopes. On arrival in Fachi, the priority lies with the camels, who need to quench their thirst. They can easily manage 100 litres of water in one drinking session. The *azalaï* then rests for a few days in Fachi, where inhabitants of the oasis carefully collect all the camels' droppings. Once dried – which does not take long in the scorching climate – these are used for fuel, as Fachi also lacks firewood. The caravan then continues east towards Bilma, another 170km away, where the merchandise is traded for salt and dates. After a week's rest, the caravan returns to the Aïr after a total of around five to seven weeks.

If it is your ambition to join a caravan to Bilma, there are a few things to consider. You need to be in very good condition, and able to cope with the harsh, hot and primitive conditions. The caravan stops only for the night, and during the day the *azalaï* keeps in motion from dawn to well after dusk. Food is little more than dried dates, tea, *takomért* (cheese), and bowls of *la boule*, a filling and nourishing porridge (see *Food and drink*, page 73). No matter how blistered your feet are and how desperate you are for a break, the caravan can't afford to stop until the next well. Also take note of the fact that the route for the *azalaï* is not the same as the one for trucks, and the chances of hitching a ride with tourist vehicles that do pass Fachi are slim.

While strict timing is essential for the journey proper, you will need to be very flexible for time. The caravans do not leave on a set date, and therefore you have to take your time to meet the guides and camel drivers to make arrangements, then wait for departure. Do not expect camel drivers to feel urged to deliver you somewhere in time to catch a plane, so you will have to allow plenty of time for your return trip. Once you have set out with a caravan, their pace is your pace.

If all of the above has not drained your enthusiasm, you are ready to take the next step: to get in touch with guides and camel drivers. Agadez is one place to try your luck, as word may have spread that a caravan is preparing for a journey. Travel agencies may be able to inform you, and you will probably need an agency anyway to take you to the point of departure, which is often from the region of Timia. If you are unlucky and do not find a caravan that will take you, it is always an option to arrange your own camel expedition through an agency. This would allow marginally more flexibility on the way, but getting to water will always determine the pace of the caravan. While you will then miss the sensation of being part of 'the real experience', bear in mind that the routine of a journey through the desert remains the same, and the experience will be a unique one anyhow.

Whether you join an *azalaï* or a private caravan, you need at least three camels to carry your personal luggage, provisions, water, fodder for the camels and yourself. Riding a camel makes a wonderful change after hours of walking, and as you will soon find out, walking makes a wonderful change after hours of riding. The combination is ideal, though your camel may not agree. As the journey is extremely strenuous for the camels, the rate to rent-a-camel will be calculated accordingly. Expect to pay around CFA5,000 per camel per day, but it could be as much as CFA10,000 for 'heavy days'. This does not include other expenses like provisions and fodder, and the fee needs to take into account the guides and camel drivers.

The journey is not over yet, though. After a rest the caravan heads south, to the region of Tanout and Zinder, or even onwards to Kano in Nigeria. It is a different kind of journey, with more waterpoints along the way, pastures for the camels, time for breaks and meals, and village markets to sell the first bars of salt at. Eventually, when all salt and dates have been sold or bartered, the caravan returns back to the Aïr region. The camels now carry heavy loads of millet, textiles, tea and sugar. When the caravan reaches home again, the journey has lasted several months, or even half a year.

GRAND TOUR Most travel agencies organise *grands raids* or 'grand tours': a round trip along the edges of the Ténéré, including a part of the fringes of the Aïr and Ténéré. Below are described those areas of interest that are usually part of the itinerary. For information on the destinations along the fringes of the Aïr, see *The fringes of the Aïr and Ténéré*, pages 190–4.

Agadez THE TENERE DESERT

7

TENERE TREE The most famous tree in Niger must be the *arbre du Ténéré* or Ténéré tree. It was the only landmark between the southeastern end of the Aïr Mountains and the oasis of Fachi. In 1973, the tree was knocked over by a Libyan lorry driver, and has been replaced by an object that only remotely resembles a tree. The original tree is now on display as an oddity at the National Museum in Niamey.

FACHI Hidden in a natural depression near the isolated Agram mountain range lies the oasis of Fachi. Given the presence of water and its strategic position along the caravan routes, Fachi survived the centuries that were often characterised by insecurity and raids. The inhabitants of Fachi therefore used to live in a fortified village or *ksar*, where they could retreat in the event of instability. This fort is now in ruins, and the Kanouri and Toubou inhabitants live in houses nearby. Thick *banco* walls keep out the heat of the day, while the narrow alleys in the labyrinth-like structure of the village provide some shade. At the other side of the oasis, near the palm gardens, are the *salines* or salt pits.

The soil around the Agram is very rich in salt and minerals, which are extracted by evaporation. When the pits are dug, a saline solution of water rich in salt and minerals, emerges, and the salt crystalises on the surface. This crust is repeatedly broken to allow the water to evaporate, and then the salt crystals are spread out to dry. While this pure salt is rich in sodium chloride, it is often mixed with sulphates, sand and argil. This mixture is then moulded into bars that are sold as salt licks for livestock. Work in the salt pits is extremely demanding, not just because it involves arduous physical labour, but the direct and reflecting sunlight turn the *salines* into a scorching oven. One cannot help but admire the endurance of the inhabitants of Fachi.

KAWAR As easterly winds prevail in this part of the Sahara, the eastern side of the Kawar mountain range is covered by sand dunes, crawling up the slopes. The western side, however, is sheltered from the sand that is blown across the desert. This lee side hides a life-bringing treasure: just under the surface of sand, groundwater is easily accessible, and it is primarily the presence of water that has brought life to the Kawar region. Small settlements are nestled all along the western side of the Kawar Mountains from Bilma to Séguédine. They used to be an important link along the 2,800km-long trade route linking the Mediterranean to the Sudanese Sahel. Houses in the region are built from *banco* and salt, giving them a particular greyish colour.

BILMA Bilma is the largest and southernmost of all settlements, and the administrative capital of the region. It used to be a real crossroads of trade and traffic, as this is where the east–west caravan route meets the north–south route from Libya to Chad. Trans-Saharan trade has declined dramatically over the last decades, and the times when caravans counted tens of thousands of camels have long gone. Whilst traffic is much quieter now, Bilma remains a compulsory halting place for all travellers, traders and tourists alike. Apart from the salt caravans from the Aïr Mountains, it is frequented by Toubou from the south. Some are camel traders, on their way with herds of young camels to be sold in Libya. Others are Toubou women from the Termit region, who have come to collect dates from their palm gardens. These women are highly praised for their stamina and their capacity to survive on very little water and food. The journey from Termit to Bilma is one of the harshest Sahara crossings as it cuts through the Grand Erg de Bilma, the notorious shifting sand dunes where many desert travellers have perished without a trace. Yet, the Toubou women ply this route every year.

The pretty village of Bilma is inhabited by both Toubou and Kanouri. The latter exploit the *salines de Kalala*, where salt is extracted in the same way as in Fachi (see page 192). The salt basins hold different concentrations of saline water, which causes different shades of browns, reds and oranges, like a rustic stained-glass window. After extraction, the salt is moulded into round bricks (*fossi*) or salt pillars (*kanutu*). Though it has a greyish colour and a coarse texture, it is said to be of better quality than the salt in Fachi. Nevertheless, even the demand for this salt dropped significantly when the much purer sea salt became available for human consumption, and now neatly stacked rows of salt pillars patiently wait to be bought by traders.

The population of Bilma also cultivates vegetable gardens. In the shade of the date palms, water is hoisted to the surface and then poured into narrow irrigation channels. These gardens are a true haven in this remote corner of an immense desert.

DIRKOU Much less attractive than Bilma, Dirkou is an important military post and an economic centre. Travellers are expected to report to the former.

SEGUEDINE The drive along the Kawar Escarpment, past Chemidour and Aney, is very picturesque. From Bilma, it is a 90km-long sequence of villages, ruined forts, semi-nomadic settlements, salt basins and gardens, alternated with uninhabited stretches that are naturally beautiful. Séguédine lies in the shade of Pic Zoumri (576m) that looks a bit forlorn in the sandy environment. From Séguédine, it is 120km to the military post of Chirfa.

CHIRFA Travellers are advised to report at what must be the remotest outpost of Niger. The village of Chirfa is located a few kilometres from the military post and is nestled around the ruined colonial fort of Pacoh. Chirfa is a gateway to the Djado Plateau, a vast and rather inaccessible region that hides many archaeological sites. If you intend to venture out there, make sure to enquire about security first, as banditry is not uncommon. Be sure to travel with a local Toubou guide in order to find the sites of importance.

DJADO AND DJABA Deeper into the valley of Orida, the landscape is of a bizarre beauty. In places, the sand is littered with upright, dagger-like black rocks. The escarpment of the Djado Plateau hides many valleys and gorges of heavily eroded rock formations and natural sculptures, and it seems the elements must have had a great time creating such strange shapes. The abandoned fortified towns or *ksars* of the twin sisters of Djado and Djaba emerge like termite mounds from the sand. They are intricate mazes of corridors and passages, and allow panoramic views from the top.

The history of these citadels is rather hazy, and their origins have not yet been determined with certainty. According to some, the *ksars* were constructed by the Sô, a legendary ethnie that later probably assimilated with other ethnies. However, at some point the Kanouri took over and inhabited the towns until they abandoned the area. A probable cause for their departure is the continuous insecurity of the zone, as raids were common. A more prosaic explanation is that the Kanouri could no longer cope with the many mosquitoes in the area. Indeed, the stagnant *mares* or ponds are infested with mosquitoes.

The area is now dominated by Toubou, who take care of the gardens and *palmeraies*. Reputedly the best dates of Niger come from this zone, that still attracts traders in August and September when they are harvested. Some kilometres to the north of Djaba is the source of Orida, sheltered among palm gardens.

TENERE DE TAFASSASSET Driving back to the Aïr region through the Ténéré de Tafassâsset is a humbling and thrilling experience. The plain is so vast and spacious that a 360° panorama reveals nothing but a shimmering horizon in all directions.

The only landmarks on the way are the 'lost tree' and the Grein dunes. The wind has transformed the plain into a corrugated surface, where fast driving is the most comfortable way to skim over the ripples. The track leads to Adrar Bous, an isolated mountain in the northernmost part of the Aïr region (see *The fringes of the Aïr and Ténéré,* page 192).

Part Four

THE SOUTHEAST

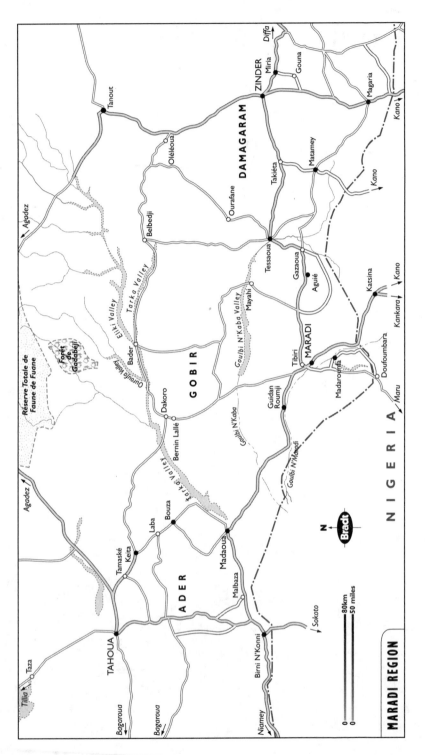

MARADI REGION

8

Maradi

While the north of the district of Maradi is dominated by monotonously undulating sand dunes formed by sand blown in from the Sahara, the valley of Maradi – south of the town of Maradi – is an ancient, heavily eroded landscape, rich in clay deposits and natural depressions that retain water during the rainy season. Two seasonal rivers or *goulbi* (the Goulbi N'Maradi and Goulbi N'Gabi) flow into the country from Nigeria during the months of the rainy season, roughly between May and October, feeding Lake Madarounfa and flooding vast areas. But even in the dry months when the landscape looks arid, permanent groundwater is more easily accessible than further north. This creates favourable conditions for agriculture allowing the cultivation of a wide array of crops like cotton, indigo, groundnuts, tobacco, niébe beans, millet and sorghum. Meanwhile, pastoralists find their way to this region when watering places and grazing become sparse elsewhere. Not surprisingly, this part of the district is one of the most densely populated areas in Niger. Most of the sedentary population is Hausa, while most of the nomads are Peul. Tuareg, as well as Kanouri and other minorities, also live in this region.

MARADI

HISTORY

The town of Maradi took its name from the Hausa title *maradi*, which means 'chief of fetishists' or 'priest-chiefs'; the *maradi* was one of the dignitaries of the court of the *sarki*, the traditional Hausa leader. The name stems from the beginning of the 19th century, when the Peul Muslim cleric Ousman Dan Fodio launched a *jihad* (holy war) in Hausaland, where the animist beliefs still prevailed (see also *Chapter 1, History,* page 17). Though the area had fallen prey to Ousman Dan Fodio just like most of Hausaland, those who strongly opposed the new Peul regime fled to the northern fringes of the city-state of Katsina. Thus, the region between present-day Maradi and Tessaoua, and especially the valley of Maradi, became a refuge and a bastion for animists. Newcomers settled here and regrouped in fortified villages, while playing cat-and-mouse with their conqueror and secretly preparing a counterattack. The neighbouring city-state of Gobir proved to be a worthy ally in the battle against the Peul oppressor.

Some years later, the Peul Mani was appointed governor of the independent state of Katsina. He imposed restrictions on the Hausa population and allowed his cavaliers to terrorise them. In 1819, the joint Hausa forces took action against the Mani under the supervision of their *sarki*-in-exile, Sarkin Dan Kassaoua. The Peul were cunningly misled, their leader was killed and his head was presented to Dan Kassaoua. After the fierce battles that followed, the Peul were eventually ousted from the region and Dan Kassaoua returned to his people. Thus, the independent city-state of Katsina, also referred to as north Katsina, was founded and its capital, until then a rather insignificant village, was renamed 'Maradi'.

During the following decades, many leaders under ever-changing entities of power were to come and go, sometimes in peace but often with bloodshed and violence. Then, at the turn of the 20th century, a new kind of oppressor moved in: the French. A whole new and artificial administration was imposed on the population, while the existing ruling authorities were moulded to fit within the new system. These changes under the new rulers were about the balance of power and control of the economy. In the religious sphere, meanwhile, the Hausa from north Katsina, and those incomers who had gradually integrated into the Hausa society, quietly embraced Islam after all. The encounter between the traditional beliefs and Islam didn't mean that animism was fully rejected, but it did lead to various syncretic religions, with new interpretations justifying the fusion. Many elements of animism lie so deeply embedded in Hausa history, that – whether it be openly or discreetly – certain rituals and customs have survived the ravages of time to this day. However, over the years Maradi became a stronghold of a more strict interpretation of Islam, whereby there is a persistent tendency to strip the essence of Islam from impurities. This means not just letting go of the old, traditional tenets, but also keeping new and unwanted influences at bay. Fundamental Islamic groups therefore criticise certain manifestations from Western, or rather Christian cultures, as they are considered to be provocative and incompatible with Muslim ethics and behaviour.

Occasionally, such criticism has led to militancy, as in 2000, days before the opening of the second FIMA (Festival International de la Mode Africaine, see page 78) near Niamey. Leaders from several Islamic organisations in the capital fiercely condemned the event as being a 'ceremony of perversion'. In response to this, Muslim activists both in the capital and in Maradi took to the streets to demonstrate against the festival. In Maradi, the situation soon turned sour and during the rioting that followed, brothels, hotels and bars, betting kiosks and churches were destroyed.

Maradi is not all about Islam, though. A visit to the town rather reveals the more visible side of this community: a lively place, buzzing with commercial activity, not in the least because of its proximity to Nigeria. Huge lorries are often parked around the big market to load or offload heavy bales or boxes; vendors walk up and down the streets, their merchandise stacked in a wheelbarrow or well balanced on their heads; cheap fuel from Nigeria is sold from old bottles, and the big market never seems to sleep.

GETTING THERE AND AWAY All four major bus companies have buses running to and from **Niamey** and **Zinder**, with stops in all the larger towns and some villages. There is some variation in departure days, fares and reporting times.

Air Transport (↘ 41 15 53) has daily buses going to Niamey (reporting time 07.30, CFA9,300). While the time is more convenient, note that these buses come from Zinder and – though it is unlikely – they could be full. However, on Tuesday, Thursday, Saturday and Sunday, extra buses start their journey to Niamey from Maradi. The price remains the same, but the reporting time is 04.30. Daily buses coming from Niamey are scheduled to leave for Zinder between 12.30 and 13.00 (reporting time 12.15, CFA3,000).

SNTV (↘ 41 08 01) also has daily buses in both directions. Air-conditioned buses (reporting time for Niamey 07.00, CFA12,850: for Zinder 14.00, CFA4,250); 'ordinary' buses (reporting time for Niamey 07.30, CFA9,565: for Zinder 14.30, CFA3,250).

Rimbo Transport (↘ 41 06 15/16 15) has daily services at similar rates between Niamey and Zinder as well. The reporting time for both directions is 07.00, while extra buses sometimes leave for Niamey, starting from Maradi instead of Zinder. Reporting time for these early departures is 05.00.

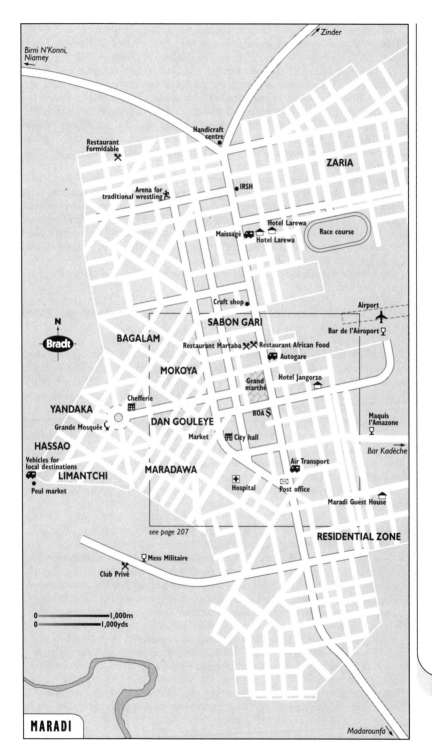

Maissagé (\ 41 13 40) has daily buses to Niamey (reporting time 07.00, CFA8,200) and sometimes extra buses starting from Maradi (reporting time 04.30). Daily buses to Zinder (reporting time 12.00, CFA3,200).

At the **autogare** you will find minibuses and *taxi-brousses* leaving when full in all directions. Though you could try your luck for certain destinations on any given day, your best chances are when vehicles leave to meet local markets. Rates vary, depending on the type of vehicle and the number of passengers travelling. The more popular destinations, their market days and fares are as follows: **Tibiri** Wednesday: CFA150–200; **Madarounfa** Wednesday, Thursday, Friday: CFA750–1,000; **Gazaoua** Friday: CFA1,250; **Mayahi** Sunday: CFA1,250–1,500; **Dakoro** Friday: CFA1,500–2,000.

The same *autogare* is also the departure point for vehicles to Nigeria. Drivers generally prefer to be paid in the Nigerian currency, the naira. Changing CFA francs to naira at the *autogare* is no problem at all. While the rates at this black market are more or less fixed, always check the official rates first. Vehicles leave daily for **Katsina**, the first sizeable town across the border. The journey takes about an hour and costs CFA2,000 or 500 naira. Some vehicles continue to **Kano** (2½ hours from Maradi; CFA2,800 or 700 naira).

On Mondays and Fridays, vehicles to nearby locations also leave from the cattle market, which takes place at the edge of town.

GETTING AROUND Taxis and *kabou-kabous* are fairly easy to find and cost CFA200 per person per trip.

LOCAL TOUR OPERATORS Maradi currently suffers from a distinct lack of tourist infrastructure. If you want to explore the region or you need information on the history of Maradi, north Katsina and the Gobir, staff at the Maradi branch of the IRSH (see *Niamey,* page 106) are very knowledgeable and helpful. The same applies for the staff at the Direction Régionale du Commerce, Industrie et Artisanat (\ 41 03 64), which is the local governmental body representing the tourist sector. There have been some temporary changes in the hierarchical structure and 'tourism' has been tossed between *directions,* but this is where experience in tourism is most likely to be concentrated. Do bear in mind, however, that neither the IRSH nor the Direction Régionale du Commerce etc should be treated as a kind of tourist office, and it is likely that you will be asked to make an appointment.

MARADI, THE GROUNDNUT CAPITAL

One product you will always find in one form or another in Maradi, is groundnuts. The French successfully introduced the groundnut as a cash crop, and for decades the economy of the region revolved around this agricultural sector. When the market value dropped, interest shifted back to other farm crops, but Maradi is still considered the centre of groundnut production. To the south of the town, the OLGA oil plant produces groundnut oil for consumption, soap and *tourteaux,* the dry ground and roasted groundnut that is used as a condiment. While the oil plant provides large-scale production, the market attracts produce from local cottage industries. Look for soap the size of big tennis balls; tiny clumps of groundnut that have been squeezed dry by hand; and sticky jars filled with oil. Also look for the *kilichi* (dried and grilled meat) variety with lots of groundnut condiment rubbed onto both sides: a delicious speciality that is hard to find elsewhere. See also *Food and drink,* page 73.

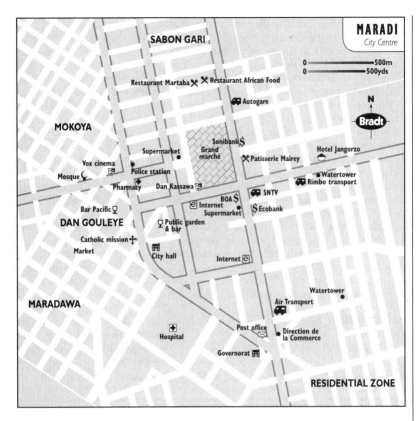

Maradi: MARADI

8

WHERE TO STAY

🏠 **Hotel Jangorzo** (80 rooms) ↘ 41 01 40. The Jangorzo has mostly spacious rooms on an equally spacious but featureless garden. This hotel has probably lost both charm and quality over the years, but given its convenient location not far from the centre of town and the friendly service, it sees many clients. Rooms are generally clean and come in various categories. *Rates from CFA6,000/8,500 (sgl/dbl) for a room with fan and shared facilities with cold water only, up to CFA14,000/16,500 for a s/c room with AC, TV and fridge.*

🏠 **Hotel Larewa** Only a 10-minute walk away from the market, but not far from the Maissagé bus yard. Under inexperienced management this hotel seems to have rapidly crumbled into a rather

sad state. Of the 2 establishments, the one next to the school is marginally better than the one across the road, which has sagging beds in musty rooms. The restaurant was closed at the time of research, but should open again shortly. *Rates are CFA5,500–8,500 for a s/c dbl with fan or AC.*

🏠 **Maradi Guest House** (14 rooms, 2 suites) ↘ 41 07 54/97 51 15 Located well outside town this is an excellent hotel with suites and spotless, comfortable rooms, many of which have 4-poster king-size beds. The pleasant, shady garden hides the smallest pool I have ever come across, but you'll appreciate sitting in the water to cool down on hot days. *Rooms from CFA30,000/40,000 (sgl/dbl) up to CFA45,000–55,000.*

WHERE TO EAT AND DRINK The restaurant at **Maradi Guest House** is pricey but excellent. The menu very much reflects the fact that this hotel was previously owned by an Italian, so you can have pizza, mozzarella and carpaccio amongst others. Birthday cakes can be ordered in advance at CFA12,000. **Hotel Jangorzo** has a bar and restaurant. A daily menu is good value at CFA3,500 and shows few surprising dishes of reasonable quality. The shelves in the bar are lamentably empty.

At **Restaurant Martaba** the indoors dining area is a bit dark and dull, but the spacious yard with some shady trees is very pleasant. Open daily from morning till midnight, it serves basic meals for around CFA500–1,500. Just next to Martaba is the small and welcoming **Restaurant African Food**. Bar **Restaurant Formidable** (↘ 97 05 71), a simple but friendly place, is open seven days a week from 10.00 until midnight. Not far from the big market is a **public garden** with an open-air bar.

A bit far out of town to be convenient, **Bar de l'Aéroport** is a small and lively place for a drink and maybe some *brochettes*. **Bar Kadèche** is another out-of-town bar with a lot of *couleur locale* and some basic dishes to choose from. Whether the many females were just visiting or looking for company was unclear. Not far from Bar Kadèche is **Maquis l'Amazone**, an open-air bar with green and blue neon lights in small secluded sitting areas.

Even further away from the centre of Maradi are Club Privé and the Mess Militaire. Though they are only a stone's throw away from each other, they couldn't be more different. **Club Privé** (↘ 41 02 62; *open daily 24hrs*) is most of all a members-only club with nightclub, frequented by expats. However, if you are passing by you can obtain a *bon de passage* at CFA5,000, which includes one-day membership, use of the swimming pool and a few refreshments. The **Mess Militaire** (↘ 41 06 01; *open daily 09.00–01.00, Sat until 05.00*) attracts a very different patronage, including soldiers and young females to entertain them. Some basic food is available, but this is predominantly a drinking place, and is particularly lively on Saturdays.

ENTERTAINMENT AND NIGHTLIFE Hotel Jangorzo has a **nightclub** which opens every Saturday and sometimes also on Fridays from 22.00. Live music – mostly rap – is sometimes played; the entrance fee is CFA1,000–1,500. Hidden behind a faint yellow wall and formerly known as Bar Prestige, the **Pacific Bar** is open during the day for drinks only. However, from 23.00 every day except Sunday, it turns into a *boîte de nuit* with rap and funky music. Two more nightclubs can be found at Club Privé and the Mess Militaire (see above).

One of the last functional cinemas in Niger is **Cinéma Dan Kasawa**, where you can see Hausa, Hindi, Chinese, European and American films for just CFA100–200. Don't expect high-tech quality. In fact, you may well find the highly empathising and enthusiastic audience far more entertaining than the film, which is a good reason to go to a Nigérien cinema in the first place. The programme starts every evening at 20.30.

SHOPPING A supermarket with a reasonable choice of produce is **Super Top Alimentation**, which opens seven days a week, 08.00–22.00 (*closed for prayer only*), while **Patisserie Mairey** (↘ 41 15 16; *open daily around the clock*) has French bread, buns and a limited choice of pastries.

OTHER PRACTICALITIES There are four **banks** in Maradi, of which only three deal with foreign currency. None of the banks takes credit cards.

$ **Ecobank** ↘ 41 17 01; open Mon–Fri 08.30–17.30, Sat 09.00–13.00. Changes cash euro and US dollars. You can also cash travellers' cheques in the same currencies; hand in your cheques with the receipt and your passport in the morning, and you can collect the money in the afternoon.

$ **BIA** ↘ 41 02 42; open 07.45–11.30 and 15.45–17.30. Takes most currencies, whether it be cash or travellers' cheques.

$ **Sonibank** ↘ 41 02 60; open 07.45–12.30 and 15.45–18.30. Changes cash euro only.

Post office ↘ 41 04 84; open Mon–Fri 07.30–12.15 and 15.00–17.45. Poste restante service charges CFA300 per letter or parcel.

Internet Connection is not ideal in Maradi, but if you are desperate for some news from home, try cybercafé Microsoft Word (↘ 41 15 24/97 46 26). Connection is slow, erratic and expensive at CFA100 per minute, but hourly rates can be discussed. Opening hours are irregular.

WHAT TO SEE AND DO

Handicrafts The **Centre Artisanal de Maradi** (↘ *41 00 61/97 02 08; open daily 08.00–18.00*) is located at the junction at the northern end of the main road leading into town. Like so many other arts and crafts centres, it has been founded by the Coopération Nigero-Luxembourgeoise (see *Handicrafts and what to buy,* page 80). The choice of *maroquinerie* or leatherwork is especially good.

Markets The marketplace is never devoid of activity, but is especially busy on Mondays and Fridays. Well worth a visit and right at the edge of town is the cattle market, most of all frequented by the colourful Peul.

Chef's Palace Under French rule, the number of sultanates in Niger was reduced to two – Agadez and Zinder – while other traditional authorities were renamed *chefferies*. The *chefferie* in Maradi is one example of a traditional *chef's* court household where protocol has remained very similar to that of a sultanate. Court members, dressed in bold-coloured garments, linger around the palace's entrance. See also Nigérien *society*, page 31.

Walk around town On Mondays and Fridays, you could go for a wonderful walk (approx two hours), combining a visit to the big market, the *chefferie* and Big Mosque, then onwards to the cattle market and finally zigzagging your way back through some very lively neighbourhoods. Glimpses of a household back yard and every street corner are true still lifes and the inhabitants will be pleasantly surprised to see some *anasara* in their quarter. You could also opt to continue from the cattle market to the Mess or Club Privé (30 minutes), but in that case you would need a guide to make sure you do not get lost: the area has dense vegetation, few road options and is virtually uninhabited.

MADAROUNFA

Once the region of north Katsina was covered in dense woodlands teeming with wildlife. Nowadays, the vegetation has been degraded to a large extent, but still this is one of the greenest regions of Niger. Along the river Goulbi N'Maradi are still clusters of woodland, and on the way to the village of Madarounfa you pass through what is now a classified forest. This means that cattle are not allowed to roam free and graze from the trees and bushes, thus leaving the undergrowth and wild grasses intact.

Most of the year the landscape looks arid and in need of water, which makes it hard to imagine that parts of this stretch do in fact occasionally flood. In 1945, an entire village was abandoned after it was completely submerged. Just by the roadside, ancient *teintureries* or dyeing pits that were used by the villagers to dye cotton with indigo and other colouring agents are still visible.

The village of Madarounfa (sometimes spelt Madarumfa) is spread out along the shore of Lake Madarounfa, with lines of baobab and gao trees of an impressive stature bringing shade. As the leaves of the baobab are an indispensable ingredient for a traditional sauce, these trees are regularly clipped and take up strange shapes. It's a picturesque and lively place, and well worth a visit or, if you have the time, a walk around the lake. Once in the village and especially if you intend to visit the tombs (see box *The 99 tombs of Madarounfa,* opposite), introduce yourself to the *préfet du département* first, and preferably walk around with a local guide.

Taxi-brousses leave to and from Maradi most days, but mostly on Wednesdays and Fridays to meet the market in Madarounfa. Otherwise you would have to have your own transport or hire a taxi for the day, but not all taxi drivers will be happy to take on the challenge of the dirt road to Madarounfa. The trip to Madarounfa takes around 45 minutes.

LAKE MADAROUNFA The river Goulbi N'Gabi ends in the natural basin of Lake Madarounfa. The highest levels of the lake are measured in July and August, well into the rainy season, when it may even flood the valley of the Goulbi N'Gabi and vast areas of land to the east. The surplus water is let out through a canal into the Goulbi N'Maradi. Then, after the rains have ended, the flow of water soon turns into a trickle and both rivers will eventually stand dry for most of the year. Though the edge of the lake also recedes, this lake, with an average circumference of 5km, is one of the very few permanent open waters in Niger. Different ethnic groups have settled down in the vicinity to make use of that precious water. Along the shore there is always a lot of activity, with children bathing, women washing their laundry or pounding millet in the shade, boys taking cattle to the edge of the water to drink and fishermen bringing in their catch of the day.

Fish is abundant in Lake Madarounfa, and while some fishermen fish from the shore or from a small boat with nets and rods, others lie directly in the water, belly down over enormous calabashes to stay afloat, and using their hands to paddle around. In December and January, the cold season, this way of fishing is less practised simply because the water temperature has dropped too much. Lake Madarounfa is also a great place for birdwatching, and you may see different species of ducks and waders, as well as teals and even pelicans.

When walking around the lake, some rectangular, knee-high walls may catch the eye. These are the sites where saints were buried well before living history. In total, there are 99 tombs around the lake and on the islands, but only 20 of them have been marked with a stone wall.

TIBIRI

After the Peul oppressors under Ousman Dan Fodio had been chased away from north Katsina and Gobir, Tibiri (or Tsibiri) was created to be the capital of the independent state of Gobir. Soon after, the relationship between north Katsina and Gobir deteriorated badly, marking the beginning of a long era of clashes between the authorities. Under French rule, Tibiri lost most of its former importance, but the core of the Hausa culture and beliefs remained remarkably intact. The potency of the animist cult never ceased to play an important role in the lives of the people.

Every year, thousands of animists from the region and even across the border come together near a seasonal lake, 12km to the west of Tibiri. The occasion is a ceremony called *'l'ouverture de la brousse'* that very much resembles the yearly gathering – with the same name and significance – in Massalata near Birni N'Konni. It is a serious occasion and should not be considered a tourist event, but if you are genuinely interested and wish to witness some of the rituals, present yourself at the local, traditional authorities first to ask permission. There is no fixed date, since – as in Massalata – the timing of the ceremony is calculated according to the lunar calendar. See also box *Arwa: ceremony of the Azna,* page 150 and box *Cultural sensitivity,* page 84.

Market day in Tibiri is on Wednesdays and you should have no problem finding transport to and from Maradi. Tibiri is located 15km north of Maradi along the main road.

According to oral history, the shores of Lake Madarounfa are the location of 99 tombs of saints. Very little is known about their origins, but in 1998 Iman Amadou and his son Malam Sani, both from Madarounfa, told the story as it had been passed on to them. This is a somewhat abbreviated version of their testimony as it was recorded:

> In his courtyard in Medina, the Prophet Mohammed told his khalifs that one day three men would appear. The khalifs were to give them 1,000 gold coins and ask them to pray for 1,000 years of peace and prosperity on earth. The Prophet handed over 1,000 coins to the khalifs. The three men took their time, though, skipping a few generations of khalifs. Every time when the khalif who was safekeeping those coins felt his time was coming to an end, he added 100 gold pieces and passed on the request to his successor.
>
> Then finally, 40 years after the death of the Prophet, the three men came to Medina. The ruling khalif asked to see the men, and though they did not speak, the khalif recognised the signs that only he could see and that assured him they were indeed the three men sent by the Prophet Mohammed. He handed over the now 1,400 gold coins and asked the men to pray for 1,400 years of peace and prosperity. After the men had finished saying their prayers, the khalif told the men to travel westbound, as their residence was to be found there. So the three men travelled all the way to Madarounfa, where they settled down. All this happened a long, long time ago, even before the village of Madarounfa was created. Since then, oral tradition speaks of 99 saints, of which only these three originate from Medina.

The testimony ends here. There seems to be no explanation for the arrival of the other 96 saints, who now supposedly all lie buried around the lake or on one of the small islands, just like the three men from Medina. The burial sites or tombs have not been thoroughly investigated either, and sceptics wonder if one would find any human remains at all. However, to the local people there is no shadow of doubt: the saints were really there, the tombs and sites are sacred and need to be left untouched. Oral history and local knowledge have been confirmed through repeated sightings of 'mysterious lights', like beams of light shining upwards to the foliage of the trees at the burial sites, and it is through such observations that the tombs have been located. Though it is said that the lights have become fainter since the advent of light pollution – which in the case of Madarounfa means torches and headlights – true believers say that they sometimes still see light coming from the tombs to this day.

TESSAOUA

The last decades of the 19th century were unsettled times in the independent states of north Katsina and Gobir. Anarchy and insecurity ruled, as former allies turned against each other, sometimes teaming up with the Peul or other forces to expand the fringes of a state or to push a kinsman forward to occupy a much-wanted position. One key figure to trigger long-lasting unrest was Mazawajé, a Muslim fanatic and leader from Maradi between 1877 and 1880. He undermined many principles that had made Maradi the bastion of animism, and was forced to take refuge elsewhere. He went on to found the state – later sultanate – of Tessaoua, from where he continued to harass his former brethren. Mazawajé was killed near Lake Madarounfa in 1890, but the warfare continued.

Nine years later, the environs of Tessaoua were the scene of the end of the Voulet–Chanoine mission (see *Chapter 1, History,* page 18). On 14 July 1899, when Lieutenant Colonel Klobb caught up with the mission, Voulet and Chanoine opened fire, killing Klobb. To Voulet's recruited men this was the last straw. As an ultimate act of revolt, they turned against their commanders, and only days later both Voulet and Chanoine were slain. All three men were buried nearby: Klobb's grave is in Dan Kori at the foot of a tamarind tree – just to the north of Tessaoua – and the graves of Voulet and Chanoine can be found at the foot of a huge gao tree south of May Jirgi, a village along the road to Zinder.

In 1927, the French colonialists dissolved the sultanate of Tessaoua, and the small town was incorporated into the French administration.

For most travellers, Tessaoua is no more than a short stop on the way to either Maradi or Zinder. Facilities are very limited, but you will always find something to eat and drink along the thoroughfare. For transport, see the relevant *Getting there and away* sections.

Patas monkey, Erythrocebus patas

9

Zinder

Sannu sannu baata hana zuwaa neesa. Say day a kwan ba a jee baa.

(Hausa proverb, meaning 'Walking slowly does not prevent from
travelling far, even if one has to spend the night along the way.'

The town of Zinder, sultanate of Tanimoune and capital of the Damagaram, was a
prosperous place and an important town along the trans-Saharan trade route when
the French first arrived. As the administrative heart of the new colony of Niger, it
seemed that its political importance would continue under the new administration.
However, the development of Zinder suddenly slowed down as the capital was
shifted back to Niamey in 1926, and from then on Zinder just lingered on as a
regional capital and centre of trade. When tourism started to develop in Niger, it
was concentrated along the axis Niamey–Agadez ignoring Zinder as its location
seemed too eccentric to be conveniently included in itineraries. Yet, Zinder
deserves to be a travel destination in its own right. Much of its history has been
preserved, and the sultanate is still of great importance to both local and regional
society.

Meanwhile, Zinder has developed into one of the leading cultural centres of
Niger, and ambitious plans to shine new light on the cultural heritage of Zinder
and the Damagaram are currently being put into effect. Literally so, as a laser-show
against the backdrop of the old town quarter of Birni is intended to boost interest
in the town and its rich history. In a way, this sums up what Zinder is about: an
embrace of old and new traditions, that quietly but steadily developed during the
years that Zinder was almost forgotten. The tourist industry is finally beginning to
take it one step further as young, locally based tour operators are dedicated to
firmly putting Zinder on the map as a tourist destination, and a starting point for
journeys to the easternmost regions of Niger.

ZINDER

HISTORY In the beginning of the 18th century, Zinder was no more than a Hausa
settlement, a village amongst other villages. It gained importance after the arrival
of the Kanouri from the empire of Bornou in the east, who founded the sultanate
of Damagaram around 1736.

Zinder remained a vassal state of the empire of Bornou until the 19th century,
when the installation of Sultan Tanimoune Dan Souleymane marked a real turning
point. Tanimoune rejected the oppressor and he severed the existing link with
Bornou. Instead, he became the new oppressor, as his army ferociously conquered
neighbouring states. Tanimoune not only expanded the political power of the
Damagaram, he also developed economic activities in the region. Zinder became a
crossroads of trade (including slave trade), where caravans coming from the north
met with Hausa merchants from the south (present-day Nigeria). In this era,

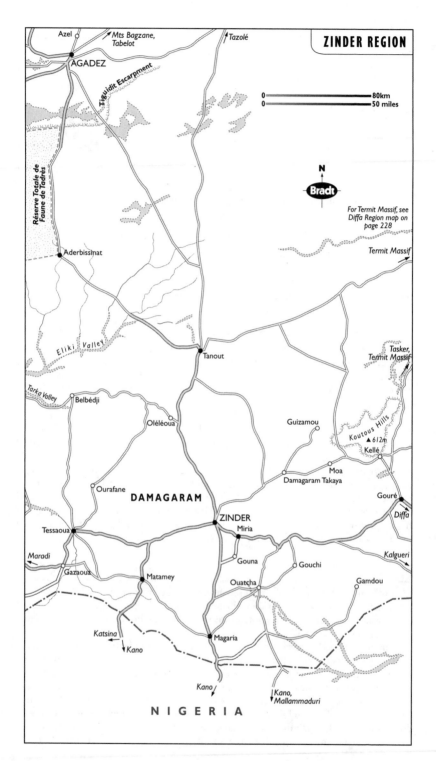

Azel

Mts Bagzane,
Tabelot

Tazolé

AGADEZ

Tiguidit Escarpment

0 ———————— 80km
0 ———————— 50 miles

N

Bradt

For Termit Massif, see
Diffa Region map on
page 228

Réserve Totale de
Faune de Tadrès

Aderbissinat

Termit Massif

Eliki Valley

Tanout

Tasker,
Termit Massif

Tarka Valley

Belbédji

Oléléoua

Guizamou

Koutous Hills

▲612m
Kellé

Ourafane

Moa
Damagaram Takaya

Gouré

DAMAGARAM

ZINDER

Diffa

Tessaoua

Miria

Maradi

Gouna

Gouchi

Kalgueri

Gazaoua

Matamey

Ouatcha

Gamdou

Katsina

Kano

Magaria

Kano

Kano,
Mallammaduri

NIGERIA

Zinder consisted of two settlements: Zengou or Zongo, the original Hausa settlement and the site to where Tuareg *caravaniers* would descend after their long journey, and Birni, the fortified quarter of the sultan and Kanouri aristocrats.

For decades, the capital of Damagaram remained a stronghold, defeating even the first of the European conquerors. Then, in 1899, the ruling Sultan Amadou Kouran Daga and his army were slain by the French, and Zinder came under French rule. Its importance within the region, and even within the French *Territoire Militaire du Niger* (Military Territory of Niger), led to a crucial decision: in 1911, the central power of the colonisers was transferred from Niamey to Zinder, making it the first official capital of the colonised territory. Owing to various factors (see *Niamey*, pages 93–4), this decision was eventually reversed, and the administrative powers were shifted back to Niamey in 1926.

By then, the space between Zengou and Birni had largely been usurped by the 'new town', with administrative buildings and dwellings in French colonial style. Zinder had become a cosmopolitan regional capital of around 20,000 inhabitants, a colourful melting pot of mostly Hausa, Peul, Kanouri, Toubou, Tuareg and French. When the political power was removed from Zinder, however, its economic importance started to dwindle too. As a regional capital and as the seat of the sultanate, Zinder is still alive. The population has grown to 180,000 inhabitants (2001), making Zinder the second-largest town in Niger.

GETTING THERE AND AWAY All four major bus companies have daily buses shuttling between Zinder and **Niamey**. The reporting time (*rendez-vous*) is at 04.30 at the various bus yards and the bus should arrive in the capital by 17.00–18.00. A ticket to Niamey costs around CFA12,500, while the bus also stops in Maradi (CFA3,000), Madaoua (CFA5,700), Birni N'Konni (CFA6,700), Dogondoutchi (CFA8,200) and Dosso (CFA9,200). SNTV has air-conditioned buses leaving on Wednesdays-Fridays-Sundays at CFA16,180.

Maissagé has a weekly bus to **Diffa** on Thursdays (CFA6,200, reporting time 05.00), while SNTV has buses leaving for Diffa (CFA6,050) and even **N'Guigmi** (CFA7,900) on Mondays and Fridays. Reporting time is at 06.00 and the bus stops in Gouré (CFA2,700), Goudoumaria (CFA3,700) and Mainé-Soroa (CFA5,200). Expect the journey to Diffa to take 12 hours, and add at least another two – more likely four – hours for the last, highly uncomfortable leg to N'Guigmi. Aïr Transport is planning to run buses between Zinder and Diffa as well, but no details were given at the time of research. Enquire at SNTN (opposite SNTV) if they have started operating trucks to **N'Guigmi** and **N'Gourti**.

SNTV and Maissagé have services between Zinder and **Agadez/Arlit** (CFA7,650/11,520) on Saturdays (both companies) and Tuesdays (Maissagé only). Reporting time is at 05.00. Depending on the state of the road and weather conditions, the journey to Agadez will take seven hours or more. Add another two to three hours for the tarred but pot-holed road to Arlit. Rimbo Transport is planning to run buses to Agadez and Arlit as well, but no schedule was fixed at the time of research. See also *Agadez*, pages 165–6. For more information or to make a booking, contact any of the bus companies: Maissagé; SNTV: �‎ 510 468); Rimbo Transport (�‎ 510 416); Aïr Transport (�‎ 510 247 or 974 724).

At the *gare routière* between the *Rond point Elf* and the Catholic mission, you will find vehicles to all the above destinations, as well as vehicles to nearby towns and villages. Usually, departures coincide with market days at the final destination, but it is always worth checking for more departures. Minibuses are slightly cheaper than the nine-seater Peugeots. Look for vehicles for **Tanout** (Saturday; CFA1,500/2,500), **Diffa** (Tuesday; CFA6,000/6,500), **Matamey** (Friday; CFA1,000), **Magaria** (Saturday; CFA1,250) and **Miria** (Sunday; CFA300)

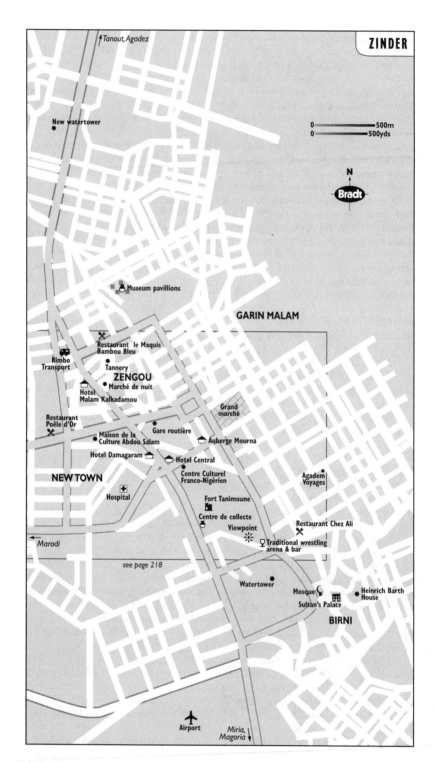

ZINDER

↑ Tanout, Agadez

0 ———— 500m
0 ———— 500yds

N
Bradt

New watertower

Museum pavillions

GARIN MALAM

Restaurant le Maquis
Bambou Bleu

Rimbo
Transport

Tannery

ZENGOU

Marché de nuit

Hotel
Malam Kalkadamou

Grand
marché

Restaurant
Poêle d'Or

Gare routière

Maison de la
Culture Abdou Salam

Auberge Mourna

Hotel Damagaram

Hotel Central

Centre Culturel
Franco-Nigérien

Agadem
Voyages

NEW TOWN

Hospital

Fort Tanimoune

Centre de collecte

Restaurant Chez Ali

Viewpoint

Maradi

Traditional wrestling
arena & bar

see page 218

Watertower

Mosque

Heinrich Barth
House

Sultan's Palace

BIRNI

Airport

Miria,
Magoria

amongst others. Minibuses regularly leave for **Kano** in Nigeria (250km, CFA3,000). Another *gare routière* with vehicles leaving for **Agadez** is located along the main road to Agadez, a few kilometres beyond the new water tower.

GETTING AROUND Zinder has relatively few **taxis**, but *kabou-kabous* or *taxi-motos* are everywhere. The typical fare is CFA200 per person per trip.

LOCAL TOUR OPERATORS

Agadem Voyages \/f 51 22 44; m 99 47 12; \ (satellite) 0088 216 218 056 39; e agademexpedition@yahoo.fr. The company is run by a dynamic Toubou who has great knowledge of the region of N'Guigmi and N'Gourti. Recommended for those who want to venture deep into Toubou country. They are located in the same quarter as restaurant Chez Ali, only a few blocks to the northeast. Ask for Mohamed Barkaï.

Gamzaki Voyages \ 51 02 80 or 98 83 31; e ericzinder@freesurf.fr; www.gamzaki-voyages.com. Run by Eric van Sprundel and Halima Ousseini, a sympathetic French–Kanouri couple. While they are new in the tourist business, already they are receiving encouraging feedback on their itineraries

to regional destinations as well as the Koutous and Termit regions. Eric speaks good English. For directions, see Auberge Gamzaki below.

Killaha Voyages \ 51 02 23 or 98 72 72; f 51 05 58; e killahavoyages@yahoo.fr. Killaha specialise in trips to the Termit Massif and the Kawar region and they offer a variety of itineraries.

Koutous Voyages \ 98 95 19. Koutous have focused on car rental and passenger transport throughout the whole region for a number of years. Though now they are eager to start working in tourism as well, thus far they lack the experience. Consider this agency if you have a clear idea of where you want to be heading.

WHERE TO STAY

🏠 **Auberge Gamzaki** \ 98 83 31; e ericzinder@freesurf.fr; www.gamzaki-voyages.com. The auberge is located along the road to Niamey, halfway between Palami handicrafts centre and Hotel Kouran Daga, at the other side of the road. A small, family-run auberge built in local Hausa style, the Auberge Gamzaki opened its doors in November 2005. *The comfortable s/c AC rooms with terrace are CFA30,000.*

🏠 **Auberge Mourna** (5 rooms) \ 99 03 06. The rooms at this homely hotel are generously decorated with wall hangings, crocheted tablecloths and ornamental flowers. The immaculate s/c AC rooms (cold water only) *start from CFA14,500 for a small dbl with no TV to CFA22,500 for a large room with TV.*

🏠 **Hotel Amadou Kouran Daga** (47 rooms) \ 51 07 42. It is located along the main road to Niamey, at the entrance to Zinder. This is easily the biggest hotel in Zinder. What it lacks in character is made up for by a reliable standard, as this hotel is clean, quiet and adequately kept. Plenty of parking space is available. *S/c rooms start from CFA7,500/10,500 (sgl/dbl with fan) to CFA13,500/18,500/25,000 for an AC sgl/dbl/triple.*

🏠 **Hotel Central** (7 rooms) (no telephone). The son of a previous owner described this place as 'a jewel in its heyday', which was in the 1960s. Since then, 7 out of the 14 rooms have crumbled to an

uninhabitable state, while the dusty remains of air conditioners are stacked in a corridor. Add to this torn and missing lampshades, broken mirrors and cracked toilet pans, and this pretty much sums up the current state of this featureless hotel. Yet, it is centrally located and if you manage to get the price down, it could still be a convenient budget place to stay. *AC rooms are CFA9,500/12,500 (sgl/dbl) while rooms with fan are CFA6,600/8,500. Camping is allowed at CFA2,000, but you share the yard with a noisy bar.*

🏠 **Hotel Damagaram** \ 51 00 69. This once must have been a real upmarket hotel, but standards have dropped: the rooms are a bit barren and the furniture has seen better days. Yet, the enclosed garden, the central location and the friendly staff make this a convenient place to stay, and in fact the hotel is often fully booked. *All rooms are s/c and cost CFA16,500 for a sgl and CFA20,000 for a dbl.*

🏠 **Hotel Malam Kalkadamou** (18 rooms) \ 51 05 68. When you are looking for real budget accommodation, try this place. Though the rooms are basic, a bit dark and definitely tatty, I thought it was a most welcoming place with an appropriate name: Malam Kalkadamou means 'do not worry, take it easy'. Perhaps it is wise to bring your own sheets and maybe flipflops for in the shower, but do enjoy the labyrinth-like corridors, the stencil

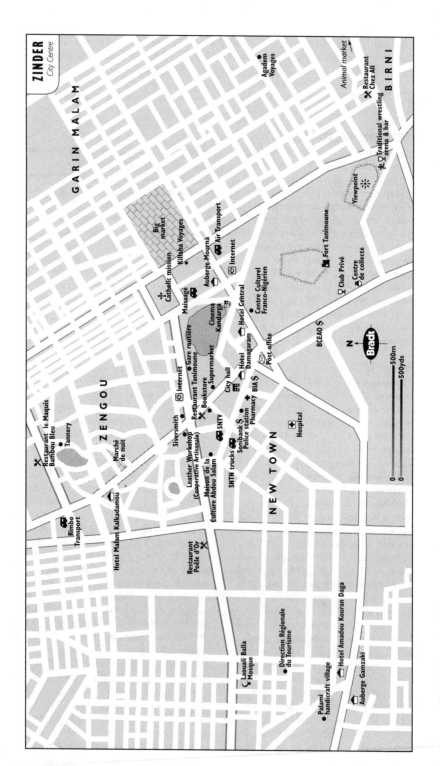

ZINDER
City Centre

GARIN MALAM

ZENGOU

NEW TOWN

BIRNI

Animal market

Restaurant
Chez Ali

Agadem
Voyages

Traditional wrestling
arena & bar

Viewpoint

Fort Tanimoune

Club Privé

Centre
de collecte

Big
market

Kilkha Voyages

Catholic mission

Maissagé

Auberge Mourna

Air Transport

Internet

Centre Culturel
Franco-Nigérien

Hotel Central

Gare routière

Restaurant Tanimoune

Cinema
Kandarga

Post office

BCEAO $

N

Bradt

500m
500yds

0
0

Restaurant le Maquis
Bambou Bleu

Tannery

Internet

Marché
de nuit

Silversmith

Bookstore

Supermarket

City hall

Hotel
Damagaram

SNTV

BIA $

Leather Workshop
(Cooperative Artisanale)

Maison de la
Culture Abdou Salam

Somibank $
Police station

Pharmacy

Hospital

SNTN trucks

Hotel Malam Kalkadamou

Rimbo
Transport

Restaurant
Poêle d'Or

Laouali Balla
Mosque

Direction Régionale
du Tourisme

Palami
handicraft village

Hotel Amadou Kouran Daga

Auberge Gamzaki

218

decorations and the terraces. Breakfast is CFA500 and meals have to be ordered in advance, but you could also opt for a bite at the *marché de nuit* across the road. Prices vary from *CFA3,100 (without fan) to CFA5,100 (s/c with fan), the best deal being a large s/c room with fan that sleeps 4 at CFA6,100.*

Å Camping Touristique ⟍ 51 05 73. Around 5km out of town along the road to Agadez *camping is allowed for CFA3,000 pp, while basic rooms with saggy beds, corrugated-iron roof and fan cost a mere CFA4,000 or CFA5,000 (s/c). Breakfast is CFA500; meals have to be ordered in advance.*

WHERE TO EAT AND DRINK
Hotel Damagaram, Auberge Mourna and Hotel Amadou Kouran Daga all serve meals. Auberge Mourna comes especially recommended, as the meals are both tasty and very well presented.

✕ Bungalow de l'Arène and another **small open-air buvette** are both situated on the premises of the Arène de la lutte traditionelle. The former invites local musicians every day to play some traditional music, but the performers have to compete with the disco music from the bar. For some reason nobody seems to feel it would make sense to switch it off to allow the soft tones and singing to be heard.

✕ Club Privé ⟍ 28 54 46. This club is well hidden next to the Centre de Collecte. It is a private club with a swimming pool and tennis court, popular with expats. If you are not a member, you will be charged CFA1,200 for the use of the pool and the same for a game of tennis, but you'll have to bring your own rackets. Not so much a restaurant but there is a kitchen, and if you have been travelling for a while, you may want to sink your teeth into a Gruyère or ham sandwich at the bar or savour an ice cream by the pool. Note that as a non-member you pay an additional 20% on top of all prices for snacks and drinks. *Open 7 days a week from 11.00 to midnight or until 02.00 on Fri and Sat.*

✕ Restaurant Chez Ali ⟍ 51 02 37. The Chez Ali serves no alcohol but otherwise has everything it takes to make this a very popular and casual place. The shady, enclosed garden is very attractive with huge trees sheltering countless weaver birds. African or some Italian meals are always available, but if you want a *mechoui (CFA25,000, see Food and drink, page 73),* this must be ordered in advance. Open 7 days a week until around midnight.

✕ Restaurant le Maquis Bambou Blue ⟍ 88 17 44. The restaurant is located inside the gate to the sports stadium. *Simple but filling meals are served for next to nothing; pay a little more for fish or chicken.*

✕ Restaurant Poêle d'Or ⟍ 29 12 79. A simple but popular hangout that serves 'potato sheeps' and various sandwiches. The *'surprise for 2' ('surprise pour 2 personnes' a platter composed of different dishes) is recommended and costs CFA3,000 only.*

✕ Restaurant Tanimoune ⟍ 98 98 08. The Tanimoune serves very affordable and succulent, straightforward meals. *Fish dishes are the most expensive at CFA2,000–2,500.*

In the courtyard at Hotel Central you can get *brochettes* only. Just outside, at the *rond point Poste* and towards Hotel Mourna, plenty of **food stalls** provide fresh and very cheap meals. More food stalls can be found at the *marché de nuit* opposite Hotel Malam Kalkadamou, which comes alive every night.

NIGHTLIFE
The **Safari Night Club** at Hotel Damagaram is open every Friday and Saturday from 22.00–04.00 and plays a wide variety of music. Entrance fee is CFA1,500.

PRACTICALITIES
For **tourist information** (⟍ 51 03 70), the only option is to go to the Direction Régionale du Tourisme. This is not a tourist office with a public function, but if you need advice on tour operators and itineraries, or if you run into serious trouble with anyone working in tourism, you will find that the staff are very willing to assist.

Banks BIA (*open Mon–Fri 07.45–11.30 and 15.15–17.15, Sat 08.00–12.00*) changes most hard currencies and travellers' cheques. BCEAO (*open Mon–Fri 07.30–13.00 and 15.00–17.30*) changes euro only. Sonibank does not deal with foreign currency. The **post office** (*open Mon–Fri from 07.45–12.15 and 15.00–17.45*).

Internet access can be found at Bureautique Excel Service, in a small and insignificant building opposite Auberge Mourna. Forget the complicated name and simply ask for the owner Ali, who is the only one who knows the password to get connected to the web. As surfing costs CFA150/minute, it is not a bad idea to write your message first offline at CFA500 per page, then get connected. The same applies for Telecentre Laksaci near *Rond point Elf* where using the internet costs CFA200/minute.

Kalou superstore is a well-stocked **supermarket**, located opposite Restaurant Tanimoune.

WHAT TO SEE AND DO

Centre de Collecte Though often referred to as the Musée Regional, the building between the districts of Zengou and Birni is in fact the Centre de Collecte (℣ *51 02 55*), the place where cultural artefacts are being collected and stored. It was founded in 1988 as part of an ambitious plan to create a combined museum, zoo and public garden. For this purpose, an immense space including the ancient race course and a *mare* (natural pond) surrounded by rocks and boulders was purchased and the Centre de Collecte was constructed in a decorative Hausa style, its door being a copy of the door to the Sultan's Palace. The population of Zinder contributed towards the plan and started handing in traditional artefacts to be exhibited in the future museum. During the decades it took to find the funds and construct the four pavilions as planned, illegally built *banco* homes and huts gradually crept in around the *mare*, occupying the site that used to be reserved for the zoo. At the beginning of 2005, the four pavilions stood empty and forlorn on the remaining empty space, their windows blocked up. Meanwhile, the Centre de Collecte serves as a makeshift museum with a rather poorly kept but interesting collecting of saddles, swords, traditional costumes, tools, etc, while a scale model of the original plans is also on display. If the above sounds rather sad, all hope now lies with the current, enthusiastic curator, who is determined to finally turn the pavilions into thematic, ethnographic exhibitions. Until that happens, the Centre de Collecte should be open daily mornings and afternoons, but doors may be closed when the curator is out on a mission. Entrance is free, but donations are appreciated.

Fort Tanimoune and viewpoint Visible from the road between the new town and Birni to the left is Fort Tanimoune. It looks like an inviting opportunity to have a panoramic view over the two sides of Zinder, but entrance is not allowed as the fort stands on military ground. However, for just as impressive views in all directions, go to the Arène de la lutte traditionelle just a little further in the direction of Birni, and scramble onto the rocky boulders on either side of the road. Watch your step: this area is also used as a public toilet.

Sultan's Palace When visiting Birni, it is hard to miss the Sultan's Palace. The striking façade depicts the sultan's emblems: a stick or *bâton*, a sword and the Koran. Below is a huge front porch, where the sultan's household – all dressed in colourful garments – is very visibly present. Around 300 people surround the sultan, and about half of them have traditional titles, linked to the specific role they play in his complex court. Once inside, the building appears to be two-faced, with some historical and traditional elements mixed with modern features such as metal doors and blinds. Some historical elements include former prison cells – where prisoners were exposed to scorpions or spiders to determine their guilt or innocence – and the impressive collection of 22 Holy Korans (all specimens that once belonged to each of the 22 previous sultans) but also numerous *gris-gris* or

When the German explorer Heinrich Barth visited Zinder in the middle of the 19th century, he resided in Birni. Like the other old quarter of Zengou, Birni had many dwellings built in refined Hausa architecture and with highly decorative façades. It was the beginning of the long and glorious reign of the ambitious Sultan Tanimoune Dan Souleymane. In 1856, a few years after Heinrich Barth had continued his voyage, Tanimoune commanded the construction of a huge wall, turning Birni into a fortified enclosure. According to legend, in order to give the ramparts indestructible strength, some Korans as well as some live virgins were incorporated in the 3m-wide structure. In places, the wall was up to 7m high. Though reputedly invincible, most of the wall was destroyed by the French in 1906. Only some giant lumps of *banco*, still showing the layers of bricks, remain to be seen today.

The presence of the French brought about many structural changes in the town, and the traditional Hausa architecture in Zengou was badly disfigured in the process. Meanwhile, most of Birni stayed intact, and a renewed interest for Hausa façades temporarily even boosted the art of decorative masonry. Yet, since then the ravages of time caused many of the once-glorious dwellings to look like stale, crumbling cakes. The abandoned house where Heinrich Barth used to stay looks even more desperate, as it has gradually deteriorated into little more than ruined walls and a signpost confirming the historical status of whatever is left of the building.

Today Birni is still visually dominated by the Sultan's Palace and the big mosque, and despite the poor state of most of the architecture, the quarter breathes history and is well worth a visit. When you do go and see Birni, you may well be in for a pleasant surprise: 2005 saw the start of a cultural project created to preserve and restore the architectural heritage of Birni. The ambitious project not only intends to rehabilitate well over 100 buildings, but also to train young masons to master the decorating skills that were almost lost to future generations.

charms that seem to have been dangling from the ceiling for ages. Another striking juxtaposition of the old and the new is hidden in one of the courtyards, where both the sultan's horses and his luxury vehicle are kept. The present sultan is the 23rd in a long tradition, and he has three wives and 23 children, many of whom live inside the palace walls. It is a home and a functional building rather than a museum, which could explain why the original structure is not always maintained in its original style and some artefacts are left to whither beyond repair.

Visitors are allowed in for a guided tour with one of the court's members (❭ 51 04 05), though some quarters will be closed when the sultan is not around. There is no official charge for the tour, but visitors are expected to contribute towards the sultan's household. Unfortunately, I had the strong impression that most of the contribution went straight into the guide's pocket, leaving very little for the remaining 299 court members.

Centre Culturel Franco-Nigérien
The **Centre Culturel Franco-Nigérien** or CCFN (*open daily, except on Sun afternoons and some holidays;* ❭ *51 05 35;* e *ccfnzr@intnet.ne*) is a lively meeting point with a stage-cum-cinema, run by a team of enthusiasts for anything that breathes traditional and contemporary culture. If you wonder what Zinder has to offer in terms of theatre, music, poetry, cinema, puppet shows, visual art, fashion and dance, pick up a monthly programme from the centre, which is just off the big square opposite the post office. Many young musicians, especially those with an interest in rap music, have found encouragement as well as a stage to perform at the cultural centre. Moreover, the

CCFN assists in recording CD albums, and the careers of many popular contemporary Nigérien musicians have been launched from here.

The CCFN is largely responsible for the organisation of two festivals and a show: **Pilotobé**, *Rencontres théâtrales du Niger* (Theatrical Encounters in Niger, a **street festival**) and *son et lumière* (sound and light show) **Wasan Ji da Gani**. Pilotobé is an annual, international theatre festival, touring between the largest cities in Niger every year (see *Public holidays and festivals,* page 77). Both the street festival and the sound and light show, on the other hand, will first of all be performed in Zinder for a number of years. The streets of the old quarter of Birni have been chosen as a background for these performances – a good decision as Wasan Ji da Gani revolves around the history of Damagaram (the region of Zinder). At the time of research, the latter events were works in progress, but the organisation of these spectacles had reached an advanced stage. By the time you read this, the show should be on in Zinder. Enquire at the CCFN for dates.

One of the largest **bookshops** in Niger is also to be found at the CCFN, but like in Niamey, most books are in French.

Handicrafts The **Village Artisanal Palami** (✆ *51 04 59; open daily 08.00–17.30*) is just beyond Hotel Kouran Daga. The name means 'The big rocks or boulders', and it is easy to see why, as it is located just out of town along the main road to Niamey, in a beautiful area scattered with huge boulders. This centre for handicrafts was set up by the *Cooperation Nigéro-Luxembourgeoise* (see *Handicrafts and what to buy,* page 80). At the village various crafts are represented; if you are looking for leatherwork only, check out the **Cooperative Artisanale** at *Rond point Elf.* You can see the artisans at work and buy directly from them. Prices are low so be restrained when bargaining. The cooperative is open seven days a week and often until late in the evening. The leather they use has already been processed and dyed. If you are interested to see how this is done, go to the **tannery** near the *mare* or pond not far from Hotel Malam Kalkadamou. It is a truly dirty and unattractive pond, but in all honesty so is the work of the tanners. They will however appreciate your visit and show you the ins and outs of their job. Also near *Rond point Elf* is a **silversmith** where you can buy directly from his stock or order something from his sample book.

Animal market The *marché du bétail* is held every Thursday. It is a lively gathering of mostly Peul, Tuareg, Kanouri and Toubou. To get to the market, walk 2km past Restaurant El Ali towards the east, beyond the end of the tar.

Special events At the end of Ramadan, people gather at the Sultan's Palace for **Hawan Kafou**. It is a traditional festival which is all about butchers and bulls. After the final prayer of Ramadan, the sultan, his court and the *chef des bouchers* – the chief of all professional butchers and their sons – ride on horseback in procession through some quarters of the old town, leading both bulls and crowd to the palace's courtyard. The final verses of the Koran are recited, after which the solemn gathering turns into an invariably spectacular scene: a kind of *corrida* or bull fight, which is best described as a battle between a man and a bull. No weapons of any kind are involved; the men have to face the huge bulls unarmed in a display of force and courage. After the event, the *chef des bouchers* receives various gifts, traditionally comprising a black and white *boubou* (traditional garment), a horse and a handsome sum of money. Some festivities are exclusively for the sultan, the butchers and their sons, and some wealthy citizens of Zinder. However, most of the event is open to the public and well worth a detour if you happen to be near Zinder towards the end of Ramadan.

Maybe less spectacular, but truly impressive all the same, is the celebration of **Tabaski**, the annual feast of sacrifice (see *Public holidays and festivals,* page 75). Huge numbers of Muslims, all dressed up for the occasion, gather at the special site for prayer. People are surprisingly tolerant towards non-Muslim visitors (not that there are many) who just want to witness the gathering. The silence, the mumbling, the sound of the starched, brand-new robes as the men kneel and bow in prayer, it is an impressive experience. After the prayer; the sultan and his household ride back to the palace, where horses stir up a lot of dust as they race up and down just in front of the palace.

Mare de Kaniya Most *mares* in town are being used as public toilets and waste dumps and are therefore best avoided. However, this pond – around 3 km out of town in the direction of Niamey – is attractive to the eye and worth a visit. The *mare* holds water throughout the year and attracts many species of birds as well as noisy frogs. Some fishing of *tilapia* and catfish is done, but most human activity is done on the shores, where farmers use the water to irrigate their gardens. On some weekends you may find vendors selling drinks, but otherwise you have to bring your own picnic if you want to spend some time. A good option is to have a taxi drop you off at the *mare*, then walk back past rocky outcrops and the *village artisanal* to Hotel Kouran Daga, from where you should be able to find a taxi to take you back into town.

MIRIA

Sometimes spelt Myrriah, this small town is located 20km from Zinder and could be a good destination for a day excursion. As the soil in this region is particularly suitable for pottery, this is one of the main activities for both men and women. The clay pots are placed in huge pits to be baked both from the inside and the outside. Ask for Mr Ibrou, a local potter, to give a detailed explanation. All around Miria are shady gardens with baobabs, mango trees and vegetable gardens. Sunday is market day.

GOURE

In Gouré you will be able to get refreshments and a meal at the **Auberge la Recreation** or in one of the small restaurants and *buvettes* along or just off the thoroughfare. There is no accommodation, but if you report at the *préfecture*, they will find you a place to stay. The *préfecture* is visible on top of a hillock to the left side of the thoroughfare. At the Y-junction, take the left (also tarred) option and find your way up the hill to the right.

After passing through Gouré the road deteriorates, forcing drivers to slow down and swerve around pot-holes big enough to cause serious damage to any vehicle. After a while, the first dunes in different shades of orange and ochre come into sight, signs of the encroaching desert.

Hardly eye-catching and sometimes even invisible from the road are the *cuvettes* or *bas-fonds*. These are natural depressions where rainwater is retained, while groundwater is more easily accessible than outside these depressions. Therefore it is easy to see why people have long since developed these *cuvettes* into lush havens, pockets of green in an otherwise rather arid landscape. Bigger trees, like date palms, provide shade for smaller crops and vegetables, as well as for goats and donkeys. The *cuvettes* are also a hideout for birds, and the longer you stand still to observe what is there, the more species you will discover. After the rains when groundwater levels are at their highest, natron surfaces, leaving a greyish crust once the water has evaporated. When you are driving a private vehicle, take a break to visit one of the many *cuvettes* between Gouré and Diffa.

KELLE

In the pretty, mountainous region of Koutous (see box below), 42km to the north of Gouré, is the village of Kellé. A few kilometres outside the village is an ostrich farm, where the ostrich *Struthio camelus* is bred in captivity. The enclosures provide ample space for these animals, that hopefully one day can be reintroduced to the wild. At present, however, they would end up being chased and killed for their meat in no time. Other captive-breeding programmes are being considered.

TASKER

The *piste* to Tasker follows the cliffs of the Koutous Hills. This marks the boundary of the region inhabited by the Hausa, and villages with *banco* houses become increasingly sparse. The landscape gradually shifts from cultivated millet fields with acacia and gao trees, to spacious pastoral zones with shrubs and grasses. Further north is the dominion of the (semi-)nomadic Tuareg, Toubou and Arabs, who live in small temporary *campements* or near the village of Tasker (200km from the main road). This is an administrative military post, and travellers are expected to report and work through the formalities. The track to the northeast leads to the Termit Massif, an isolated mountain range that sees few visitors.

TERMIT MASSIF

The landscape changes dramatically on approaching the Termit Mountains or Massif. The southern part of the massif consists of a long range of heavily eroded, black sandstone formations, intersected by crevasses, valley depressions, crumbling walls and cone-shaped peaks, while the northern part – the Gossololom region – consists of rocky islands that emerge from the sand. The highest point is 710m.

A MONKEY'S CRY IN THE KOUTOUS HILLS

Yohan Quilgars

This morning at dawn, the dew felt very refreshing. What a happy contrast to see the moist green grass in the sand! The rest of the year – nine months out of 12 – it turns into yellow straw or simply ceases to exist, completely grazed down to the roots by ruminants. I sit down and take my time to enjoy the cool morning and the landscape that surrounds us. In the distance, at the foot of the rocky hills, a pastoral nomad passes by with three sheep. Without doubt he is on his way to the weekly market in Kangama. A little further away, an old man with a hesitant tread leaves for his field with his grandsons, carrying hoes and spades over their shoulders.

After breaking camp, we head towards the southern part of the Koutous mountain range. We hope to reach the village of Doukoutou before night falls. Kiari and Souleymane nimbly herd the donkeys that carry our gear. After about an hour, we scramble our way up the mountain and take a rest near a hidden waterpool along the hillside. Though most bigger villages in the region have wells, they are often out of use. At this time of the year, it is a joy to be able to make use of such rain-fed reservoirs. We continue our journey through a landscape with the contrasting colours of bare rock, green pastures and millet fields. Along the way, we take our time to meet and greet farmers, who explain their work in the fields in the rainy season.

A narrow passage between the rocks leads us to a platform that ends in a sudden, sheer drop: a magnificent panorama over the lush plains to the south of Koutous unfolds. We need to find a passage for the donkeys, but the rough terrain and steep crevasses do not offer an easy way out. Even Kiari has never passed through here before. The threat

The desert sand tries hard to invade the massif, comprising black rocks and ochre sand. Along the massif are Toubou settlements, and while the inhabitants may be shy at first at the sight of travellers, their hospitality and curiosity soon prevail. Precious are the moments to share time, tea or even a meal with these families. Conversation is limited to signs and gestures, unless you travel with a Toubou guide who can act as an interpreter.

The Gossololom region is extremely rich in archaeological finds, dating back from the Palaeolithic to post-Neolithic periods. A whole range of quartzite acheulean stone tools, microliths, bifaced tools and chopping tools, axe heads made of volcanic rock and potsherds have been found. Some of the sites had to be excavated layer by layer, but often the first researchers just stumbled upon large fields of archaeological remnants that had been left undisturbed for thousands of years. Some metallurgic sites at Do Dimmi contained different types of iron-smelting ovens, and a remarkable fact is that the Toubou still master the same techniques to acquire metal objects from iron ore. Some sites with relatively recent rock engravings show cattle and giraffe, while several post-Neolithic tombs are found throughout the Termit Massif.

Only decades ago, in the 1970s, the Termit region was a sanctuary for many wildlife species. Animals that are now extinct or near-extinct found shelter in the many corners of the mountains, but they have been hunted down rigorously despite their endangered status and hunting restrictions. Once a haven for wildlife, the sad balance seems irreversible (see SOS *Faune du Niger: Addax survey*, page 226).

As the Termit region meets the criteria to be classified as a UNESCO World Heritage Site, plans are under way to give the region a protected status at last.

The Termit Mountains are an outstanding, if not almost forgotten travel destination. Very few travellers visit this isolated pocket of beauty, with good opportunities for a multiple-day camel trek. It also provides a rare opportunity to

of an oncoming thunderstorm from the east forces us to decide to make camp at the platform, and this will allow us time to explore and search for the best option that will lead us down to the plain, a few hundred metres below.

While dark clouds are approaching, red monkeys start to make a hissing, almost mocking noise, as if they are making fun of us. Their strident cries echo all around us. I ask Kiari if he can explain what these cries mean, and his answer comes in the form of a legend:

> One day, a mountain monkey was on his way when he passed a heron, pitched on a rock. 'Good morning, Mr heron!' said the monkey with courtesy. The heron, in return, responded by saying 'Pitchi-Potcho!' which the monkey automatically took for an insult. Annoyed, the monkey trapped the heron, grabbed it by one of its legs, and dragged it along behind him. Soon thereafter they came across a hare, who asked the two to reveal the reason for this grotesque situation. The monkey explained his side to the story and told about the insulting manners of the heron. The heron explained to the hare that 'Pitchi-Potcho' was in fact a most respectful salute in the language of the herons. The hare then suggested that the two had better put an end to the misunderstanding, and to reconcile.

The story shows that, while it may be difficult to understand a language one does not know, it is the lack of comprehension between people that leads to the worst of errors.

It seems I had wrongly accused the monkeys of mockery...

'What do you think of the Addax gazelle?' I asked a young Toubou man.

'That's good meat!' he replied.

'But do you not think they are beautiful?'

'Yes, it's beautiful meat.'

'I see, but what I meant is: are you not concerned that they will vanish from the area?'

'Well, yes, that would be a pity. But if that happens, there will still be Dorcas gazelles and that is good meat too.'

In September 2004, a survey of the Termit Massif and the more eastern Erg de Tin-n-Toumma was conducted. The survey was initiated by the Nigérien association SOS Faune du Niger (see *Giving something back*, page 88), and the primary objective of the mission was to get a realistic estimate of the Addax population. Besides that, other species – mostly the Sahelo-Saharan antelope species – could also be monitored. The survey was conducted with the use of 4x4 vehicles and an aircraft, and an area of 9,300km was systematically transected.

The survey showed that the last viable, wild population of Addax in Niger consists of no more than around 100 individuals. The Dama gazelle is on the brink of extinction, and while the Dorcas gazelle is doing relatively well, it is still listed as 'extremely vulnerable'. The scimitar-horned oryx is believed to be extinct. Other animal species that show a dramatic decline in numbers are the Barbary sheep (*mouflon* in French), the cheetah and the ostrich, while the Nubian and Sudan bustards are also struggling. The overall result is unanimous: wildlife protection is urgently needed to try and beat the odds. Captive breeding could well be a last resort to save some species from extinction.

Incredibly, after the survey was conducted and the results were published, a hunting party from Libya caused havoc among the remaining herds of gazelle, as these were chased and shot with the use of vehicles and automatic weapons. Without any doubt, the outlook for some species has become even grimmer after this hunting frenzy.

In the beginning of 2005, conservation plans to boost and improve management of the Réserve Naturelle Nationale de l'Aïr et du Ténéré or RNNAT were launched (see box, pages 190–1), and these also include a programme concerning the Termit Massif. The idea is to create a national reserve that links up with the RNNAT, so that the whole area will be protected under the same laws and regulations. The task to actually monitor and patrol the zone is immense, while it is essential that the local population is involved in a way that is beneficial to them, so the people become convinced that wild animals are more than just 'beautiful meat'.

catch a glimpse of the wildlife. The few travel agents that operate in the southeast of the country are able and more than willing to discuss itineraries that combine visits to local communities and the Termit Massif. See *Zinder*, page 217, and other sections in this chapter.

10

Diffa

If you think that Zinder is a far-off travel destination, the real challenge starts when you continue east, towards Diffa and Lake Chad. A glance at a road map shows that N'Guigmi – near Lake Chad – is where the road ends, but maps can be deceptive: the real road literally fades eastwards from Gouré, changing from a rather pot-holed to a heavily pot-holed road, and eventually to a road where you wish there hadn't been any tarmac in the first place. Then at last, between Diffa and N'Guigmi, the sealed road threatens to end, allowing plenty of opportunity for cars and trucks to get stuck and block the way for trailing vehicles. So yes, it's a challenge, but also the promise of a journey into a very little-explored region.

For independent travellers using motorised public transport only, options are virtually restricted to the main road. If that sounds unadventurous, bear in mind that only few travellers get here, and just stepping off the road means entering a rural, unspoilt world filled with the authentic and the traditional. Curiosity becomes a mutual thing, hospitality is an innate characteristic of the population, but a soft bed and a shower are rare commodities. It is the land of the nomadic Peul, but also of the Toubou and the Kanouri, ethnic groups that are very little known. The Toubou are a people of the desert and their women are renowned for their tremendous capacity to cope with harsh living circumstances.

When I spoke with a young Toubou in N'Guigmi about their origins and the remoteness of their present homeland, he cut me short: 'Our grandfathers came from Tibesti in Chad, but now we are at the other side of an invisible boundary so we call ourselves Nigériens and that is fine. We are here now, at a day's or more travelling from any big town, at the end of the tarmac. But it suits us, it is not the end of the road to us. There is a whole world out there and travelling just needs a different approach. I could be back in Tibesti in a week from now.'

So all is relative, and travelling to the end of the road does not mean the journey has to stop there. But the infrastructure – whatever that means in this context – gets increasingly limited. Some independent onward-travel options do exist, but those are really not for the faint-hearted. The easiest way to explore the region off the main road would be to make use of one of the few travel agencies that are based here (see below and also see *Zinder,* page 217). Do not expect the same expertise, as you would find in Niamey or Agadez, though. Experience is a quality that needs time to develop, and here the tourist industry is but a young child, eager to grow up and learn. That doesn't necessarily have to be a disadvantage. The few travel agencies I managed to track down in the area are invariably run by people with interesting backgrounds, hence a very useful expertise after all. Most of them are native to Niger or are long-time residents, many of them have been working in the field for NGOs for many years, and all of them are very willing to give any excursion or expedition their best shot. So by all means, if you do enjoy deviating from the beaten track, there is a world out there to explore.

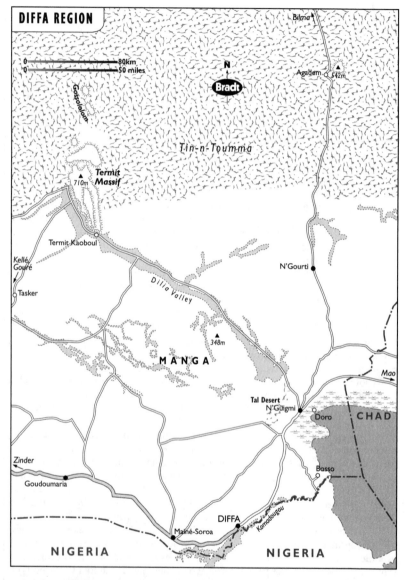

0 ————— 80km
0 ————— 50 miles

N

Bradt

Bilma

Agadem ○ ▲ *542m*

Tin-n-Toumma

Gossololom

▲ **Termit**
710m **Massif**

Termit Kaoboul

Kellé
Gouré ↙

○ Tasker

Dilla Valley

N'Gourti ●

▲
348m

M A N G A

Mao

Tal Desert
N'Guigmi ○ ● Doro   C H A D

Zinder

Goudoumaria ●

Bosso ○

DIFFA ●   *Komodougou*

Mainé-Soroa ●

N I G E R I A   N I G E R I A

MAINE-SOROA

Finding a meal and a drink along the main road is possible, but there are no hotels in Mainé-Soroa. However, when you enquire at the local NGO Initiatives et Actions (signposted on the left-hand side of the thoroughfare, when coming from Zinder), they will put you up somewhere. The NGO also happens to be the base of **Goondal Tours** (*PO Box 46, Mainé-Soroa;* ☏ *540 229/205 or call 229 and ask to be put through to ext 063*), run by Maïtouraré Boukary, one of the driving forces behind the NGO. His background ensures a very humane approach to tourism, summed up in the name of the agency: 'goondal' means 'being together' or 'living together' in the language of the Peul. The programme offered by Goondal Tours focuses on encounters between two different worlds (the industrialised world versus the traditional world of pastoralists), with plenty of opportunities to share ideas to enhance mutual understanding and appreciation. The role of a guide-cum-translator (some English is spoken) is crucial. Itineraries vary from an overnight stay with a Peul family, to long expeditions to the Koutous Plateau, the Termit Massif, and the Dilia Valley.

DIFFA

At Goudoumaria (halfway between Gouré and Maïné-Soroa), you have entered the region of Diffa, a region that extends from the Nigerian border and the river Komadougou in the south, to the southern edge of the Grand Erg de Bilma in the north. Other than a few rocky peaks near the oasis of Agadem (542m), the landscape undulates between 300m and 400m in altitude. Most of the region consists of sand plains and shifting sand dunes, while a combination of severe droughts, bush fires and logging cause severe desertification in other areas. The environment provides harsh living conditions, and it hides some little-visited but beautiful landscapes, like the riverine areas, Lake Chad, the pristine white dunes of the Erg du Tal, the Dilia Valley – stretching from N'Guigmi to the Termit Massif – and the hidden gardens, called *cuvettes*.

Most of the population are Kanouri or Béri-béri, who are settled along the river Komadougou and in the vicinity of Lake Chad, the most densely populated areas. The nomadic Peul are dispersed over the whole region, while the Toubou and Arab minorities live in the area to the north of N'Guigmi. Some other minority groups include the Boudouma.

The sleepy town of Diffa is located at 1,360km from Niamey and has approximately 25,000 inhabitants (2001).

GETTING THERE AND AWAY Maïssagé has buses going to **Zinder** every Saturday. Reporting time is at 05.00 and the fare is CFA6,200. SNTV has two weekly buses to Zinder on Wednesdays and Sundays. Since these buses start from N'Guigmi, the reporting time is at 09.00, while the fare is CFA6,150. The SNTV buses to **N'Guigmi** pass through Diffa on Mondays and Fridays. Reporting time is at 16.00 and the fare is CFA1,750. Though the heavily pot-holed stretch to N'Guigmi is 120km only, the journey could take well over three hours and more if the bus – or any vehicle the bus is trailing – gets stuck in the soft sand where the tar is missing completely. Delays may take several hours.

Local transport leaving from the *gare routière* is paid for preferably in niara, but CFA francs are also accepted. Vehicles for **Maïné-Soroa** and **Zinder** leave daily when full and cost CFA1,000 and CFA5,000 respectively. Whilst the road to **N'Guigmi** does require 4x4 vehicles really, most of the traffic is ordinary, battered minibuses (CFA2,000). Note that the section between Diffa and N'Guigmi is closed to all traffic from dusk till dawn. Vehicles leaving for **Bosso** (CFA1,500 or 400 naira) sometimes continue into Nigeria (Maidougouri, CFA2,500 or 600 naira). From there, you can travel onwards to Cameroon and Chad.

GETTING AROUND Diffa has a couple of taxis, but do not waste your time by the roadside waiting for one; you may be stuck there for a long while. The chances of finding a *kabou-kabou* are much better, though in all fairness, Diffa is a small town and everything is well within walking distance.

LOCAL TOUR OPERATORS A very accommodating, local woman has set up the **Agence Kanem Bornou Voyage** or **AKBV** for short (*PO Box 37, Diffa;* \ *54 01 12; f 54 02 82*). It is a small enterprise with a mission: to promote and develop eco-

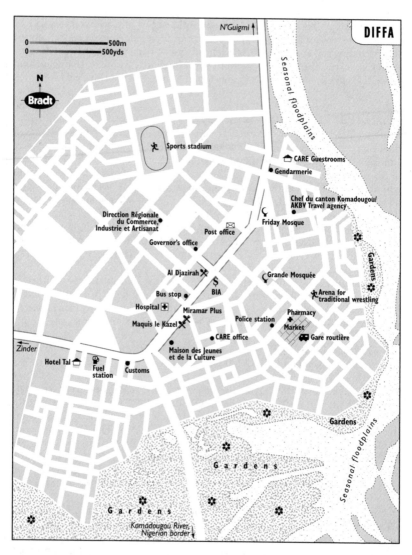

N'Guigmi

0 ————— 500m
0 ————— 500yds

N

Bradt

Seasonal floodplains

☆ Sports stadium

⌂ CARE Guestrooms

● Gendarmerie

Chef du canton Komadougou/
AKBV Travel agency

Direction Régionale
du Commerce,
Industrie et Artisanat ●

Post office ✉

Ç Friday Mosque

● Governor's office

Gardens

Al Djazirah ✗

$ BIA

Ç Grande Mosquée

Bus stop ●

Hospital ✚

Miramar Plus

Maquis le Kazel ✗

Police station ●

Pharmacy ✚

Market

☆ Arena for
traditional wrestling

● CARE office

🚌 Gare routière

Gardens

Maison des Jeunes
et de la Culture

Zinder

Hotel Tal ⌂

⛽ Fuel
station

Customs

Gardens

Gardens

Seasonal floodplains

G a r d e n s

Gardens

Komadougou River,
Nigerian border ↓

tourism in the region. While international tourist boards discuss the importance of 'poverty alleviation through community-based tourism', this lady embodies the true sense of that phrase. She intends to work closely with some small communities of various ethnic groups, carefully designing programmes that enrich both the local population and the visitors. She is fully licensed and has the support of the Direction Regional du Commerce, Industrie et Artisanat, the governmental body that monitors tourist activities. The agency does not yet have an office. You can contact Mme Falmata Kazelma (or her husband Moussa Maïkano) directly or enquire at the aforementioned Direction (see map *Diffa* above). If that fails, just ask around at the stalls and shops along the main road.

WHERE TO STAY The only official hotel in Diffa is **Hotel Tal**, formerly known as Hotel Kanady (℣/f *54 03 32*). The old rooms have been replaced by brand-new ones in an annexe which was constructed in 2000. However, this is one fine example of a rather nice building falling apart before it was actually finished. It didn't help when some of the furniture was stolen, and the overall result is sadly a pitiful shell. Rates start at CFA7,500 up to CFA19,000, which is way over the top.

Fortunately the **Case de passage du CARE** (no telephone) is available for tourists, though employees and guests from this NGO get priority. You'll have to ask at the CARE office for permission to stay in one of the rooms before heading out to the guesthouse. Two bathrooms with cold water only are shared between three clean rooms that sleep up to four people each. These are very good value at CFA10,000 per room. No restaurant available.

WHERE TO EAT AND DRINK Hotel Tal has a restaurant on the former premises. Most dishes are a variety of 'starch and sauce', but you could order in advance and have half a guinea fowl for CFA1,800 or rabbit for CFA4,000.

Along the thoroughfare is **Restaurant Maquis le Kazel**, a pleasant and shady garden where you can have 'scrimble' omelette and 'stock au pair', which turned out to be a juicy pepper steak. Fizzy drinks – including bitter lemon – are imported from Nigeria.

PRACTICALITIES The **BIA** bank (*open Mon–Fri 08.00–11.30 and 15.00–17.00*) changes cash euro to CFA only. For naira, find the moneychangers at the *gare routière*. They change euro and CFA without much ado at very reasonable rates. A **Western Union** branch is at the **post office**.

WHAT TO SEE
River Komadougou Yobé and gardens The River Komadougou Yobé (or Komadougou) marks the boundary between Niger and Nigeria, meandering along the border for 150km before flowing into Lake Chad. It is lined with gallery forest, rich in vegetation and wildlife, a lush and green ribbon in an otherwise arid landscape. The river passes Diffa at a distance of around 6km, flooding the plains between Diffa and the border after the rains. These plains are Diffa's treasury, as the river supplies the water to irrigate a whole patchwork of gardens and fields. Levels are at their highest between July and October, while the river stands dry in February and March. Only a few remaining *mares* or ponds supply the necessary water for crops, livestock and a rich variety of birds.

Crops include wheat, rice, onions and tiny hot peppers, but the winner is the sweet red pepper or paprika. A walk across the market, or better still, a walk along the road leading to the border reveals the importance of this 'red gold'. The peppers are spread out to dry, or mountains of the dried, crinkly fruit await transport. In dry conditions (most of the year in Niger), peppers can be preserved for months, and so you may find the red peppers from the region of Diffa at markets elsewhere in the country.

Bosso At 85km from Diffa, this Béri-béri village is located between the Nigerian border, the river Komadougou and Lake Chad. *Barques* or pirogues shuttle passengers between Bosso and the small islands like Guidira, a fishermen's port. Fishing is undertaken in the same way as from Doro (see page 237). Besides fishermen, many artisans live in this village, and they produce fine leatherwork and objects made from palm leaves. Vehicles leave from Diffa in this direction especially to meet the market, which is on Sundays. Onward travel to Nigeria is possible from here.

Though N'Guigmi seems to be the end of the road, the town is in fact an important commercial centre that serves as a link between the Manga region (see map *Diffa region,* page 228), Chad and Nigeria, and even Libya. Regional trade involves smaller ruminants and food provisions, but the trans-Saharan trade is mostly about camels. The weekly camel market in N'Guigmi is frequented by Toubou and Arabs, who buy and sell animals that are destined to traverse the Sahara to be sold again in Libya, and it is one of the liveliest markets in the area (see box *Camel market in N'Guigmi,* page 236).

Trans-Saharan trade suffered greatly from insecurity during the 1990s as a result of the armed Toubou rebellion that affected the region stretching from N'Guigmi and along and across the border with Chad. To a certain degree, the reasons for the Toubou to rebel against the government are similar to those that triggered the Tuareg rebellion in the northwest of the country: living in the periphery of the Nigérien territory, the Toubou felt they were ignored by the central administration, that imposed taxes on the population but did little to improve their living standard. The non-indigenous governmental representatives were accused of being corrupt and insensitive to the needs of the local population, even after the serious droughts of the 1980s.

In addition to this, internal conflicts between ethnic groups and between the different Toubou clans (see *Ethnic groups,* page 29) seriously complicated social co-habitation in the region. Camel raids, traditionally a not uncommon practice among the Toubou, also seriously affected the Peul pastoralists. It became virtually impossible for the Peul to raise camels, as Dazza Toubou frequently raided the herds – claiming that the Peul were not worthy of keeping camels – leaving the Peul little choice but to focus on breeding ruminants and donkeys instead. Another complicating factor was the arrival of the Mohamid Arabs in the 1980s, non-indigenous Muslim pastoralists from Chad who claimed pastures and wells, in disregard of local customs. As they tried to settle disputes, the different groups were caught between the traditional or religious authorities on one side, and the governmental court of justice and the military on the other.

As conflicts escalated, violent clashes were commonplace during the years of rebellion. Eventually peace accords were signed by all parties, officially marking the end of the armed conflicts. The most important conditions to the accords were that the government should invest more in the region to improve the quality of life in general, while decentralisation was considered of great importance to create the right precedents for the internal peace process. After the municipal elections of 2004, all parties involved could start working towards better relationships and agreements between ethnies and clans within their respective local areas.

Little of the underlying problems are felt during a walk in N'Guigmi. As the situation has calmed down over the years, life has returned to what it used to be, and is once again centred around local and regional trade. At the end of the tar, N'Guigmi is a surprisingly lively and colourful town.

GETTING THERE AND AWAY For **Diffa** and **Zinder**, you have the choice between twice-weekly buses or *taxi-brousses.* SNTV has sturdy but battered buses running to Diffa (CFA2,000) and Zinder (CFA8,000) on Wednesdays and Sundays. The reporting time is at 05.00 and their bus depot is along the main dirt road. Buy your ticket one day in advance. Minibuses and 4x4 vehicles leave daily from the *gare routière,* which is not far from the barrier. It is sometimes possible to book a seat in advance, otherwise make sure you get there early in the morning. By 08.00, most vehicles will have left. You could opt to hitch a ride at the barrier with a service

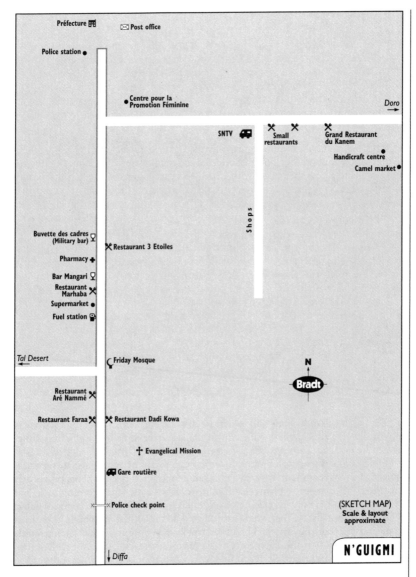

Préfecture
⊠ Post office
Police station ●

● Centre pour la
  Promotion Féminine
                                                        Doro →

SNTV 🚐   ✗ ✗   ✗
             Small   Grand Restaurant
             restaurants du Kanem
                                    Handicraft centre ●
                                    Camel market ●

Shops

Buvette des cadres ♀
(Military bar)   ✗ Restaurant 3 Etoiles

Pharmacy ✚

Bar Mangari ♀
Restaurant ✗
Marhaba
Supermarket ●
Fuel station ⛽

← Tal Desert

                ⌇ Friday Mosque   N

                                        Bradt

Restaurant ✗
Aré Nammé

Restaurant Faraa ✗   ✗ Restaurant Dadi Kowa

                ✝ Evangelical Mission

                🚌 Gare routière

                ⤬ Police check point   (SKETCH MAP)
                                          Scale & layout
                                          approximate

                                          N'GUIGMI

↓ Diffa

vehicle (if you are lucky) or with a truck (if you are not so lucky). The latter option will be rough, very rough, unless you get off the truck each time a stretch of tar is missing. Note that the section between N'Guigmi and Diffa is closed to all traffic from dusk till dawn.

Onward travelling to **N'Gourti** and **Agadem** by public transport is possible, though do not take this option lightly. If you are lucky, you'd get some space at the back of a pick-up truck, but you are more likely to end up between dozens of local people, on top of a big truck laden with goods. There is no fixed schedule, but ask around at the barrier, at the police station or at any truck that seems to be heading north. The duration of the trip very much depends on the vehicle and the number of breakdowns but to give a rough estimate: count on two days for N'Gourti

The road connecting Diffa and N'Guigmi, as well as the border region between Niger and Chad (north of Lake Chad), has a dubious reputation where safety is concerned. Vehicles are occasionally halted and passengers are forced to hand over their money. These robberies are usually about money only, and victims get away unharmed and with their other belongings untouched, after an otherwise shocking experience. It does not stop drivers from travelling into 'risky areas', and local people just put up with the inconvenience, as they tend to call it.

When I travelled to N'Guigmi and beyond, I took a few simple precautions. While I would normally carry money and documents on my body, I put everything in my luggage, which was then secured on the roof. I happily boarded the vehicle, prepared to hand over the cash I carried, just about enough to please potential robbers. Nothing happened that day, nor during the time I spent in the area. During various trips I took from N'Guigmi, I left most valuables behind in the private house where I was lodging. I would have done the same had I been staying at the Catholic mission.

Meanwhile, I have had reports from other travellers who were invited to stay at the private house of the guide I had previously also travelled with, and whom I considered a reliable person. When these travellers returned with their guide from an excursion to the Grand Erg du Tal, a handsome sum of their money they had left behind was missing. Not all of it, though, which is exactly why they didn't discover the theft until they had reached their next destination.

There is no general rule in matters concerning safety, as individuals may not always appear to be who they really are and circumstances may change. It is sensible to enquire about the current situation, then make your choice about eventual precautions. The bottom line is not to exaggerate the risks, nor to underestimate them. Precautions very much depend on the circumstances, and a little luck is always welcome.

(135km along a sandy *piste*), and two more days for Agadem. Travelling by truck is physically very challenging, while you would also have to be fully self-supporting. For more detailed warnings, see *Chapter 2, Getting around,* page 69.

Unless you intend to continue northbound to Bilma, you have to seriously consider your return trip. I got two different, contradictory comments on **return options**. One version explains that heading north is easier than coming back, and here is why: some nomads take herds of camels from N'Guigmi to Bilma or Libya where the animals are then sold. Instead of walking all the way back, the camel traders often return by truck. Therefore, trucks travelling from the north towards N'Guigmi are often full (very, very full!) once they reach Agadem or N'Gourti, and you may find yourself stuck in a very desolate place. The second version explains just the opposite: there would be more vehicles coming from Libya, than vehicles travelling north, in which case you should have no problem in finding a ride back to N'Guigmi. That makes you wonder what happens to all the trucks from Libya, but I could not get a plausible answer. The only positive news, possibly overruling the above, is that oil companies are trying their luck in the region of N'Gourti, and more vehicles may be plying the section between N'Guigmi and N'Gourti than in past years.

If you haven't been put off yet, if you even consider travelling onwards to **Bilma**, then the lack of comfort will reach yet another degree. Not just because the distance nearly doubles, but the terrain gets increasingly demanding. The only way to Bilma is by crossing the Grand Erg, the vast area of thick sand and shifting sand dunes. Think twice, and do share your experience with us.

When the destination of your choice is **Chad**, bear in mind that you will need a visa, plenty of water and stamina. While more or less the same warnings apply, it can be done, as has been proved by the adventurous couple Thomas and Bethany Eberle. This is their account:

> From N'Guigmi to Mao (Chad) it's a very challenging, two-day trip through pure sand and the dry bed of Lake Chad. The only transport options (almost daily) are cheap, old and badly serviced Toyota pick-up trucks which are incredibly crowded: luggage and about 25 people piled on top, legs and water canisters dangling outside. The sand, heat, squeeze and long prayer, customs, repair and whatever stops plus the frequent acacia bushes at close range make this ride very uncomfortable. Try to pay extra to ride in the cabin or at least secure a space in the middle of the vehicle and bring and defend your own big water canister. The nights will be spent in the open, so come prepared. From Mao to N'Djamena there is a real road with the last bit surfaced and Jeeps that do the seven-hour trip.

PRACTICALITIES The authorities urge visitors, especially those who want to explore the region, to report at the police stations. The police will then supply a *Feuille de Route* or route approval, which includes personal details, mode of travel (independent or with an agency), and the itinerary. This is a security regulation, and though it is not compulsory, you are strongly advised to shake hands with the police and let them know your plans. The police station is at the end of the tarred road.

WHERE TO STAY The only accommodation is at the **Mission Evangélique** in Quartier Sabon Karé. Ask for Barkaï Batouré. Rooms are clean and comfortable, but they have one single bed each which is meant for one person only. Unless you can make it credible that you are a (mixed) married couple, there is little point in asking whether you can share one room. Nine rooms have shared facilities and cost CFA3,000, while three self-contained rooms with fridge cost a mere CFA5,000. The quiet premises are kept clean, while the filtered water is safe to drink.

WHERE TO EAT AND DRINK There are quite a number of small, basic restaurants with a limited choice of meals. The better ones seemed to be **Restaurant Aré Nammé** (meaning 'come and sit you down', for grilled meats and fish), **Restaurant Maraba**, both along the tarred road, and **Grand Restaurant du Kanem** along the wide dirt road.

For an alcoholic drink and some traditional live music on weekends, try **Bar Mangari**. The **Buvette des Cadres** doubles as a video club during the daytime. In the evenings, you can have *brochettes* and grilled meat, and cold drinks to wash them down. Live music is sometimes staged here. If you fancy a fruit juice, one shop in the 'shopping street' has an ample choice of bottled and pre-packaged juices.

WHAT TO SEE AND DO
Market and shops There is a surprising amount of commercial activity in N'Guigmi. One street has tiny shops lined up one after the other (see N'Guigmi map, page 233), while especially on market day (Sunday) a lot of trading takes place in three rows of stalls and workshops. This provides a good opportunity to see various artisans at work, as they make numerous products: camel saddles, metal utensils and leatherwork to name but a few. Along the wide street leading to the market, traders from Libya display their colourful carpets and blankets. If you are wondering about the piles of greyish lumps, this is natron, imported from Chad and used as animal salt licks and raw material for the production of soap. The biggest attraction on Sundays is the camel market (see box on page 236).

10

At the edge of N'Guigmi, wooden poles stick out of the ground on a wide open space. This is the location for the weekly camel market. Every Sunday, Toubou, Tuareg and Arabs come trickling in, herding groups of camels and other livestock. When the camels are tied to the poles, the pastoralists – mostly men, but sometimes whole families – make themselves comfortable along the edges of the town, brewing tea while catching up with news from other traders. This market gathering knows no hurry; serious bargaining doesn't start until halfway through the afternoon. Hundreds of camels quietly await their fate as men dressed in all possible colours discuss the health and strength of their animals. As the sun sets, the whole scene turns to glowing shades of pastel; a magnificent sight.

Market activities pick up again on Monday morning, and some camels produce gruesome sounds as they are being branded by their new owners. Then one by one the herds are led away to start their long journey to Nigeria, sometimes all the way to Libya. By 11.00, only some stray goats are left to search for anything edible. Otherwise the area is silent again.

Centre pour la Promotion Féminine This women's centre – not far from the Préfecture and the post office – was founded in September 2004 and aims to educate women through discussions, counselling and courses. The battle against illiteracy is one issue, and another goal is to teach women practical skills, like knitting, and how to use a sewing machine. All items that are produced are for private use or for sale. You can order directly from the women, but even if you do not need anything, just pop in for a chat. This is an inspiring environment, very informal and welcoming.

LAKE CHAD

The IGN map represents Lake Chad by a permanent lake somewhere in Chad, surrounded by an immense seasonal floodplain that may or may not receive water, while the ITMB map shows Lake Chad as an impressive pan dotted with countless seasonal lakes, stretching out over hundreds of kilometres and touching the dot representing N'Guigmi. Indeed for many years the water reached as far as N'Guigmi, and what is now the site for the camel market used to be the lake's edge. A series of severe droughts in the 1970s caused the water to recede. At one point, you would have had to travel for over 85km and into Chad to meet the water's edge.

Lake Chad consists of two major basins that are fed by different rivers – the Chari, Logone and El Beid rivers (Cameroon) that provide almost 90% of the water – and rainwater. The Komadougou River (along the Niger–Nigeria border) provides very little water due to the construction of dams upstream. Since the depressing droughts that caused the water to retreat from Niger, the water level has risen significantly again. In January, when the water level is at its highest, it now reaches as far as the village of Doro (see opposite).

All along the lake's edge and from small islands there is a lot of fishing activity. Fishing used to be the livelihood of ethnic groups like the Boudouma, but after losing their entire livestock as a result of the serious droughts, even some Peul families have taken to fishing. Some fishermen use nets and rods from wobbly dugout canoes, while another peculiar method is also practised: some fishermen take to the water using an enormous calabash as a floating device. They lean all over the calabash as if it were a small surf board, trying to keep their balance while using their hands to paddle across the water. They catch fish bare-handed. Most of the catch is dried and smoked before being exported to Nigeria.

The abundance of fish (carp, catfish or *silures*, and *capitaines*) attracts a lot of birds. Herons, kingfishers, plovers and other waders are everywhere, while the vegetation is also teeming with many species of birds.

DORO

After the droughts, fishermen had no choice but to move along with the receding, then rising water. They created temporary settlements or looked for places where water was never too far off. One of the newly built, semi-permanent villages is Doro. This Béri-béri name means '*port de pêche*' or 'fishermen's port', which pretty much sums up the reason for the existence of this village. In the dry season when the lake retreats, however, the real port is 5–10km from the village. Women – with a very dark skin and deep facial scarring – are responsible for the construction of the huts, made from wooden sticks and endless bundles of reed.

The village is 45km from N'Guigmi. Though there is no regular transport to Doro, some vehicles do ply this rough route. Ask around in N'Guigmi, and if you can't catch a ride, you will have to rent a 4x4 vehicle. On the way to Doro you will pass small Boudouma settlements and a peculiar cattle breed that is typical to this region: the *kouri*. Their horns are both bulky and large, but contrary to popular belief, they do not help the animals to stay afloat as they swim across flooded areas of the lake.

N'GOURTI

Located 135km to the north of N'Guigmi, in the east of the Manga region, is the administrative post of N'Gourti. Like N'Guigmi, the population is an ethnic mix of Toubou, Arabs and some Peul pastoralists, while a minority of Hausa and Djerma military, civil servants and traders add to the colourful amalgam of inhabitants in this remote desert town. In 1998, the community of N'Gourti and environs had an estimated 33,000 inhabitants.

Various legends explain the creation of N'Gourti, and one of these claims is that the first inhabitants were the Manga, a sub-group of the Kanouri. It is said that at the bottom of the *cuvette* or depression, a hippo lived in a pond. The Kanouri word for 'hippopotamus', is '*n'gurtu*'.

AGADEM

The oasis of Agadem has some beautiful palm gardens and a ruined colonial fort. The dry salt pans are no longer exploited.

> ### TAL DESERT
>
> Two areas of pristine white sand dunes are within easy reach of N'Guigmi. The smaller area, the Petit Erg du Tal is only a couple of kilometres away from the town, while the eastern most edge of the Grand Erg du Tal is 18km from N'Guigmi. By 4x4, it takes less than an hour before entering the enchanting sand dunes. By camel, you need a day to get there. The transition from ochre sand and thorny bushes to the white sand is abrupt. The Grand Erg du Tal is around 5–8km in width, while it stretches out for 120km. The landscape is beautiful under any circumstances, but it becomes truly mesmerising at full moon, as the fine sand reflects and glistens like snow. Walk into the dunes until you see nothing but sand, and do stay overnight!

DILIA VALLEY

When the climate was much more humid, a wide river carried water from the Termit Massif over a distance of 200km to Lake Chad. Now it is a linear fossil riverbed, kilometres wide and aligned by dunes. In this semi-desert zone with an annual rainfall of less than 200mm, the vegetation is limited to mainly grasses, shrubs and some acacia species. As there are only a few water points along this riverbed, the human population is sparse. Nomadic Toubou may pass with their herds of camels or temporarily camp near a well, military vehicles occasionally patrol in the area, but otherwise the valley is reserved for the wildlife. Dorcas gazelle are regularly seen, and while the number of bustards have dwindled over the last decades, this is still a good zone to spot Arabian and Nubian bustards, pallid harriers and golden nightjars. If you are really lucky you may even spot the Pharaoh eagle owl.

The Dilia Valley provides a good approach to the isolated Termit Massif, which is described in *Chapter 9, Zinder,* pages 224–6.

Baobab tree, *Adonsonia digitata*

Appendix I

LANGUAGE

FRENCH

You should, you must… (Though this expression could be taken as an order, it is more likely to be meant as an encouragement)	*Il faut…*
You must be patient, you'll have to wait	*Il faut patienter*
Take another helping, take some more (food)	*Il faut augmenter*
You should add/offer more (bargaining)	
Across the river, at the other bank ('behind the river')	*Derrière le fleuve*
Though literally this means 'straight away', in real terms it means 'not yet'	*Tout de suite*
Time is elastic	*Le temps est elastique*
Shall we go?	*On y va?*
How is the cold (the temperature)?	*Ça va le froid?*
And the tiredness?	*Et la fatigue?*
Crunching/chewing *kola* nuts	*Croquer du kola*
Fasting	*Le carême*
Rush hour at the end of the day	*La descente*
4x4	'Quatre-quatre' (pronounced 'kat-kat' – 'a' as in last))
Cabin or front seat(s) of a vehicle	*La cabine*
Generally used to describe a rough or sandy track in arid or desert regions.	*Piste*
Water tower	*Chateau d'eau* (or 'chateau')

DJERMA

General popular greeting	*Fofo!*
Answer to 'Fofo'	*Fofo!*
Good morning/how was the night?	*Mate aran weete?*
Good afternoon/how was the day?	*Mate a wicira?*
How are you? (singular)	*Mate ni go?*
How are you? (plural)	*Mate aran go?*
How is the family?	*Mate almayaalo?*
Fine (general answer to all of the above)	*Baani samay walla*
What is going on?	*Ifo no?*
What is wrong?	*Baani? Ifo no?*
Welcome	*Fonda kaayan/kubayni*
Thank you	*Ngoyya/fofo*
What is your/her/his name?	*Mate ni ma? Mate a ma?*

My name is Amadou	*Ay ma Amadou*
His/her name is …	*A ma…*
See you later	*Kala a tonton*
Goodbye/see you some time	*Kala han fo*
Good night	*Iri ma kani baani*
Have a good day	*Iri ma weete baani*
That's fine, OK	*To! A boori!*
Do you speak French?	*Ni ga waani faransi sanni?*
I speak a little French	*Ay ga waani faransi sanni kayna*
I don't speak Djerma	*Ay si waani Zarma sanni*
What did you say?	*Ifo no ni ne?*
I did not understand	*Ay mana faham*
Yes/No	*O or Oho/Ha'a*
Come! Don't come!	*Ka! Wa si ka!*
Let's go	*Iri ma koy*
I come from…	*…no ay fun*
When? On what day? Where?	*Wati fo? Han fo? Manga?*
Today/Tomorrow/Yesterday	*Hunkuna/Suba/Bi*
Where is…?	*Man no…go?*
I don't know	*Ay si bay*
Where is the *autogare*?	*Man no mooto teesamo go?*
Near the market	*Habo jare ga*
Where are you going?	*Man no ni go ga koy?*
I am going to…	*…no ay go ga koy*
How much is it?	*Marje no i ga bana?*
Where then?	*Kala man ga?*
Help me with my luggage	*Sambu ay se ay jiney*
I get off here	*Ne no ay ga zumbu*
Excuse me/Go on	*Alhakunnan/Bisa.*
I am hungry	*Haray no ay ga*
I am thirsty	*Hari jaw no ay ga*
Stop here	*Gaayi*
Is it far?	*A ga mooru?*
What is this?	*Ifo no wo-ne?*
Help me	*Wa ay ga*
Shop/hotel/a well	*Faadi/otal/day*
Is there a room?	*Fu go no wala?*
The place of the village chief	*Kwaarakoyo kwaara*
Rice/fish/sauce	*Mo hawru/hamiisa/foy*
Milk/water	*Wa/Hari*
Millet paste/couscous	*Hayni hawru/guni*
Meat/beef/mutton/chicken	*Ham/haw ham/feeji ham/gornyo ham*
Bread/salt	*Buuru/ciiri*
What is wrong with you?	*Ifo ga du ni?*
I am sick/ill	*Ay sinda baani*

HAUSA

General popular greeting	*Sannu!*
Answer to 'Sannu'	*Sannu!*
Good morning/how was the night?	*Ka kwana lafiya?*
How are you? (singular/plural)	*Kana lafiya?/Kuna lafiya?*
How is everyone?	*Suna lafiya?*
How is the family?	*Ina gida*

Fine (general answer to all the above)	*Lafiya lau*
What is going on?	*Yaya ne?*
What is wrong?	*Mi ya faru?*
Welcome	*Sannu da zuwa*
Thank you	*Yawwa*
What is your/her or his name?	*Mi ke sunanka?/Mi ke sunanshi/sunanta?*
My name is Maryama	*Sunana Maryama*
His/her name is…	*Sunanshi/sunanta…*
See you later	*Sai an jima*
Goodbye/see you some time	*Sai wata rana*
Good night	*Mu kwana lafiya*
Have a good day	*Mu yini lafiya*
That's fine, OK	*Ya yi kyau/Na ji*
Do you speak French?	*Ka iya faransanci?*
I speak a little French	*Na iya faransanci kadan-kadan*
I don't speak Hausa	*Ban iya Hausa ba*
What did you say?	*Mi ka ce?*
I did not understand	*Ban gane ba*
Yes/No	*Awo* or *Eh/A'a*
Come! Don't come!	*Taho! Kar ku zo!*
Let's go	*Mu tahi*
I come from…	*Daga … na hito*
When? On what day? Where?	*Yaushe? Wace rana? Ina?*
Today/Tomorrow/Yesterday	*Yau/Gobe/Jiya*
Where is…?	*Ina ne…?*
I really don't know	*A gaskiya ban sani ba*
What do you want?	*Mi kake so?*
Where are you going?	*Ina za ka?*
I am going to…	*…za ni*
How much is it?	*Nawa ake biya?*
Where then?	*Kenan ina za ka sabka?*
Help me with my luggage	*Daukar mini kayana*
I get off here	*Nan ne zan sabka*
Excuse me/Go on	*Ka yahe ni/Wuce*
I am hungry	*Yunwa nike ji*
I am thirsty	*Kishirwa nike ji*
What is wrong with you?	*Mi ya same ka?*
I am sick/ill	*Ba ni lafiya*
Stop here	*Tsaya nan*
Is it far?	*Nesa ne?*
Let's go	*Mu tahi*
What is this?	*Mi nene wannan?*
Help me	*Ku sanya mini hannu*
The place of the village chief	*Gidan mai gari*
Shop/hotel/a well	*Kanti/otal/Rijiya*
Is there a room?	*Akwai daki?*
Rice/fish/sauce	*Shinkafa/kihi/miya*
Milk/water	*Nono/ruwa*
Millet paste/couscous	*Tuwon hatsi/tuwon tsaki*
Meat/beef/mutton/chicken	*Nama/naman shanu/naman rago/naman kaji*
Bread/salt	*Burodi/gishiri*
Riverbed that is dry for most of the year, but which may flood during the rainy season	*Kori*

TAMASHEK There is no uniform way to write Tamashek, as the Roman alphabet was not designed to write this language. An adapted alphabet is sometimes used for Tamashek, which is similar to the Roman alphabet but with extra vowels and consonants. For convenience, Tamashek can also be written using the Roman alphabet, although this is a poorer representation of the language. In order not to complicate your first efforts to speak some Tamashek, I have used the 'ordinary' alphabet. Some indication of pronunciation is mentioned below. Do not worry about a loss of nuances, and try to pick up the different fine sounds as you go.

a: as in 'master'
e: as 'a' in 'lake'
i: as 'ee' in 'feet'
o: as in 'dog'
u: as in 'you'
x: as 'ch' in 'loch'
gh: as if you are scraping your throat

Good day	*Man edis*
Good evening	*Man ekilli*
How are you?	*Maduwan igan?*
All is well	*Alher ghas*
How is your health?	*Man elam?*
How is the family?	*Man aghiwan?*
And the cold/heat?	*Man esamed/tufuk?*
Good night	*Edis n alher*
See you again (soon)	*Arsaghat*
Thank you	*Tanimert*
My name is Fatima	*Isin nin Fatima*
What is your name?	*Misin nam?*
Where are you from?	*Minde du tigmada?*
I am going that way	*Den akke*
I will come back later	*Orgezaghin marda*
Where are you going?	*Minde tikkam?*
Where do you live?	*Minde tik sara?*
I stay at hotel…	*Izibbe dagh hotel…*
I am looking for…	*Ussuk agamaya…*
I am leaving tomorrow	*Awizli age tufat*
How much does it cost?	*Manaket?*
That is too much	*Yi zuwat*
I agree	*Orde*
I don't understand	*Wer tat issena*
I do not speak Tamashek	*Chawela Tamajaq*
Can you help me?	*Tifragam adi tilalam?*
Please	*War ge mil ka nak*
Where is…?	*Man…?*
I need a doctor	*Are enasmagal*
I am sick/ill	*Turna age*
Today	*Aghorawa*
Tomorrow	*Tufat*
Yesterday	*N-dazal*
I do not know	*Wer issena*
Yes/no	*yo/kay*
Sun/moon/stars	*Tufuk/tellit/etran*
Milk/water	*Akh/aman*

Bread/rice	*Tagilla/tafaghat*
Onion/tomato/dates	*Temizlilit/tamatunt/tayni*
Do you have…?	*Talam…?*
Water is life	*Aman iman*
Riverbed that is dry for most of the year, but which may flood during the rainy season	*Oued*

Agadez cross

Appendix 2

BOOKS, DOCUMENTS AND ARTICLES There is an ample choice of books covering topics on Niger, provided you can read French. So unless stated otherwise, the following selection of books is written in French. Most of these books I found in Niamey, in one or another of the bookstores mentioned on page 106, while publications by the IRSH (Institut des Récherches des Sciences Humaines) can be bought directly from the IRSH in Niamey.

Background reading

Adamou, Aboubacar *Agadez et sa région* Etudes Nigériennes No 44, Institut des Récherches des Sciences Humaines, 1979. In-depth history of Agadez and environs.

Aghali Zakara, Mohamed and Drouin, Jeannine *Recherches sur le Tifinagh; Elements sociologiques* Librairie Orientalistes Paul Geuthner, Paris, 1978. A study of the tifinagh script.

Aghali Zakara, Mohamed *Contes Touaregs Nigériens* Nouvelle Imprimerie Niger, 1995. Traditional Tuareg stories.

Beckwith, Carol and van Offelen, Marion *Nomads of Niger* Harvill, HarperCollins, London, 1983. An excellent photographic work about the Bororo Peul, their society and traditions. In English.

Bernus, Edmond and Echard, Nicole *La région d'In Gall-Tegidda-N-Tesemt (Niger) Part V Les populations actuelles* Etudes Nigériennes No 52, IRSH, 1992. About the (mostly Tuareg) population from the Ingal region, their crafts and their society.

Boureïma, Alpha Gado *Niamey, Garin kaptan Salma (Histoire d'une ville).* Printed for educational purposes in Niamey, this book describes the history of the town of Niamey from its earliest days well into independence.

Claudot-Hawad, Héléne *Touaregs, apprivoiser le désert* Découvertes Gallimard, 2002.

Crisler, T Jameson, and Brouwer, J *The Birds of 'W' National Park, southwest Niger* Malimbus, journal of the West African Ornithological Association, 25:4-30, 2003. In English.

Decoudras, P-M et al *Bonjour le Sahara du Niger* Guide pour voyageurs curieux, Les créations du Pélican, Lyon, 1994. A beautiful collection of stories, history, photographs, and comprehensive information on the Nigérien Sahara.

Devisse, J et al *Vallées du Niger* Brochure d'une exposition, 1994. Description of archaeological finds along the river Niger (including Mali), illustrated with colour photographs.

Fuglestad, Finn *A History of Niger 1850–1960* Cambridge University Press, 1983. Many developments and events put into a historical perspective. In English.

Gado, Boubé et al *Eléments d'archéologie ouest-africaine' deel IV: Niger* DARA/IRSH/CRIAA/Sépia, 2000. A compact explanantion of archaeology, and a survey of Niger during the archaeological periods.

Gado, Boubé *Les traditions de Lougou, de Birnin Lokoyo et de Massalata* IRSH, 1986 A series of interviews with Azna animists from different regions.

Lamarque, François *Les grands mammifères du complexe WAP* ECOPAS, Niger, 2005. A beautiful publication about the WAP Transboundary Park, with a comprehensive guide on 51 mammals of this complex.

Le Coeur, Marguerite *Les oasis du Kawar (Une route, un pays) part I: Le passé précolonial* Etudes Nigériennes No 54, IRSH, 1985. Pre-colonial history of the Kawar region.

Masquelier, Adeline *Prayer Has Spoilt Everything* Duke University Press, Durham and London, 2001. An in-depth study of the Bori cult of Dogondoutchi, with many descriptions of possession rituals and other ceremonies. In English.

Nicholas, Guy *Dynamique de l'Islam au sud du Sahara* Publications Orientalistes de France, 1981.

Salifou, André *Le Niger* Editions l'Harmattan, 2002. A much-praised work about the history of Niger and contemporary issues and politics by the highly respected historian André Salifou.

Spittler, Gerd *Les Touaregs face aux sécheresses et aux famines* Editions Karthala, Paris, 1993. Also available in German (*Dürren, Krieg und Hungerkreisen bei den Kel Ewey (1900–1985)*).

Spittler, Gerd *Hirtenarbeit, die Welt der Kamelhirten und Ziegenhirtinnen von Timia* Köln, 1998.

Vernet, Robert *Le sud-ouest du Niger de la préhistoire au début de l'histoire* Etudes Nigériennes no 56, 1996, IRSH Niamey/SEPIA Paris.

Nigérien literature

Adamou, Idé *Sur les terres de silence* Editions l'Harmattan, 1994. Poetry.

Adamou, Idé *Talibo, un enfant du quartier* Editions l'Harmattan, 1996.

Bania, Mamadou Say *Le Niger et ses merveilles* Imprimerie Brunaud, France, 1989.

Hama, Boubou *Contes et légendes du Niger (parts I–VI)* Editions Présence Africaine, different years. Six anthologies of stories and legends from different ethnic groups in Niger.

Hama, Boubou *Kotia Nima* Présence Africaine, 1969.

Hama, Boubou *L'Extraordinaire aventure de BiKado, fils de noir* Présence Africaine, 1973.

Hawad *Caravane de la soif* Edisud, 1985. Tuareg poetry.

Hawad *Testament nomade* Editions Silex, 1988. Tuareg poetry.

Ibrahim, Issa *Les grandes eaux noires* 1959.

Kanta, Abdoua *Le Deraciné* 1972. Received the 'Prix Unesco'.

Kanta, Abdoua *L'aîné de la famille* Hâtier, 1977.

Konate, Issoufou *Tate, l'enfant de Mokoyo* Les Editions des Diasporas, Cotonou, 2004. The story of a young boy from Maradi, and the choices he has to make to achieve his dreams.

Mamani, Abdoulaye *Sarraounia, le drame de la reine magicienne* Editions l'Harmattan, Paris, 2001. The legend of the Sarauniya, written as a historical novel.

Mayaki, Djibo *Le poids d'un milieu* Published by the Centre Culturel Franco-Nigérien, 1978.

Oumarou, Idé *Gros Plan* Dakar, 1979. Grand Prix Littéraire d'Afrique Noire winner.

Ousmane, Amadou *L'Honneur perdu* Niamey, 1993.

Salifou, André *Tanimoune* Présence Africaine, 1973. The story of the Tanimoune sultanate adapted for theatre.

USEFUL WEBSITES While it is difficult to find good books about Niger in English, there is a wide choice of interesting websites. Unless stated otherwise, the following websites are in English.

General information

www.cia.gov CIA World Factbook

www.britannica.com Encyclopaedia Britannica

www.infoplease.com Almanac, atlas, encyclopaedia, dictionary; numerous links to other useful sites

www.nigerphonebook.com Niger's yellow pages; incomplete but worth a try

www.afriqueindex.com/Pays/Niger.htm Site with thematic references to a wide range of Nigérien sites (French)

www.afrol.com/countries/niger More general information and lots of links

www.unicef.org/infobycountry/niger-statistics.html A whole array of statistics

www.world66.com/niger General information on various destinations and some practicalities

www.worldatlas.com/webimage/countrys/africa/ne.htm General information and geography facts

www.agadez-niger.com/ In French, but very interesting with up-to-date information as well as history, forum discussions and pictures

www.sul.stanford.edu/depts/ssrg/africa/niger.html With many links to other sites about Niger

Natural history

www.africanbirdclub.org/countries/Niger/introduction.html Comprehensive site about birds in Niger, information on good birding areas, checklists, and a general natural history of Niger

http://malimbus.free.fr/ Information on local bird species.

Local news

www.republicain-niger.com Nigérien weekly newspaper (French)

www.allafrica.com PanAfrican News Agency (PANA)

www.auniger.com General information and some recent news reports, as well as some radio programmes (French)

www.nigerportal.com A regularly updated website with a wide scope of news and dozens of links. You can even listen to local radio stations and check what is in the Nigérien newspapers (French)

www.izf.net/izf/Actualite/RDP/niger.htm Another good (French) site with compact up-to-date reports

www.planeteafrique.com/Niger In French, with many direct links to Nigérien newspapers, news reports and general information (French)

www.izf.net/Guide/Niger With many links to newspapers and other sites (French)

www.tamtaminfo.com Recent reports and direct links to most Nigérien newspapers (French)

www.rfi.fr Website for the Radio France International station. Features well-researched reports by local and international journalists (French)

Travel information

www.oanda.com/convert/classic To work out the current exchange rates

www.fco.gov.uk For a link to Foreign and Commonwealth Office (FCO) Travel Advice Notices for up-to-date information and for information on UK representations worldwide

www.bbc.co.uk/worldservice For up-to-date radio frequencies

www.icrtourism.org/capetown.html For official statements about responsible tourism and the Cape Town Declaration about this subject

Culture

www.tuaregs.online.fr About the Tuareg way of life, culture, history, news

www.agadez.org In French, with items about Agadez, and a link to the local newspaper *Aïr Info*

www.clapnoir.org/accueil/gauche.htm About African cinema with links to Nigérien cinema, worldwide festivals and events, portraits, reports (French)

www.Us.imbd.com/Sections/Countries/Niger/ With descriptions of over 20 Nigérien films

www.hostingproject.info/goza Listen to Nigérien rap from different groups (French).

www.planeteafrique.com/fofomag A link to *Fofo* magazine, with information on Nigérien modern music (French)

Projects and NGOs

www.niger-ue.net Governmental site (in French) with links to the Ministry of Tourism and Artisanat. Most interesting is the information about the Syrene project (see *Giving something back* on page 88) and SAFEM (see *Public holidays and festivals* on page 78), both dealing with poverty alleviation through the promotion of arts and crafts.

www.snvworld.org About the Dutch development organisation

www.unesco.org UNESCO (United Nations Educational Scientific and Cultural Organisation) was founded in 1946 and 'is working to create the conditions for genuine dialogue based upon respect for shared values and the dignity of each civilisation and culture'. Also for information on World Heritage Sites and other classified sites in Niger

www.friendsofniger.org See page 90 for more information

www.rain4sahara.org See page 89 for more information

www.unicef.org/infobycountry/niger_1415.html 'For every child: health, education, equality, protection'

WIN £100 CASH!
READER QUESTIONNAIRE

Send in your completed questionnaire for the chance to win £100 cash in our regular draw

All respondents may order a Bradt guide at half the UK retail price – please complete the order form overleaf.

(Entries may be posted or faxed to us, or scanned and emailed.)

We are interested in getting feedback from our readers to help us plan future Bradt guides. Please answer ALL the questions below and return the form to us in order to qualify for an entry in our regular draw.

Have you used any other Bradt guides? If so, which titles? . . . .
. . . .
What other publishers' travel guides do you use regularly? . . . .
. . . .
Where did you buy this guidebook? . . . .
What was the main purpose of your trip to Niger (or for what other reason did you read our guide)? eg: holiday/business/charity etc. . . . .
. . . .
What other destinations would you like to see covered by a Bradt guide?
. . . .
Would you like to receive our catalogue/newsletters?

YES / NO (If yes, please complete details on reverse)

If yes – by post or email? . . . .

Age (circle relevant category) 16–25   26–45   46–60   60+

Male/Female (delete as appropriate)

Home country . . . .

Please send us any comments about our guide to Niger or other Bradt Travel Guides. . . . .
. . . .
. . . .
. . . .

Bradt Travel Guides
23 High Street, Chalfont St Peter, Bucks SL9 9QE, UK
✆ +44 (0)1753 893444 f +44 (0)1753 892333
e info@bradtguides.com
www.bradtguides.com

CLAIM YOUR HALF-PRICE BRADT GUIDE!

Order Form

To order your half-price copy of a Bradt guide, and to enter our prize draw to win £100 (see overleaf), please fill in the order form below, complete the questionnaire overleaf, and send it to Bradt Travel Guides by post, fax or email.

Please send me one copy of the following guide at half the UK retail price

Title	Retail price	Half price
. . .	. . . .	. . . .	. . . .

Please send the following additional guides at full UK retail price

No	Title	Retail price	Total
. . .	. . . .	. . . .	. . . .
. . .	. . . .	. . . .	. . . .
. . .	. . . .	. . . .	. . . .

Sub total . . . .

Post & packing . . . . . .

(£1 per book UK; £2 per book Europe; £3 per book rest of world)

Total . . . .

Name . . . .

Address . . . .

Tel . . . .   Email . . . .

☐ I enclose a cheque for £ . . . . made payable to Bradt Travel Guides Ltd

☐ I would like to pay by credit card. Number: . . . .

Expiry date: . . . / . . .   3-digit security code (on reverse of card) . . . . .

☐ Please add my name to your catalogue mailing list.

☐ I would be happy for you to use my name and comments in Bradt marketing material.

Send your order on this form, with the completed questionnaire, to:

Bradt Travel Guides/NGR
23 High Street, Chalfont St Peter, Bucks SL9 9QE
☎ +44 (0)1753 893444   f +44 (0)1753 892333
e info@bradtguides.com   www.bradtguides.com

Bradt Travel Guides

www.bradtguides.com

Africa

Africa Overland	£15.99
Benin	£14.99
Botswana: Okavango, Chobe, Northern Kalahari	£14.95
Burkina Faso	£14.99
Cape Verde Islands	£13.99
Canary Islands	£13.95
Cameroon	£13.95
Eritrea	£12.95
Ethiopia	£15.99
Gabon, São Tomé, Príncipe	£13.95
Gambia, The	£12.95
Georgia	£13.95
Ghana	£13.95
Kenya	£14.95
Madagascar	£14.95
Malawi	£12.95
Mali	£13.95
Mauritius, Rodrigues & Réunion	£12.95
Mozambique	£12.95
Namibia	£14.95
Niger	£14.99
Nigeria	£15.99
Rwanda	£13.95
Seychelles	£14.99
Sudan	£13.95
Tanzania, Northern	£13.99
Tanzania	£14.95
Uganda	£13.95
Zambia	£15.99
Zanzibar	£12.95

Britain and Europe

Albania	£13.99
Armenia, Nagorno Karabagh	£13.95
Azores	£12.95
Baltic Capitals: Tallinn, Riga, Vilnius, Kaliningrad	£12.99
Belgrade	£6.99
Bosnia & Herzegovina	£13.95
Bratislava	£6.99
Budapest	£7.95
Cork	£6.95
Croatia	£12.95
Cyprus see North Cyprus	
Czech Republic	£13.99
Dubrovnik	£6.95
Eccentric Britain	£13.99
Eccentric Edinburgh	£5.95
Eccentric France	£12.95
Eccentric London	£12.95
Eccentric Oxford	£5.95
Estonia	£12.95
Faroe Islands	£13.95
Hungary	£14.99
Kiev	£7.95
Latvia	£13.99
Lille	£6.99

Lithuania	£13.99
Ljubljana	£6.99
Macedonia	£13.95
Montenegro	£13.99
North Cyprus	£12.95
Paris, Lille & Brussels	£11.95
Riga	£6.95
River Thames, In the Footsteps of the Famous	£10.95
Serbia	£13.99
Slovenia	£12.99
Spitsbergen	£14.99
Switzerland: Rail, Road, Lake	£13.99
Tallinn	£6.95
Ukraine	£13.95
Vilnius	£6.99

Middle East, Asia and Australasia

Great Wall of China	£13.99
Iran	£14.99
Iraq	£14.95
Kabul	£9.95
Maldives	£13.99
Mongolia	£14.95
North Korea	£13.95
Palestine, Jerusalem	£12.95
Sri Lanka	£13.99
Syria	£13.99
Tasmania	£12.95
Tibet	£12.95
Turkmenistan	£14.99

The Americas and the Caribbean

Amazon, The	£14.95
Argentina	£15.99
Bolivia	£14.99
Cayman Islands	£12.95
Costa Rica	£13.99
Chile	£16.95
Chile & Argentina: Trekking	£12.95
Eccentric America	£13.95
Eccentric California	£13.99
Falkland Islands	£13.95
Peru & Bolivia: Backpacking and Trekking	£12.95
Panama	£13.95
St Helena, Ascension, Tristan da Cunha	£14.95
USA by Rail	£13.99

Wildlife

Antarctica: Guide to the Wildlife	£14.95
Arctic: Guide to the Wildlife	£14.95
British Isles: Wildlife of Coastal Waters	£14.95
Galápagos Wildlife	£15.99
Madagascar Wildlife	£14.95
South African Wildlife	£18.95

Health

Your Child Abroad: A Travel Health Guide	£10.95

NOTES

NOTES

Index